Remke Kruk is Professor Emeritus of Arabic at the University of Leiden. Starting with *The Arabic Version of Aristotle's Parts of Animals: Books XI–XIV of the* Kitāb al-Hayawān (1979), she has published on a wide range of subjects, notably in the field of Graeco-Arabic natural philosophy. She was the editor, with Gerhard Endress, of *The Ancient Tradition in Christian and Islamic Hellenism* (1997). She has translated various classical Arabic texts and is co-editor of the series *Aristoteles Semitico-Latinus*.

'*The Warrior Women of Islam* is a groundbreaking scholarly examination of a topic that has long deserved more detailed study. The book offers a fascinating and insightful investigation into the representation of women warriors as found in a major narrative genre of pre-modern Arabic literature, the popular epic [...] The author's incisive analysis is unique in that it encompasses every major example the genre and hence provides a panoramic view of the subject. The summation of decades of study by the author, this is a major contribution to the field.'
   – Peter Heath, Chancellor, American University of Sharjah, UAE

'Remke Kruk has written a delightful and indispensable study on a tradition of popular Arab storytelling little known or appreciated beyond its indigenous cultural and religious borders [...] Kruk expertly guides the reader through stories that should challenge common western perceptions of the Middle Eastern woman, medieval or modern.'
   – David Waines, Professor Emeritus of Islamic Studies, Lancaster University

THE WARRIOR WOMEN OF ISLAM

FEMALE EMPOWERMENT IN ARABIC POPULAR LITERATURE

Remke Kruk

Published in 2014 by I.B.Tauris & Co Ltd
6 Salem Road, London W2 4BU
175 Fifth Avenue, New York NY 10010
www.ibtauris.com

Copyright © 2014 Remke Kruk

The right of Remke Kruk to be identified as the author of this work has been asserted by her in accordance with the Copyright, Designs and Patents Act 1988.

All rights reserved. Except for brief quotations in a review, this book, or any part thereof, may not be reproduced, stored in or introduced into a retrieval system, or transmitted, in any form or by any means, electronic, mechanical, photocopying, recording or otherwise, without the prior written permission of the publisher.

Library of Middle East History, vol. 54

ISBN: 978 1 84885 926 5 (hb)
      978 1 84885 927 2 (pb)

A full CIP record for this book is available from the British Library
A full CIP record is available from the Library of Congress

Library of Congress Catalog Card Number: available

Typeset in Minion Tra by AtriTeX Technologies Pvt. Ltd., Chennai, India

Photography by Ole Eshuis

On the occasion of the four hundredth anniversary of the Leiden Chair of Arabic, founded in 1613, I dedicate this book to all my venerable male predecessors and to my intrepid female successor.

Contents

Preface		ix
A Note on Transliteration		xiii
Abbreviations		xv
A Note on the Illustrations		xvii
List of Illustrations		xxi
Acknowledgements		xxv
1	Arabic Popular Epic: An Introductory Note	1
2	Warrior Women in the Arabic Tradition	15
3	*Sīrat Dhāt al-Himma* 1: Princess Dhāt al-Himma and Her Many Battles	37
4	*Sīrat Dhāt al-Himma* 2: Prince ʿAbd al-Wahhāb and His Warrior Wives	63
5	*Sīrat Dhāt al-Himma* 3: The History of Ghamra the Daughter of ʿUtārid	93
6	Warrior Women in *Sīrat ʿAntara* 1: Ghamra the Daughter of Fāʾiz	111
7	Warrior Women in *Sīrat ʿAntara* 2: Hayfāʾ, Zarqāʾ and ʿUnaytira	131
8	Prince Hamza al-Bahlawān: In Praise of Traditional Womanhood	147
9	*Sīrat Baybars* 1: Lionesses	163
10	*Sīrat Baybars* 2: Warrior Queens	175
11	King Sayf ibn Dhī Yazan, the Soft-Hearted 1: Qamarīya	187
12	King Sayf ibn Dhī Yazan 2: Tāma	201
13	King Sayf ibn Dhī Yazan 3: Munyat al-Nufūs	213
14	Final Observations	223
Notes		227
Bibliography		253
Index		265

Preface

In this book I describe the role of warrior women in a particular branch of Arabic narrative literature, namely popular epic. The genre consists of long adventure tales about champions performing all kinds of heroic deeds, and some of these champions are female. These tales, we must assume, were composed by men for a male audience, and, accordingly, the stories do not tell us about the ambitions of women, but about the tastes of men.

My primary intention in writing this book is that it should be informative. While addressing the field of Arabic studies, it also aims at the wider public. To many people, this branch of traditional Arabic literature is almost unknown, and the stories about the women featuring in it have received little attention, even in gender-orientated literary studies. One of the main reasons is that most of them are not easily accessible. Here I intend to tell a number of the stories, occasionally including translated passages to give an idea of the language and style in which they were told. Theoretical questions are occasionally brought up, but do not form the main focus. For the benefit of Arabists, I have taken care to include extensive references to the Arabic texts.

Other points of attention are the transmission of the texts and the manner and context of their performance. These texts were not only read, but also formed the stock-in-trade of professional storytellers from medieval times until very recent days. In explaining their practices, I will partly speak on the basis of my own observations of narrative performance in Morocco.

I hope to convince people that popular epic is not only a rich source of material but also makes fascinating reading. The Arabic narrative tradition has more to offer than *The Thousand and One Nights*, however inexhaustible that collection may be as a source of enjoyment as well as of scholarly interest.

My fascination with popular epic started in the late 1980s, and my first article on warrior women in the epics appeared in 1993. Although I was by no means the first to write on this topic, reactions showed that the subject was very little known even among Arabists. Since then, I have published a series of articles on popular epic, several of them on warrior women. For the present book I have drawn upon these earlier publications, added a substantial amount of new material, and amply made use of the many new publications on popular epic that have appeared during the past twenty years.

Research in popular epic is time-consuming. Most of the texts in this genre contain many thousands of pages, the plots are often complicated and the narrative constantly switches from one plot line to another. The text editions are cheaply produced, contain many misprints and differ considerably from each other. They are often produced by a printer who doubled as a bookseller, and they are frequently undated. For this reason the bookseller, if known, should always be mentioned in the bibliographical information: it is the only way to discern one undated edition from another. Researchers also have to deal with the problem that many libraries, even (or maybe especially) venerable university libraries, do not stock these popular works. Luckily, this was not the case with the Leiden University Library, although, for a wider variety of editions I still depended heavily on my own private collection.

Given the size of the texts, the publication of Malcolm Lyons's three-volume *The Arabian Epic* (1995) was an enormous step forward in this field. It offered a general analysis of the narrative aspects of the genre, extensive summaries of all the printed epics, and motif indices. Browsing, although still time-consuming, became much easier, and it was possible to compare material on a much wider scale. I could certainly not have written this book without *The Arabian Epic*.

In writing about these tales and translating them, one has to deal with various problems of terminology. First there is the question of the genre itself: do we refer to it as epic, romance, saga, adventure tale or something else? These are all Western terms, coined for literary genres that do not, or at least not fully, correspond with this particular Arabic genre. As a result, various terms are used, and they all have their uses as well as their disadvantages.

Another matter is the titles allotted to the protagonists. The Arabic *amīr* has many meanings, and although it has entered Western usage in the form of 'emir', this word cannot be used on all occasions. I have translated it in a number of ways: prince, governor, chief and leader. *Fāris*, 'rider', offers a similar problem. Sometimes I have translated it as 'knight', sometimes as 'horseman'. Women may be called *amīra*, translated as 'princess', or *malika*, 'queen' or 'princess'. In none of these cases should the terms that are used evoke the system of hierarchic nobility in which the European terms belong.

Arabic names are always a baffling problem for the general reader, because they are complicated as well as often including similar elements. Although I have tried to include as few names as possible in my accounts of the stories, the number of protagonists is still fairly staggering. To facilitate reading, I have provided an alphabetical list of names at the beginning of each chapter featuring a number of protagonists.

As to literature: many fascinating publications on the topic have appeared, and, unavoidably, I had to be selective. Only such literature as was used for specific references has been included in the Bibliography.

A Note on Transliteration

Full diacritics have been used only in the index. In the text, the Arabic *hamza* has been indicated by ', Arabic *'ayn* by ', and long vowels by ¯. Arabic *thā'* has been rendered by th; *dhāl* by dh; *khā'* by kh; *ghayn* by gh; *qāf* by q. With a view to readability, no diacritical dots have been used to discern Arabic consonants. Thus t stands for *tā'* as well as *ṭā'*; h for *hā'* and *ḥā'*; d for *dāl* and *ḍād*; z for *zāy* and *ẓā'*, and s for *sîn* and *ṣād*.

Abbreviations

References to the five most frequently used epics are as follows:

'Antara
: Sīrat 'Antara ibn Shaddād (Cairo: Maktaba wa-mat-ba'a Mustafā al-Bābī al-Halabī, 1381/1961–2), 12 vols, 58 parts (ajzā'), bound in 6 (sometimes 8) bindings.

Baybars
: Sīrat al-Zāhir Baybars (Cairo: al-Hay'a al-misrīya al-'āmma li-l-kitāb, 1996–7), introduction by Gamāl al-Ghitānī, 5 vols. Pagination is continuous through all five volumes.

Dhāt al-Himma
: Sīrat al-amīra Dhāt al-Himma (Cairo: Maktabat al-Hanafī, n.d.), 70 parts (ajzā'), 7 vols.

Hamza
: Qissat al-amīr Hamza (Cairo: Maktaba wa-matba'at al-mashhad al-Husaynī, n.d.), 4 vols.

Sayf
: Sīrat fāris al-Yaman al-malik Sayf ibn Dhī Yazan (Cairo: Maktaba wa-matba'at al-mashhad al-Husaynī, 1391/1971), 4 vols.

A Note on the Illustrations

Arabic popular epic has its own tradition of illustration, which deserves to be treated more broadly than is possible within the present context. Some brief remarks will have to suffice here.

Manuscripts of Arabic popular epics are rarely illustrated, for these tales were not considered prestigious enough to be written down in expensively produced manuscripts lavishly provided with illustrations.[1] Such illustrated manuscripts are, in any case, rare in the Arabic tradition, where the pictorial aspect is far less prominent than in the Persian tradition with its wonderful miniature paintings.

From the late nineteenth century onwards, however, we find a wide range of pictures illustrating the epics that were used for home decoration. Images of the most popular heroes as well as of a limited set of action scenes were depicted in various techniques. There are textiles (embroidery or block prints), poster prints and (especially in Syria and Tunisia) reverse glass paintings. *Sīrat 'Antara* dominates the scene, then come pictures of 'Alī and Ra's al-Ghūl from the stories about the legendary early conquests: a genre related to popular epic. The style of the pictures often shows a connection to the kind of illustrations found in manuscripts of popular tales other than the epics, such as stories from *The Thousand and One Nights*;[2] in manuals of chivalry, such as that of al-Aqsarā'ī;[3] and sometimes of the *maqāmāt* of al-Harīrī.

A number of Syrian and Tunisian artists became famous for their reverse glass paintings, and their work found its way into museum collections such as that of the Linden Museum in Stuttgart and the Musée des arts et traditions populaires in Sfax (Tunisia). A good idea of the Tunisian tradition can be obtained from Mohamed Masmoudi's *La peinture sous-verre en Tunisie*. Reverse glass paintings of this kind, with designs taken from older pictures, were later produced for the popular and tourist markets.

In these pictures, women are represented in traditional roles. 'Abla, 'Antar's proud and sometimes ruthless wife, is usually shown as watching with trepidation from her *howdah* as her husband strikes

xvii

off an enemy's head. No representations of martial women or women in general engaging in violence are known to me from this tradition. This is surprising, because they are not completely absent in the wider Islamic pictorial tradition. Persian miniatures exist of Alexander fighting the Amazons and of beloveds fighting each other on horseback, such as Prince Humāy and Princess Humāyūn.[4] The famous illustrated manuscript of *The Adventures of Hamza* commissioned by the Mughal emperor Akbar contains pictures of women shooting with bows, wrestling or cutting off an enemy's head (Plates 15, 16 and 17). Apparently such images did not find their way into the Arabic tradition.

The Arabic illustrations usually have a fairly standardized character and the number of representations that appear is limited. We see 'Antar and 'Abla together, seated on camels or on horseback; or 'Antar slaying an enemy with 'Abla looking on from a *howdah* (Plates 8 and 10). A common representation of 'Abdallāh ibn Ja'far, hero of an Islamic conquest cycle popular in North Africa, is that of the hero fleeing on horseback with his beloved seated behind him (Plate 1).

The pictures are not always representative of what is told in the texts. The scene of 'Abdallāh ibn Ja'far just mentioned is of minor importance in the written text. There the beloved even remains nameless, while she receives a name in the reverse glass paintings: Yāmina. Another example is a reverse glass painting of 'Antar on horseback attacking a dragon with his spear in the characteristic posture of St George, as the incident of 'Antar's dragon-killing is only a very minor event in *Sīrat 'Antara* itself, in which he does not even fight the dragon on horseback, as the picture suggests, but dismounts in order to attack it (Plate 12).

The latter example also demonstrates that pictorial representation of the heroes were, to a certain extent, dependent on images that were already current, sometimes in a different context: paintings of St George killing the dragon were well known in Christian Arab communities, and the image was simply reused. A related phenomenon can be noticed in printed editions, which are sometimes illustrated by crude drawings. In a picture of 'Antar and his tribe travelling in Arabia, the artist, clearly not an accomplished draughtsman, used the images that for him were iconic of travel in Arabia, namely the travel scenes traditionally found in Egyptian murals to celebrate the pilgrimage to Mecca. These often included trains, lions, soldiers with rifles, and camels, and all of these are found in the picture of 'Antar's tribe travelling through pre-Islamic Arabia (Plate 9).

A Note on the Illustrations xix

This brings us to the printed editions and the visual representations that they have to offer.

In these editions, illustrations gradually start to be included, albeit sparingly. They are initially of an unsophisticated nature, which makes them no less interesting, as examples demonstrate, but they gradually become more accomplished.

In the older editions women were almost always shown in a traditional role, very rarely as martial figures. In that respect, the picture of 'Abla killing the Persian ruler Ardashīr with a knife in the 1971 Cairo edition of *Sīrat 'Antara* is an exception (Plate 13), strongly contrasting with a Cairo edition of *Sīrat Sayf ibn Dhī Yazan* of that same year, where the brave Princess Shāma, beloved of Sayf ibn Dhī Yazan, is represented as a kind of Spanish princess with a fan (1: 177), and 'Āqisa, Sayf's fierce foster sister, who saves him from numerous difficult situations and flies all over the world with him, is only shown as taking loving care of him when he is ill (1: 281). Queen Qamarīya, Sayf's depraved but almost undefeatable mother, is seen sitting in prison, sadly pining away (1: 265). Regrettably, the quality of the print is too poor to reproduce these latter pictures.

A quite different picture, however, is seen in a Turkish version of the story: Qamarīya is depicted as a voluptuous odalisque sitting on a stone with a sword in her hand and a threatening look on her face in Ali Bey's Turkish translation of the *sīra* published in 1847.[5]

In more recent editions a gradual shift can be observed. Illustrations show less stereotypically feminine women and regularly attempt to represent them in a way that fits their image in the actual text. This is particularly noticeable in the case of women engaging in acts of violence. In an undated, but obviously fairly recent abbreviated version of *Sīrat Sayf*, we see Tāma threatening her rival Nāhid with a sword (Plate 21) and 'Āqisa attacking Sayf's evil mother Qamarīya (Plate 22).

While the covers of the older editions are usually not illustrated, or at best have a simple line drawing or woodcut in traditional style (Plate 2), editions published after *c*.1980 often have bright cover illustrations which confirm the outline given above. They often show the hero engaging in battle and, in several cases, he is fighting a dragon (Plate 20). The hero fighting a dragon was clearly seen as an appropriate illustration of his heroism.

A shift can be noticed in the representation of women on these covers. If they do appear, it is no longer exclusively as beautifully dressed, seductive females. A cover picture for *Sīrat ʿAntara* shows a woman, probably ʿAbla, awkwardly wielding a sword (Plate 14).

The change in cover representations of Princess Dhāt al-Himma is a case in point. The seven large, hot-pink volumes of the 1980 Beirut edition of *Sīrat Dhāt al-Himma* have a picture on their covers showing the princess sitting on a throne, beautifully dressed, with not a trace of armour in sight (Plate 6). Of the covers of three reprints of older Arabic studies on *Sīrat Dhāt al-Himma*, two present beautifully dressed princesses, but the third shows a drawing of a young woman on horseback raising a sword.[6] Most striking is the English translation (produced in Egypt) of Shawqī ʿAbd Al-Hakīm's little book on Princess Dhāt al-Himma. It shows the princess on horseback, galloping to the attack, wearing a helmet and coat of mail and brandishing her sword. Her face does not look Arabic: she bears a marked resemblance to the actress Lucy Lawless in her role of Xena, warrior princess, heroine of an American television series that was popular in the Middle East in the 1990s (Plate 7). It looks as if Xena helped to pave the way for illustrations in which the warrior women of Arabic popular epic are finally allowed to present themselves in their full strength.

List of Illustrations

1. 'Abdallāh ibn Ja'far fleeing with his beloved al-Yāmina. Reverse glass, modern copy. Bought in Tunis, 1995. (Collection Remke Kruk)
2. Combat scene. Cover of *Taghribat Banī Hilāl al-Kubrā al-Shāmīya al-aslīya* (Cairo: Maktaba wa-matba'at al-mashhad al-husaynī, n.d.)
3. Abū Zayd al-Hilālī killing al-Harrās. Reverse glass, modern copy. Bought in Tunis, 1995. (Collection Remke Kruk)
4. Alexander fighting the Amazons. Bibliothèque nationale de France, Paris, painting from a MS of Qazwīnī's *'Ajā'ib al-makhlūqāt*. Carole Hillenbrand, *The Crusades: Islamic Perspectives* (Edinburgh: Edinburgh University Press, 1999), plate 8.
5. Jāziya (or Zāziya). Reverse glass. Micheline Galley and Abderrahman Ayoub, *Histoire des Beni Hilal et de ce qui leur advint dans leur marche vers l'ouest. Versions tunisiennes de la geste hilalienne* (Paris, 1983), between pp. 152 and 153.
6. Cover of *Sīrat al-amīra Dhāt al-Himma*, 7 vols (Beirut: Al-Maktaba al-thaqāfīya, 1400/1980).
7. Cover of Shawqi 'Abd Al-Hakim, *Princess Dhat Al Himma: The Princess of High Resolve*, trans. and intro. by Omaima Abou Bakr (Cairo: Ministry of Culture, 1995).
8. 'Antar and 'Abla. Reverse glass, modern copy, initialled B.R. on the back. Bought in Tunis, 1995. (Collection Remke Kruk)
9. Bedouin tribe travelling through pre-Islamic Arabia. *Sīrat fāris fursān al-hijāz abī l-fawāris 'Antara ibn Shaddād*, 8 vols (Beirut: Al-maktaba al-'ilmīya al-hadītha, n.d.), vol. 1, 165.
10. 'Antar killing an enemy. Poster print. Bought in Damascus by Wim Raven, c.1975. (Collection Remke Kruk)
11. Princess al-Jaydā' captured by 'Antar. *Sīrat fāris fursān al-hijāz abī l-fawāris 'Antara ibn Shaddād*, 8 vols (Beirut: Al-maktaba al-'ilmīya al-hadītha, n.d.), vol. 1, 433.

12. 'Antar killing a dragon. Reverse glass, modern copy. Bought in Tunis, 1995. (Collection Remke Kruk)
13. 'Abla kills Ardashīr. Sīrat 'Antara ibn Shaddād, 8 vols (Cairo: Maktaba wa-matbaʿat al-mashhad al-Husaynī, 1391/1971), vol. 5, 172.
14. Cover of vol. 1 of Sīrat 'Antara ibn Shaddād, 8 vols (Beirut: Al-maktaba al-shaʿbīya, n.d.)
15. Two girls wrestling on a roof. Painting from the manuscript of the Persian version of *The Adventures of Hamza*. John Seyller, *The Adventures of Hamza: Painting and Storytelling in Mughal India*. With contributions by Wheeler M. Thackston, Ebba Koch, Antoinette Owen and Rainald Franz (Washington, DC: Freer Gallery of Art and Arthur M. Sackler Gallery, Smithsonian Institution, in association with Azimuth Editions Limited, London, 2002), no. 67 (detail).
16. Princess Mihrdukht shoots her bow. Painting from the manuscript of the Persian version of *The Adventures of Hamza*. John Seyller, *The Adventures of Hamza: Painting and Storytelling in Mughal India*. With contributions by Wheeler M. Thackston, Ebba Koch, Antoinette Owen and Rainald Franz (Washington, DC: Freer Gallery of Art and Arthur M. Sackler Gallery, Smithsonian Institution in association with Azimuth Editions Limited, London, 2002), no. 76 (detail).
17. The woman Khos-Kiram beheads a spy. Painting from the manuscript of the Persian version of *The Adventures of Hamza*. John Seyller, *The Adventures of Hamza: Painting and Storytelling in Mughal India*. With contributions by Wheeler M. Thackston, Ebba Koch, Antoinette Owen, and Rainald Franz (Washington, DC: Freer Gallery of Art and Arthur M. Sackler Gallery, Smithsonian Institution in association with Azimuth Editions Limited, London, 2002), no. 66 (detail).
18. Baybars and his four companions. Print on cardboard. Bought in Tunis, 1997. (Collection Remke Kruk)
19. Cover of a one-volume abbreviated version of *Sīrat al-malik al-Zāhir Baybars* (Beirut: Dār al-kutub al-shaʿbīya, n.d.).
20. Cover of a one-volume abbreviated version of *Sīrat Fāris al-Yaman al-malik Sayf ibn Dhī Yazan* (Beirut: Dār al-kutub al-shaʿbīya, n.d.), 139–140.

21. Tāma threatening Nāhid. *Sīrat Fāris al-Yaman al-malik Sayf ibn Dhī Yazan* (Beirut: Dār al-kutub al-shaʿbīya), 104.
22. ʿĀqisa attacking Qamarīya. *Sīrat Fāris al-Yaman al-malik Sayf ibn Dhī Yazan* (Beirut: Dār al-kutub al-shaʿbīya), 107.
23. Cover of *Sīrat al-malik Sayf ibn Dhī Yazan Fāris al-Yaman*, 4 vols (Beirut: Maktabat al-tarbīya, 1404/1984).

Acknowledgements

Many friends and colleagues over the years have inspired and supported me in my research into Arabic popular epic. It is impossible to name them all. There are a few, though, to whom I feel particularly indebted: Mariëtte van Beek for bringing me into contact with Sī Mlūd, one of the last traditional performers of popular *sīra*, and Claudia Ott, with whom I spent fascinating days in Marrakesh attending Sī Mlūd's performances. I benefitted greatly from her wide knowledge, enthusiasm and insights, especially regarding the musical aspects of the performance. Most of all, my gratitude extends to the late Sī Mlūd himself, whose friendly willingness to answer our questions and to let us attend his performances greatly contributed to my understanding of *sīra* tradition.

I am most grateful to the Netherlands-Flemish Institute in Cairo (NVIC) for organizing a conference on popular epic on the occasion of my retirement in 2007 and to those colleagues who participated in it and contributed to the resulting conference volume edited by the organizer of the conference, Sabine Dorpmueller. Special thanks go to Peter Heath, whose casual remark during the conference that he expected my continuing work on warrior women to result in a book gave me the final push to sit down and actually write it.

Then there is Maaike van Berkel, whose continuing active interest in my work on popular epic has meant more to me than she may have realized; Arnoud Vrolijk, to whom I never apply in vain for bibliographical help, information and cheerful discussions on scholarship; and Asghar Seyed-Gohrab, who keeps me inspired by invitations to the many conferences and workshops that he organizes. David Waines encouraged the project and paved the way to publication by putting me in touch with Alex Wright of I.B.Tauris, who has been a most pleasant and efficient editor. Finally, there is Susan Spectorsky, colleague and dear friend, who read the manuscript as it grew and provided many useful suggestions, and Frans Oort, my continuing support, who as usual let me benefit from his clear mathematical sense about organizing texts and life in general. To all of them, my deepest gratitude.

CHAPTER 1

Arabic Popular Epic: An Introductory Note

In the minds of most people, Arabic popular storytelling is equivalent to the tales of *The Thousand and One Nights*. This is not surprising, for since it first became known in Europe early in the eighteenth century through Galland's translation,[1] the tales from *The Thousand and One Nights* became so popular in the West that they eclipsed most of the rest of the Arabic narrative tradition.

Even now, few people realize that, in the vast sea of Arabic storytelling, the tales of *The Thousand and One Nights* occupy only a minor place. Other collections of tales exist, and large numbers of stories circulate in the oral tradition of the Arab world. There is also another vast corpus of popular narrative texts that was popular among Arab audiences from medieval times up to the twentieth century. This is the genre known as popular epic, *sīra shaʿbīya*. It is also referred to by various other names: heroic romance, popular romance, saga or chivalric tales.[2] The genre consists of usually lengthy heroic tales centred around a specific hero, often based on a historic character, and his companions. The exploits of these heroes are the subject of huge cycles of adventure stories, amounting to thousands of pages. They are composed in prose or in rhymed prose, sometimes a mixture of both, and often include poems as well. One of the most famous, the *Sīra Hilālīya*, which tells about the adventures of the tribe of Hilāl, is mostly in verse form.

The Arabic word for this type of literature is *sīra*, 'geste'. *Malhama*, epic, is another term that is used. We might call them heroic tales, chivalric romances or even adventure stories. These long tales formed the stock-in-trade of professional storytellers, who recounted them in daily instalments to an enthralled audience. This tradition went on until the twentieth century, and still exists locally. It should be kept in mind that

1

the tradition of telling these long epic tales stands apart from the more casual telling of various kinds of short stories, which may happen in any place or context, including the family circle.[3]

The epics were handed down in oral as well as in written form. Storytellers, often specialists in the performance of a specific epic, recited the tales in public spaces, and, along with these oral performances, manuscripts of the texts circulated widely. Owners of manuscripts, often storytellers themselves, but also booksellers, divided up the text into small volumes, which they rented out to readers.[4] From the nineteenth century on, cheap printed editions became available, and the texts have been regularly reprinted up to the present day.

These narratives usually present legendary versions of historical events, and famous historical figures play leading roles in them. Fantastic elements play a major part in some of them, less so in others. A number of stock characters appear in all of them, varying in appearance and character. The periods, geographical regions and social backgrounds in which the tales are set differ widely. The *Sīrat Banī Hilāl*, still performed in Egypt, is a legendary account of the westward emigration and adventures of the Arabian tribe of the Banū Hilāl.

Sīrat ʿAntar, about the legendary pre-Islamic Bedouin hero ʿAntar ibn Shaddād, is set in the context of rivalries between Bedouin tribes, and this is also a major element in *Sīrat al-amīra Dhāt al-Himma*, which describes the adventures of Princess Dhāt al-Himma and her warriors in their continuing struggle with the Byzantines. *Sīrat al-malik al-Zāhir Baybars* is a legendary account of the exploits of the Mameluke sultan Baybars, who lived in the thirteenth century.

Sīrat al-malik Sayf ibn Dhī Yazan is full of tales of wonder about the adventures of the legendary Yemenite king Sayf ibn Dhī Yazan, while *Qissat al-amīr Hamza al-Bahlawān* tells the story of the pre-Islamic Arabian prince Hamza and his conflict with the Persians. The latter tale is of Persian origin, and it is very widespread in the Islamic world. Widely varying versions exist in Urdu, Malay, Turkish and Arabic.[5] Also of Persian origin is *Qissat Fīrūzshāh ibn al-malik Dārāb*, about the adventures of the Persian prince Fīrūzshāh.

Less well-known works in this genre are the *Sīrat al-Iskandar* (about the adventures of Alexander the Great)[6] and the *Sīrat al-Hākim bi-amr Allāh* (about the Fatimid caliph of that name; not yet available in print).[7] The list is not complete, and continues to be expanded by new finds. While the epics mentioned here are all extremely lengthy, four to six thousand pages or even more, there also exist relatively short ones, such as the story of Princess al-ʿAnqā, 'The Phoenix' (still unedited), and various others.[8]

No proper definition of the genre has as yet been given, and, consequently, opinions differ as to the works to be included in the corpus. The story about the picaresque rogue ʿAlī Zaybaq demonstrates the scholarly dilemma: it is not a heroic tale at all, but since most of the works in this genre contain a certain amount of picaresque elements in the form of the ʿayyār, the trickster character who plays a prominent role in many epics, this has led scholars to include ʿAlī Zaybaq in the corpus. Another problem is that there is a certain amount of overlap with the stories about the legendary exploits of the Arabs in pre-Islamic and early Islamic times, and the equally legendary accounts of the first Islamic raids and conquests (*maghāzī* and *futūḥ* literature). The story of the hero ʿAbdallāh ibn Jaʿfar and the conquest of North Africa, popular in the Arabic as well as the Berber tradition of the Maghrib, is a good example.[9]

Development of the genre

We do not know exactly how old these popular epics are, at least not in the form in which they have come down to us. Clearly, the fact that many feature a specific historical figure offers us a *terminus post quem* for the epic in which this person appears, but that is about all. We know that tales about the hero ʿAntar and about Princess Dhāt al-Himma, her son ʿAbd al-Wahhāb and their companion Baṭṭāl were already circulating in the tenth century, but we do not yet know exactly when and why these tales were converted into the long epic narratives that we know as *sīra shaʿbīya*, popular epic. The influence of the Persian narrative tradition is likely, but the exact connection has not yet been sufficiently researched.

The first actual evidence of long semi-historical tales circulating in Arabic dates from the twelfth century. Samawʾal al-Maghribī (d. 1174) mentions in an autobiographical note that in his youth he was very fond of reading 'the great compilations of tales such as that about the tales of ʿAntar and about the tales of Dalhama and al-Baṭṭāl', until he came to realize that these tales were mostly written by booksellers, and then he started to look for real historical tales, such as the works of Miskawayh and Ṭabarī.[10] We also know about a physician who lived in the middle of the twelfth century, who was nicknamed 'al-ʿAntarī' because he earned money by copying the tales of ʿAntar.[11] Precisely what form these tales were in and how long they had been in existence we do not know. They may not have been exactly like the *sīra*s as we know them. All we can say is that the references to the Crusades included in the *sīra*s of 'Antar and of Dhāt al-Himma as we currently know them demonstrate that they cannot be older than the twelfth century, although they very likely contain material that is older. Similar problems exist concerning the *Sīrat Banī Hilāl*, which occupies a position of its own because, much more than the others, it has been passed on by oral tradition and is always performed in dialect Arabic.

The other *sīra*s are of a slightly later date, but even there our knowledge is restricted by the fact that no manuscripts of these texts older than the fifteenth century have come down to us.[12] These MSS originated from the milieu of the professional storytellers who composed or reworked the *sīra*s and passed them on through a mixed oral and written tradition. In doing so, they made use of the narrative material that formed the stock-in-trade of their profession. Storytellers, reading from written texts or performing orally without the help of books, adapted their material to the taste of their public. Successful plots and motifs were used again and again and crop up in different *sīra*s, sometimes virtually unchanged. The diversity of the MSS of each particular *sīra* shows that the written versions of the *sīra*s were part of a living process in which the interaction of written and oral tradition was a basic element.

Narrative aspects

A few remarks must suffice here about the narrative aspects of the epics. For a more elaborate treatment the reader is referred to Malcolm Lyons, who deals extensively with these matters in the first volume of his *The Arabian Epic* (1995).

Although each *sīra* has its own specific subject matter and approach, as a whole they have much in common. The adventures in which their heroes become involved partly take place in well-known geographical settings, but also often take them to mysterious faraway countries where they may meet strange beings and monstrous enemies. Actual geographical distances are hardly taken into account, and time has laws of its own in this type of literature. Thus, the passing of time hardly affects the heroes' physical appearance, and when they are grandparents they are just as redoubtable in battle as in the prime of their youth.

The stories are often extremely complicated, because they involve a vast number of characters who, in the course of events, each go their separate ways until their paths cross again. So the narrator has to jump from one plot line to another in order to catch up with what is happening on the wider scene, exactly as is done in modern television series involving a number of characters whose lives are interrelated. A further complication, especially for the non-Arab reader, is that many characters bear the same first names, and one quickly becomes confused reading about all these ʿAmrs, ʿUmars and ʿAbdallāhs, not to mention the staggering number of Maryams and Fāṭimas that appear on the scene.

Just as in a television series, the story can be expanded continuously by linking a new episode to the previous episode. If, for instance, the lovers in a modern television soap are finally united, this could bring the series to a conclusion. Instead, however, a former lover turns up in the next instalment. Mistrust and discord between the couple arise, and everything starts all over again. The equivalent in Arabic popular epic is the cloud of dust that appears at the horizon after an adventure has been brought to a good end. The cloud announces the arrival of a group of warriors, enemies or friends, and a new series of adventures is set in motion. A narrative device repeatedly used in modern soaps also frequently occurs in the epics: a character who is presumed dead suddenly reappears, sometimes with a much altered appearance, for instance as a result of magical tricks involved in his disappearance.

Protagonists

A vast number of protagonists appear in these epics. Many of them are fictional versions of historical figures, which offer us an interesting view of the way in which these persons were perceived on the popular level. Among the protagonists are a number of stock characters, adapted to the needs of each particular narrative. One, of course, is the hero, whose status and career is described according to the usual framework of heroic literature all over the world. The circumstances of his birth and early youth are unusual; he often acquires an extraordinary sword and an exceptionally powerful steed at the start of his career; he has to set out on a quest to win his beloved or to gain recognition. A remarkable aspect of the Arabic epic is that a number of the heroes are people of low social status, handicapped in their career by their birth and physical appearance. Many of them are black, and some even start out as slaves. Some of the heroes are female, in some cases black women.

Early in his life the hero usually acquires a faithful companion and helper, who, in Arabic popular epic, is generally a sort of trickster figure, the 'man of wiles'.[13] The Arabic term is *ʿayyār*. The *ʿayyār* possesses characteristics that enable him to cross all kinds of boundaries, natural, social and practical. He speaks a number of languages, is a master of disguise and, in some cases, has supernatural powers. As a typical trickster, he is a creature of marginality, not bound by convention. He can subvert the existing natural or social order by doing things that run counter to accepted patterns and social codes. All this puts him in an excellent position to make all kinds of unexpected moves. He may, for instance, appear out of the blue in unlikely places and thus save the hero from almost certain death. In general, he acts as the narrator's deus ex machina, propelled onto the scene when the narrative has come to a point where there seems no way out.

Aspects of the *ʿayyār* may also be encountered in other characters, sometimes the hero himself. An example is Abu Zayd al-Hilālī, the leading protagonist of the *Sīrat Banī Hilāl*. Princess Dhāt al-Himma, who will be studied extensively in Chapter 3, also has some *ʿayyār* traits, and we meet a real female *ʿayyār* in the person of ʿUdhayba, daughter of Battāl, the prominent trickster character of *Sīrat Dhāt al-Himma*.

The hero's opponent appears in many forms. There are foreign enemies of all kinds to battle against, while rivalries within the hero's own group may also threaten him and lead to armed conflict. Often the hero's opponent is one particular major villain, for instance a Christian posing as a Muslim and occupying a powerful position, who continues his evil actions throughout a whole *sīra*.

A protagonist noteworthy in the context of this book is the warrior woman. Female warriors appear in most of the epics, and in some of them they are especially prominent. They may be foreign princesses trained from youth in the chivalrous arts, but also Arab women, usually Bedouin girls, who have mastered the art of combat. More will be said about them in the next chapter.

Polygamy

A great advantage of the Islamic setting of the stories is that the hero can legally be involved in continuous love affairs. Some of these may be clandestine, but most lead to marriage. Even though the legal number of four simultaneous wives cannot be exceeded, the possibilities are virtually unlimited because a wife may die or be left behind in a foreign city with the right to consider herself divorced after a certain period of time has elapsed. A quick count of the marriages concluded by ʿArnūs, one of the protagonists in *Sīrat Baybars*, yielded 13. A further advantage of these marriages is that sons born from long-forgotten wives may turn up at any moment, offering fresh possibilities for narrative developments.

Attitudes to Arabic popular epic

Remarkably, this vast corpus of material has, for a long time, hardly been taken into account in histories of Arabic literature. While Western interest in these texts flared up early in the nineteenth century, manuscripts of them were collected and included in European library collections, and some scholars studied their contents and wrote about them, these works did not become part of the general picture of Arabic literature. They usually received only a brief mention, if at all, in introductions to the Arabic literary heritage. In the last five decades, however, there has been renewed scholarly interest in this branch of literature, and a number of publications from the hands of Arab as well as Western scholars have appeared. Giovanni Canova's extensive overview of recent developments and publications demonstrates how much is happening in this field.[14] In spite of all this, the study of popular epic is still something of a marginal field in the sense that it is self-contained: its results are rarely taken into consideration in the study of mainstream culture. Many scholars, too, are still not aware of the close connections between popular *sīra* and the literary tradition of the elite.[15]

Very little of this material is available in translation, and this is one of the reasons why these narratives have remained almost unknown to the non-Arab public. A great step forward was the appearance of Malcolm Lyons's three-volume *The Arabian Epic* in 1995, which provided motif indexes as well as extensive summaries of nearly all the epics available in print.[16] By providing summaries, Lyons continued in the line of Rudi Paret, who, in 1924, published a summary of *Sīrat al-malik Sayf ibn Dhī Yazan*, and so for the first time presented the non-Arab reader with a full survey of one of the epics.

One might wonder why scholarly interest in this branch of Arabic literature took so long to develop, and why it was considered irrelevant to the study of classical Arabic writing. A possible answer is that, in their approach to Arabic literary culture, Western scholars took their lead from Arab scholars and implicitly saw these tales as substandard literature, not worthy of attention.[17] The negative attitude of Arab literates towards these stories in the past was based on the fact that they presented fictional, often fantastic accounts of events; that their style and composition were different from formal classical poetry and prose; and that their language often did not conform to the rules of classical Arabic. Some, such as the tales about the adventures of the Banū Hilāl, were even composed exclusively in Arabic dialect. And although a medieval Arab scholar with an exceptionally open mind, such as the famous Ibn Khaldūn (1332–1405), argued that the literary quality of a text did not depend on the use of correct classical grammar and that, accordingly, the songs of the Banū Hilāl could not be considered worthless simply because they were written in dialect, the large majority of scholars were of a different opinion, as various indications in Arabic sources make clear.

Thus, it was seen as unadvisable for children to copy out texts of this kind.[18] This was not only because it would teach incorrect grammar. Objections were also, and even predominantly, of a moral nature. Religious scholars frowned upon these stories. They considered it a frivolous pastime to occupy oneself with such literature instead of devoting attention to serious texts and religious duties. Some of these scholars explicitly expressed such opinions in their writings, thus presenting modern scholars with rare snippets of information about the role and existence of popular epic in their particular time. Ibn Taymīya (d. 1328), the austere theologian who became the leading religious authority for the Wahhābī form of Islam currently practised in Saudi Arabia, sternly condemned listening to heroic tales,[19] and the theologian Ibn Kathīr (d. 1373), speaking about the epic *Sīrat Dhāt al-Himma*, remarked: 'it is nothing but lies, falsehood, stupid writings, complete ignorance and shameless prattle which is only in demand by fools and lowly ignoramuses. The same is true of the fabricated epic of 'Antar al-'Absī.'[20] Over a century later, the law scholar al-Wansharīsī (d. 1508) cites a *fatwā*, a juridical ruling, that forbids selling fictional historical tales and similar untruthful texts.[21]

Medieval Muslim scholars were not alone in their condemnation of fictional literature. Views towards frivolous, that is, not morally uplifting, pastimes, including reading chivalric romances, were no different in medieval Europe, as is demonstrated, for example, by a passage in Dante's *Divina Commedia:* in the section on Hell (Canto 5 v. 127),

Dante describes how Francesca and her friend were led astray by reading about the adventures of Lancelot and so ended up in Hell.

Religious condemnation, however, has rarely kept people from enjoying themselves, and the very fact that scholars fulminated against reading and listening to heroic tales demonstrates that they were actually quite popular. As to the Arabic heroic tales, the existence of substantial numbers of manuscripts confirms this. Yet the generally accepted notion among Arab literates seems to have been that the popular epic, along with other aspects of popular culture, had no real connection to classical literary culture and, accordingly, was not worthy of attention in scholarly discourse. This attitude prevailed until quite recently, and the idea of treating this genre of literature as something worthy of scholarly study did not become generally accepted in the Arab world until the 1960s, when the first publications in Arabic about this literary genre began to appear.[22]

Readership, audience and performance

Since Arab literates of the past (i.e. from the twelfth century onwards) usually did not consider popular epic, *sīra*, worthy of attention, we have very little information as to how these stories circulated and were passed on. We know that this happened both through written copies and through oral performance, but how exactly such performances took place cannot easily be ascertained. Luckily, the reports of foreign (usually European) travellers to the Middle East offer invaluable information, running from brief remarks about the activities of storytellers to lengthy descriptions of actual performances. From these descriptions it is clear that there were considerable differences in practice, not only between regions and periods, but also regarding the specific work that was performed.

The most elaborate report is that of Edward William Lane, who provides us with extensive information about the professional storytellers of Cairo in the nineteenth century. Settling in Cairo in 1825, Lane noted down all kinds of details of everyday life, which he brought together in his invaluable book, *An Account of the Manners and Customs of the Modern Egyptians*.[23] He gives extensive information on the professional storytellers whose stock-in-trade were the popular epics, such as the *Sīrat al-amīra Dhāt al-Himma* (also called *Sīrat al-mujāhidīn* or *Sīrat Dalhama*), the *Sīrat ʿAntara* (or *Sīrat ʿAntar*), *Sīrat Baybars* and the *Sīrat Banī Hilāl* (or *Sīra Hilālīya*). Specific details are added about the performance tradition:

Sīrat Banī Hilāl, always performed orally, without recourse to written texts, was the exclusive domain of specialist performers and was accompanied by music, unlike the other epics. A narrator's histrionic talents were put to use particularly in the performance of *Sīrat Baybars*, something that is also reported from Syria.[24] Reciters of *Sīrat ʿAntara* formed a separate group and always read from books, sometimes also reciting other *sīra*s.

Lane also describes the setting of the performance: the storyteller took his place on a little stool placed on an elevation built against the outside wall of a coffee house and then started reciting his tale, surrounded by his audience. Although, as Lane remarks, some of the storytellers also had *The Thousand and One Nights* in their repertoire, it is obvious that the *Nights* were not nearly as popular as the long heroic adventure tales of the *sīra*s, which were told in daily instalments over long periods of time: the equivalent of modern television series. Modern research among storytellers in Morocco has confirmed that professional storytellers had a much better chance of obtaining a steady audience, and thus a steady income, by performing *sīra* recitations than by recounting the relatively short *Thousand and One Nights* stories.[25]

Locations for storytelling differed from region to region. In Middle Eastern cities, coffee houses were a common venue, while in southern Egypt performances of *Sīra Hilālīya* took place (and still take place) in the context of festive family gatherings or public festivals.

Observations made in Morocco in the first half of the twentieth century by Roger Le Tourneau show that in North Africa sessions were held outside the city gate or in open spaces in the city. It is clear that the use of written texts was not as clearly defined here as in the Cairo scene described by Lane. Literate storytellers might read from books, but others memorized even the longest narratives. Ba Dris, the Moroccan storyteller described by Le Tourneau, was an illiterate *babouche* (slipper) seller, and recited the three long *sīra*s forming his repertoire completely from memory.[26]

With the arrival of radio and television in the twentieth century, *sīra* performers gradually began to disappear, although the tradition continued for a long time in some places. Even today the *Sīra Hilālīya* is still performed in Egypt as part of a living tradition.[27] The performance tradition of the *Sīra Hilālīya*, however, stands apart from that of the other *sīra*s. Its performance is the exclusive domain of specialists. With regard to other *sīra*s, sometimes attempts have been made to revive and continue the tradition, as was done in Damascus.[28]

Probably one of the last traditional *sīra* performers, apart from those of the *Sīra Hilālīya*, was the Moroccan storyteller Sī Mlūd, whose sessions I

Arabic Popular Epic: An Introductory Note

attended together with Claudia Ott in 1997, three years before his death. Those sessions took place in Dār al-Barūd, a somewhat rundown city park close to the Kutubīya minaret in Marrakesh. It no longer exists today. Sī Mlūd had recited *sīra* literature there on a daily basis since 1961. The reciting traditionally took place from afternoon prayer until sunset prayer, but because of his advanced age Sī Mlūd had, during the last years, reduced this to one hour before sunset prayer.

Seated on a little stool, he read from books, reciting very fast in a sing-song manner, and occasionally interacting with the public. His audience, between fifty and eighty people, sat around him on the ground, sometimes renting a piece of cardboard to sit on from the 'cardboard man' who formed part of the setting, which also included a tea-maker and a passing biscuit-seller. Reciting was stopped abruptly when the call to sunset prayer sounded from the Kutubīya and everybody left immediately, putting a few coins into Sī Mlūd's hand.

Several people among the almost exclusively male audience had attended the sessions in the park even before Sī Mlūd took over from a predecessor in 1961. They knew the titles of all the well-known *sīras*, and could easily sum them up, including *Futūh al-Shām*, a work on the legendary conquest of early Islam. Yet they had very outspoken preferences as to which *sīras* they wanted to hear performed, and, clearly, *Sīrat 'Antara* and *Sīrat al-amīra Dhāt al-Himma* (called *al-Wahhābīya* in Morocco) were the two favourites, with *Sīrat Baybars* as a possible third (we were not sure whether the latter had actually been recited in recent years). So there was an explicitly stated preference for *sīras* that had Arab history as their subject matter, and this decided which *sīra* was going to be performed next. Reciting for about one hour every day, it took Sī Mlūd one year and three months to finish *Sīrat al-amīra Dhāt al-Himma*. *Sīrat 'Antara* would take a couple of months less.[29]

Visual representations

The popularity of *sīra* literature up to the second half of the twentieth century also manifested itself in the form of visual representations. In particular, scenes from *Sīrat 'Antara* and the *Sīra Hilālīya* were often depicted on reverse glass paintings, embroideries, cheap poster prints and block prints on textiles. Nowadays these are popular objects for the tourist market.

Some of the popular printed editions include illustrations, usually consisting of fairly crude and simple drawings. Then there is a traditional form of visualizing the epics, which so far has received little attention. This is the 'wonder box', the *sundūq al-'ajab* or *sundūq al-furja*. It was used throughout the Arab world to illustrate a story with pictures, a simple device equivalent to the magic lantern used in the West. The wonder box appears, for instance, in Ahmad Sefrioui's novel *La boîte à merveilles* (The Wonder Box), about a young Moroccan boy.[30] It also appears in the title of a work by the Palestinian author Emile Habibi.[31]

In letters dated 28 March and 7 April 2001, Salma Jayyusi, a prominent authority on Arabic literature, told me about her childhood experiences with this contraption in Acre, and she gave me permission to quote her letters:

> *Sundūq al-'ajab* was a small longitudinal metal box with metal studs on the outside and the appearance of something that has been touched, hugged, and cajoled by hundreds and hundreds of children. It had a peephole through which people could look at a demonstration of pictures which the proprietor rolled for the viewer to see: 'Antar embracing 'Abla, Sayf ibn Dhī Yazan flying on the wings of 'Āqisa, etc., all from legends and folk tales. He also carried a bench on which we sat (never mind the cleanliness which obsessed my mother) and would peep through the hole to witness the moving scene. A very primitive kind of cinema with the man there bellowing in sing song voice what he had memorized of the story of this hero or that. It was a decrepit box falling apart all the time, but it was the most cherished thing to come to the neighbourhood now and then.

The pictures were painted or drawn on a strip of paper which was wound around a vertical cylinder, with the outer end attached to a second cylinder. By turning the cylinders, the narrator could roll the pictures along while telling his story. The practice, reported to be two centuries old, was recently revived by a Palestinian storyteller who adopted the professional name Abū al-'Ajab, built his own wonder box and uses it in his storytelling.[32]

Recent developments

While public performances of *sīra* in their traditional setting are dwindling, the texts themselves are still published regularly. They are cheaply produced for the popular market, either as full texts or in abbreviated form. The genre has also proven its vitality in other ways, namely by moving on to new media. This started with audio cassettes. Audio cassettes of the *Sīra Hilālīya* became quite popular in southern Egypt in the later part of the twentieth century. A complete set of the *sīra* as performed by one particular singer (Arabic: *shāʿir*, poet) consisted of some twenty cassettes. When my colleague Marcel Kurpershoek and I tried to collect a full set of the *Hilālīya*, visiting small cassette shops in Luxor in the 1990s, we discovered that at least four different sets were in circulation, each recorded by a different singer.

In addition, the *Sīra Hilālīya*, along with several other *sīras*, has been given a new lease of life as a television series. In Ramadan in particular, TV versions of the old epic story cycles such as the *Sīra Hilālīya*, *Sīrat ʿAntara* and *Qissat al-Zīr Sālim* have been broadcast. So the old tradition continues to live on in a new form, and one waits with interest to see what the future developments will be. Why shouldn't the great traditional heroes find their way into the graphic novel or the digital gaming industry? They certainly have the potential.

CHAPTER 2

Warrior Women in the Arabic Tradition

Warrior women in Arab culture

Muslim equivalents of Catwoman, Wonder Woman and similar heroines, ruthlessly fighting all sorts of enemies, including religious zealots and terrorists, may seem a rather unlikely phenomenon. Yet they make striking appearances in popular graphic novels, such as the series *The 99* by Kuwaiti author Na'if al-Mutawa.[1] There is also Jalila, who appears in *Protector of the City of All Faiths*.[2] They form the most recent representations of Arab warrior women in popular fiction. Few people, possibly not even their creators, will realize that these martial women stand in a long tradition. To discover that such martial females appeared on a large scale in Arabic fictional literature of the past is, to most people, a great surprise: the fact does not tally at all with their expectations of Muslim culture.[3] How this relates to actual historical reality is another question, and a brief discussion of the matter may be in order here.

Were warrior women, especially young and beautiful girls well trained in the martial arts and eager to engage in combat, a familiar phenomenon in the Islamic world? Popular imagination certainly suggests it, and not only Arabic popular imagination. In *La Gerusalemme liberata*, the Italian poet Torquato Tasso (d. 1595) makes Tancredi, the brave young Crusader, engage in battle with an unknown Muslim knight outside the walls of Jerusalem. Tancredi fatally wounds his opponent, discovering too late that the supposed enemy knight is his beloved, the Muslim girl Clorinda.[4]

Similar female knights also frequently occur in Arabic and other Middle Eastern literatures of the Islamic period, such as Persian, Turkish and Urdu.⁵ It raises the question whether these stories had a basis in historical fact, either in Islamic times (that is to say, roughly after 600 CE), or, possibly, in the distant pre-Islamic past. As to pre-Islamic times: it certainly is possible, but there is little actual evidence. Archaeological research in Central Asia has unearthed burial sites probably dating from 300 BC of what were possibly female warriors of high standing, but the interpretation of the finds is still speculative. Yet they offer at least an indication that, at some point in the past, women in these regions may have taken part in armed combat.⁶ Otherwise, the idea that warrior queens and warrior women existed in the Middle East is mostly based on legends going back to antiquity, legends that continued to circulate in later Middle Eastern traditions.

Thus, the Amazons of Greek mythology found their way to the East in various ways. They appear in the scientific tradition because there is a reference to them in a work of Hippocrates that became very widespread in the Arabic tradition,⁷ and that is how Marwazī, a physician who lived around 1100 and who wrote a book on various kinds of living beings, came to speak about these 'Amāzūnas' in his *Book on the Natures of Living Beings*:

> Galen says that their women (i.e. people in Asia, such as the Ionians and Turks) fight like men and that they cut off one of their breasts so that their entire strength should go into their arms, and their bodies grow slim (enabling them) to jump on to the backs of the horses. Hippocrates has mentioned these women in some of his works. He calls them Amāzūnas, which means 'those who possess but one breast', for they cut off the other and they are only prevented from cutting off the (remaining) breast by the necessity of feeding their children for the perpetuation of their race. (The reason why) they cut off one breast in order that it may not hamper them in shooting arrows on horseback.⁸

Marwazī comes back to these women in a later chapter devoted specifically to deviant forms of male and female,⁹ such as men with feminine and women with masculine characteristics: 'Masculine women are those whose femininity has coarsened and whose nature has become close to that of men who are brave, gallant and courageous. There are many categories of such women. There are those who set out to encounter valiant warriors and to venture into battle, in the way that 'A'isha (with whom God may be pleased) did on the Day of the Camel,¹⁰ and like some of the women of the Turks and the daughters of the Byzantines do.'

Another source of information about the Amazons, far more widespread than this scientific tradition, is the legendary biography of Alexander the Great, which has left ample traces in the Christian and Islamic literatures of the Middle East, including Arabic popular epic. A famous episode describes Alexander's meeting with an Amazon queen, and this also occurs in accounts circulating in the Arabic tradition. There Alexander meets an Amazon queen called Baryānūs.[11] This is not the only occasion in the Arabic Alexander tradition where Alexander meets a warrior queen. In *Sīrat al-malik Iskandar*, a popular *sīra* based on the Alexander legends circulating in the Arabic tradition, Alexander (here a champion of monotheism) meets Queen Rādīya, 'an expert in the field of astrology and the art of battle. Moreover, she was very beautiful and skilled in equestrian sports and riding the giraffe.' No battle takes place, because the queen and her people, who are already secret monotheists, quickly convert.[12]

Also of a legendary nature are the stories about Zenobia, the famous third-century queen of Palmyra. Various elements of what is said about her in classical sources, such as that by Trebellius Pollio, may eventually have found their way into the Arabic tradition as motifs in the warrior women tales. Stories about Zenobia's tomboy youth match what is being told in Arabic popular epic about the youth of warrior women such as Princess Dhāt al-Himma: the girl scorns womanly activities, preferring to wander about in the wilderness, shooting game with her arrows. The same source tells about Zenobia in battle, saying that she was not recognizable as a woman, hiding her female body under armour and her long flowing hair under a helmet.[13] This is also a familiar motif in Arabic warrior women stories. As to Zenobia herself: in the Arabic historical tradition she does not appear as a woman carrying arms and participating in battle, but as a brave woman who challenges a powerful man in the crudest possible way and has him killed.[14]

Tales about fearsome Georgian queens have left their traces in the Arabic popular tradition, such as in *Sīrat al-amīra Dhāt al-Himma*.[15] Then there is the Berber queen known as al-Kāhina, who led Berber resistance against the Arab invasion, and who continues to play a part in the Algerian popular imagination.[16]

Islamic history itself has known female rulers, although not in great numbers, but few of them actually wielded power.[17] They were usually just figureheads for a man behind the throne. None of them is reported to have led armies or participated in combat, not even the few who actually exercised power, such as the Yemeni queen Arwā, who lived in the first half of the eleventh century, and was also known as Sayyida Hurra,[18] and Dayfa Khātūn, sultan of Aleppo on behalf of her young grandson from 1236 to 1242 CE.[19] Shajarat al-Durr, sultan in name of Egypt in the thirteenth century, did not play an important political role, but, remarkably enough, she found her way into Arabic popular epic and became a prominent character in *Sīrat Baybars,* where she personally kills her husband Aybak with a knife.

It has often been stated, both by Arab historians of the past and by modern scholars, that Arab women played an active role in the tribal conflicts of pre-Islamic days (*ayyām al-ʿarab*) and in the raids and wars of conquest of early Islam (*maghāzī* and *futūh*). References of this kind are indeed found in Arabic sources, but they are rare and usually very brief. A noteworthy case is that of the prophetess Sajāh, who set herself against Islam. She married another prophet, Musaylima, and in 632, the year of the Prophet Muhammad's death, she made ready to attack Medina with the tribe that had put itself under her command.[20]

To the same period belongs a report that was later passed on by the historian Tabarī (d. 922/923), namely that women actively fought in the Battle of the Yarmūk, which took place in 636 CE). One of them is mentioned by name: Juwayrīya, the daughter of Abū Sufyān. According to the same report, her husband also took part in the battle.[21] Here, too, it is hard to decide how much is based on historical fact. There is little evidence that women actually fought in combat. Their role was mostly restricted to encouraging the men and occasionally killing, at the men's request, wounded enemies.[22]

Occasionally we come across a brief reference to women getting involved in warfare in later times, and the very fact that this is presented as something very unusual is to be noted. The historian Ibn al-Athīr tells us that Umm ʿĪsā and Lubāba, the two sisters of a certain Sālih b. ʿAlī, joined him in the campaign in to Byzantine territory in the year 756 CE because they had vowed to go on holy war if the reign of the hated Umayyads came to an end. This happened in 750, and so they set out to fulfil their vow. Nothing, however, is said about the sisters carrying armour of any kind.[23] Another case is that of a woman participating in battle during the time of Caliph Hārūn al-Rashīd. The account is noteworthy because it demonstrates the negative attitude towards martial women at the time. The woman, Laylā bint Tarīf, was the sister of a dissident leader, the Kharijite al-Walīd ibn Tarīf, and, when an army was sent against her brother, she accompanied him in battle, carrying arms and wearing a helmet and a coat of mail. She started to attack people and was recognized. Yazīd, the leader of the caliph's army, went up to her and struck the backside of her horse with his spear, telling her in strong terms to go away because she had brought shame on her father's clan. She felt deeply ashamed, and Yazīd was generally applauded for his action.[24]

This all indicates that a woman engaging in warfare was a very rare and unusual phenomenon in Arab history, especially a woman donning formal battle equipment. It was no different in later centuries. In the heat of battle women might occasionally help fight off the enemy, as is mentioned by 'Usāma ibn Munqidh (d. 1188) in his memoirs: when Ismaili Shi'ites besieged his home base, the fortress of Shayzar, in 1109, an old woman named Funun put on her veil, took up a sword and rushed into battle.[25] That, however, is a very different situation from an army incorporating women as a matter of course, and Arab historians of the Crusades note with amazement the presence of armed women in the Frankish army, such as Eleanor of Aquitaine, wife of Louis VII,[26] without giving any indication that the phenomenon of women participating in warfare was familiar to them. They find it quite fascinating, however: 'Amongst the Franks are women knights (*fawāris*). They have coats of mail and helmets. They are in men's garb and they are prominent in the thick of the fray. They act in the manner of those endowed with intellect (i.e. men) although they are ladies.'[27]

While here we see Arab historians expressing their amazement about what they saw in European armies, the opposite also occurs. A famous case that has been the subject of much scholarly discussion is an account about a contingent of some three hundred African women forming part of the Almoravid army during the siege of Valencia in 1094. It is found in the *Primera Crónica General*, a chronicle probably dating from the first part of the fourteenth century, and the African women feature in the chapters devoted to El Cid, Rodrigo Díaz de Vivar. According to the account, the women panicked and ran off, and so contributed to the defeat of the Almoravid army instead of being a support. The affair is highly intriguing, but it would take us too long here to discuss its various implications.[28]

Fiction

Literary fiction, however, presents its own view of reality, and while female warriors may not have been a prominent feature in actual Islamic history, they frequently occur in the legendary literature about the wars and conquests of early Islam.[29] Rosenthal's remark about the Battle of the Yarmūk as described in *Futūh al-Shām* (The Conquest of Syria), a work that he classifies as 'prose romance', aptly illustrates this: 'A stellar cast of heroic women fills the traditional role of Bedouin women of inciting the men to bravery and, moreover, doing brave deeds themselves far beyond any historical reality.'[30] The stories about warrior women in this kind of literature are full of themes and motifs that are familiar from popular epic, a genre that is closely related to the legendary stories about early Islamic wars and conquests. An example is the case of Zalfā in the legendary account of the conquest of Yemen. She converts to Islam and attacks her own father, the monstrous Yemeni ruler Ra's al-Ghūl.[31] The young girl who is attracted to Islam (often in the form of a brave and handsome Muslim warrior), converts and sets herself against her father, fully prepared to kill him if he refuses to convert, is a familiar figure in Arabic popular epic.

In popular epic, warrior women occur in great variety, although they are more prominent in some epics than in others. This chapter attempts to give a survey, necessarily brief, of the role and nature of these warrior women.

Amazons?

A few words as to terminology may be in order. In speaking about the warrior women of the Arabic *sīra*s I consistently try to avoid the term Amazons, and this may need some explanation. What, exactly, is an Amazon? Obviously, she is some kind of woman warrior, and popular usage tends to apply the term to virtually every type of woman who takes up a martial role. For many people, the association with the Amazons of Greek mythology, the martial females who excluded males from their society, has all but disappeared, and all kinds of martial women are denoted as 'Amazons'.

This, however, does not contribute to a clear evaluation of the warrior woman's role and function in a particular context. Although, for many people, the word 'Amazon' may have lost most of its specific meaning, for others it still has the connotation of the classical Amazon myth. A vital characteristic of the Amazon myth is that it presents a female-dominated society and, by so doing, puts the accepted values of the male-dominated social order at stake. This challenge to male domination often takes the form of a negative if not outright hostile attitude towards men in general, without, however, necessarily rejecting them as a possible means of sexual gratification. Common denominators of the myth in its various forms are the women's refusal to accept restriction to the non-public sphere and to act as childbearers for men. As such, 'Amazon' is a very clearly defined concept. This concept, however, does not apply to the majority of martial women in Arabic popular epic, and using the term would be likely to create confusion. Many of the warrior women in *sīra* literature form happy unions with men, bear them sons and daughters which they raise with motherly care, and do not form part of exclusively female societies that present a reversal of the accepted social order.

This does not mean that traces of the classical myth are completely absent from Arabic literature. Adapted versions of it are well in evidence in the Arabic (and, more generally, the Islamic) tradition, as was pointed out above. Intriguing in this respect are the more or less standard opening scenes of many warrior women stories, in which the male hero suddenly comes upon a community of females, well-trained in the chivalrous arts, living in an isolated castle or in a monastery. Often, the leading heroine in these cases makes a remark about her having no need for men but feeling 'more inclined towards the ladies'.

These episodes are, at first sight, puzzling, and have given rise to various suggestions, such as that they may be based on Islamic observations of Christian nunneries or point to the existence of female equivalents of *futuwwa-* or *'ayyār*-like organizations; that such equivalents existed in Persian society has been suggested by Hanaway.[32] I doubt that the solution lies in any of these directions; these episodes have every semblance of being a literary remnant of the traditional Amazon myth.

In several of these stories, some of the concepts discussed in, for instance, Tyrrell's study of the development of the Amazon myth, are well in evidence: the opposition between the customs of the female community and those of patriarchal society; allotting specific exclusive domains of life to males and females; attitudes towards sex, marriage and reproduction, and children.[33] Yet the challenge of patriarchal society rarely takes the form of a complete reversal of the social order. One of the most intriguing cases is an episode in *Sīrat Sayf ibn Dhī Yazan* in which an exclusively female society is presented, having as its counterpart an exclusively male community. Chapter 13, one of the chapters devoted to *Sīrat Sayf ibn Dhī Yazan*, will discuss this further.

Source texts

In this book I have based my research on printed popular epics, leaving aside the still unedited works, of which there are quite a few. The material is vast and stories featuring warrior women are numerous. Since I decided to concentrate attention on some of the most striking and representative warrior women tales, not all the epics could be treated in separate chapters. Five epics will be dealt with extensively. *Sīrat al-amīra Dhāt al-Himma*, with its leading warrior princess and vast number of warrior women, will, of course, get ample attention, and so will *Sīrat ʿAntar*. The *Tale of Prince Hamza* (this epic is called *qissa*, tale, instead of *sīra*) contains a number of warrior women episodes, and is especially interesting because Hamza, the leading hero, expresses his disapproval of women engaging in such activities. Then there is *Sīrat Baybars*, in which warrior women trained in formal armed combat on the battlefield still occur, but play only a minor role. Foreign queens acting as army leaders, but without taking part in battle, frequently appear, though, and there is also the phenomenon of the lady of independent mind, full of initiative and prepared to kill by whatever means that comes to hand when the situation demands it. Finally, there is *Sīrat Sayf ibn Dhī Yazan*, an adventure tale full of fairytale elements that features several striking female characters prepared to take up arms if necessary. They deserve special attention, and so does the episode of the Island of Maidens that occurs in the *sīra*.

The *Sīrat Banī Hilāl*, or *Sīra Hilālīya*, on the other hand, will not receive prominent attention, although it contains a number of fascinating female characters, including brief appearances of warrior women. Several of the women married to the protagonists are warrior women,[34] and there is, for instance, the Maiden of the Languorous Eyes, who not only has been taught the sciences and the recitation of the Qurʾān, but has also been trained in horsemanship and rides into battle.[35]

Most prominent is al-Jāziya, the sister of Hasan, one of the leading heroes. She is the leading female protagonist of the *sīra*, renowned not only for her beauty and political acumen, but also for her horsemanship. She plays a prominent part in the expeditions and the discussions of the Hilālī tribe, but not as a warrior woman regularly participating in battle, like many of the women in *Sīrat Dhāt al-Himma*. When al-Jāzīya girds herself in battle armour, it is for dramatic effect. She makes a most impressive appearance in the *Dīwān al-Aytām* (The Book of the Orphans), one of the lesser known parts of the *Sīra Hilālīya*. Abū Zayd, the leading hero of the *Sīra Hilālīya*, by then completely blind, is mounted on his horse and led into battle. Al-Jāzīya, in full armour, rides forth beside him leading an army of orphans to seek vengeance for the death of her brother Hasan.[36] In spite of these occasional appearances in arms al-Jāziya does not quite fit into the context of this book, and we will not discuss her further.

The tale (*qissa*) of Prince Fīrūzshāh is, like that of Hamza, connected to the Persian narrative tradition, and features several warrior women.[37] Princess 'Ayn al-Hayāt, the leading female protagonist, is well trained in the martial arts. We see her, for instance, fighting another woman in single combat during a tournament organized as part of her wedding festivities.[38] Earlier in the story, in the course of a nightly escapade to meet her lover Prince Fīrūzshāh, she kills a slave with her sword when she discovers him having illicit sex. Subsequently, she also kills three servants who are trying to capture the slave's murderer.[39]

In two short epics, the small *sīra* of King 'Umar [ibn] al-Nu'mān included in *The Thousand and One Nights* and *Sīrat Sayf ibn Tījān*, martial women also make an appearance. *Sīrat al-Iskandar*, about the legendary adventures of Alexander the Great, is noteworthy for the Amazons who appear in it. These tales will occasionally be referred to in passing.

Warrior women: general characteristics and motifs

Warrior women in these epics come in all sorts of guises. They may be foreign women encountered as opponents, but also women of sound Arab stock. They may be young and beautiful but also old and ugly, in which case they are usually enemies. They may also be advanced in years but respected for their wisdom. They may appear in the roles of mother, daughter, sister or wife and are always free women, although the vicissitudes of war may sometimes bring them into slavery. Sometimes they are not female warriors trained in the arts of war who habitually engage in combat, but just intrepid women who do not hesitate to take up the sword or any another weapon when the situation demands it. We will meet several of these women in *Sīrat Baybars*.

A number of standard motifs appear in the warrior women stories. The warrior girl has often acquired her skills by being educated as a boy for a variety of reasons. There is the motif of the girl who will only consent to marry a man who manages to defeat her in combat. Many suitors unsuccessfully take up the challenge until finally the hero steps in and wins the contest. Familiar, too, is the motif of the warrior girl or woman who engages in combat in male disguise and reveals her female charms (hair, face, breasts) at a crucial moment, unsettling her opponent to such an extent that she can easily unhorse and capture him.

Then there is the motif of hero worshipping. In stories about young warrior girls we regularly come across the motif of the girl's fascination for a famous hero from the enemy camp who is held captive by her own people. She visits him in prison, asks him questions and boasts about her own martial prowess, which she would like to test by duelling with him. All this usually leads to her desertion of her own people and marriage to the hero. A remarkable motif that sometimes turns up is that of the warrior girl who protects her meek father or bosses him around.

Heroic cycle

In heroic literature, the hero's special status is usually brought into focus by elements such as his unusual birth and youth, proving his special status early in life by a remarkable heroic feat, the acquirement of special, often miraculous, armour or weapons (usually a sword) and an extraordinary kind of mount. Also, he usually finds a faithful helper. His life follows a well-defined pattern involving quests, winning a maiden, victory over enemies and a heroic death. Of the vast literature on the subject, I will here just refer to Jan de Vries's analysis of the 'heroic cycle', the hero's life pattern,[40] and to Peter Heath, who has analysed the specific form of this pattern in *Sīrat ʿAntar*.[41]

In ʿAntar's life, all the heroic signs can clearly be seen. How, then, does this work out in the case of warrior women with a major heroic status? Do we find the same elements? Is the pattern adapted to their specific case? Can we speak of a specifically feminine type of heroic cycle? Two warrior women are particularly interesting in this respect because they both play major leading roles and follow a heroic career with a specific goal. Princess Fāṭima Dhāt al-Himma (see Chapter 3) is the most obvious case; the other is ʿUnaytira, ʿAntar's daughter (see Chapter 7). Both will be treated more extensively in the next chapters, but here we may note some significant points about their heroic careers.

Relatively few of the standard elements summed up above are present in the case of Princess Dhāt al-Himma. Her childhood and youth are indeed unusual: she is rejected by her father because she is a girl and raised outside the family. At the age of five, she is abducted and cut off from her family. Already at a very young age she is remarkable for her pride and physical strength, and trains herself in the art of war: from reeds and branches she fabricates her own weapons, and she teaches herself to fight on horseback. When she is about seven years old she kills a man who threatens her honour. No special kind of weapon or unusual horse comes her way, but she has another remarkable quality: she is noted for her piety, which borders on the asceticism. She has no interest in marriage or children.

Yet the narrator clearly feels that it would diminish her heroic status as a woman if she did not become a mother, preferably the mother of a son. So she gives birth to ʿAbd al-Wahhāb, destined to become the second leading hero in *Sīrat Dhāt al-Himma*. While respectable conception of the child demands that she is legally married to his father, her relations with this man, whom she detests, are restricted to the absolute minimum. He soon disappears from the scene, killed by his son ʿAbd al-Wahhāb. From that moment on, her life is devoted solely to war in the service of God, together with her son. Her death is not particularly heroic: she dies of old age after a long and respectable heroic career.

Marriage and, more specifically, motherhood are thus particularly feminine elements in her career, the equivalent of winning a maiden in that of a male hero. Piety takes the place that, in male heroic careers, is often reserved for loyalty to king and people.

The career of ʿUnaytira, ʿAntar's daughter, shows more resemblance to the standard pattern, and, in fact, to that of her father. There are her unusual birth and childhood: she is born after his death, and, for a long time, she is not aware of the fact that she is ʿAntar's daughter. She is unusually big and strong for her age. When she is five years old she wrestles down dogs and wolves and shoots arrows at the servants. She goes out with her head wrapped up in a turban and is generally taken for a boy. An opportunity arises for her to demonstrate her valour and strength when she joins an expedition and a huge lion approaches. She rushes forward, attacks it and kills it with a sword forged from lightning, originally owned by her father ʿAntar.[42]

Equipped with this miraculous sword, her valour proven by the fight with the lion, she can now launch on a full heroic career. Revenge for her father's death soon becomes her major quest, in which she is joined by her two half-brothers. Yet the narrator clearly feels that this does not complete her heroic career: marriage, motherhood and piety are still missing. So, ultimately, she meets the Prophet Muhammad, who has recently emerged preaching the religion of Islam. She converts, and, at the insistence of the Prophet, she gets married. To the end of her life, she bravely continues to fight for the cause of Islam, accompanied by her husband and their five sons. She is finally killed in battle, and the Prophet speaks words of mourning over her: a true heroic end.

As to the careers of minor warrior women in the epics, there are a number of common elements that occur. Some of the women have an unusual childhood, growing up as boys or being taught the art of combat by their fathers. If they are Christian, they often live in the company of other young women, with whom they engage in martial games, notably wrestling. They are usually endowed with beauty (if they are young), physical strength and prowess in combat. They may express their unwillingness to marry, sometimes adding that they will only marry a man who defeats them in single combat. They often roam about on their own in the wilderness, especially if they are Arab girls. They may run into a male champion and defeat him in combat or be defeated by him. Such combats are full of erotic tension, and, after many adventures, the warrior woman usually ends up marrying her opponent or one of his companions. If she is Christian, she converts to Islam. A familiar theme is that of the warrior girl who kills her father, or sometimes her mother, after having been converted to Islam.[43] Clearly patricide or matricide does not carry any blame when the parent involved is an unbeliever or otherwise shows ethically unacceptable behaviour.

Once married, she usually soon becomes a mother, though many of these women continue to take part in battle, often in the company of sons and sometimes of daughters, as is demonstrated by the Kurdish warrior al-Hayyāj and his wife Ghaydā', a warrior couple who have joined the army of Dhāt al-Himma and 'Abd al-Wahhāb with their seven daughters. The daughters are so dedicated to the cause of Islam that they categorically refuse any suggestion of marriage and repeatedly state that the only bridal dress that they will ever need is a shroud,[44] having died fighting the *jihād*.

Summarizing, we see that the basic elements of a warrior woman's heroic career in these epics consist of her being trained from youth in the art of war; meeting a future husband and engaging with him in combat; marriage and motherhood; and continuation of her heroic career as part of a larger group of warriors. This does not necessarily mean that all these elements need to be present; sometimes a noteworthy warrior woman does not become a mother because her marriage soon comes to an end and she continues her martial career on her own.

In the next chapters, a number of cases will be examined in detail. Here we will present some additional material dealing with women of foreign extraction as well as purely Arab girls.

Foreign queens and princesses: general

A frequently occurring type is the foreign warrior princess or queen. Very often she is Byzantine. She is referred to as *malika*, queen, and may be the daughter of an emperor or a local ruler. She is described as a woman of great beauty, but here one should not imagine slender ethereal beauty: she may be quite sturdy. Karna, queen of a faraway Christian region, has the strength of forty men and can lift a camel with such force that its legs remain permanently bent.[45]

The warrior princess knows the art of war and may seriously engage in warfare, leading armies and conquering cities. Such a woman is Malatya, daughter of the Byzantine emperor Lāwūn (Leo), who, in *Sīrat Dhāt al-Himma*, founds the city bearing her name, Malatya. Princess Malatya had always been interested in political affairs, attending her father's sessions behind a screen, and, together with her sister Bāgha, she led an army to fight the Muslims, to their father's delight. They formed a very serious threat, and only with much effort and cunning did Princess Dhāt al-Himma manage to defeat and kill them.[46]

A number of such Byzantine warrior women appear in *Sīrat al-amīra Dhāt al-Himma*, which has the continuing war with the Byzantines as its setting, but they do not usually come to such a bad end. A closely related work, the history of King 'Umar al-Nu'mān and his sons, a small *sīra* incorporated in *The Thousand and One Nights*, also contains a long episode featuring a Byzantine warrior princess named Ibrīza (often written as Abrīza in translations).

The story of Ibrīza, just like that of several princesses in *Sīrat Dhāt al-Himma*, starts with a group of young girls gathered together in a castle, palace or monastery. Their leader is a beautiful princess. The girls amuse themselves by competing with each other in martial games, in particular wrestling. A Muslim champion accidentally passes by, secretly watches the proceedings and is discovered. He is invited to participate and to engage in various contests, in which the princess is victorious. He claims that he lost because he was too distracted by her beauty to concentrate. Wrestling is a favourite type of contest in these situations because it offers the narrator ample opportunity to describe the man's sensation during the intimate contact with the girl's body. Usually this is the beginning of a love affair leading to marriage, although Ibrīza's case is untypical in this respect: no marriage takes place, although the prince in question stays very close to her and even houses her in his father's palace. This leads to her doom: his father rapes her, she gets pregnant, flees and dies after giving birth.

The story of Nūra, also in *Sīrat Dhāt al-Himma*, starts in the same way as that of Ibrīza: the Muslims notice a monastery and one of their champions, Battāl, goes to find out about it. He looks through the windows and sees ten beautiful girls singing and drinking wine with three monks. In their midst is a girl of dazzling beauty. The girls start amusing themselves by wrestling and the beautiful leader defeats them all. Then an old nun comes in and starts telling stories about the wars between the Arabs and the Byzantines, dwelling extensively upon the heroic deeds of Battāl. This makes Nūra, the leading girl, very eager to meet him, even though up until then she had only been interested in the company of women. She calls Battāl's name, and, to her great surprise, Battāl answers her call from outside and steps in through the window.⁴⁷ He joins them, and he and Nūra immediately fall in love. Then he asks permission to bring in his friends and nine more Muslim champions step in, all to be defeated by Nūra in wrestling matches. The men all claim to be defeated by her beauty rather than her martial prowess, a claim that she is prepared to acknowledge because they all have the appearance of valiant warriors. She orders her girls to lead them away to the country of the Byzantines, but then grants them their freedom.⁴⁸

Other episodes in *Sīrat Dhāt al-Himma* with a similar beginning are the stories of Princess Nūr al-Nār and of Princess Alūf. Nūr al-Nār lives with ten girls in a palace, is discovered by Prince ʿAbd al-Wahhāb and engages in a wrestling contest with him.⁴⁹ In this case, the meeting has no follow-up in the form of a love affair. It is different in the case of Alūf, a clever and valiant Byzantine princess raised as the only girl in a family with ten brothers. She meets an Arab emir in much the same manner as Ibrīza met her prince, and subsequently becomes involved with the Umayyad prince Maslama and marries him.⁵⁰

Alūf, just like Nūra, initially states that she is not interested in men or in marriage. She is more interested in books, and anyhow she prefers the company of women: 'my heart inclines towards the ladies'.⁵¹ This is a familiar topos in the warrior women stories. One might be tempted to see here something of a lesbian slant, but there is little support for such an interpretation. The female communities forming the setting of these stories belong to the wider motif of female societies where men are excluded: the women's castles, cities of women and women's islands that we encounter not only in fantastic tales, including popular epic, but also in travel literature all over the world. *Sīrat Sayf ibn Dhī Yazan* contains a long episode of this kind, to which we will return in a later chapter.

Along with Byzantine warrior princesses, a vast number of other foreign warrior women make their appearance in the various epics. They may be of African, Georgian, Persian or Indian origin, or their provenance may remain somewhat vague – some undefined region in the Middle East or an island of unclear geographical location. Ghamra bint Fā'iz, in *Sīrat ʿAntar*, is of part-Ethiopian descent. The martial women whom Sayf ibn Dhī Yazan meets in the *sīra* full of fantastic adventures that bears his name come from somewhere along the upper regions of the Nile, or from faraway mythical island empires. It is a similar situation in *Sīrat Sayf al-Tijān*, a short *sīra* even more fantastical in content than *Sayf ibn Dhī Yazan*. The warrior girls in *Qissat Hamza al-Bahlawān*, on the other hand, are all Middle Eastern but from largely unspecified areas.

Foreign queens and princesses: old women

A special category is formed by the warrior women who are not young and beautiful but old and ugly. If such old women belong to the enemy camp, as they usually do, the narrator may describe them in very coarse terms.

This, however, is not the case with Shamtā', 'the Grizzle', a fearsome old lady with a large following who appears in *Sīrat Dhāt al-Himma*. She personally defeats a whole family, a father and his ten sons, taking them captive. Their mother is desperate, for nobody else dares to attack her. Luckily her foster son Junduba appears and manages to defeat and kill Shamtā. Then he averts the wrath of her followers by saying that it was shameful for them to obey an old woman, an *ʿajūz*.[52]

The description of Shamtā' is still fairly neutral. Only her name, 'the Grizzle', refers to the body hair that often appears in descriptions of threatening old women. Shawāhī Dhāt al-Dawāhī, the indomitable Christian old lady in *The History of King ʿUmar ibn al-Nuʿmān* in *The Thousand and One Nights*, does not get off so easily, and neither does the Georgian queen Bakhtūsh, discussed below. They are depicted in a most unpleasant manner, with much attention given to their revolting old bodies and shameless behaviour. They are sexually repulsive as well as threatening, and their cunning and undiminished physical strength make them redoubtable enemies.

Shawāhī is the grandmother of Princess Ibrīza, but this is not clear when she first enters the story. Shawāhī insists on wrestling with Ibrīza after she has seen how the princess defeated all her female companions and tied them up. This has incited her anger. Ibrīza consents with great reluctance: 'Well, let us wrestle then, if you are up to it.' She throws the old woman down in barely a minute.[53]

It is a curious interlude, not usually part of the widespread motif of a community of young girls living in a castle or monastery and engaging in martial games. It seems to have no other function than to put Shawāhī, who will turn out to be a dangerous opponent, in a negative light from the start. To this end, the narrator presents her in a most disgusting way. A central element is that she refuses to accept that her aged body is no longer attractive and thinks that she can still successfully compete with a young girl. She insists on wrestling naked, which offers the narrator ample opportunity to set off her ugly body against the beauty of the nubile young girl. Hairs sprout everywhere on her body: 'the hair on her body stood upright like the spines of a hedgehog'.[54] Worst of all, she produces a couple of loud farts.

In the sequel of the story, Shawāhī turns out to be a redoubtable opponent. She acts as counsel to her son, the Christian king Hardūb, and when he is killed she stops at nothing to avenge his death. She leads armies, scales walls, cleverly disguises herself to trick the enemy and does not hesitate to cut off someone's head when the situation asks for it. Transgressing various social codes, wily and donning clever disguises, she is something of a trickster, a female *'ayyār*. Only by a mean and despicable ruse of her Muslim opponents is she finally defeated and cruelly put to death.[55]

While there is possibly a nasty insinuation of incestuous lesbianism in the previous case, the sexual preferences of Queen Bakhtūs in *Sīrat Dhāt al-Himma* are of a different nature: she has a voracious sexual appetite and is described in very coarse terms. She is a very unattractive lady. She is one hundred and sixty-three years old and extremely ugly. In spite of her age she is a fearsome warrior, who has killed many champions in her raids on the Turks and Turcomans. She is widely feared, especially after she skinned the head of a defeated enemy, filled it with cotton and wool, and hung it on a gate to show people what happened to those who opposed her. She constantly drinks wine, eats a whole pig for breakfast as well as for supper and likes to engage in sexual intercourse from sunset until morning, not stopping for a minute; when her partner shows signs of flagging she crushes his head under her armpit until his eyes pop out and his temple bones are pulverized.

So when she captures a group of Arabs, their fate looks grim. She orders them to be beheaded. Midlāj, a giant of a man and a former brigand, opposes her. She throws him down, and is impressed by what his worn old underpants, which do not cover much, reveal to her. The sight makes her drool. She takes Midlāj with her, plies him with wine and orders him to give her the benefit of the equipment she saw when he was down on the ground. They engage in intercourse all night, alternating sex with drinking and eating. Midlāj speaks words of love to her, saying that he no longer wants to be a Muslim. Overjoyed, she finally falls asleep, overcome by drunkenness and snoring loudly. Taking the sword that hangs above her head, Midlāj puts the tip on her breast, leans on it and impales her to the ground.[56]

Arab warrior women: some examples

While the women described above are all of foreign descent, Princess Dhāt al-Himma is a Bedouin woman of true Arab stock. So are many other warrior women in the epics, including the two warrior princesses in *Qissat Fīrūzshāh*, who come from Yemen. Among these Arab heroines there are some of the most delightful characters of popular epic, such as the headstrong Ghamra, the daughter of 'Utārid, from *Sīrat Dhāt al-Himma*, who will be studied extensively in Chapter 5, and Jaydā' from *Sīrat 'Antar*, with whom she has much in common.

Considerations of space mean that only a limited number of warrior women can receive more than passing attention in this book. Yet it would be a pity to omit Hind and Zahra, two Arab girls who feature in episodes of great charm. Their stories, serving as brief illustrations of what has been said above, conclude this chapter.

Example of a warrior woman story 1: Hind

Hind, the daughter of King Qays in *Sīrat 'Antar*, is a very accomplished and spirited Arab girl. She is described in a delightful episode, in which the flippant verbal exchange, which includes many verses, between Hind and her suitor, Rabī'a ibn Zayd, plays at least as prominent a part as their duelling on the battleground. Rabī'a is a very handsome and successful young man. He is beautifully dressed, wearing a red turban embroidered in gold and decorated with pearls and precious stones. A jealous companion, thinking that he is too big for his boots and could do with a lesson, suggests to Rabīʻa that Hind, the daughter of King Qays, would be the perfect wife for him.

Hind is widely famed for her beauty, intelligence and warrior skills, having been taught by her father to write as well as to handle arms. She is a valiant girl who has defeated many famous knights. She has many suitors, among them powerful tribal chiefs, but she has refused them all, going off into the desert to lead her own life. Of course, this is a challenge that Rabīʻa cannot resist, although his mother tries to hold him back. He sets out to find Hind's tribe and tells her father Qays that he has come to ask for his daughter's hand. Qays, seeing his beauty and hearing about his lineage, seems agreeable, but considers him too young for what he wants to take on. Rabīʻa soon finds out that Hind makes her own decisions. She admits him into her tent for a talk but treats him with disdain, saying that he is nothing but a small boy: 'I smell milk on your mouth, and find no intelligence in you.' She also criticizes him for sitting down on the same level as her, uninvited. Full of confidence, he tells her about his martial feats and impressive lineage. She briefly pulls aside the curtain between them, allowing him to see her beauty. Then she orders him to go away and propose to someone else, because she is way out of his class, even if tried to win her with the sword. She has defeated much more impressive opponents, but is prepared to fight him in a duel. He refuses, saying that the Arabs would heap shame on him for fighting a duel with a woman. She insists, however, saying that if she wins she will make him herd camels, and if he wins he can do whatever he wants with her. But he walks off angrily.

His mother insists on patience, and only after some time has passed does he decide to try again. This time he goes to meet Hind without his turban, his hair falling down to his ankles, and his sword in his hand. She is intrigued and impressed by his hair. Why does he wear it so long? Because it is the mark of his tribe, he replies. 'Well, well,' she says, 'I will cut off those locks with a Yemeni sword and take them after I have defeated you on the battlefield.' 'Hind, no knight has managed to cut them off in the turmoil of the battlefield,' he answers, 'so how would a woman manage to do that? But if you pull them to your bosom at the time of embracing they will be yours, oh woman of noble character!' He then walks out, leaving her dazzled by his beauty.

His deeds, however, impress the tribe of Qays, and they insist that Qays gives him Hind in marriage. Hind, however, is adamant: she would rather fight him to the death. When her father arranges a duel between Rabīʿa and one of his most valiant champions, Hind is so impressed by Rabīʿa's martial prowess that she immediately calls for her horse and armour. After an exchange of poetry, they engage in combat. Her horse tires and she asks for a short delay in order to get another. Rabīʿa agrees in a most charming and chivalrous manner. Hind recites more poetry, but he criticizes her: this poetry is not right, because fighting is a serious business. He proceeds to attack with full strength and finally she has to give up: 'I surrender myself to you, take me as your handmaid.' Taking away her spear, he tells her to dismount and to go on foot to her people and soldiers, while he remains mounted on his horse. Obviously she has now submitted completely, and, to make the position clear, she says: 'I testify that I will consent to your being my husband and I your wife.' The situation mirrors their first meeting, but in reverse: while previously she insisted that he should be seated on a lower level, this time Rabīʿa, towering over her on his horse, has firmly gained the superior position.

Together they walk over to Hind's father and Rabīʿa officially asks for her hand, giving a full account of his lineage and descent. The proposal is accepted and the wedding is organized straight away. It lasts for three days, after which the couple withdraw for ten days. On the next morning, Hind's mother comes to visit and, to her amazement, finds Hind alone, without her husband. Rabīʿa, as it turns out, has gone away to collect a suitable dowry, so that it will not be said that he married Qays ibn Masʿūd's daughter without offering a bride price.[57]

Example of a warrior woman story 2: Zahra

It is not only in *Sīrat ʿAntara* that an intrepid young warrior girl gets carried away by male beauty. Zahra, who appears in a brief episode in *Sīrat Dhāt al-Himma*, finds a very elegant compromise between her warrior pride and her love for a young man more remarkable for his beauty than for his martial prowess. He is the son of Baṭṭāl, the trickster, which explains why the narrator does not hold his lack of martial prowess against him. As Baṭṭāl's son, he is also something of a trickster, and thus he can go against all kinds of social codes. He can even lack the ability to fight without losing status.

The episode runs as follows. Prince Qashʿam, son of Prince ʿAbd al-Wahhāb and thus one of Princess Dhāt al-Himma's grandsons, goes out hunting in the course of an expedition. Having strayed far away, he suddenly sees a castle that reaches almost to the clouds. He notices a gazebo. Its door opens and ten girls appear, among them a girl of breathtaking beauty. Her name is Zahra. Qash'am is immediately smitten with her, and tries to impress her by elaborating on his descent and martial prowess. She, however, is not at all impressed by his boasting. Soon Qash'am's companion Madhbahūn appears and is equally impressed by the girl, who, in her turn, is very taken by his handsome appearance. Unpleasant words are exchanged between the two men, and Qash'am goes off to his father to complain about Madhbahūn and to call on his father's help. The girl's father is fetched, and before Qash'am's father has had time to ask the girl in marriage for his son, Madhbahūn's father, the wily Battāl, jumps in and claims her for his own son before anyone realizes what is happening.

There is a general uproar. Zahra's father consults his daughter: whom does she want? The blond and elegant one, not the gaunt dark-skinned one, is her answer. However, she will only marry the man who defeats her on the battleground, and she is prepared to duel with both suitors. Qash'am, the famous champion, is elated; his rival, who is not a fighter, definitely does not stand a chance. But it works out differently. She unhorses Qash'am after having confused him by taking off her veil, and then it is Madhbahūn's turn.

In the previous story, Hind happily submits to the handsome Rabī'a once he has defeated her, and she gives up her martial attitude. Here, Zahra decides not even to fight, dazzled by the young man's beauty. It is interesting to see in what terms male beauty is described in these stories: Hind's suitor, Rabī'a, has amazing hair, falling down to his ankles when he takes off his lavishly decorated turban; Zahra's young man, Madhbahūn, also has beautiful long hair, and wears beautifully embroidered clothes. But, in his case, there is more: he has some distinctly feminine traits and this is exactly what attracts the accomplished warrior girl. We see here an interesting switch of gender roles.

Stepping onto the battleground, although he is not very skilled at combat, Madhbahūn

> uncovered his arms, which were like crystal; he let down his tresses of hair, which were like black adders. His face was like the moon on the night of its fullness, his eyes like those of a gazelle, and his body like a willow branch. His neck was like that of a silver jar, and he had folds in his belly like a woman.

To the girl, he is irresistible:

> 'Welcome, you who surpass the crescent of the moon and the eyes of gazelles, and who looks like a lady! Rejoice, for you have reached your goal.' [...] Trying to help him, she added: 'Coolness of the eyes, grant me delay! You have hit me without spearhead, thrown me down without sword. Jump in and renew your attack, for I am like a little bird in your hand.' Madhbahūn fell upon her like a bone-breaking eagle, yelling at her. Her limbs became flaccid and her strength disappeared. He stretched out his hand, drawing her towards him, and she simply threw herself over as his captive.

The couple are married straight away.[58]

Questions

For the moment, these examples must suffice. They demonstrate how each of these stories, while largely using the same motifs, develops its own characters and provides its own particular emphasis. The material also raises a number of obvious questions. Given that these stories were composed by and for men, they clearly reflect male anxieties and desires. Humiliating and killing a threatening old woman or forcing a beautiful but headstrong girl into submission are obvious examples. But why did male audiences so clearly enjoy hearing about male heroes being defeated and humiliated by a woman, without ensuing suitable punishment for the woman? How could they accept that leading male protagonists expressed their delight about being married to women who could protect them? I will come back to these matters in the final chapter.

CHAPTER 3

Sīrat Dhāt al-Himma *1:*
Princess Dhāt al-Himma and Her Many Battles[1]

Protagonists

- 'Abd al-Wahhāb, leading hero of the Kilābī tribe, son of Fātima Dhāt al-Himma
- Abū Muhammad (Abū Muhammad al-Battāl), major Kilābī hero, known for his wiliness. See Battāl
- 'Antar, hero of *Sīrat 'Antar*
- Bahrūn, son of Maymūna and 'Abd al-Wahhāb
- Banū 'Āmir, Bedouin tribe
- Banū Kilāb (or Kilābīs), Bedouin tribe to which Dhāt al-Himma belongs
- Banū Sulaym, Bedouin tribe, rivals of the Banū Kilāb
- Banū Tayy, Bedouin tribe
- Battāl, see Abū Muhammad al-Battāl
- Dāhiyat Banī Tayy, 'Calamity of the Banū Tayy', nickname of the young Dhāt al-Himma
- Dalhama, see Dhāt al-Himma
- Dhalhama, see Dhāt al-Himma
- Dhāt al-Himma (Fātima), leading female hero of the Kilābī tribe, mother of 'Abd al-Wahhāb
- Dhū l-Himma, see Dhāt al-Himma
- Fātima Dhāt al-Himma, see Dhāt al-Himma
- Ghamra, Arab warrior woman, daughter of 'Utārid
- Ghaydurūs, enemy king
- Hadlāmūs, fearsome enemy champion

- Hārith, member of the Banū Tayy, master of the young Fātima Dhāt al-Himma
- Hārith, son of Zālim, cousin of Dhāt al-Himma, later her husband
- Hārūn al-Rashīd, Abbasid caliph
- Iftūnā, daughter of Ghaydurūs, warrior woman
- Jaʿfar al-Sādiq, sixth Shiʿite imam
- Kūshanūsh, enemy king
- Maʾmūn, Abbasid caliph
- Mansūr, Abbasid caliph
- Marzūq, foster brother of Dhāt al-Himma
- Maymūna, Ethiopian warrior princess, fourth wife of ʿAbd al-Wahhāb
- Mazlūm, father of Fātima Dhāt al-Himma
- Muʿtasim, Abbasid caliph
- Mutawakkil, Abbasid caliph
- Nūra, Byzantine warrior princess, marries Battāl
- Qannāsa, Arab warrior princess, daughter of Muzāhim, third wife of ʿAbd al-Wahhāb
- Sharīha, name given to the young Dhāt al-Himma
- Shūma, wife of Shūmdaris
- Shūmdaris, evil monk
- Suʿdā, foster mother of Dhāt al-Himma
- ʿUlwā, Arab warrior woman, second wife of ʿAbd al-Wahhāb
- ʿUnaytira, daughter of ʿAntar, warrior woman
- ʿUqba, chief *qāḍī* (judge), crypto-Christian, villain of the *sīra*. Related to the Banū Sulaym
- Wāthiq, Abbasid caliph
- Zālim, brother of Mazlūm, uncle and father-in-law of Dhāt al-Himma

A year and three months, that is how long it took Sī Mlūd, the Moroccan storyteller, to complete *The Adventures of Princess Dhāt al-Himma, her son Prince ʿAbd al-Wahhāb, Prince Abū Muhammad al-Battāl, ʿUqba the sheikh of misguidance and the wily Shūmdaris*. This involved reading to his faithful audience every day from afternoon prayer to sunset, sitting on his little stool in the park near the famous Kutubīya in Marrakesh.[2] The *sīra* takes up more than six thousand densely printed pages in its modern edition. It is written in rhymed prose, with poems inserted every now and then.

From what Sī Mlūd and his audience told us when we spoke with them in 1997, it was clear that *The Adventures of Princess Dhāt al-Himma* was one of their favourites, next to *The Adventures of ʿAntar*. In their view, these *sīra*s dealt with Islamic history, a subject they greatly preferred over fantastic tales such as *The Thousand and One Nights* or *The Adventures of King Sayf ibn Dhī Yazan*, which they saw as 'tales full of lies and sorcery'.

Is *The Adventures of Princess Dhāt al-Himma* a tale about historical events? Certainly, but it is largely fictional history, with only a superficial connection to actual historical fact. The *sīra* is divided into two sections of very unequal length. The five 'parts' forming the first section are set in the age of the Umayyad dynasty, and the remaining sixty-five parts in the era of the Abbasids. A number of caliphs, Umayyad as well as Abbasid, feature in the epic, as do many historical figures from their entourage. Viziers (notably the Barmacids), governors and army leaders well known from history make their appearance. The *sīra* comes to an end under the rule of the caliph Wāthiq, who reigned from 842 to 847. His successor, Mutawakkil, is mentioned briefly on the last page.

The *sīra* presents a fictionalized version of events that took place during this period. The fact that we are dealing with fiction, however, does not mean that the text is without interest for the historian. *Sīra* literature was very popular, and thus must have been instrumental in shaping people's perception of history.[3] So this literature is not without importance for a proper understanding of political views and sensitivities, even up to the present day.

The oldest known reference to the *sīra* dates from the autobiography of the twelfth-century Samaw'al al-Maghribī, mentioned in Chapter 1. The oldest manuscripts of the text that we have today date back to the fifteenth century.[4] Events in the *sīra* are often immensely complicated, but two main themes run throughout the work: the rivalry between the two Bedouin tribes that play a major role, namely the Banū Kilāb (or Kilābīs), to which Dhāt al-Himma belongs, and the Banū Sulaym. The tribes are closely connected and settle in the same town (Malatya). They operate under the same commander-in-chief, but their constant rivalry often leads to serious conflicts.

The other major theme of the *sīra* is the constant war of the Muslims against the Byzantines and their allies. There is a historical basis to this. Border conflicts with the Byzantines were a constant in the first centuries of Islam, and yearly seasonal campaigns were a routine matter. *Sīrat Dhāt al-Himma* is not the only epic tale in which these campaigns play a role. Other, closely related, epics have the same setting. One is the relatively short *sīra* about King 'Umar al-Nu'mān and his sons Sharkān and Dā'u l-Makān, which has been incorporated in to *The Thousand and One Nights*. Another is the Turkish *Battālnāme*, in which the hero

Battāl, who also plays a major role in *Sīrat Dhāt al-Himma*, is the leading character. On the Byzantine side, there is the short epic *Digenes Akritas*, which is set in the same historical context.

Connected to the two major themes of the *sīra* there are a vast number of subplots, involving intrigues at the caliphal court in Baghdad as well as in Byzantine surroundings, and expeditions to foreign regions to fight all kinds of enemies. Love affairs, abductions and stolen children are all part of the picture. The supernatural hardly features in *The Adventures of Princess Dhāt al-Himma*, unlike in other *sīra*s.

A good overview of the contents and background of *Sīrat Dhāt al-Himma* can be found in Marius Canard's entry 'Dhū l-Himma' in the *Encyclopaedia of Islam*. A lengthy and detailed summary taking up 160 pages is given by Malcolm Lyons in the third volume of his *The Arabian Epic* (1996). Shawqi 'Abd al-Hakīm retold some of the events in a small volume that also appeared in English translation.[5]

Although the *sīra* is generally referred to as *The Adventures of Princess Dhāt al-Himma*, after its leading protagonist, it is not the only title under which it is known. Sī Mlūd and his Marrakesh audience called it *al-Wahhābīya*, after its second leading protagonist, Princess Dhāt al-Himma's son, 'Abd al-Wahhāb. This title is not used in any of the manuscripts or printed editions, unlike another title, namely *Sīrat al-Mujāhidīn*, *The Adventures of the Holy Warriors*. This last title emphasizes the main theme of the *sīra*, the continuing wars between the Muslims and the Christian Byzantines.[6]

The number of personae who make their appearance in the *sīra* is vast. We will just mention some of the main protagonists. Five of these are mentioned in the title of the work: Princess Dhāt al-Himma, her son 'Abd al-Wahhāb and Battāl, their companion and helper. On the enemy side, there are 'Uqba and Shūmdaris. 'Uqba is the primary villain of the *sīra*. He is a learned Muslim judge, a *qādī*, who is favoured by the Abbasid caliphs and appointed as their court judge. The wife of the caliph Hārūn al-Rashīd, Zubayda, especially trusts 'Uqba and supports him under all circumstances. 'Uqba is secretly a Christian. He is extremely wily and is constantly working against the Muslims, especially the tribe that Dhāt al-Himma and her son belong to. He himself is related to their rival tribe. Shūmdaris, the second villain whose name appears in the title, is a Christian monk and also a major enemy of the Muslims. He is assisted by his wife Shūma. The Abbasid caliphs who actually appear in the epic start with Mansūr and end with Wāthiq. An especially important role is played by the caliphs Hārūn al-Rashīd, Ma'mūn and Mu'tasim.

In this chapter Dhāt al-Himma, the most prominent warrior princess of Arabic epic literature, is our main focus of interest. She makes her appearance in the sixth part (or *juz'*), the part that starts with the rise of the Abbasid dynasty. In actual history, this event took place in the year 750. Dates, however, are not mentioned in the *sīra*, although events roughly follow actual historical sequences. Dhāt al-Himma's name is given in different forms: Dhū l-Himma, Dhalhama or Dalhama. The latter form, meaning 'she-wolf', is probably the original form.[7] She belongs to the tribe of the Banū Kilāb, who settled near the border of the Byzantine Empire and are constantly at war with the Christians. Dhāt al-Himma, 'the woman of high resolve', is one of the tribe's most renowned warriors.

Dhāt al-Himma: heroic status

Dhāt al-Himma's major heroic status is demonstrated by her story, which contains many of the standard elements of the heroic biography.[8] The pattern, however, is not followed in every the detail and has been adapted to her role as a woman.

Prominent elements of the heroic life cycle, as exemplified also in 'Antar, the archetypical Arab hero, are unusual circumstances of birth and youth; precocious physical development and warrior skills; and obtaining an extraordinary piece of weaponry, usually a sword, an unusual mount and an unusual helper. The hero then proves his heroic status by defeating a daunting enemy, often a lion. A career of impressive raids follows, which gains the hero great prestige with the tribe and finally leads to paternal acknowledgement: the 'unusual birth' scenario usually implies that the hero's father does not acknowledge or accept the child, or is unaware of its existence.

All these elements, except the unusual mount, are, in some form or other, also found in the accounts of prominent female warrior heroines. Examples that we will encounter in later chapters are, for instance, the stories of Ghamra the daughter of Fā'iz and of 'Unaytira, the posthumously born daughter of 'Antar. Not all the elements are necessarily found in each story, and there may also be adaptations: the 'monster' defeated and killed by the young Dhāt al-Himma is a man who threatens to rape her when she is still a small girl.

As to remarkable arms, no mention is made of a famous sword or piece of armour acquired by Dhāt al-Himma. All that sets her apart in this respect are the arrows and spears she fabricated for herself from sticks and reed stalks when she was a little girl, not having access to other arms.

Does she have a 'helper'? Her foster brother Marzūq in a way performs that role, but this comes to an end when she feels betrayed by him because he helps her husband to consummate their marriage against Dhāt al-Himma's will. He may have done so with the best of intentions, but she is furious and no longer trusts him. She soon acquires another helper, however. The traditional 'helper' in Arabic popular epic is usually the *ʿayyār*, a trickster-like character called, by Malcolm Lyons, the 'man of wiles'.[9] *Sīrat al-amīra Dhāt al-Himma* has a prominent 'man of wiles' in the person of Muhammad al-Battāl, the clever but good-for-nothing boy who grows into a brave warrior but who is far more noteworthy, and useful, for his *ʿayyār* qualities. He will indeed act as a helper to Dhāt al-Himma. The relationship between them is discussed in more detail later on.

As a further introduction to Dhāt al-Himma's personality and character we can say that she is very pious and universally respected for it: 'Once she had started praying, she would not be diverted from her prayer even if a thousand swords appeared over her head intending to kill her.'[10] Because of her piety, she is often more loyal to the caliph than his behaviour towards her and her tribe warrants. She always gives him the benefit of the doubt, however, even if there is ample evidence that he has been set against her and her Kilābī warriors by evil influences.

As a warrior she is unsurpassed. She is widely respected as an army leader and she is a clever strategist. She regularly clashes about matters of strategy with her son ʿAbd al-Wahhāb, of whom she is otherwise very fond: she is desperate when he is lost and is feared dead, and when she has a dream in which her son is freed from the claws of a bird of prey, she immediately concludes that he must still be alive and sets out to rescue him.[11] Moving scenes occur when they see each other again after such episodes. On one occasion, even the caliph Muʿtasim cannot hold back his tears when he witnesses the reunion of Dhāt al-Himma and ʿAbd al-Wahhāb.[12] More about the relationship between them will be discussed in the next chapter.

Dhāt al-Himma has always shunned marriage. She was forced by the caliph to marry, and the birth of her son was the result of marital rape. Yet she is a devoted mother to her son. In a way, she also acts as a mother figure to the tribe as a whole: the men look to her for guidance, and she deals with them much in the way a mother would with a bunch of unruly boys. She can get especially exasperated when the men get involved in rivalry about a woman and start behaving in a most childish manner.

Early life and career; motherhood

Dhāt al-Himma's history starts with a conflict between her father Mazlūm and his brother Zālim about the leadership of their tribe, the Banū Kilāb. Both their wives are pregnant, and they decide that the one to whom a son is born will become chief. Zālim's wife gives birth to a boy, and Zālim then sends his trusted midwife over to his brother, because he fears that they may attempt to cheat him if the other baby turns out to be a girl.

> She [the midwife] sat with Mazlūm's wife for a while, and then she went into labour and gave birth to a daughter as beautiful as the full moon, with strong arms and limbs and splendid shoulders. Her mother became disheartened, worried and sad, for she was afraid of her husband Mazlūm. He said to her, putting it as nicely as possible: 'I may lose the chieftainship. If you want, you may kill her, and say to the Arabs and their leaders that a son was born to us, but that he died.'

The midwife objects, saying that it would be unacceptable to kill the girl. It would be much better to pay another woman to bring her up, and if that is what they decide, she herself is prepared to go and tell Zālim that the baby was a boy but that he died. Zālim is certain to believe her.[13]

This duly happens. The girl, who is named Fātima, is given to a woman called Su'dā, who has a baby boy of her own, Marzūq. She looks after the little girl, and at night she brings her to her own mother to be nursed. Her father, on the contrary, does not even want to see her, 'because men do not like girls, especially when they lose advantages because of them'. In this way Fātima grows up. When she is five years old, she looks like ten, 'and she had become not only very beautiful, but was also gifted with purity and an excellent character. Praise to Him who created her in that way! When she entered her sixth year, her father started to worry about her, fearing that something shameful might befall her, because she was not aware of having another mother than Su'dā.'[14]

Her father apparently fears that because his daughter is not aware of her noble descent and thinks that she belongs to the servant class, she may consider herself unprotected and consequently feel that it is hard for her to ward off sexual advances. He need not have worried, for little Fāṭima has an inborn sense of her own nobility, as becomes clear when Suʿdā and the two children, Marzūq and Fāṭima, are abducted by another tribe, the Banū Ṭayy.[15] When the Banū Ṭayy ask Suʿdā the name of her daughter, having noticed that there is no resemblance between them, she answers:

> 'She is my daughter, but she does not have an easy name. Call her whatever you want.' 'Then we will call her Sharīha.' 'That is your affair,' she said, 'she and I are now your slaves.' When Fāṭima, who could not bear to be humiliated, heard this she said to Suʿdā: 'Stop saying such things! If you don't, I will kill myself by my own hand, by the protection of the magnanimous Arabs and by Him Who raises the seven heavens[16] and calls the dead forth from their graves and tombs! For I am neither a slave girl nor a servant. How could a slave serve a slave like himself?' Thus she spoke, for she had always pulled her veil closely over her face, very different from the way in which slave women dress and the sun had never seen her face.

To have a tan is, of course, a sign that a woman is forced to work outside, without being able to stay out of the sun. Only women of noble families could afford to protect their skin against the sun by staying indoors. By always covering her face, Fāṭima has instinctively found a way to preserve this mark of her noble birth.

> Then she said to Suʿdā: 'If you do this again, I will kill myself, for I serve nobody but the Creator, sublime and exalted is He. Our people will undoubtedly come and free us from our misfortunes, and bring disaster on the Banū Ṭayy.' Then she cried and recited a poem, after having said the blessing of the Prophet, Taha the Messenger.

The Banū Ṭayy are much impressed by the poem she recites, and immediately recognize her as 'a brave Arab girl, an invincible champion'. When the spoils are divided, Suʿdā and the two children are allotted to a kind and noble man, who treats them with great courtesy. They are given the task of herding the camels and horses, and Fāṭima is left free to roam about wherever she wants. She cuts branches and reeds to make them into weapons, and teaches herself the art of fighting on horseback. When a camel stallion is unruly she manages to subdue it with her shouts. Everybody is very impressed by her.

Just like other motifs of the warrior woman theme, the description of the warrior heroine's tomboy childhood goes back a long way. It is found in classical antiquity, for instance in legendary accounts of the life of Zenobia, the famous third-century queen of Palmyra. Anthonia Fraser, in her *Warrior Queens*,[17] tells how the fourth-century author Trebellius Pollio, in his account of the life of Zenobia, elaborates on her boy-like preferences during childhood: she scorned womanly exercises and instead wandered the forests, killing does and stags with her arrows. She also liked to wrestle with young men, being careful at all times to preserve her virginity. Such wrestling parties are not mentioned in Dhāt al-Himma's case, but they occur in many other stories about warrior women (see Introduction).

Chastity is another widespread motif in warrior women stories, well known from the legends about the Amazons and female communities in general. Sexual relations are only allowed, on a very restricted basis, as a means to produce children. A connection is often made between the woman's fighting prowess and her virginity. This motif is not widespread in Arabic warrior women stories, but, in this, Dhāt al-Himma is an exception. She is not interested in sexual relations with men, and at one point it is even suggested by her prospective father-in-law that the loss of her virginity will put an end to her martial prowess and make her more tractable.

As to the little Fātima/Sharīha, who is not yet known as Dhāt al-Himma, her preoccupation is solely with the Lord: she fasts during the daytime, and she is not interested in the things of this world. Her reputation spreads and she becomes known as 'Sharīha the Pious'.[18] She also possesses great beauty and her speech is excellent. Everybody loves and respects her. Her master Hārith continues to treat her with great kindness. One day he finds her in tears, full of rage because, being out in the field on her own, she had been harassed by a prominent member of the tribe who wanted to seduce her, thinking that she was an unprotected slave girl. He chides the man in front of his companions, saying that he should ask for her hand properly or otherwise leave her alone. "'Me, marry your slave girl, Hārith? Never, not even if refusal would mean my death!'" The next day he seeks her out in the field, abusing her because she has dared to complain to her master. She chases him off with stones and goes back to her master, trembling, saying that she will kill the man if he harasses her again. Her master brings the affair to the attention of the king who also speaks to the man.[19] It was all just a joke, he says.

Fāṭima, upon hearing this, asks and gets the king's permission to kill the man if he bothers her again: "'Calamity girl! Yes, if he bothers you again, he is your affair.'"

Furious, the man approaches her again at the next opportunity and she does indeed kill him, her fellow camel herders looking on in shock. She goes back to the house of her master, 'blazing like a viper'. He asks, "'What kind of disaster has overcome you, you calamity of souls?'" When she tells him that she has killed her attacker, he is very angry. He drags her to the king, chief of the tribe. The family of the victim has already gathered there to claim revenge, and when they hear that the killer is a slave girl referred to as Dāhiyat Banī Ṭayy, 'Calamity of the Banū Ṭayy', they say that her master Ḥārith will have to pay with his life for her crime, since he is the one who is legally responsible for her deed. Finally, however, they agree instead to accept a blood price of a thousand camels. Ḥārith is desperate: how will he be able to feed his family after having paid such a huge price?

Note that this is the second time that Fāṭima receives a new name, in this case a sobriquet. From now on she becomes known as Dāhiyat Banī Ṭayy, 'Calamity of the Banū Ṭayy'. It is all part of establishing her definitive identity.

As for her unfortunate master, in his desperation he is about to whip Fāṭima, who is bound in chains. She says that she has a better solution: if he gives her a horse and armour, she will go out and collect the blood money herself. Ḥārith is very sceptical, but complies with her wishes, and before long she arrives home with four thousand camels obtained in a raid, having killed their owner.[20] The tribe is much impressed, and people decide that she deserves a better name: after 'Calamity of the Banū Ṭayy', a sobriquet emphasizing her troublesome character, she now obtains a honorific name, Dhāt al-Himma, 'she of high resolve'.[21]

Her success in obtaining the blood money has given her a taste for raiding and collecting booty, and she continues in this line with great success. Her spoils are divided equally between her and her master, Ḥārith. Her fame becomes so widespread that, at some point, a delegation of the Banū Ṭayy, led by Ḥārith, politely comes to ask her help against the tribes of the Banū ʿĀmir and the Banū Kilāb.[22] She consents, not realizing that this means fighting her own tribe, the Banū Kilāb. As is to be expected, her actions soon lead to confrontations with family members. In a few successive raids she first drives off the herds of her father Mazlūm. Suʿdā, her nurse, realizes what is happening, but does not see fit to inform Fāṭima about her real descent.[23]

Soon Fātima and her father Mazlūm meet in battle, resulting in a combat where Mazlūm is at a disadvantage because he keeps being overwhelmed by feelings of love and tenderness towards Fātima.[24] As a result, she plays with him 'like a small child with a little bird', eventually unhorsing him and taking him captive. Back in the camp, she orders him to be executed the next day. Her master Hārith suggests a delay in order to enable the other members of the Banū Tayy to come and witness the execution. Meanwhile Suʿdā, seeing her old master in this condition, is in despair, and she decides that it would be unforgivable not to tell Fātima that the man whom she is about to have beheaded is, in fact, her father. Upon being told this, Fātima is less surprised than expected: the news fits in with the qualms she had during her combat with Mazlūm: "'Every time I thought about striking him while we were fighting, my heart started to throb with tenderness and my joints trembled and slackened, and it was clear to me that he was experiencing the same feelings.'"[25]

Fātima and Suʿdā quickly go to free Mazlūm from his bonds, and Suʿdā, at Fātima's request, tells him that Fātima is his daughter, the girl who was given to her, Suʿdā, to bring up.

> When Mazlūm heard this from Suʿdā, he threw himself down on his knees to thank God Most High, saying: 'Praised be God, Who brought forth this lioness from my loins! Praise to Him for bestowing this blessing!' When the princess knew that he was really her father, she stood up and began to kiss his hands and feet, his breast and his brow. As to him, he pressed her to his breast and began to kiss her brow, saying: 'God has forgiven everything that has happened in the past, my daughter. Praise to Him that we have got to know each other!' And he wept with joy.

Here, for the first time, Fātima is referred to as *amīra*, princess. She is finally adopting the identity that she will keep throughout the *sīra*, that of Princess Dhāt al-Himma. For a while though, she will still regularly be referred to as Dāhiya, 'Calamity', the name which used to instil such fear among the Arab tribes.

Of course, Fātima has to inform the Banū Tayy about her newly discovered identity, which fills them with amazement. Then her father takes her home, she still dressed in male attire, and introduces her to her mother: "'Do you know who this turbaned person is?" She took a long look, and blood was stirred by blood. She said to her husband: "Cousin, you ask me whether I know this person – I really do not know who this is, but I feel a stir in my blood when I see him." "This is not a boy," he said, "it is your daughter Fātima.'" A happy reunion takes place.[26]

Not long afterwards, Fātima meets her uncle Zālim and her cousin, another Hārith. The confrontation is much less pleasant than that with her father. Zālim is a nasty and treacherous character, and he is not at all pleased that his brother has escaped execution: he had already appropriated his brother's share of their inheritance. His son Hārith, a brave warrior, is very much impressed by Fātima's beauty and martial prowess, and is eager to marry her. It is a logical step, for marriage between paternal cousins was, and is, the preferred type of marriage among the Arabs; hence Fātima's mother addressed her husband as 'cousin'. The idea has his father's full support, for he thinks that there is a good chance that 'when she belongs to him, her inviolability will be broken,[27] her energy will diminish and her power will disappear'.[28]

When Zālim approaches his brother about a possible marriage between their children, Mazlūm tells his brother that the decision is not his: on no account can he speak on his daughter's behalf, but he is willing to plead his nephew's case with her. Fātima practically explodes at the suggestion: she would never consider marriage, not even if the king of Persia proposed to her:

'Father, I do not need a lord and master. I am created only for wrangling, not for men and the marriage bed. Only my sword, my coat of mail and my battle gear will lie with me. The only thing that I will treat with loving care is my horse's foal, and the only eyeblack I will aim for is the powder of windblown dust. I swear by God that if you mention this again I will definitely leave your tent and go and settle in the wilderness, living in the plains and rugged terrains.'

Ashamed, her father gets up and embraces her, saying that from now on he will simply go along with what she likes and dislikes.[29]

Here we see how the young Fātima firmly discards every aspect of traditional feminity: she has no interest at all in caring for babies or enhancing her beauty.

So, as far as Fātima and her father are concerned, the idea of marrying her cousin Hārith is definitely off, in spite of the presents that have been sent by Hārith's father, Zālim, to smooth the way. Zālim's attitude to Fātima is clearly demonstrated by the way he refers to her as 'that girl Dhalhama'.[30] Yet the young Hārith is still deeply in love. His father keeps pleading his son's case with Fātima, in spite of her emphatic statement that she does not want a husband. He asks her why not. Hārith is superior to her in all respects: "If it is about wealth: he is very wealthy. If it is beauty: by God, he is more beautiful than you. If it is his chivalrous skill: he is more skilful in that respect and more courageous than you." This is too much for Fātima and she agrees to meet her cousin in combat, saying that if he manages to defeat her, she will consider that as her dowry and accept him in marriage. Of course, he does not stand a chance. She thrusts the butt of her lance against his shoulder and throws him from the saddle. Hitting his head, he lies there unconscious. Deeply humiliated, his father has to drag him away from the battleground.[31]

Yet Zālim sees fresh opportunities for his son when a new caliph, Manṣūr, comes to power as a result of the dramatic overthrow of the Umayyad dynasty. Hārith's case is put before the caliph. The context in which this happens is noteworthy: the Bedouin tribes have just arrived at the caliph's court in Baghdad in order to swear their allegiance. They are received hospitably, and the caliph is vastly amused to watch their simple ways of eating and comporting themselves. It is obvious that their customs seem quite primitive to him, and this also applies to the curious matter that is put before him: a girl's unwillingness to marry a perfectly suitable cousin. The caliph asks her in private about her objections, and she answers him quite vehemently that it is not a matter of disliking her cousin, but has to do with her own feelings:

> 'I am a woman who does not like to be close to men, for God has made me detest the tents of women and of ladies secluded by curtains. As you see, I love to fight, to gird myself with polished swords and long lances. I do not want to be bundled together with the women, oh merciful caliph. My sword is my anklet, dust is my eyeblack, and my horse is my family. What would I do, oh Prince of the Believers, with Hārith or other creatures[32] such as he?'[33]

The caliph is more amused than impressed, and laughs. Then Hārith jumps up, saying that he promises to marry her only on the condition that she will be to him 'the sky that I look up to, not the earth that I tread on'. Reassured, the caliph says to Fātima that, since God has created women for men, and women need a husband to protect them from other people's glances, he orders her to consent to the marriage. She sits there silent and full of shame. Her uncle remarks that her silence implies her consent. Islamic law indeed assumes that a virgin is too shy to give her explicit consent to marriage, and that her silence indicates that she has no objection.³⁴

The marriage is immediately concluded. Nothing further happens though. Bride and bridegroom each sit in their own tents, and Hārith 'could not feast his eyes on her, and had not obtained what he wanted'. It will take a while before anything further happens on this count, for an attack is launched on the Muslims by a Byzantine warrior princess and her sister, and all hands are needed to counter the attack. The Byzantine princess, Malatya, founds a city which takes her name, and, after the princess and her armies have been defeated, this city, Malatya (in Greek: Melitene, nowadays the Turkish city of Eski Malatya), will become the home base of the Banū Kilāb and their rival tribe, the Banū Sulaym.

When all this is over, the matter of the unconsummated marriage of Fātima and Hārith again becomes an issue. Hārith, deeply frustrated, consults 'Uqba, the villainous *qādī*. 'Uqba suggests drugging Fātima with the help of her trusted foster brother Marzūq. Marzūq, who does not approve of Fātima's attitude towards her legal husband, agrees to put a soporific into her drink. Hārith's behaviour on the occasion is not very impressive:

> 'Have you done it, Marzūq?' 'Yes, go in, for I have put her into your power.' When he heard Marzūq's words, Hārith said to him: 'Please, you go in first and shake her arms, so that I can see what she does.' Marzūq went up to her, shook her, and see, she was like a log of wood. When Marzūq saw her in that condition, he regretted what he had done.

It is all in accordance with the law, however, he thinks, so he tells Hārith to go ahead. In a daze, Hārith tries to take Fātima's clothes off, but is faced with underwear offering such sound protection that, in the end, he has to cut it partly away to reach his aim. When it is all over, he gets up and leaves her bleeding. Happily reciting a poem he walks out, to the disgust of Marzūq, who angrily chases him away, refusing the money Hārith has offered him. Hārith goes to inform his father and his uncle, confessing to the latter that he considered fleeing after what he had done. '"Why should you flee from your own wife? You have only done what is good and proper, so be happy that your time of fretting and patient endurance is over."'³⁵

As we see, all the men in whom Fātima had put her trust have finally betrayed her. In the end, feelings of male solidarity and the men's confidence that they know what is best for a woman have left her completely isolated. Yet her father goes and sits at her door to look after her when she comes to. He says calming words, prevents her killing Marzūq and repeats that women have only been created for men, and that she would do better to accept this.³⁶ She sits there, full of shame and misery, promising to kill Hārith as soon as she can get hold of him. Feelings of sickness and general weakness soon make it clear that she is pregnant, and in due course she gives birth to a strong and beautiful baby boy, bravely hiding her pain during the delivery process.

To everybody's great consternation, the baby is black. Questions immediately arise among the attending women, but Fātima says that she has nothing to hide, her case is perfectly clear and it is up to God to create a baby in any shape He wants, white from black and black from white. One of the women points out that anyhow the boy will bring shame on her, saying that it is better to cut the umbilical cord and hide the whole affair. Thinking the matter over, Fātima decides that there is nothing she can be blamed for. Her marriage, after all, was conducted by the caliph himself. She has no need of marriage, however, preoccupied as she is with higher things, and she would prefer to forget the whole matter as soon as possible. On no account, however, should the baby be killed: he is a gift from God. He is named 'Abd al-Wahhāb and is put with a foster mother, history repeating itself. The rumour is spread that Fātima has given birth to Hārith's child, but that he died. Hārith is sad to hear the news and also worried because Fātima, wanting to take revenge, is out looking for him, although 'Abd Allāh, their commander-in-chief, eventually persuades her to cease.³⁷

Fātima keeps a close eye on her son, and, when he is four years old, she starts teaching him the Qur'ān and the basic religious duties. When he is six years old he wants 'a horse to practise the art of chivalry among the champions', and from then on Fātima gradually starts taking him under her wing, having become very fond of him.³⁸ Her secret, however, is betrayed by a slave girl, who spreads the rumour that Fātima has given birth to a black baby, the result of a love affair 'with some servant or other'.³⁹ The news soon reaches Hārith and his father. They are extremely angry and Hārith states emphatically that the child cannot possibly be his son.

Heated discussions follow. Dhāt al-Himma is miserable, but is cheered up by her little son, by then seven years old, sitting on her knee. Feeling his strong arms, she says that he will be a real holy warrior, and he comforts her by saying that God has created him black because of something that happened earlier, and they should not protest to Him about it. He creates what He wants.

Then 'Abd al-Wahhāb cried profusely, and having pronounced blessings on the Prophet, he recited the following verses:
Even though I am black, my heart is as white as the light of day,
Colour can be no blame for a person when his deeds are full of glory.
The only honour lies in right behaviour for the Day of Resurrection, the Day of the Final Decision.[40]

At last, the decision is taken to go and consult a specialist, a Meccan shaykh very knowledgeable in matters of family resemblances. He establishes beyond doubt that Hārith is 'Abd al-Wahhāb's father.[41] Objections and doubts, however, still continue, and finally everybody agrees that the imam Ja'far al-Sādiq, descendant of the Prophet and the sixth imam of Shi'ite Islam, is the only one who can bring light to the affair.[42] The imam explains that the child is black because he has been conceived during menstruation. Semen has become mixed with blood, and the child's dark complexion is the physiological result of this. The case is not unique, he says, and the obvious physical resemblance between 'Abd al-Wahhāb and Hārith sufficiently confirms that they are father and son.

Thus, Dhāt al-Himma is exonerated from guilt, but Hārith still refuses to accept the child as his own. Not even the fact that the caliph, too, takes Dhāt al-Himma's side after the Prophet has, in a dream, confirmed Ja'far al-Sādiq's views, can make him change his mind.[43] The affair further increases Dhāt al-Himma's hatred of her cousin, and relations between them are broken off.

When 'Abd al-Wahhāb, who, until then, has been raised by a nurse, is six years old, he starts asking for a horse, and from that time on Dhāt al-Himma takes him under her wing, personally instructing him in the art of chivalrous warfare. When he has reached the point where he considers himself his mother's equal on the battleground she puts him to the test by attacking him in male disguise, and is pleased to find him as unmovable as a rock.[44] Not long afterwards, he kills both his father and grandfather in battle. Thus, he takes revenge for the way they have treated his mother and himself, and also frees Fātima Dhāt al-Himma from the marriage bonds that still tied her to Hārith.

From now on, Dhāt al-Himma and 'Abd al-Wahhāb together will lead the Kilābī tribe, soon to be joined by Abū Muhammad al-Battāl, who, in *The Adventures of Princess Dhāt al-Himma,* plays the role of 'ayyār, 'man of wiles'; the trickster character who, in Arabic popular epic, acts as companion and helper to the main hero. Battāl is the archetypical ʿayyār: he speaks seventy languages, is a master of disguise, has no qualms about transgressing social and moral boundaries, often displaying clownish behaviour, and always comes up with a crafty trick to outwit the enemy.[45]

Dhāt al-Himma and Baṭṭāl

Within the triumvirate formed by Dhāt al-Himma, ʿAbd al-Wahhāb and Baṭṭāl, Baṭṭāl acts as 'helper' to both Dhāt al-Himma and her son. Yet his relationship with Dhāt al-Himma is much closer than that with her son. Baṭṭāl is, in many ways, Dhāt al-Himma's alter ego, her real friend. She is very fond of him and is deeply worried when nothing has been heard from him for a while.[46] On another occasion, when he has again disappeared without trace, both she and ʿAbd al-Wahhāb are so upset that they even ask the detestable qāḍī ʿUqba whether he has of news of him. Dhāt al-Himma sends out spies in every direction and weeps day and night, stating that she is more worried about Baṭṭāl's disappearance than she was when ʿAbd al-Wahhāb was lost.[47]

The bond between them is strengthened by the fact that Dhāt al-Himma herself also has trickster-like aspects. In Baṭṭāl's company, her marginal, unconventional side can unfold and is allowed to blossom. She may not do outrageous things herself, but she cannot help being amused and laugh when Baṭṭāl acts or speaks in a way totally incompatible with the code of manly honour, for instance unashamedly showing cowardice. She may even cover for him when this brings him into trouble. It all curiously contrasts with her piety and generally high moral standards.

She is quite prepared to use unconventional, sometimes even less than honourable, means in order to reach her goal. She will secretly sneak into enemy dwellings or climb up using a rope, or let herself be admitted on trust and then kill unarmed people. Just like the ʿayyār, she regularly appears out of the blue in critical situations and saves the day. She speaks at least one foreign language (Greek) and often acts in disguise, not just donning male attire in battle, as is customary for warrior women, but also, for instance, dressing up as a Turk or a Slav, or letting Baṭṭāl disguise her as a venerable old Christian priest and convincingly playing the part. It is unthinkable that Prince ʿAbd al-Wahhāb would do such things; he is a straightforward hero of the usual type. It emphasizes Dhāt al-Himma's transitional aspects: she cannot be fixed exclusively into one category, and may switch roles if the situation requires it. She can move between different worlds and strata, from male to female, from Islam to Christianity, from pious lady to wily rascal, from devoted mother to fierce warlord. It makes her, in a way, a doubly marginal character, as a woman and as a trickster.

It is noteworthy that the twelfth-century scholar Samaw'al al-Maghribī refers to the *sīra* as the '*dīwān* (one of the terms used for *sīra*) of Dalhama and al-Battāl', without mentioning 'Abd al-Wahhāb. This may indicate that, early on, Princess Dalhama (alternatively: Dhū l-Himma or Dhāt al-Himma) was seen as the main hero of the epic, with Battāl as the usual trickster companion of the main protagonist.

Dhāt al-Himma as a warrior

Abd al-Wahhāb's importance in no way diminishes Dhāt al-Himma's role as a leading warrior and army leader in the epic. Her high moral standards are an important aspect of this; she is universally respected. She does not battle for honour or riches: she is a female *mujāhid*, a fighter for the cause of Islam. She shrugs when people suggest that she has other motives, such as when a rival tribe, the Banū Sulaym, complains to their commander that Dhāt al-Himma does not consider the consequences of her actions, but just rushes into battle to prove that her reputation for courage is well deserved.[48] As a result, they are now all in deep trouble. The commander laughs, and Dhāt al-Himma says to him that for sixty years she has only wanted one thing from God. He asks the princess what this might be and she replies, to die as a martyr, fighting for His cause.

Dhāt al-Himma's exploits are too numerous and varied to be recounted here in detail, so a few examples will have to suffice. On many occasions she leads huge armies into battle, such as when, only just recovered from a serious illness, she decides not to wait for news of her son, but to set out for the Byzantine lands.[49] Her son 'Abd al-Wahhāb has disappeared during the course of a war with the frightening foreign king Kūshanūsh, who has conquered Constantinople and is now on his way to Baghdad. Dhāt al-Himma decides to march on to Constantinople, as had been planned earlier, and sets out at the head of 70,000 men. The gates of the city are locked just in time and she does not manage to get inside. She goes instead to the fortress of Shaytaban, where, as it turns out, Prince 'Abd al-Wahhāb and a number of other Kilābī champions have been imprisoned by Kūshanūsh, together with the Byzantine emperor and his vassals. Dhāt al-Himma, joined meanwhile by Baṭṭāl and his servant, attacks the fortress, making use of a secret passage, and the prisoners are freed. A moving scene between mother and son takes place: 'When the princess saw her son her heart went out to him, and when he looked at her he recognized her, although she looked like a ghost.[50] Crying, he started to kiss her and to ask how she was. She told him about her illness.'[51]

Dhāt al-Himma is a redoubtable opponent in battle. When the Kilābīs are confronted with another enemy, the terrible Hadlāmūs, she sets out for combat. She jumps on her horse, not even putting her foot in the stirrup, and attacks Hadlāmūs while reciting a poem. They battle for a long time, until her lance is struck from her hand and he manages to knock her from the saddle with his shield. Quickly, he, too, dismounts, and after a struggle he lifts her on his shoulder. Her men look on in shock. But she is not that easy to defeat:

> and lo, Princess Dhāt al-Himma had got hold of Hadlāmūs's head, squeezing with all her might till the blood spouted from his ears. Then she gave him a tremendous blow on the head so that his teeth fell from his mouth and he dropped down unconscious. She fell upon him, while he had no idea where he was. She put her hands under his armpits and lifted him on her shoulders. So he came back being carried, while he first had been the one who was the carrier.[52]

It is not only on the battlefield that Dhāt al-Himma performs brave deeds. She often volunteers to undertake risky actions on her own.[53] When her daughter-in-law Maymūna is held captive in a castle she makes a rope from silk to throw down to the warriors who have come to save her. They discuss who will be the first to climb up. 'Abd al-Wahhāb, Maymūna's husband, offers to go up first, but there is no question of this: Dhāt al-Himma firmly takes on this risky task herself. She ties the rope around her body, climbs up and so gets into the castle, which they soon manage to take over.

On another occasion she manages to be admitted into a monastery, hoping to capture her enemy *qāḍī* 'Uqba and the evil monk Shūmdaris. She is dressed as a monk, with a white beard pasted on her chin by Baṭṭāl and her sword hidden under her clothes. As soon as she is inside she kills a monk and pulls off her beard. She is recognized too soon to prevent the two scoundrels escaping, but finds the fatally wounded caliph Ma'mūn, who had been abducted by 'Uqba and his friends.[54]

A somewhat similar situation occurs when she sails with Baṭṭāl to a castle where the caliph Wāthiq is held captive. Dhāt al-Himma is dressed like a Slav and mutters a foreign language. They present the commander of the castle with the ring of the Byzantine emperor, previously stolen, in order to prove that they are acting on his orders. The caliph is handed over to them, and Dhāt al-Himma is admitted to the castle on the pretext that she wants to pray in the church. Once inside, she finds that everybody is unarmed and she kills the whole garrison.[55]

In these adventures, she does not always escape unscathed: she is regularly wounded or captured, and during captivity she is often treated with extreme harshness. She is tortured, threatened with rape or left to starve. All this she bears with stoic patience.

During one of the episodes Dhāt al-Himma and her grandson Bahrūn, lost in the wilderness and exhausted, are brought to King Ghaydurūs.[56] Bahrūn speaks to the king about Dhāt al-Himma's prowess on the battlefield, and the king tells him that he has a daughter, Iftūnā, who is also a redoubtable warrior woman and has a large entourage of warrior girls.[57] Clearly, Dhāt al-Himma is presently not in a condition to fight, starved and exhausted as she is after her time in the wilderness. The king decides to give her time to recover, and then he proposes to match her against his daughter and his other champions.[58] Iftūnā, accompanied by a hundred of her girls, goes to visit Dhāt al-Himma. She finds her praying and reciting the Qur'ān.[59] She looks like a ghost and is obviously still very weak, but her spirit is unbroken. They have a conversation during which Dhāt al-Himma remarks that if she had not been starved and exhausted, she would never have been taken captive. This angers Iftūnā, who is proud of her warrior skills and those of her girls, and she decides to let Dhāt al-Himma wrestle with one of them. Dhāt al-Himma kills the girl and also the next twenty who are put against her.

A subsequent fight with Iftūnā herself remains inconclusive, and the same happens when they meet each other in single combat ten days later. King Ghaydurūs then takes over and a tremendous battle follows. The king strikes off the head of Dhāt al-Himma's horse.[60] On foot, she strikes off his horse's legs in return. They continue wrestling and she deals him a blow on the head, 'a real Kilābī Arab blow', which leaves him unconscious. His men rush in to kill her, but Iftūnā calls them off and Dhāt al-Himma is put in chains. When the king comes round he orders that she be set free immediately, and offers her his kingdom if she consents to marry him and to convert. She turns red with anger: '"You Byzantine dog, who has brought upon himself the wrath of the Living,

The Eternal! How can I leave the religion of the Eternal in which I was brought up?'" She does not want marriage but just to serve God, and would be happy to undergo all kinds of torture and punishments for His sake. Eventually, the king decides simply to let her die of hunger and thirst.

Of course, she is soon freed by Baṭṭāl through a complicated set of ruses involving, among other things, a fake marriage to Ghaydurūs. They flee, taking Iftūnā with them, for Dhāt al-Himma sees her as a possible bride for her son ʿAbd al-Wahhāb.

Dhāt al-Himma and other women

Dhāt al-Himma's contacts with Iftūnā show the curious mixture of admiration, sympathy and rivalry that is typical of her relations with other warrior women. It also brings us to the more general question of her relationships with women. It is clear that she has little interest in conventional women. There are few instances in the *sīra* that elaborate on her contacts with women other than warrior girls, or at least with women who play active roles in the hostilities. There are, of course, her mother and her foster mother Suʿdā, but very little is said about Dhāt al-Himma's relationship with them. Suʿdā she criticizes for not being proud enough when they have been captured, and contact with her mother is mainly restricted to a short reunion scene when Dhāt al-Himma is presented as the long lost daughter.

She chooses a bride for her son, ʿAbd al-Wahhāb, who duly bears him two sons and dies of jealousy and grief when he marries a second wife. No mention is made of any views expressed by Dhāt al-Himma on this matter. On the other hand, she states unambiguously that they have to go and save ʿUlwā, ʿAbd al-Wahhāb's second wife, a warrior woman herself, when she is held captive under threatening circumstances.

Many warrior girls and women cross her path, foreign as well as Arab, and Dhāt al-Himma often becomes engaged in tremendous fights with them, in the course of which serious invective is exchanged. Yet there is usually an undercurrent of mutual respect for each other's prowess and skill. The women whom Dhāt al-Himma has to confront in battle are generally young, but she manages to defeat them in spite of their youth and physical strength.

That these women, or girls, are young and beautiful, and sexually highly attractive, is a complicating and disruptive factor. They often manage to confuse their male opponents to the point where these men are no longer able to offer proper resistance. During combat the girl may, for instance, suddenly expose her long hair, her breasts, or even throw off her clothes altogether, and then make short work of her totally bewildered male opponent. Such behaviour causes the men to fall helplessly in love, so that they can think of nothing but how to make the woman their own. As a result, all kinds of rivalries arise, causing rifts between members of the tribe and even close friends. Men no longer care about the basic rules of proper behaviour, so obsessed are they with the thought of how to make the girl their own.

It is all very exasperating to Dhāt al-Himma, and she usually has to step in and solve the matter with brute force. She will rush in and defeat a female opponent who continues to put men out of action in combat. When a girl has been defeated and forcibly married to one of her enemies, Dhāt al-Himma will do anything, including personally wrestling her down and tying her up, in order to get the marriage consummated. She is especially inclined to take action when the men closest to her, ʿAbd al-Wahhāb and Baṭṭāl, are morally or physically in danger from a warrior princess.

Much of the above can be seen in the history of Nūra, a Byzantine warrior princess of great beauty, valour and skill.[61] Baṭṭāl meets her when he accidentally surprises her and her girls in her father's castle while they enjoy practising martial arts. They invite him in, and Nūra challenges him to wrestle with her. He immediately falls in love with her. Hostilities between her father and the Muslims begin soon afterwards, with Nūra fighting on her father's side.

This is the start of a long series of events during which Nūra again and again manages to get the better of the Muslims. A series of Muslim champions, including ʿAbd al-Wahhāb and even the caliph Harūn, fall in love with her. She fights them, defeats them in combat, sometimes gets captured, but escapes again and again. Dhāt al-Himma meets her early on, during an episode in which Nūra's girls have defeated and captured a series of Kilābī champions in succession, among them ʿAbd al-Wahhāb. Nūra fights in the rearguard, and Dhāt al-Himma, who wants to meet her, asks whether anybody has seen her. Nūra, in her turn, is looking for Dhāt al-Himma. Eventually they meet in combat.[62] Dhāt al-Himma is hampered by one of her own men, who, upon seeing Nūra, is completely smitten with her, and in trying to come near to her throws stones among Dhāt al-Himma's feet and causes her to stumble. Nūra, approaches Dhāt al-Himma, who is on the ground, but who gets up, loudly screaming invective at Nūra. In the subsequent wrestle she lifts Nūra up bodily and takes her away. Dhāt al-Himma is impressed by her beauty: "'Well, I have never felt inclined towards men, and have never wanted anyone but the King Most High; but if this girl had been a man, I would have lost my head.'"

Dhāt al-Himma treats Nūra well while she is a captive, and later on, when their roles have changed and Dhāt al-Himma is the prisoner of the Byzantines, Nūra, in her turn, protects Dhāt al-Himma. While Dhāt al-Himma clearly feels sympathy and respect for Nūra, she is also exasperated by the havoc she causes in the hearts of the Muslim men, including her son 'Abd al-Wahhāb and her trusted companion Battāl. They all seem to take leave of their senses as soon as Nūra appears on the scene. Personally, she favours Battāl as Nūra's prospective husband, but this leads to such trouble with her son that she even has to fight him in order to bring him to his senses. Carefully trying not to hurt his feelings, she brings him down, meanwhile praising his courage in order to cover his embarrassment. She asks him very seriously "'by the sanctity of the breast that suckled you'" not to let his passion run away with him.[63]

Whatever sympathy she may feel for Nūra, eliminating her as a cause of strife and disorder (*fitna*) has first priority with her. So she remains watchful, even after the wedding of Nūra and Battāl has finally taken place and the couple have retired. Not trusting Nūra, Dhāt al-Himma storms in just when Nūra offers Battāl a poisoned drink. She hotly denies it, but her guilt soon becomes clear and Dhāt al-Himma throws herself upon Nūra. The ensuing fight leaves Nūra totally exhausted. Dhāt al-Himma, not prepared to take any more risks, ties her up firmly before leaving the couple alone again.

As we have seen, female sexuality as a source of *fitna* has to be brought under control at all costs, even if this involves making the woman forcibly helpless.[64]

Several of the warrior women whom Dhāt al-Himma encounters, and often also battles with, will eventually become her daughters-in-law. Qannāsa, whom she attacks and defeats in order to save her son 'Abd al-Wahhāb, is an example. Her history will be told in the next chapter, along with that of Maymūna, another of 'Abd al-Wahhāb's wives. Maymūna is a headstrong young girl, who, after a quarrel, refuses to be reconciled with 'Abd al-Wahhāb, but instead fights and defeats him in combat.[65] Finally, Dhāt al-Himma herself decides to fight her and wins. This earns her Maymūna's love and respect, and soon she wants nothing better than to marry 'Abd al-Wahhāb. The wedding takes place and

Maymūna becomes Dhāt al-Himma's staunch supporter, assisting her on the battlefield.

It is only later in the story, when Maymūna has undergone a complete change of personality left her husband to join the Byzantines, that embittered battles between her and Dhāt al-Himma take place. By that time all sympathy between them has gone, and it is Dhāt al-Himma who finally kills her.

Two of the women mentioned here, Nūra and Maymūna, are foreign princesses, while Qannāsa is an Arab princess of unclear tribal background. Ghamra the daughter of 'Utārid, a Bedouin princess who is dealt with extensively in Chapter 5, is closely related to Dhāt al-Himma's own tribe. She is a brave and headstrong girl who refuses to be forced into marriage and, not surprisingly, Dhāt al-Himma has great sympathy for her. When, at some point, she cuts herself loose from the tribe and departs to other regions, Dhāt al-Himma is very sorry to see her go, for she had become very fond of her.

As we have seen, Dhāt al-Himma's relationships with those warrior women show real interaction, emotionally as well as otherwise. They often act together during battles and forays, in excellent comradeship. Little, on the contrary, is said about her relationships with other women. Women belonging to the enemy camp are extremely cruel to her. These are often family members of her arch-enemies: 'Uqba has a treacherous daughter, and the evil monk Shūmdaris has an equally evil wife, Shūma. Shūma is a fierce opponent who takes an active part in fighting and harming the Muslims, even though she is not, strictly speaking, a warrior woman. She is very cruel: on one occasion she holds Dhāt al-Himma captive and the princess is about to be executed. Shūma calls in her son to rape Dhāt al-Himma before she dies, so that the latter's son 'Abd al-Wahhāb will have to bear the burden of his mother's dishonour. Of course, she is saved in the nick of time.[66]

The end of Dhāt al-Himma's life

After many thousands of pages, during which Dhāt al-Himma continues to act just as bravely as she did in her youth, the story is gradually brought to a conclusion. Qāḍī 'Uqba, her arch-enemy, is finally executed, Constantinople is taken and 'Abd al-Wahhāb's son Zālim is installed there as governor, reigning for twenty years before he dies as a result of an accident.[67] 'Abd al-Wahhāb and Dhāt al-Himma go on a pilgrimage and continue living near Mecca until Dhāt al-Himma falls ill and dies.[68] ʿAbd al-Wahhāb survives her by a few months.[69]

Battāl did not accompany them to the Hijāz, but remained with the caliph al-Wāthiq, Muʿtasim's successor, who eventually gave him permission to go and live in Byzantine Ankūrīya (Ankara). The caliph dies soon afterwards. The Byzantine reconquest then begins. Soon Wāthiq's successor, Mutawakkil, has to be informed about the Byzantine recapture of Malatya.[70] Battāl is deeply sad that he has to witness these events, unable to do anything about them. When he dies he is buried in a mosque in Ankūrīya, where eventually a gilt dome is built over his tomb. The link to Turkey need not be a surprise for us, for Battāl, as Seyed Battal Gazi, is an important hero in the Turkish epic tradition. Several localities still claim to house his grave, the most important being Seyitgazi in Eskişehir Province.

Chapter 4

Sīrat Dhāt al-Himma 2: *Prince ʿAbd al-Wahhāb and His Warrior Wives*[1]

Protagonists

- ʿAbd al-Wahhāb, leading hero of the Kilābī tribe, son of Fātima Dhāt al-Himma
- Abū Muhammad, see Battāl
- Al-Rashīd, see Hārūn al-Rashīd
- Alūf, Byzantine warrior princess, converts to Islam
- ʿAmr ibn ʿUbaydallāh, chief of the Banū Sulaym and chief army commander
- Anqūsh, Yemeni king
- Armānūs, Byzantine king, marries Maymūna
- Ashmītūs, a Byzantine king
- Bahrūn, son of Maymūna and ʿAbd al-Wahhāb
- Battāl (Abū Muhammad al-Battāl), major Kilābī hero, known for his wiliness
- Būhinmā (Bohemond), son of Maymūna and Armānūs
- Damdamān, Ethiopian king, father of Maymūna
- Daygham, son of ʿAbd al-Wahhāb and his first wife
- Dhāt al-Himma (Fātima), leading female hero of the Kilābī tribe, mother of ʿAbd al-Wahhāb
- Fātima, daughter of Mazlūm: see Dhāt al-Himma
- Ghamra, Arab warrior girl, daughter of ʿUtārid
- Hārith, father of ʿAbd al-Wahhāb
- Hārūn al-Rashīd, Abbasid caliph

- Hayyāj al-Kurdī, Kurdish warrior fighting with the Kilābīs, father of seven warrior daughters
- Ibrāhīm, son of 'Ulwā and 'Abd al-Wahhāb
- Iftūnā, Byzantine warrior princess, converts to Islam
- Ja'far al-Sādiq, sixth imām of Shi'ite Islam
- Karfanās, enemy king, marries Maymūna
- Madhbahūn, son of Nūra and Battāl
- Ma'mūn, Abbasid caliph
- Marjāna, Christian girl, converts to Islam
- Maymūna, Ethiopian warrior princess, fourth wife of 'Abd al-Wahhāb
- Mayrūna, Byzantine warrior princess, concubine of 'Abd al-Wahhāb
- Mazlūm, father of Fātima Dhāt al-Himma
- Mu'tasim, Abbasid caliph
- Nāfi', emir in charge of the fortress Kawkab
- Nūra, Byzantine warrior princess, marries Battāl
- Nūr al-Nār, Christian princess, converts to Islam
- Qannāsa, Arab warrior princess, daughter of Muzāhim, third wife of 'Abd al-Wahhāb
- Qarāqūnā, enemy king
- Qash'am, son of 'Abd al-Wahhāb and his first wife
- Rāshid ibn Damra, Kilābī warrior, father of 'Abd al-Wahhāb's first wife
- Sayf al-Hanīfīya (also: Sayf al-Hanafīya), Muslim name of Sayf al-Nasrānīya
- Sayf al-Nasrānīya, son of Mayrūna and 'Abd al-Wahhāb
- 'Ulwā, Arab warrior woman, second wife of 'Abd al-Wahhāb
- 'Uqba, chief *qādī* (judge), crypto-Christian, villain of the *sīra*. Related to the Banū Sulaym
- 'Utārid, chief of a Yemeni tribe, father of Ghamra
- Zālim, son of Qannāsa and 'Abd al-Wahhāb
- Zanānīr, Byzantine warrior princess, converts and marries Battāl's servant Lu'lu'

Al-Wahhābīya, that is how people in Marrakesh refer to *Sīrat al-amīra Dhāt al-Himma*, as was noted in the previous chapter. It clearly demonstrates the fact that 'Abd al-Wahhāb, the son of Princess Dhāt al-Himma, is at least as important a protagonist as Dhāt al-Himma herself, and probably even more important, at least in the eyes of the Moroccan audience. The fact that he is a man may have something to do with this. He is the second of the three leading Muslim heroes referred to in the *sīra*'s full title, *The*

Adventures of Princess Dhāt al-Himma and her son ʿAbd al-Wahhāb and Abū Muhammad al-Battāl (etc.).

ʿAbd al-Wahhāb is noteworthy not only as a major hero, but also for his personal circumstances: he has been raised and trained by a warrior mother, and all his wives, except the first, are also accomplished warrior women. His relationship with these women will be the subject of this chapter.

As is usually the case with major heroes, ʿAbd al-Wahhāb's birth and early youth have various unusual aspects, starting with his conception. As mentioned in the previous chapter, his mother, Princess Dhāt al-Himma, was forced by the caliph to marry her cousin al-Hārith, whom she loathed. She refused to have marital relations with her husband, and when she could not be persuaded, he finally decided to drug her in order to be able to consummate the marriage. When Dhāt al-Himma subsequently gave birth to a son, the baby turned out to be black and her husband Hārith refused to acknowledge the child. However, a Meccan shaykh, a specialist in detecting physical resemblances, confirmed Hārith's fatherhood beyond doubt. How the child came to be black is explained by the imam Jaʿfar al-Sādiq, descendant of the Prophet and a famous scholar: this was caused by the fact that he had been conceived during menstruation. Thus Dhāt al-Himma is exonerated from guilt, but Hārith continues to consider the child a bastard, and relations between them are completely cut off.

When ʿAbd al-Wahhāb, who until then has been raised by a nurse, is six years old, he starts to ask for a horse and, from this time on, Dhāt al-Himma takes him under her wing, personally instructing him in the art of chivalrous warfare. On reaching the point where he considers himself his mother's equal in combat she puts him to the test. After having warned him that there are robbers operating along the road, she hides herself and attacks him in male disguise, trying to unhorse him. He does not move an inch, though, and she laughs heartily when he grabs her by the arms and pulls off her veil. ʿAbd al-Wahhāb is very embarrassed when he sees who his attacker is.[2]

Five thousand black warriors have already been placed under his command, and from now on he is fully equipped to take up a leading role in the forays and battles of his tribe, the Banū Kilāb (or Kilābīs).[3] Soon he engages in his first battle, confronting an enemy party which includes his grandfather on his father's side, and kills a large number of enemies. In a subsequent battle he kills his grandfather as well as his father. Returning, he meets his mother, who is aghast when she sees how badly wounded he is and quickly summons the surgeon to sew up his wounds.⁴

The episode brings into focus the tension between Dhāt al-Himma's feelings as a mother and as the tribe's prominent leader in battle. As a staunch and almost unbeatable warrior herself, she is proud of her son's martial prowess, but she also has to deal with her motherly feelings of anxiety. And even though, from now on, they will jointly lead the tribe of the Banū Kilāb, usually in harmony, the fact that they are mother and son regularly causes emotional tensions, most frequently in situations where 'Abd al-Wahhāb refuses to accept his mother's judgement on the best way to handle tricky situations. She may, for instance, chide him about taking unnecessary personal risks, to which he may react with insulting remarks: '"No, my son, come back, do not go and fight this Byzantine and do not give me something to carry that I cannot bear." When the prince heard this, he looked greatly amazed, and said: "Dhāt al-Himma, off with you, go and spin with the women and leave it to your son to fight brave opponents. Even if a thousand Byzantines came to fight me, distress and misery would be their share!"'⁵ (Note the extremely insulting use, in Arabic, of his mother's honorific name instead of the usual polite 'princess' or 'mother'). 'When the princess heard the words of her son she became extremely angry. She did not say another word to keep him back, and did not answer him. Anger clearly showed in her eyes.'

Dhāt al-Himma leaves the battlefield, goes to her tent and takes off her equipment. Then she prepares her revenge. Disguised as a Byzantine knight, she attacks her son and defeats him, saying:'"So, you did not care for full-bosomed companions [i.e. the weaker sex]? How does it suit you to be tested by the lion of the forest?" Then she took off her veil. A face like the full moon appeared, and lo, it was Princess Dhāt al-Himma.'⁶

She regularly comes to 'Abd al-Wahhāb's rescue when he finds himself in difficult situations. In some of these cases she confronts and defeats a female warrior whom she considers to be a serious threat. The girl in question may later become her daughter-in-law, and be on excellent terms with her.

First wife: unnamed

Dhāt al-Himma's role as a parent also involves monitoring her son's relations with women. When he reaches adulthood and has distinguished himself in his first armed conflict, returning seriously wounded, she decides that it is time for him to marry: 'She firmly bandaged his wounds and he returned to Malatya, for it was the princess' intention that 'Abd al-Wahhāb should marry before going to the land of the Byzantines. When his wounds had healed she asked the sister of Prince Rāshid ibn Damra in marriage for him. This Rāshid was a very prominent member of the Banū Kilāb, a famous knight and renowned champion.'[7]

We never get to hear the name of the girl. She dutifully fulfils her wifely role by bearing 'Abd al-Wahhāb two sons, Qash'am and Daygham. Her life, however, is not a happy one, for 'Abd al-Wahhāb, with his mother's approval, soon concludes a new marriage. The woman he marries is the sister of an ally from Iraq who wants to join the Banū Kilāb permanently, and who wants to strengthen the bonds by marrying his sister 'Ulwā (this time the bride has a name) to 'Abd al-Wahhāb. Princess Dhāt al-Himma is all in favour of it, and the wedding takes place.[8]

As to the fate of the hapless first wife: 'Prince 'Abd al-Wahhāb was very happy with 'Ulwā, and he left his [first] wife, the sister of Rāshid, alone. He had begotten from her two male children. One he had named Daygham, and the other Qash'am. When he married 'Ulwā and left her [his first wife] alone, she was pregnant with Qash'am. She gave birth to him and then died of jealousy. 'Abd al-Wahhāb was sorry that he had left her alone, but he found consolation in 'Ulwā.'[9]

Second wife: 'Ulwā

While 'Abd al-Wahhāb's nameless first wife simply fulfils the traditional role of a wife, his subsequent wives have other accomplishments. His second wife, 'Ulwā, it later transpires, is an accomplished warrior woman. She will play an active part in the tribe's exploits, accompanied by Ibrāhīm, the son she bears 'Abd al-Wahhāb. Her martial capacities are not immediately obvious, for after she has married 'Abd al-Wahhāb we do not hear much about her for a while. Apparently she stays at home while her husband becomes involved in other adventures, one of which leads to his third marriage (more about this later), and another to a brief affair with a Byzantine princess.

'Ulwā appears on the scene again when the women and children of the Banū Kilāb, including 'Ulwā and her son Ibrāhīm, are taken captive by the Byzantines during an attack on Malatya.[10] For a while no trace can be found of them, and this finally draws 'Abd al-Wahhāb's attention, after he has been involved in a complicated situation with the caliph and the Byzantines: "'This affair has made me forget my son Ibrāhīm and his mother 'Ulwā, of whom nothing has been heard and no trace has been found; there is no help and no power except with God, the High, the Almighty." And he did not sleep for the rest of the night until the light of daybreak appeared.'[11]

Finally the news arrives that 'Ulwā and her son are being held captive in the castle of a Byzantine king, Ashmītūs.[12] Their captivity has already lasted four years. An expedition is sent out to get them back and a long series of adventures follows.[13] Meanwhile the situation of 'Ulwā and Ibrāhīm has become very dire indeed, for Ashmītūs has been urged to kill them both in order to remove 'Abd al-Wahhāb's incentive to attack the Byzantine fortresses. 'Ulwā finally manages to send a letter to her husband telling him about their imminent execution. To strengthen her appeal, she also includes a love poem that 'Abd al-Wahhāb once composed for her.

The messenger is a Christian monk who had been so impressed by the piety and continuous worship of 'Ulwā and Ibrāhīm that he started to ask them about their religion, which 'Ulwā explained to him in detail: the discussion of the tenets of their respective religions takes up nearly a whole page. Convinced by the superiority of Islam, he converts.[14]

'Abd al-Wahhāb is devastated when he receives 'Ulwā's message. Action is immediately undertaken, although surprisingly not by 'Abd al-Wahhāb. It is Princess Dhāt al-Himma who feels morally obliged to answer 'Ulwā's call for help. She suggests dividing the army in two groups, one staying behind with 'Abd al-Wahhāb, while she herself will swiftly take a band of elite warriors to the enemy castle and try to prevent the execution of the prisoners.[15]

Meanwhile, another party, namely Battāl and a group of his followers, secretly depart, disguised as Christians, to see what they can do. They are successful, for they arrive at Ashmītūs's castle just at the crucial moment. 'Ulwā has been brought out naked with her son Ibrāhīm, and people prepare to stone them. The monks are moved by the sight of 'Ulwā's beautiful body and say to Ashmītūs that he should try to convert her and spare her life. Ashmītūs gives one of them permission to try. 'Ulwā, however, rejects the suggestion, in spite of the monk's promise to marry her, and points out the superiority of her own religion. The monks give up, stating that they see beheading and crucifixion as a fit punishment for her. The henchman is about to lift his sword when a cry is heard in Greek: 'Leave off from her!' The surprised Christians see a stranger approaching, who speaks Greek beautifully.

The stranger (it is, of course, Baṭṭāl, in Byzantine disguise) makes himself known as a messenger who has been asked to fetch ʿUlwā and Ibrāhīm so that they can be exchanged for one of Ashmīṭūs's brothers, who is held captive by the Muslims. ʿUlwā and Ibrāhīm are handed over and they depart, but they are intercepted by a Byzantine party and Baṭṭāl is recognized. A fight follows. Baṭṭāl and ʿUlwā try to kill their opponents, but they are captured. Baṭṭāl later escapes, but ʿUlwā and Ibrāhīm are taken back to Ashmīṭūs's castle. ʿUlwā is so worried about what is going to happen to her and her son that she is unable to eat anything. They are locked up again in the castle, and later on in a cave, away from the other captive women and children.[16] There ʿAbd al-Wahhāb, having defeated Ashmīṭūs and freed the captive women and children, finally finds them, nearly starved to death: 'Ibrāhīm was like a ghost, he could not utter a sound because he was completely starved, and it was no better with his mother ʿUlwā. Tears abundantly flowed from ʿAbd al-Wahhāb's eyes when he saw them.'[17] A moving family scene follows. Then they go back to the castle, where Princess Dhāt al-Himma hails ʿUlwā with congratulations.

In this episode ʿUlwā appears for the first time as an active warrior woman. As we see, her ability to fight is presented here without any particular emphasis: that she can handle arms seems to be taken for granted. While most warrior women are allotted at least one big combat scene involving a major opponent, usually shortly after they have made their first appearance, nothing like that occurs in ʿUlwā's story. Yet it is clear that she knows how to conduct herself in warfare. Her name appears regularly in the summaries of the main heroes taking part in a certain foray. Female warriors, in any case, feature prominently in these lists: see, for instance, an occasion where all three of ʿAbd al-Wahhāb's wives, ʿUlwā, Qannāṣa and Maymūna, go into conflict together with Ghamra, the daughter of ʿUṭārid (see Chapter 5), and Nūra, the wife of Baṭṭāl.[18]

ʿUlwā also acts independently if the situation requires it. At some point she and Qannāṣa find themselves in the Hijāz, where they had gone after ʿAbd al-Wahhāb and Qannāṣa's son Ẓālim had been captured. ʿUlwā starts bringing together a group of warriors in Yemen to go to Baghdad. Qannāṣa goes back to her own castle to collect her men and then 'sets out for Iraq to free her son Prince Ẓālim and Prince ʿAbd al-Wahhāb, for longing for them had killed her for many nights and days'.

When word is received that the two have been freed, Qannāsa and ʿUlwā happily continue on their way to Baghdad, where ʿAbd al-Wahhāb is delighted to see them. The extra troops they bring are also received with great joy. The caliph Muʿtasim, seeing them, is greatly amazed by the huge army and asks where it has come from. They told him that the two wives of Prince ʿAbd al-Wahhāb, Qannāsa and ʿUlwā, had arrived. The caliph laughed with joy and said: "With his wives and his mother Dhāt al-Himma, this man possesses something that nobody else has."[19]

On another occasion, when ʿAbd al-Wahhāb has been captured again and ʿUlwā hears that he has escaped and is fighting his way through Byzantine territory, she decides to go and join him with ten thousand men. Having captured three hundred enemy ships, she comes to ʿAbd al-Wahhāb's rescue when he is besieged in a Byzantine fortress.

Among ʿAbd al-Wahhāb's wives, ʿUlwā, in a way, stands between his unnamed, completely traditional first wife, who died from jealousy, and the two very independent warrior women, both unconnected to the tribe, whom he subsequently marries. Unlike these women, ʿUlwā is solidly embedded in the Kilābī tribe, where she has a true family network. ʿAbd al-Wahhāb, for instance, financially supports her deceased brother's widow and son.[20]

ʿUlwā is excessively devoted to her son Ibrāhīm, who remains somewhat in her shadow and does not play as prominent a part as ʿAbd al-Wahhāb's other sons. He disappears fairly early from the scene, killed by a lance.[21] The account of his death is drawn-out and tragic. Contrary to what his companions thought when they saw the lance pierce his body, Ibrāhīm was not killed immediately. When Battāl returns to the battlefield to look at the victims, he hears a faint moaning and discovers Ibrāhīm still alive. He carries him to the house of his father, who sits with him through part of the night, kissing his brow, weeping and saying over and over again: "'Ibrāhīm, this is farewell, and when will we be together again? This is parting, and when will we meet again?'" Ibrāhīm opens his eyes and answers that they will meet again before the King, the Creator, adding: "'Father, pass on my greetings to my mother. Wipe my blood on my shirt and bring it to ʿUlwā. May God give her strength to endure this trial.'" Then he pronounces the confession of faith and gives up the ghost. Amidst loud wailings of all the companions, he is wrapped in his clothes and sent to Āmid, where his mother is.

This scene has an obvious connection to an earlier episode, during which Ibrāhīm has been captured by the Byzantines. ʿUlwā, returning from a foray, runs into ʿAbd al-Wahhāb and they talk about the lost Ibrāhīm. ʿUlwā weeps, reproaching her husband that he has not made enough of an effort to get Ibrāhīm back. She says that, of course the loss of their son is not as unbearable to him as it is to her, because he still has many sons left. But if he does nothing to get Ibrāhīm back, she will call in all the Arab tribes to help. Shocked, he tries to console her, saying that, of course emotions do not work that way: why does she have to suppose that love for one person must necessarily be at the cost of love for another?[22]

ʿAbd al-Wahhāb's poignant grief about Ibrāhīm's death obviously supports his reaction to ʿUlwā's unjust reproaches, and so does his explicit statement that "'none of my sons occupies the place of priority in my heart'".[23] This is his reaction to what people were saying when his son Qashʿam comes to greet him. He presses him to his heart, kissing him on the forehead and crying for the loss of his brother Ibrāhīm. Seeing this, the people respond: "'Prince, you at least have other sons to console you for the loss of him.'"

It might seem as if ʿUlwā's resentment about ʿAbd al-Wahhāb's other marital relations and paramours focuses mainly on the many sons resulting from these relationships. ʿUlwā, however, just like ʿAbd al-Wahhāb's first wife, can be deeply jealous of other women. This aspect comes to the fore in the affair of Nūra, a Byzantine warrior princess who, for a long time, keeps the Arabs busy. Again and again she is caught but escapes, dealing with her opponents in a most ruthless manner. A number of the Arab heroes are hopelessly in love with her, among them Battāl (who eventually marries her) and ʿAbd al-Wahhāb, a fact which causes unpleasant rivalry between them. The caliph Hārūn, too, is smitten by Nūra. The childish behaviour of the men in the whole affair very much exasperates Princess Dhāt al-Himma and she repeatedly interferes, as described in the previous chapter.

ʿUlwā, too, is vexed by the matter. She is jealous because of her husband's feelings for Nūra, and also very worried about the rift this has caused between Battāl and ʿAbd al-Wahhāb, both of whom behave as if they are completely out of their minds. At some point, when ʿAbd al-Wahhāb has been taken prisoner and Nūra is still in his house in Malatya, ʿUlwā decides on an elaborate intrigue to get Nūra out of the way. She goes to the camp of her stepson Daygham, who leads the tribe in his father's absence. Daygham, supported by the tribe, has more or less decided to give Nūra to Battāl, who is also in the camp. ʿUlwā arrives with the same suggestion:

'Know, my son, that I definitely have a say in the matter, for my heart has suffered direly because of this Greek whore of a girl who has brought upon us all those disasters. She has caused all kinds of misery between your father and this prince Abū Muhammad, while before they were such good friends and brothers. Personally, I suffer from a jealousy such as no human heart has ever felt and the heart and mind of no creature have ever experienced! Come on now, give her to Battāl, and send her to him this minute, for I have heard what he has done with you and how he has freed you from captivity and arrest.'

Daygham answers that this is exactly what he had in mind. He urges her to go and fetch Nūra straight away from 'Abd al-Wahhāb's house. 'Ulwā, however, says that, to her regret, this is not possible: Nūra is no longer there. Daygham asks, "'Mother, is she no longer in the house where my father left her?'" and 'Ulwā replies, "'Know, my son, that when the army of the caliph al-Rashīd left Āmid, Prince 'Abd al-Wahhāb worried about what the caliph might do to Nūra, and he sent her away to Prince Nāfi' in the fortress of Kawkab with a thousand horsemen of the Banū Kilāb and a hundred of the noble blacks.'" Battāl is devastated. 'Ulwā then manages by a ruse to shut Nūra up in her own house, safely away from the quarrelling men.[24]

Remarkably, there is no evidence of jealousy on 'Ulwā's part in connection with Qannāsa and Maymūna, the later wives of 'Abd al-Wahhāb.

Concubine: Mayrūna[25]

'Abd al-Wahhāb's first love affair after he has married 'Ulwā does not result in marriage. It is a brief relationship with a Byzantine warrior princess called Mayrūna. It is significant because it contains many of the standard elements of the warrior woman theme as it is developed in *The Adventures of Princess Dhāt al-Himma*. For that reason it deserves to be treated at some length, with a few illustrative extracts of translation.

The story starts when Mayrūna, daughter of the Byzantine head patriarch, is sent abroad to be married to the king of Portugal. The party is intercepted by Muslim warriors of the Kilābī tribe. Daygham, one of Prince 'Abd al-Wahhāb's sons, appears, running, saying that he has been attacked by a very fierce warrior and that if one of his companions had not come to his rescue he would certainly have been killed. Then the companion in question appears, badly wounded, and says that if a number of the blacks had not come to save him he would now be dead. Prince ʿAbd al-Wahhāb goes to see what is happening and sees a young warrior chasing the blacks all over the place. The story then continues:

> Looking at this knight, Prince ʿAbd al-Wahhāb saw a young man with beautiful posture, a nice way of speaking, and beautifully proportioned. They attacked each other and started the usual twisting and turning. The dust hid them from the glances of the onlookers. The Byzantine looked at ʿAbd al-Wahhāb, and lo, he saw that he was a man unlike any other, and a champion unlike other champions. He made the sign of the Cross over his face, saying: 'By the Messiah and the true religion, I would never have thought that there could be another man such as ʿAbd al-Wahhāb in the Muslim community and the Mohammedan tribe! I have always wanted to see him and been eager to meet him.' 'Would you know the black man [i.e. ʿAbd al-Wahhāb] when you saw him?' asked ʿAbd al-Wahhāb. 'No, for I have never seen him. I have heard about him, but I do not know him.' 'Well, young man,' said ʿAbd al-Wahhāb, 'I am ʿAbd al-Wahhāb, shield of the grave of the Prophet, the repentant.'
> When the young man heard that this was the Prince, he went back again and took off some of his clothing, after having been [almost completely] hidden from him. He turned out to have breasts like ivory boxes, attached to the upper part of a chest like marble, supported by a slim waist that rose from folds of white silk. The knight drew his sword and attacked Prince ʿAbd al-Wahhāb with a heart stronger than rock and a soul bolder than the current of the sea. ʿAbd al-Wahhāb did not pay the slightest attention to him. When the Byzantine saw that ʿAbd al-Wahhāb stood there motionless, he was stupefied and completely out of his depth. He stood still, totally confused. Then he threw off his remaining clothes and stood there in a thin Venetian shirt, under which sides were visible enfolding a slim waist and other things that baffled the minds of the onlookers and left people totally confused. The Prince found it all a marvellous sight.
> Then the knight shouted in great excitement: 'Famous champion and renowned knight, are you not ashamed that you, the knight of the age, the giant of all times, the most outstanding of brave warriors, are struck with exhaustion facing the ladies?'(The narrator said:) Those sweet words, that were like cool water, made Prince ʿAbd al-Wahhāb laugh. He looked at fourteen tresses of hair interwoven with jewels and nicely arranged, and stepped back.

'What kind of conversation is this?' asked Abū Muhammad al-Battāl. ʿAbd al-Wahhāb started to tell him what had happened, saying: 'Abū Muhammad, I am afraid that God, praise to Him, He is exalted, will see me having fought someone because of some earthly passion while before I only used to fight for His sake.' Abū Muhammad was full of admiration for the purity of his intention and the goodness of his heart. While he stood there confused, a knight suddenly broke through the lines and split the thousands of the Banū Kilāb asunder like a charging lion. He did not stop before he had reached the battleground and fiercely attacked the knight mentioned before. He grabbed him by the arm, shaking him so vehemently that his heart nearly fell out. He dragged him from the saddle and took him prisoner, leading him away somewhere, cowering and humbled. ʿAbū Muhammad! Go to that knight!' said Prince ʿAbd al-Wahhāb, 'for he is an excellent friend and helper!' Abū Muhammad went forward, saying: 'Champion of the chiefs and knight of the camp sites, you have pleased the exalted King and done a beautiful deed! To which noble and esteemed Arabs do you belong?' The knight answered: 'What kind of curiosity is this? Do not be so curious or I will come and take your soul from between your sides!' 'I am a believer, professing God's unity, and I have spoken to you only with deference, having come to bring you the happy tidings that the Prince wants to offer you many robes of honour, large amounts of money, ample quantities of jewels, and horses and foals.' ʿAbū Muhammad, you have a very short memory!' said the knight. 'I am Fātima the daughter of Mazlūm, handmaid of the Living, the Eternal.'[26]

ʿAbd al-Wahhāb's mother, Fātima Dhāt al-Himma, arrives just in time to save him from a dire situation. She had been warned by the Prophet in a dream and straight away set out from Malatya to save her son. ʿAbd al-Wahhāb is much relieved that his dilemma has been resolved, and, no longer hampered by his conscience, he attacks his Byzantine opponent immediately. The Muslims soon defeat the Byzantine party, gaining many spoils and slave girls in the process.[27]

They return to Malatya, with ʿAbd al-Wahhāb 'happy because of the daughter of the patriarch [i.e. Mayrūna], his appetite for her increasing'.[28] In Malatya they are cordially received by commander Prince ʿAmr ibn ʿUbaydallāh and *qāḍī* ʿUqba, who, as usual, is plotting behind their backs. When he sees the captives, ʿUqba says that Mayrūna's exceptional beauty makes her fit only for the caliph. When Mayrūna is auctioned, Battāl buys her and sends her to the house of ʿAbd al-Wahhāb.[29] ʿUqba is angry and secretly sends Hārūn a message about what has happened. Baṭṭāl, who has foreseen this, has already urged ʿAbd al-Wahhāb to sleep with her, for if a letter should then arrive from Hārūn ordering the girl to be sent to him, ʿAbd al-Wahhāb could say that he has already taken her as a concubine, not knowing about the caliph's wishes. A letter indeed arrives, and ʿAbd al-Wahhāb answers it, explaining the situation. All this correspondence, by the way, is done using carrier pigeons.[30]

The caliph is extremely angry and ʿUqba makes use of the situation by persuading the worried commander, ʿAmr ibn ʿUbaydallāh, to take both ʿAbd al-Wahhāb and Baṭṭāl captive. The latter has them put in boxes and sends them to the caliph, together with Mayrūna. ʿUqba, however, has arranged for a party of Byzantines to intercept them, and so Mayrūna is brought back to Constantinople, where her delighted father immediately gives her in marriage to the man who rescued her.

We hear no more about her until much later, when the Kilābīs are confronted by a young Byzantine warrior, the seventeen-year-old Sayf al-Nasrānīya, 'Sword of Christendom'. Shortly before ʿAbd al-Wahhāb is scheduled to face this young man in combat he has a strange dream. Dhāt al-Himma, consulted about it, thinks that it announces a joyful event. The subsequent account of the combat between ʿAbd al-Wahhāb and young Sayf al-Nasrānīya contains the usual elements of a father–son anagnorisis in popular epic. While engaging in combat, ʿAbd al-Wahhāb is suddenly overwhelmed by emotion, even to the point where he starts crying. His young opponent supposes that he is overcome by fear of being killed, and insultingly suggests that it would probably be better if he withdrew from the combat. Angered, ʿAbd al-Wahhāb attacks. At a certain point the two dismount and continue wrestling on foot, and that is when they discover that they are wearing identical bracelets. Explanations follow, and it turns out that Sayf al-Nasrānīya wears the bracelet – one of a pair of magic bracelets protecting against poison – that ʿAbd al-Wahhāb once gave to Sayf's mother Mayrūna. All is now clear. Sayf is ʿAbd al-Wahhāb's son, raised by Mayrūna and her husband, the Christian king. He converts to Islam, joins the Kilābī army and from now on will go by the name of Sayf al-Ḥanīfīya,[31] 'Sword of the true religion'.

We encounter here a number of standard elements: there is the Byzantine princess who easily defeats the Muslim champions; her girlish enthusiasm about meeting the great champion; the erotic tension between the brave young princess and the legendary hero; the provocative way in which she challenges him; and the role of his mother, who forcibly eliminates the girl whose erotic influence threatens to affect her son's martial prowess. Finally, there is the emergence of a son whose existence was not previously known to his father, and then we get all the standard elements of the father–son anagnorisis as it commonly appears in Arabic popular epic: the son appearing as an enemy knight challenging his father; the father's unexplainable strong emotion upon seeing the boy; the wrestling; and the token by which he recognizes his son. Often, but not in the present story, this is followed by a reunion of the hero and the boy's mother.

An uncommon element in this particular episode is the hero's moral dilemma when he realizes that his eagerness to battle with the girl results from erotic passion rather than from the wish to fight for the sake of God.

Third wife: Qannāsa[32]

'Abd al-Wahhāb's third wife, Qannāsa, enters the story in such an ominous manner that it is hardly imaginable that she will turn into one of the pillars of the Muslim army. She is first heard of when the governor of Mecca comes to the caliph with a complaint that a nearby region is being terrorized by a warrior princess residing in a mountain castle. Her name is Qannāsa, daughter of Muzāhim, the latter being a true Arab name meaning 'he who competes'. Qannāsa is very much her own woman and her father does not play a part in the story. Yet his name demonstrates that she is of Arab stock and not a foreign princess. This explains why the matter of her religion is not an issue in the story. Clearly, the narrator considers her, and also her son, to be part of the Muslim community, and the only issue is whether they will become warriors for the cause of Islam instead of Bedouins raiding for booty. As we will see, Qannāsa is a remarkable character: brave, intelligent, cool-headed and with a good grip on her emotions. Her personality remains consistent throughout the story.

Qannāsa, we are told,

> stands at the head of five thousand trampling heroes on horseback. She has given them a free hand where the high-ranking daughters of the Arabs are concerned, and many a greedy man has joined her. Her followers have struck out against Upper and Lower Egypt, they have seized caravans and goods, and have led into captivity women, young people and children. Moreover, when people tell her that somewhere

a charming and handsome youth is to be found she goes there in person, captures him by force and takes him, against his will, away to her castle. She then marries him for three days, and on the fourth she takes him up onto one of the towers and strikes off his head. In this manner she has killed a great number of people.[33]

The governor's request to the caliph is to free them from this affliction. Prince 'Abd al-Wahhāb volunteers to go and destroy this woman with his brave warriors. His mother, Princess Dhāt al-Himma, insists on joining him, partly to protect him, and they set out for the castle of Qannāsa. She watches them approach from afar and sends her men forward, but it is soon obvious that the Kilābīs are too strong for them. Qannāsa is impressed. She has watched the battle and two of the warriors stood out to her: 'Among them was a knight brown of face, of pleasant appearance, of charming character and pleasant nature and impression. I also saw another knight of great courage and skill, a ferocious lion, except that his way of riding was like that of a woman, and if my estimation is right and my divination does not fail me she is the bravest fighter on horseback of her time. And lo, I will go out against them.'

She makes herself ready for battle and lines up her men. Prince 'Abd al-Wahhāb, looking on, is impressed: 'By God, I have seen warriors and have experience with battle lines and armies: never did I see a better formation than hers!' Qannāsa jumps on her horse, spurring it on with such force that she breaks its ribs. A second horse is brought; she breaks its spine. The third horse turns out to be strong enough, and she challenges a Kilābī warrior to come forward and fight her in single combat. The first young warrior to do so is easily defeated and taken captive: 'You do possess a certain amount of knightly virtue, but you lack a strong arm.' 'Abd al-Wahhāb is next, but when his attention is diverted by cries for help from a companion, Qannāsa rips open an old wound. His guts spill out and he almost loses consciousness. She grabs him and takes him away to the castle. As so often happens, he is eventually saved by his wily companion Battāl, who, with his glib tongue, tricks Qannāsa into letting Princess Dhāt al-Himma into the castle. A tremendous fight between the two women follows:

> They fell upon each other, and the inevitable fight between them began. Iron fell upon iron with such resonance that it sounded like music, and what music! They were like two mountains colliding, two seas clashing. In Qannāsa the princess met an opponent such as she had never en-

countered before [...] They hacked away until they could hardly breathe any more. The balance between them began to tilt; Qannāsa found that she was no longer equal to her opponent and the princess inferred this from the fact that Qannāsa struck out in the most destructive manner because she found every way blocked in front of her.

Qannāsa and her men are eventually defeated. Qannāsa, it is said, was the most beautiful woman of her time, and

> the prince asked for her hand and married her on the spot. Battāl arranged the marriage contract. The prince consummated the marriage and found her to be a virgin, just as God had created her. This greatly surprised him. She realized what was on his mind and said: 'Prince, I suppose you are thinking of what you have heard about me, about my marrying a large number of men and striking off their heads?' 'Yes,' said the prince, 'I have heard about that; what then did you do?' She said: 'When I heard about a warrior I went to his people to get him, and then I caught him on the battlefield or struck him down with my spear. But when I was alone with him after I had married him I thought of the way in which I had captured him, and this made the idea that I would be his wife and he my master so repulsive to me that I withheld myself from him and struck off his head in order to prevent him from going back to his people and telling them how things stood with me. In this way fear of me settled in their hearts while I remained a virgin, as you see.' The prince rejoiced about this and stayed with her a number of days.[34]

The device used by the narrator to turn Qannāsa suddenly into a virtuous woman is brilliant. She could hardly have become an acceptable heroine in the sequel of the story with all these affairs behind her, even though they had happened under the cloak of marriage.

Qannāsa's admission that these men lost their sexual attraction for her when she had managed to defeat them is a point of interest. One might ask whether this is a standard element in the relationship between warrior women and their male opponents. In one sense it is a variation of the common motif of the warrior girl who only consents to marry a man who manages to defeat her in combat. In a slightly different form, the motif also appears in the case of Ghamra, the daughter of 'Utārid, who will be dealt with in the next chapter. Her love for her cousin turns into disdain when she defeats and humiliates him in combat after he has rejected her love.

After ʿAbd al-Wahhāb has spent some time with Qannāsa he moves on to new adventures. Qannāsa is reluctant to join him, for she prefers to remain in her own castle. For a long time it looks as if she has disappeared from the scene for good.

One day, however, the Muslims are confronted with a new enemy, a fierce young man of huge stature, who wields an iron mace of fifty kilos with which he easily strikes a camel in two. His name is Zālim, 'Son of the Stranger'. He attacks the Muslims, eager for booty. The caliph Hārūn sends out a letter asking for help, saying that Zālim wants to destroy the Kaʿba and other holy places in Mecca, and to build a new 'Holy House' in his own country. There is no evidence that this actually was Zālim's intention – at one point he even swears by the Meccan sanctuaries. The narrator clearly takes care not to present him in such a way that he destroys the audience's goodwill towards him for good. It is not long, indeed, before we hear that there was nobody in a foreign country or in Yemen more beautiful of face and with more noble characteristics than he.[35]

The usual series of attacks, fights, captures and escapes follows, and eventually the moment arrives when Zālim and ʿAbd al-Wahhāb face each other in combat. ʿAbd al-Wahhāb is full of admiration for the man's strength and wishes that he were part of the Muslim army, for then he would treat him like his own son. While his mind is on this possibility, Zālim rips open the old, sewn-up wound in ʿAbd al-Wahhāb's belly. Blood and guts gush out and ʿAbd al-Wahhāb loses consciousness. Instead of killing him, Zālim, full of respect for his opponent, ties up the wound and carries him off to his camp to be treated. Princess Dhāt al-Himma, very anxious about her son's fate, sneaks into the camp with some of her companions and carries him off, but is stopped by Zālim, who had come to check on the patient before going to sleep. Having recaptured the prisoner, Zālim sends him to the castle of his mother, 'a very important lady', with orders to arrange medical care for him.

When ʿAbd al-Wahhāb looks at the castle, he immediately recognizes it: 'By God, this is the castle that belonged to my wife Qannāsa! No doubt she has died and authority over the castle has passed to someone else. Everything will have changed, and this devil [i.e. Zālim] now rules this place.' But Qannāsa is still there. She is not aware of the wounded prisoner until her son Zālim arrives and tells her his name. It is a big shock to her but she remains quiet, thinking over her situation.

> She was no longer as beautiful and handsome as she once had been, but she was still just as strong, her body was just as stout, and her

speech just as eloquent. She went and did not halt before she had come to Prince ʿAbd al-Wahhāb, and when her eye met his, a scream rose from deep inside her belly and she threw herself upon him. She started to shiver and tremble, and she became crazy with love for him. (O ye gentlemen). For Zālim was the son she had had from Prince ʿAbd al-Wahhāb.

Afraid that her son might leave her to join his famous father, she had told him that his father had been a very brave foreign knight who had died when Zālim was still a small child.

In spite of her renewed rush of love for her husband, Qannāsa keeps a clear head and gives herself time to think. She sees to it that ʿAbd al-Wahhāb gets the best possible care, but covers her face with a veil so that he does not recognize her. Soon afterwards, the Muslim army arrives in front of the castle and Zālim informs his mother that it is led by the caliph and by Princess Dhāt al-Himma, the mother of ʿAbd al-Wahhāb, a woman whose martial prowess he greatly admires. Qannāsa urges him to go out and fight, promising that she will join him later. Soon he is engaged in combat with Dhāt al-Himma herself. Then, however, a shout is heard from the ramparts: '"Princess, stop hitting my son Zālim!"' It is ʿAbd al-Wahhāb, who stands there with Qannāsa at his side. After Zālim had left the castle, she had gone to ʿAbd al-Wahhāb, who had almost recovered, and said to him: '"So this is how men deal with women!"' He immediately recognized her voice. The next thing we hear is that the couple appear together on the ramparts, ʿAbd al-Wahhāb clearly having been informed of the existence of his son.[36]

Thus, the family is reunited, and after the little matter of Zālim's marriage to a girl he loves has been taken care of, Qannāsa happily joins the Kilābīs. Together they set out on new forays. From now on, Qannāsa and her son will be among the prominent champions of the Muslims and continue to take part in the events almost to the end of the *sīra*.[37]

As to Qannāsa's role, she does not simply follow the tribe's lead but often acts on her own initiative. She also keeps her castle as a base and sometimes returns to it, as we saw above: when ʿUlwā goes to get reinforcements from Yemen, Qannāsa fetches them from her own castle. When ʿAbd al-Wahhāb and the other leading Kilābīs are captured she takes over the command, defeats and captures an opponent in a duel,[38] kills another enemy leader and eventually defeats the caliph's army.[39]

Her behaviour and character remain consistent throughout the story. She is courageous and independent, and sometimes gets involved in adventures not unlike those of modern thriller heroes. Such a case is the episode where the villainous *qāḍī* ʿUqba, the crypto-Christian taken captive, persuades his gullible and naive black guards to set him free and encourages them to plunder the town and rape the women. He looks everywhere for the warrior women, for he knows that Qannāsa, Nūra, Zanānīr and the daughters of Hayyāj al-Kurdī are in town, but he can find no trace of them. He makes the black warriors search the houses, for he is especially eager for the rape of Hayyāj's pious daughters, who are married to the sons of ʿAbd al-Wahhāb. These women lived only for the war against the Christians, and ʿUqba considers it to be a particularly noble Christian deed to dishonour them. Finally, the women are brought out, but Qannāsa is not among them. She has escaped with Nūra just in time, and, while they are trying to get away, Qannāsa suddenly comes across a well which is the entrance to a subterranean stream. Desperate to escape, she slips into the hole and is swept away by the water. Nearly drowned, she notices that the stream has run into a wider space and she manages to get out. She walks on until, close to exhaustion, she sees light coming from an opening. When she reaches it and looks out, it turns out that she has come to a spot where the stream runs out into the open through a tunnel under the wall, and she realizes that this is the perfect place from which to enter the town and take it.

After she has recovered somewhat, she goes to the camp where Princess Dhāt al-Himma is waiting. The princess has no news of the others and is constantly pestered by ʿUqba, who promises to bring her the captive Kilābī women in exchange for the caliph Maʾmūn. 'And lo, there Qannāsa suddenly came in. She gave Dhāt al-Himma the general picture of what had happened to her and seemed completely distracted, unable to speak because of her terrifying and exhausting experience. When the princess had heard all this, she stood up and said: "Come on, let us go to that place straight away and get what we want from those misguided people!"'

Qannāsa persuades the princess to wait until dark and she agrees. After darkness has fallen, they sneak into the town with a large number of companions, sliding on their bellies. Qannāsa and the princess are the first to emerge from the hole, just when the other warrior women pass by, having left their hiding place in an attempt to reach safety under cover of darkness. Qannāsa hears Nūra mention her name, expressing her fear that something has happened to her, and makes herself known:

"'I am the Huntress, turned into the Diver!'"(Qannāsa, turned into al-Ghawwāsa – the Arabic words for 'huntress' and 'diver' rhyme.) When the others have also crept out of the passage the attack is launched and the town is recaptured.[40]

As to Qannāsa's relationship with 'Abd al-Wahhāb, initially the latter's attitude towards his wife seems somewhat detached, to say the least. He practically forgets her existence after the honeymoon until they are reunited by accident. Yet the narrator regularly emphasizes his attachment to her in the later part of the story, for instance when Qannāsa finds herself in a dangerous situation and 'Abd al-Wahhāb is not aware of this in the heat of battle: 'Had he known about her, he surely would have come to her succour even if she had been in a sea of fire; to this end, he would have faced any kind of danger.'[41] Their support is mutual: Qannāsa also comes to his help on a number of occasions.

Just as Qannāsa is a far more colourful and assertive character than 'Ulwā, her son Zālim is far more prominent than 'Ulwā's son Ibrāhīm. In fact, Zālim is one of the leading characters of the story, a very brave fighter, who even outlives 'Abd al-Wahhāb and Dhāt al-Himma: he is the last hero of the *sīra* to die. Qannāsa and her son act independently of each other, but Qannāsa's attachment to her son regularly comes into the picture, such as in the episode where Zālim has been banished by the caliph to the Maghrib, North Africa. In spite of this hostile treatment of his son, Prince 'Abd al-Wahhāb answers the caliph's call for support in a difficult situation. This angers Qannāsa, who sees it as a breach of loyalty towards their son. She goes out to join Zālim and Baṭṭāl, who have come to confront the caliph with an army of North African Berbers. They say that she is welcome to join them, and, without further ado, she dons the typical Berber clothing with the veil. She refuses to go back, for she is angry with 'Abd al-Wahhāb, who clearly is less attached to Zālim than to his other sons, such as Sayf, because he only got to know Zālim once the boy was already grown. This is a slip on the part of the narrator, for just like Zālim, Sayf grew up with his mother and only found out that 'Abd al-Wahhāb was his father when they met in combat.[42]

As we have seen in the case of 'Ulwā, 'Abd al-Wahhāb's attitude towards his sons is a delicate point with all his wives. They all fear that their own son may be less important to 'Abd al-Wahhāb than the sons from other marriages. This comes up especially in situations where the fear exists that the son in question may be dead. Another point that arises in that context is that men and women have different ways of showing their emotions: for example, there are 'Ulwā's reproaches to 'Abd al-Wahhāb about his lukewarm reaction to their son's disappearance, and his shocked reaction. While, in the case of Qannāsa, friction occurs when Zālim has disappeared and 'Abd al-Wahhāb travels extensively to discover his whereabouts, getting very irritated by the fact that Qannāsa does nothing but cry, sitting together with Battāl's wife Nūra, whose sons have also disappeared.[43]

Fourth wife: Maymūna[44]

Maymūna, 'Abd al-Wahhāb's fourth wife, also at some point brings up the argument that 'Abd al-Wahhāb has a number of sons and thus is less vulnerable as a parent than his wives: '"You, as you know, have other sons besides him and your pity is not exclusively focused on one of them, but I, I have only the one boy."'[45]

Like 'Ulwā and Qannāsa, Maymūna is a warrior princess but she is of foreign origin. She is the daughter of Damdamān, an Ethiopian king whom the Muslims, led by Dhāt al-Himma and 'Abd al-Wahhāb, set out to defeat. Maymūna had already begun to train herself in the art of war when she was very young, and the fact that she grew up with seven brothers greatly contributed to her skill in this field. At the time that she met 'Abd al-Wahhāb she had already earned fame as a warrior. She had raided the land of Anqūsh, a Yemeni king, who fell in love with her but was refused 'because she had no desire for men'. This is a familiar topos in the warrior women stories: it also occurs, for instance, in the stories of the princesses Alūf and Zanānīr in *The Adventures of Princess Dhāt al-Himma*.[46] Maymūna is a hot-headed girl and even her father is in awe of what she might do if thwarted: she killed her brother Maymūn in a conflict over the division of spoils.[47] This tendency not to shun violence even when her closest relatives are involved will reach extreme proportions later on in the story, and the narrator is possibly giving an early warning here about the way in which her character is going to develop. She will also kill her father and, eventually, even her son.

Maymūna first meets 'Abd al-Wahhāb when he is taken captive by her father and is being tortured. Maymūna immediately falls in love with him. She puts a halt to the torture and takes him away to a place where he can be comfortable. She writes him a letter offering him her love. He declines, but the relationship between them is full of erotic tension.[48]

Her actions to keep him safe eventually lead to battle with her father. Initially, she has qualms about fighting her father in person, but she kills him in utter despair when he untruthfully tells her that he has slain ʿAbd al-Wahhāb. In fact, ʿAbd al-Wahhāb has secretly left the castle and disappeared. Maymūna is very hurt by this, and when she runs into him later on a combat between them takes place, which is won by Maymūna. ʿAbd al-Wahhāb asks for her forgiveness, but she says that she would rather die in the most horrible manner than be reconciled with him.[49]

She then rides off. Other efforts at reconciliation also fail. A combat takes place between Maymūna and ʿAbd al-Wahhāb's son Zālim, whom she also defeats. Finally, Dhāt al-Himma herself takes the field against her and wins. This earns her Maymūna's love and respect, and it also breaks down her resistance about reconciliation with ʿAbd al-Wahhāb. She expresses the wish to be married to him and the wedding takes place shortly after.[50]

As ʿAbd al-Wahhāb's wife, Maymūna becomes a paragon of the Muslim army and a staunch supporter of Dhāt al-Himma, whom she often assists in battle.[51] During one of the forays she is abducted by an enemy king, Qarāqūnā. She is pregnant at the time and when the baby is born Qarāqūnā threatens to kill the boy if Maymūna continues to refuse his sexual advances. When she remains steadfast, he throws the baby into the sea. The small son of Nūra, the wife of Baṭṭāl, who has been captured along with Maymūna, is also killed, or at least supposed to be killed. Not unexpectedly, the two boys will turn out to have been miraculously saved and will make their appearance later on in the story. The setting in which this happens follows a familiar pattern: the Kilābīs come up against a young Christian prince by the name of Bahrūn and his equally young vizier Madhbahūn, who shows a strong resemblance to al-Baṭṭāl. In due course, Nūra recognizes Madhbahūn as the baby son whom she lost when she was Qarāqūnā's captive, and Madhbahūn quickly converts to Islam.[52]

Maymūna, in her turn, sees in Prince Bahrūn a resemblance to her lost baby son, but ʿAbd al-Wahhāb says that it is highly unlikely that Bahrūn is indeed their lost child and Maymūna gives up the idea. Hostilities are resumed. At some point, Dhāt al-Himma and Maymūna pursue and capture Bahrūn, and Dhāt al-Himma is about to kill him when Maymūna 'saw that his colour was hers' (meaning that he was dark-skinned) and recognized a charm that used to belong to her. Maymūna then explains the whole history of the loss of her baby son, and Dhāt al-Himma translates it all into Greek for the benefit of Bahrūn. Only then does he realize that the warrior he fought – Maymūna – is, in fact, a woman, and not just any woman but his own mother.⁵³ Now he finally understands how he came to be of a different colour from that of the Byzantines among whom he grew up. The mystery of how he came by the charm and what the name written on it meant is also solved.

It is noteworthy that, in Maymūna's combat with her son, we have one of the rare cases where the motif of the father–son combat and the subsequent recognition scene is applied to a mother–son situation. It is not the only instance in Maymūna's history where a narrative device is adapted to fit a female protagonist, as we will see.

When Bahrūn's identity is revealed, his mother and grandmother embrace him and take him to meet his father, ʿAbd al-Wahhāb, and his half-brothers.⁵⁴ ʿAbd al-Wahhāb welcomes his newly discovered son with joy. Bahrūn refuses to convert to Islam, but does not exclude the possibility that, in due course, he may have a change of mind. Meanwhile, he joins the band of Kilābī warriors and accompanies his mother on their forays.⁵⁵ The picture may seem idyllic, but this event marks a turning point in Maymūna's history. From now on, loyalty to her non-Muslim son will have priority with her, and it will ultimately be the incentive that drives her away from her husband and from the Muslim community. This also sets in train her moral downfall: as the story develops, she will become more and more depraved. In the course of events, she will subsequently marry three enemy kings, and each marriage will mark a further stage in her moral downfall.

It all starts with Bahrūn's love for a Christian girl called Marjāna, at the time when he was still unaware of his real parentage. The girl dislikes him because he is black, but says that she might accept him if he manages to defeat her in combat. Before this happens, however, Marjāna has converted to Islam through a complicated series of events. It is pointed out to Bahrūn that now he can only marry her when he also converts, and when he refuses to do so, the caliph Muʿtasim marries her himself.⁵⁶

Bahrūn, whose deeper loyalty still lies with the Byzantines, considers killing his mother Maymūna, but then decides to see first whether she is prepared to help him: '"Mother, I need something from you." "What, my son?" And he complained about his burning passion, saying: "If I cannot have her I will die." Well, this woman was his mother anyway, and she had no son but him.' Maymūna promises to help Bahrūn. She forsakes Islam, leaves her husband ʿAbd al-Wahhāb and returns to the Byzantines with four thousand of her black warriors, whom she persuades to convert to Christianity. She then proceeds to tell Marjāna about Bahrūn's love. Marjāna says that she cannot possibly marry him since she is now a Muslim. Maymūna grabs her and flees with her, together with Bahrūn. When Marjāna's disappearance is discovered in the morning, the caliph summons ʿAbd al-Wahhāb and asks him to swear his innocence. The caliph says that the girl is his wife, and that whoever has taken the girl has violated his honour (*hurma*). ʿAbd al-Wahhāb swears on the triple divorce of all three of his wives, ʿUlwā, Qannāsa and Maymūna, and on the freeing of all his slaves that he knows nothing about the affair.[57]

His son Zālim is then sent in pursuit of the fugitives. Zālim is deeply shocked by the behaviour of his stepmother Maymūna, and tries to find excuses for it. "'She has struck me in the face with her sword, but she only did this in order to make sure that Bahrūn could hold nothing against her.'" ʿAbd al-Wahhāb is deeply miserable. Crying, he says that because of this girl Marjāna he has lost his wife, his son and four thousand black warriors. The caliph takes pity on him. He consents to divorce Marjāna and to leave her to Bahrūn, of course on the condition that he converts to Islam. Bahrūn is told about this and wants to comply, but Maymūna has already passed the point of no return. She dissuades her son from following his inclination, saying that their first priority is to save *qāḍī* ʿUqba, the villainous crypto-Christian, and to get him to Constantinople, taking Marjāna with them. ʿAbd al-Wahhāb is not prepared to leave Marjāna, now a Muslim girl, to an unbeliever, not even if that person is his own son. He also wants to make a last effort to persuade Maymūna to mend her ways and come back to him. So he rides out to meet Bahrūn 'the accursed' and the 'foolish and ignoble' Maymūna.[58]

> ʿAbd al-Wahhāb came and looked at Maymūna, seated on horseback amidst her black warriors. He said to her: 'Have you become an unbeliever after having believed?' 'No, by the Merciful, the Compassionate!' she answered. 'But necessity overcomes prudence. You, as you know, have other sons besides him and your pity is not exclusively focused on one of them, but I, I have only the one boy. I cannot bear to be parted from him and my soul cannot bear to be far away from him. I am a Muslim, and not of his religion. You know that we have rendered you many useful services, but you have brought my son into dire straits because of a Christian girl. If you give her to him, we will return, but if not, it will be sufficient ground for us to desert you, to fight you and to shed your blood.' The world turned black

in 'Abd al-Wahhāb's eyes, and he answered: 'Woman, can you be a Muslim, a person who states that God is One and that the Prophet Muhammad is His Messenger, and still want that miserable unbeliever, an adherent of the Christian faith? This must not be, even if it be the death of me! Return to the One Lord, the One, the Unique, the Everlasting, Who has not given birth and Who has not been born, and Who has no equal! That is better than to follow the boy.' 'You are right,' she answered, 'this is not permitted in the religion of the Living, the Eternal; but Bahrūn's unbelief will not last.' 'If such is your intention,' he said, 'then I will definitely take the girl away from him and from you.'[59]

Maymūna tells him not to talk nonsense, since this will definitely mean battle. Upon hearing her words, 'Abd al-Wahhāb orders his Kilābīs to capture Maymūna and Bahrūn. A fight follows in which Bahrūn wounds his father. In a last effort, Dhāt al-Himma sends a message to Maymūna, reproaching her for her apostasy. She says that 'Abd al-Wahhāb is on the verge of death and urges her to return. Maymūna indeed makes a final effort to let Bahrūn convert to Islam, pointing out to him that he has blocked her way to paradise, but he refuses.[60]

Then the Byzantine king Armānūs arrives. Armānūs is greatly taken by Maymūna and wants to marry her. This induces Maymūna to make the final step in cutting her ties with the Muslims. Her further downfall is marked by a series of marriages: first to Armānūs, then to the island king Karfanās, then finally to the latter's son-in-law, a Frankish king.

Maymūna thus accepts Armānūs's proposal, saying that he is more attractive to her than 'the black man, the son of Fātima [i.e. Dhāt al-Himma]'. She converts back to Christianity. To emphasize the fact that she is now lost beyond all hope, the story tells how the Prophet appears to 'Abd al-Wahhāb in a dream and tells him that he has cursed Maymūna. From now on, the epithet 'the accursed' will habitually be attached to her name. The Prophet also shows 'Abd al-Wahhāb a beautiful woman as a replacement for his lost wife.[61] This presents an intriguing point. According to the Muslim tradition, dreams of the Prophet, by definition, tell the truth, so the reader wonders whether this is a houri from Paradise or an actual new wife. Nothing, however, is said about a new marriage of 'Abd al-Wahhāb in the sequel of the story, although at least two promising females, both accomplished warrior women, make their appearance. The first is Iftūnā, a brave warrior girl, who, in Dhāt al-Himma's opinion, would make a good wife for 'Abd al-Wahhāb.

She falls in love with someone else, however, and gradually fades from the story. One gets the impression that the narrator, for some reason, decided to discontinue the storyline which he originally had in mind and started to follow another track. The other girl who looks promising as a future wife is Nūr al-Nār, a converted Christian princess. ʿAbd al-Wahhāb is impressed by her, and she accomplishes brave feats in freeing him and his companions from captivity. She, too, disappears from the scene without getting further involved with ʿAbd al-Wahhāb.

Maymūna bears her new husband, Armānūs, a son, Būhinmā, to whom she teaches the art of chivalrous warfare.[62] From now on, however, she goes from bad to worse. That she has really crossed a threshold becomes clear during subsequent battles, for instance when she sets the undefended camp of the Kilābīs on fire and kills everybody, including religious scholars and Qurʾān reciters. Even ʿAbd al-Wahhāb is finally of the opinion that she has to be killed unless she returns to Islam. But while Maymūna, who initially just wanted to follow her Christian son, has now definitively cut off her ties with the Muslims, her son Bahrūn makes an about-turn and converts to Islam. The reason is his love for Iftūnā, the accomplished warrior girl whom Princess Dhāt al-Himma sees as a suitable bride for her son ʿAbd al-Wahhāb,[63] and who has converted to Islam. Iftūnā, however, is not interested in Bahrūn's suit.

In converting to Islam, Bahrūn has taken a definitive step. On no account can he be reconciled again with his mother, who is now full of aggression towards Islam. Her infatuation with her new husband, Armānūs, has also completely obliterated her love for her former husband and her son. Bahrūn, now a true believer, will come to a tragic end, although eternal happiness awaits him. This is announced by a dream in which he finds himself in the seventh heaven, embracing a houri. He tells ʿAbd al-Wahhāb about his dream, saying that he no longer has any fear of meeting his Maker. He then sets out to fight his mother Maymūna. She kills him in combat, without any mercy.

As if this is not enough, she loses any sense of decency that she may have had left in the sequel of the story. Her hunger for power and riches is even stronger than her love for her new husband, Armānūs. When he is captured she refuses to spend money on a ransom, saying that Armānūs is no dearer to her than Bahrūn was. She claims that she is only interested in fighting for the Messiah. Yet she manages to free Armānūs from ʿAbd al-Wahhāb's tent in a subsequent raid, and she is not prepared to put her power over him at risk by letting him take an interest in other women. Thus, she reacts quite fiercely when two beautiful sisters, both brave warrior girls, are captured and Armānūs is full of attention and concern for them.⁶⁴

After having been involved in a number of other battles, Maymūna meets another king, Karfanās, who is advancing on Constantinople. They engage in combat, and when Karfanās discovers that he is fighting a woman, he falls in love with her. Maymūna is easily persuaded to marry him, in spite of the fact that she is still married to Armānūs and is the mother of his son Būhinmā (Bohemond), who is seven years old. She even remarks that this is not the first time that she has concluded a bigamous marriage, for she married Armānūs while she was still the wife of 'Abd al-Wahhāb.⁶⁵

Karfanās, who comes from a faraway island, is a most disgusting person. We can say that he reflects Maymūna's darkest side. He, too, kills his father (although by mistake) as well as his son, the latter by cracking his skull with his hand, a favourite habit of his. He also uses this method to kill the girls with whom he sleeps. Maymūna, however, explains to 'Uqba that she loves him "first for his courage, secondly for his magnanimity and thirdly because he is excellent for a good romp in bed. That is exactly why I love him." "May God keep him strong," was 'Uqba's reaction.⁶⁶ For a while Maymūna and Karfanās jointly fight the Byzantines, and there also occurs a confrontation with 'Abd al-Wahhāb and Dhāt al-Himma. In particular, facing the latter in the course of battle is a great shock to Maymūna:

> She called out to the knight: 'By your religion, who are you?' The knight answered: 'Woe to you, you harlot! I am the woman fighting the Holy War, the perseverant, the helper of God's religion, and thus I hope to achieve success in the hereafter. I want to deal you a blow that sets your head flying.' When Maymūna heard this she was sure that her end was near, and her determination wavered. 'Dhāt al-Himma,' she said, 'do not think that I wanted to do your son 'Abd al-Wahhāb any harm, that was not my intention at all. I just saw that he was getting tired in his fight with Karfanās and so I went up to him, talking in Arabic, trying to make peace.' 'Woe to you, stop this importunity, you unbeliever!' answered Dhāt al-Himma.

Dhāt al-Himma attacks and quickly takes Maymūna captive, but she is later exchanged for 'Abd al-Wahhāb's son Sayf al-Hanīfīya. Soon afterwards, Karfanās is killed by 'Abd al-Wahhāb.⁶⁷ Maymūna escapes and tries to rally Karfanās's men, but without success.

She then joins Karfanās's son-in-law, a Frankish king, promising him support and marriage.⁶⁸ 'Abd al-Wahhāb, however, defeats them, and she goes with the king to his country. From there, they later start out again to fight the Muslims. Maymūna is now filled with hatred not only for the Muslims but also for Armānūs: when she hears that his army has been defeated, she laughs and says that it is typical of him to be careless and to give up easily. She says that she will certainly take vengeance on him, on behalf of Karfanās as well as herself.⁶⁹

It is during one of the subsequent battles that Maymūna finally meets her fate. She comes up against Princess Dhāt al-Himma. Both have previously had dreams about a confrontation. Maymūna dreamt that she killed Dhāt al-Himma with a lance. Dhāt al-Himma dreamt that Maymūna struck her with a lance that subsequently turned into a snake. Dhāt al-Himma then struck her with the snake, which turned into a red shawl wrapped round Maymūna's neck. During their actual combat, Dhāt al-Himma is indeed wounded by Maymūna with a lance, but she manages to pull it out and to kill Maymūna with it.⁷⁰ She is elated, and 'Abd al-Wahhāb thanks God with all his heart for having delivered them from 'this woman'. Maymūna's husband, still leading his people, bravely fights on until the sword is struck from his hands and he and his people have to give up. When 'Uqba, the villainous *qāḍī* hears about Maymūna's death he sits down is his tent, pulling out his beard, and weeps over her, 'because she was a real treasure to him, and a support. She kept the hearts of the Muslims constantly busy, and he loved her very much for that.'⁷¹

With Maymūna's death by the hand of Dhāt al-Himma the long Maymūna episode comes to an end. In terms of narrative symmetry, this is a satisfactory ending. It was Dhāt al-Himma who made Maymūna decide to join the Muslims and to marry 'Abd al-Wahhāb, and it is also Dhāt al-Himma who finally strikes her name from the record. It is another indication that the story was carefully composed, even though the switch in character and the disgusting behaviour that Maymūna presents in the second part of the story suggest the opposite. The road to her later unpleasant behaviour, however, had already been paved when she was first introduced, for from the very beginning she is depicted not only as a brave but also highly volatile and somewhat disquieting character.

By the time of Maymūna's death the narrator has exploited the possibilities of her colourful and exciting character to the full. Again and again her story has been propelled onwards and extended by 'linking' new episodes to the story. The linking is done with the usual narrative devices of the genre: abductions take place, ruses and subterfuges are planned, and new enemies appear on the scene in abundance. A remarkable point is that a device often used in the case of (polygamous) male heroes, namely letting the hero engage in a new love affair leading up to a new marriage, is also used in Maymūna's history: in her case, too, a new episode often begins with a new paramour appearing on the scene. This is very unusual for a woman.[72] In order to make it possible, the narrator had to bring about a gradual change of character, using a narrative device which is used effectively in serial storytelling to the present day. The following remarks to this effect, made by the producer of a popular Dutch soap series, explain the system rather aptly: 'You may for instance turn a sympathetic character into an unsympathetic one, so that the other protagonists have to react to this new attitude. That is how you push the story forward.'[73]

In Maymūna's case, the effectuated change is so radical that she ultimately becomes a monster of opportunism and depravity, such that her well-deserved death is the only satisfactory way to conclude the story.

Pattern

There is an obvious pattern in 'Abd al-Wahhāb's marriages: each woman he marries is more independent than the previous one, and less inclined to follow the conventional pattern of marriage. The narrator gets bolder and bolder, and with him the women. 'Abd al-Wahhāb's nameless first wife is completely traditional, and expresses her grief about her husband's new marriage only in a passive way: by helplessly dying of jealousy. 'Ulwā, the second wife, is a warrior woman and perfectly able to take her own decisions, but is less outspoken, less colourful and enterprising than the third wife, Qannāsa. Finally there is Maymūna, initially too headstrong to marry; once she is married and is faced with dilemmas and new opportunities, she shakes off the bonds of wedlock without any qualms whatsoever and goes her own way.

CHAPTER 5

Sīrat Dhāt al-Himma 3:
The History of Ghamra the Daughter of ʿUtārid[1]

Protagonists

- ʿAbd al-Wahhāb, leading hero of the Kilābī tribe, son of Fāṭima Dhāt al-Himma
- ʿĀmir, son of Ashʿath, cousin, later also husband, of Ghamra
- ʿAmr, Ghamra's name in her male impersonation
- ʿAmr ibn ʿUbaydallāh, chief of the Banū Sulaym, later commander-in-chief of the tribes
- Ashʿath ibn ʿAwf, brother of ʿUtārid
- Banū Kilāb (or Kilābīs), Bedouin tribe to which Dhāt al-Himma and ʿAbd al-Wahhāb belong
- Banū Sulaym, Bedouin tribe, rival of the Banū Kilāb
- Dhāt al-Himma (Fāṭima), leading female hero of the Kilābī tribe, mother of ʿAbd al-Wahhāb
- Ghamra, daughter of ʿUtārid ibn ʿAwf, Arab warrior woman
- Jaydāʾ, Arab warrior woman, beloved of Khālid
- Jawdar, Jaydāʾ's name in her male impersonation
- Khālid, beloved of Jaydāʾ
- Maʾmūn, Abbasid caliph
- Marjāna, Christian warrior princess, converts to Islam
- Maymūna, Ethiopian warrior princess, fourth wife of ʿAbd al-Wahhāb
- Muʿtasim, Abbasid caliph
- Nūra, Byzantine warrior princess, marries Baṭṭāl

- Qannāsa, Arab warrior princess, daughter of Muzāhim, third wife of ʿAbd al-Wahhāb
- ʿUlwā, Arab warrior woman, second wife of ʿAbd al-Wahhāb
- ʿUqba, chief *qāḍī* (judge), crypto-Christian, villain of the *sīra*, related to the Banū Sulaym
- ʿUtārid ibn ʿAwf, chief of a Yemeni tribe, father of Ghamra
- Zālim, son of Qannāsa and ʿAbd al-Wahhāb

In Arabic, *ghamra* means 'flood'. It is still a common name for girls. In modern Arabic, the word may also be used in a metaphorical sense, meaning 'emotional exuberance', and, as such, it is an appropriate name for Princess Ghamra, one of the heroines in *The Adventures of Princess Dhāt al-Himma*. She is quite an ebullient character, a high-spirited girl who gives free rein to her emotions.

The context in which the story of Ghamra unfolds is the military exploits and adventures of the Banū Kilāb and the Banū Sulaym, the rival Bedouin tribes that play such a leading role in this epic. At this point, the two tribes have made Malatya, the former Byzantine Melitene, their home, using it as a base for their raids against the Byzantines and other enemies. The Banū Kilāb are, as usual, led by Princess Dhāt al-Himma and her son ʿAbd al-Wahhāb, and the Banū Sulaym by Prince ʿAmr ibn ʿUbaydallāh, who also acts as commander-in-chief.[2]

Ghamra and her family appear on the scene just after the Abbasid caliph Maʾmūn has died and the caliphate has been taken over by his brother Muʿtasim. In the story, Ghamra does not enter the stage as a girl, but as a young man of radiant beauty by the name of ʿAmr, not to be confused with Prince ʿAmr ibn ʿUbaydallāh mentioned above. Only when the story is well under way do we discover that ʿAmr is, in fact, a girl, and then we realize that certain narrative elements in the preceding part have already paved the way for this. It remains unclear why Ghamra's parents decided to bring her up as a boy. That there was a specific reason for doing so is implied in various passages, but the audience is kept in the dark as to the nature of this reason. It gives the story a somewhat truncated aspect.

The explanation is that the narrator used a motif familiar from other stories, and that this particular element, the reason for bringing her up as a boy, fell by the wayside. An example, next to that of Dhāt al-Himma herself, is the story of Jaydāʾ and Khālid from *Sīrat ʿAntar*. There, too, we have a daughter and son, respectively, born to two brothers who were not on good terms with each other. When Jaydāʾ was born her father did not want to give his brother, whose son was born at the same time, the opportunity to mock him. So he named her Jawdar and brought her up as a boy.[3] Just like Ghamra in the present story, Jaydā'/Jawdar falls in love with her cousin, but in this case they get married after the initial difficulties have been overcome and live together happily until Khālid, to Jaydā''s bitter grief, is killed in battle.

The story of Ghamra has some noteworthy aspects. One is that she virtually operates on her own, even though at some point, much against her will, she is formally married. It is an aspect that she has in common with Princess Dhāt al-Himma herself, the heroine of the *sīra* in which Ghamra's story is included. Unlike Princess Dhāt al-Himma, though, Ghamra does not give birth to a son, which is a most unusual deviation from the pattern. It might suggest that her marriage has not even been consummated. Another point worthy of attention is the change of role that takes place between Ghamra and her father: it is Ghamra who plays the active and protective role, while her father is a noble but meek character, intent upon the avoidance of conflict and aggressive confrontation.

Ghamra, or 'Amr as we will call the girl for the time being, appears on the scene in the same way as so many new characters in this kind of literature: under a cloud. Not a metaphorical cloud, but an actual cloud of dust that appears in the distance and announces the arrival of new protagonists, in this case an unknown emir accompanied by a thousand horsemen. Their approach is watched with amazement, for they are mounted on Arabian horses and dressed in the finest white cloth from Iraq and Egypt. Their leader is a man of impressive stature, showing all the marks of noble character, status and wealth. Most of all, however, people's eyes are drawn towards the young warrior who rides next to him:

> Next to the emir rode a young man of radiant youth, dressed in clothes as sheer as air and with black tresses of hair that fell over his saddle bow like bunches of grapes. The beauty of his face made that of the full moon pale. Everybody who saw him stood speechless, saying: 'This is not a human being! Praised be God, Who created the appearance of everything that exists!'[4]

Such descriptions of male beauty are not at all uncommon in this particular cultural convention. The luxuriant hair may seem somewhat unusual, and might be taken as a pointer that the young man is not actually a man. However, it also occurs in stories where the gender aspect is not an issue.[5]

The people arriving are 'Utārid ibn 'Awf and his young son 'Amr, come to join the Bedouin warriors on the Byzantine border with a large group of followers. When the leaders of the tribes come out to meet them, 'Utārid explains his origin and lineage. He refers to himself as 'king of the land of Sheba and Bilqīs'. So Yemen is his land of origin, the land of the Queen of Sheba, called Bilqīs in the Qur'ān. As is explained later on, the tension between 'Utārid and his aggressive and unpleasant brother Ash'ath threatened to cause a rift among his people, and 'Utārid decided to leave the leadership of Yemen to his brother and to emigrate to the north. Arranging for his womenfolk and children to follow shortly after, he travelled north with his warriors in order to join the Banū Kilāb, to whom he was related, and the Banū Sulaym, among whom he had friends.

Presents are exchanged on a large scale and 'Utārid is received with joy in Malatya. His son 'Amr soon begins to find his way there. His fame quickly spreads, and when he rides out everybody tries to catch a glimpse of him. Children, men and women climb on roofs, towers and elevated buildings to see his face. As a knight he is almost the equal of Prince 'Abd al-Wahhāb. He defeats all the other young warriors on the battle-ground and it is no different with spear throwing and lance thrusting. He engages in a contest with Zālim, the much respected son of Prince 'Abd al-Wahhāb, as well as with all his companions, and manages to defeat them all. When 'Abd al-Wahhāb and 'Amr ibn 'Ubaydallāh hear about this, they greatly rejoice about having such a champion in their midst. Soon the young prince 'Amr becomes to them the most cherished of all the young men, dearer even than their own sons. It takes quite some effort to placate the feelings of jealousy and dismay aroused by this among the other young warriors. 'Amr handles the matter with friendliness and tact, giving them a share of all the presents he receives and treating them with the utmost generosity. In this way he soon becomes accepted by the group.

One day 'Amr goes out hunting in Byzantine territory and runs into a large party of Armenians, a thousand horsemen who have set out to raid the Islamic lands.[6] He kills a number of them, takes the others captive and captures the spoils. Among the captive monks in the party is 'Uqba, the villain of the whole epic. He is a treacherous crypto-Christian, who again and again manages to ingratiate himself with the Abbasid caliphs and so maintain an influential position at court. The fact that he is related to the Banū Sulaym, the rival tribe to 'Abd al-Wahhāb's Banū Kilāb, makes him all the more dangerous to the Kilābīs, and he often manages to do them severe harm. Knowing what will be in store for him if young Prince 'Amr takes him to the Muslim camp, 'Uqba manages to play a trick on him, drugs him with the *banj* that he always carries behind his ear,[7] ties him up and escapes, together with the other prisoners. When 'Amr does not come home his mother gets very worried. His father, together with a group of his people, follows his son's tracks. They become involved in a hard struggle with a Byzantine army and matters look very bad for them. Fortunately, Prince 'Abd al-Wahhāb comes to their rescue with his Kilābī warriors. They chase off the enemy, free the young 'Amr and set out for home with a large quantity of booty. People flock to gaze at the booty and also at the young prince:

> Nobody could get enough of looking at him, because he was the most unique person of his day in beauty and handsomeness, the Joseph of his time in comeliness, with eyes larger than those of a gazelle[8] and a manner of speaking that satisfied the hungry to such an extent that they no longer needed food, and that cured the sick straight away when they heard it.[9]

The repeated emphasis on 'Amr's extraordinary beauty and charming behaviour (remember his tact in dealing with the other young warriors) is, of course, not accidental. At this point in the story, 'Amr's female identity has not yet been disclosed and these descriptions help to lead up to that.

Not long afterwards, another cloud of dust is spotted on the horizon, announcing yet another party arriving from Yemen. This time they are 'Utārid's old mother and his sister-in-law, the wife of his brother. She is also the cousin of 'Utārid's wife. Longing for her son 'Utārid, the old mother kept pestering Ash'ath, her other son, to make arrangements for her to visit his brother. Supporting her mother-in-law, Ash'ath's wife declares her eagerness to visit her cousin, 'Utārid's wife. The problem, however, is then to find someone suitable to accompany them. Ash'ath's son 'Āmir would have been the obvious person, but this, as it turns out, cannot easily be accomplished. 'Āmir is a wild and unruly boy, who, from an early age, preferred deserted areas and the company of wild animals over that of his family. When he was twelve years old he left his family to go and wander about in the wilderness. His father traced him and tried to persuade him to come home but to no avail.

Supporting himself by highway robbery and plunder (perfectly respectable pastimes according to traditional Bedouin tribal standards), 'Āmir roams about until he is twenty years old. His absence is a constant source of grief to his mother. From time to time he pays her a secret visit, avoiding his father, but these occasions are few and far between.

Since 'Āmir is thus not available, Ash'ath organizes a party of a hundred horsemen to accompany his mother and wife. But just at that time 'Āmir happens to visit his mother, not having seen her for three years. His mother persuades him to join them in their visit to his uncle 'Utārid. Upon hearing that his uncle has joined the great prince 'Abd al-Wahhāb, 'Āmir agrees, for it has long been his wish to get acquainted with the renowned Kilābī heroes and he had already made plans to go there on his own. The idea of going to see whether his uncle is treated well there has an extra appeal for him, for it will offer him an opportunity to show those people who they are dealing with if the reports are not good.

So 'Āmir and the women depart. They arrive in Malatya and 'Utārid is very pleased to welcome his mother, his sister-in-law and his nephew 'Āmir, 'a handsome, very clever young man with black hair'.[10] Having heard about 'Āmir's preference for solitude, he houses him and his mother in a house that is set apart from the rest. Here we should note the succinct description of 'Āmir's handsomeness, considerably less exuberant than that of Ghamra/'Amr.

Once they have settled in, 'Āmir is soon invited by the other young men to join them on the training ground for some good jousting. At this point the narrator, in a somewhat awkward switch, reveals the female identity of 'Utārid's son 'Amr, saying:

> 'Utārid had a daughter whose name was Ghamra. She watched her cousin while he was playing, and a tremendous love for him sprang up in her heart. The girl saw how brave and skilfully her cousin comported himself on the playground, and how handsome and beautiful he was, and she completely lost her head. She did not sleep a wink that night but lamented her situation to her mother, saying to her: 'I cannot bear to be without him. Either you go and tell his mother the whole story, or I will inform her about this matter. I am Ghamra, not 'Amr!'

Her mother chides her, but Ghamra does not want to listen. Then her mother has a suggestion:

'If this is how things stand, you ought to know that you have not fallen in love with a stranger, but that he is your cousin, a man of your own flesh and blood. Tomorrow his mother will come over, and then I will take off your clothes in order to wash your hair. When she sees you then she will know the truth.'[11]

This takes place and 'Āmir's mother understands the whole situation. She immediately goes to her son and tells him about his beautiful cousin Ghamra, describing her in glowing terms. She says that he should definitely pay attention to her, for the man who snaps her up will be a lucky man indeed. 'And then she repeated to him the whole case and the reason why they had kept silent about her.' We, the audience, would also have liked to know this reason, but no more is said about it. In fact, the story at this point demonstrates again its awkward adaptation of the Jā'ida story: when 'Āmir becomes aware of the fact that his cousin 'Amr, whom he undoubtedly had already met on the battleground, is in fact his cousin Ghamra, how then could he subsequently behave as he does? The problem, however, is easily glossed over by the narrator.

'Āmir does not pay the slightest attention to his mother's words, but immediately goes out hunting, subsisting on lions' meat. Meanwhile, the girl frets and worries, spending sleepless nights. At last she asks what has happened and she is told that 'Āmir has not said a word to his mother after she had told him about Ghamra and her feelings. The aunt is easily persuaded to try another time and describes Ghamra in even more glowing terms. Her son, however, begs her to stop: he is not interested in full-bosomed companions. He just wants to go and hunt the lions in their thickets and to accomplish brave deeds on the battlefield, charging into enemy lines to let heads fly.

Ghamra, being informed of his reaction, is deeply miserable, but also extremely angry. She answers that people will talk for a long time about the way she will deal with him. 'Who is this dog, to say that he will rather go and hunt wild animals? He will see what happens!' Her mother, too, takes it very hard, and says that 'Āmir might have acted differently if he had known how beautiful of face and figure and how intelligent her daughter is. Ghamra lets herself be persuaded by her mother and aunt that once 'Āmir has seen with his own eyes what an exceptional beauty she is, he may reconsider his decision. Mother and aunt know all the ploys to circumvent the strict rules of convention in order to let the prospective husband catch a glimpse of a girl's face.

'Āmir's mother will bring him over for a visit to his aunt, who dearly loves to see him. Ghamra must then stand behind the curtain and when he raises his head, she too must raise her head and show herself to him with uncovered face. 'Even if he were a king he would not be able to restrain himself!'[12]

The prospect gives Ghamra the strength to bear her grief and passion, and she recites a love song. 'Āmir lets himself be persuaded to go and visit his aunt. She welcomes him with joy and they sit down to talk. Ghamra's mother, less than tactful, comes straight to the point:

> 'My son, I want all this beauty and perfection [namely, 'Āmir's] only for that heartbreaker, that supple twig, for she, my son, is your cousin, of your own flesh and blood, and you are the one who most deserves her.' 'Āmir averted his eyes to the ground in embarrassment. Sparks flew from his nostrils. He raised his head, looking away from them to the side of the room, and there Ghamra showed herself in all her beauty as if she were a frightened gazelle, like the moon on its fourteenth day. When he saw her, he knew that this was the only reason why they had made him come over. He turned to his aunt and said: 'Know, oh princess, that if I should be eager to join myself to full-bosomed girls, I would love most of all to take one of my relatives. Such, however, are not my feelings. I do not want to be distracted by women from what I want to do. My only purpose is to meet heroes and to encounter chieftains.' (He recites some verses to that effect.) Ghamra's mother was very much embarrassed. As to Ghamra herself, her gall bladder almost ruptured from anger, shame and passion, and had it not been for fear of the people, she would have thrown herself upon him. She came to her senses, however, and restrained herself.[13]

'Āmir decides to depart immediately. He orders his people to load up the presents which he has received and informs his uncle 'Utārid, who clearly has been kept completely in the dark about what has happened, of his intentions. 'Utārid bestows still more presents upon his nephew, and so do Prince 'Abd al-Wahhāb and Prince 'Amr ibn 'Ubaydallāh. 'Āmir and his company make themselves ready to depart in the last part of the night, 'when Canopus rises'. They ride off, and when Ghamra watches them go her heart is torn apart. For three months she remains steeped in misery. She is sick with love, unable to get up from her bed but not getting any sleep. When her father hears about her condition, 'he brings in astrologers and people who know about charms'.¹⁴ Meanwhile, the heroes of the Banū Kilāb and the Banū Sulaym come and visit her without having any suspicion that she is, in fact, Princess Ghamra and not Prince ʿAmr. Her condition gets worse and worse, and she is close to death.

For those who are familiar with the themes and motifs of Arabic literature on love, in particular the love poetry, this part of the story is highly amusing. The development of the well-known themes, such as the despair about unrequited love, the sleeplessness, the pining away till death is near, is interrupted time and again by Ghamra's rebellious actions. The fact that the narrator plays here with elements from 'high' literature demonstrates how strongly this so-called popular literature is connected to the literary tradition of the cultural elite, in which the 'malady of love' plays an important part.¹⁵

Soon some of Ghamra's former spirit returns and she tells her mother that she will go hunting: 'No better way to forget about my misery.' Her mother agrees; it makes no sense to go on pining for someone who is not interested. Here, again, a famous motif from classical Arabic poetry is brought to mind: in the traditional Arabic ode, the *qaṣīda*, the transition from the poet's complaint about his lost love to the episode in which he sets out for new adventures is made by stating that it makes no sense to continue grieving about a beloved who is unattainable, and by exhortations to pull oneself together and get on with life. So Ghamra puts on her male attire, jumps on one of her horses (the horse is described extensively) and sets out. She rides until she is far out in the field and completely alone. Then she recites a poem about the misery of unrequited love, and, having done so, she continues:

> 'Pour soul! What fun is it to see your beloved faring well while you are steeped in misery yourself? Go look for him and erase all traces of him, then you will rid yourself of all your heart's pain and the misery of love.' So she set out for the country from which her people originated and the area where her tribe lived. She went on without ever going near houses or habitations. She sought shelter with the Bedouin tribes who received her hospitably, saying: 'This is Prince ʿAmr, the son of ʿUtārid ibn ʿAwf, the king of the land of Sheba and Bilqīs!' On and on she went, crossing the land until she arrived in her own country. She knew where to look for her cousin and went to a forest where, according to what she had heard, he might be found. She hid there for three days because she was convinced that he was in that forest. She found it extremely boring, having to stand there like this. On the

fourth day, just when she considered entering the woods in order to attack him, a horseman suddenly emerged on a marked horse, a horse pitch black like a raven, with a split upper lip,[16] sturdily built, with hooves shining like dirhams.[17]

The horseman carries a lance and sword, and is dressed in costly attire. He has been killing animals day after day, so that all the wild animals have fled the area. Ghamra/'Amr recognizes him immediately. She pulls her clothes closely around her and draws her sword. With her quiver on her back and sitting high on her horse, she calls out to him with altered voice and challenges him in the most insulting terms: 'Piece of scum! Wicked kind of man! Ladies' pet! Take care, for I am going to kill you and free the Arabs of your presence!' He laughs, however, and answers that she clearly does not know who he is, taking him for just any kind of rabble. However, she knows exactly who he is, saying that isn't he 'Āmir the son of Ash'ath, the most despicable among men? She tells him that she has come here especially to give him a taste of the cup of death. But if he will do as ordered, she may be prepared to let him off lightly. She'll just take his clothes and his horse, for she is a young man trying to collect the bride price for his cousin whom he has asked for in marriage. Her father is willing to consent, but asks for a huge price. So 'Āmir's horse and apparel will make a good start. She orders him just to hand them over: 'Actually to fight you would be below me, that is too dishonourable an act.'

This makes 'Āmir, about whose pride and prowess we have already heard, see red, and he reacts as expected. A tremendous fight follows that lasts throughout the day. Never has 'Āmir met a warrior of this calibre. Finally, Ghamra manages to strike him down with a blow of her lance from the rear. She jumps upon him and pulls off his helmet and clothes until he has only his trousers left. These too she demands: if he does not hand them over she will strike off his head. He implores her to let him keep this essential bit of covering, but she is adamant. Those trousers may be sold for half a dinar, after all! And she leaves him 'just as naked as on the day his mother brought him into the world'. She rides off into the wilderness while he sits there until darkness falls, deeply humiliated. He decides to go to the house of his nurse under cover of darkness and look for something to put on.

Ghamra, meanwhile, rides on until she arrives at the tribe of her uncle, 'Āmir's father. She, too, heads for the house of the nurse, who only recognizes her after she has taken off her coverings. 'Dear girl, what brings you here?' asks the nurse. Ghamra tells her the whole story, from beginning to end, and declares in the strongest of terms that she will never take a husband. She hands the nurse ʿĀmir's helmet, his apparel and his horse, and asks her to pass on to him the following words when he arrives: 'Piece of dirt among the Arabs, you say that you want nothing to do with full-bosomed companions but only want to hunt the lions in the forest, to plunge into the battle ranks and to strike off heads. So, let this be your place!'[18]

Then she returns to Malatya. She feels completely herself again. Everybody is happy to see her back, for they had been afraid that she, Prince ʿAmr, had been killed in the land of the Byzantines. When her father asks her the reason for her long absence she says that she had longed for the spicy smell of the desert plants in her native land. Missing those aromatic smells had affected her health in the urbane surroundings of Malatya, and, when she realized this, she had set out for the wilderness to get well again. Only to her mother does she tell what has really happened, and her mother is very proud of her. Ghamra states emphatically that ʿĀmir no longer means anything to her, and that she has even come to detest him heartily. She quickly puts the whole episode behind her, and soon she, or rather he, is just as cheerful and handsome again as previously.

The role of the mother is to be noted: rather than trying to persuade her daughter to adapt to the traditional role model, she encourages her to take her fate in her own hands, even if this implies highly unconventional behaviour.

'Āmir, meanwhile, is in quite a different position. After Ghamra has left him, he waits until dark before going back to the village. Covering his private parts with his hands, one in front and one on his backside, he walks on until he reaches the house of his nurse. He tells her what has happened and asks her to go and fetch some clothes from his mother's house. To his astonishment, however, the nurse has all his clothes waiting for him. He is very embarrassed. How has she come by them? The nurse explains that the redoubtable horseman whom he just met was in fact somebody very close to him, someone who had no wish to shame him before the Arabs. The knight in question had been his cousin Ghamra, who had wanted to teach him a lesson: in spite of all his boasting about fighting heroes and killing lions, he had been defeated by 'a coquettish and attractive girl, one of those ladies'. The nurse further informs him that Ghamra has sworn that ʿĀmir will never be her husband.[19]

We would expect a response of shame and anger from ʿĀmir, but his reaction is completely different: passion flames up in his heart, and he is overwhelmed by love and longing for his cousin. He goes to his mother's house, trembling like a leaf. For ten days he remains in this condition, not uttering a word. His father is very worried. The nurse tells ʿĀmir's mother what has happened and she in turn informs her husband, who thinks that the solution is obvious: he will go to Malatya with his son, carrying a large number of presents, and will ask for Ghamra in marriage. It is the only solution, for, as he says, his son is clearly wasting away, getting thinner and thinner, and this may well end in death if no action is taken. ʿĀmir, as opposed to Ghamra earlier on, here follows the true pattern of the 'malady of love': he completely lacks the strength or willpower to do anything about his condition, and only by the intervention of others can he be prevented from succumbing to love.

His father steps in, reminding his son of the opportunity that he had let slip when Ghamra declared her love. He says that all may not be lost; if they all go to Malatya, Prince ʿAbd al-Wahhāb may well be persuaded to exert his influence so that ʿĀmir will be able to marry Ghamra. This suggestion cheers ʿĀmir up considerably and they depart with a large entourage. ʿĀmir, emaciated by his passion for his cousin, counts the stages. Messengers are sent ahead to announce their arrival. All the leaders ride out to meet them, and the noble and forgiving ʿUtārid is delighted to greet his brother. Ashʿath, in tears, embraces him, reciting verses to ask forgiveness for the harm that he has done to his brother. Celebrations go on for ten days. On the eleventh day Ashʿath brings out the presents. All the men are gathered together in the big house of Prince ʿAbd al-Wahhāb, as is their custom on Thursday evenings: they talk, listen to the Qurʾān, and poems are recited. Ashʿath apologizes again for his behaviour to his brother and says that he has come to ask the hand of ʿUtārid's beautiful daughter, Princess Ghamra, on behalf of his son ʿĀmir. He describes in detail the huge bride price that he is willing to pay. His address brings tears to people's eyes: 'It fell on people like cold water on a thirsty liver.' For they had not known that ʿUtārid had another child besides ʿAmr, and, of course, it did not occur to them straight away that this newly revealed Ghamra might actually be the same person as Prince ʿAmr.

Ghamra/ʿAmr herself, foreseeing trouble, is not present. ʿUtārid feels very embarrassed that he now has no option but to explain the whole situation concerning his 'son'. When they hear that ʿAmr is in fact a girl, people are very astonished. A girl, and yet what bravery! 'What an excellent girl! Fantastic!' says Princess Dhāt al-Himma. All the members of the Banū Kilāb and the Banū Sulaym, without exception, hope that

The History of Ghamra the Daughter of 'Uṭārid 105

'Uṭārid will refuse to marry her to his nephew so that they can propose to her themselves. Prince 'Amr ibn 'Ubaydallāh, the leader of the Banū Sulaym, said: 'There exists no other girl like her on earth! I would very much like to be in the same situation as Prince 'Abd al-Wahhāb, who has women who can protect him as well as themselves! That 'Uṭārid has played a sly trick on me!'[20]

It may seem quite surprising that men from a traditional Arab culture would utter such views. It is, however, not so exceptional in Middle Eastern literature. A passage from the story of Kan Turali in the Turkish *Book of Dede Korkut* illustrates this:

'Father, you want to have me married, but can you find a girl who would be my match? Father, I want a girl who must get up before I do. She must be able to mount her horse before I mount my black stallion. She must be able to reach the bloody land of the infidels before I do, and she must bring me an enemy head,' said the son. Kanli Koja said: 'Son, you do not want a girl. You want a brave warrior, so that you can eat and drink and have a good time at her expense.' 'That is true, Father.'[21]

Everybody eagerly waits for 'Uṭārid's reaction. He, however, points out that it does not do to act rashly in a matter like this. An honourable man has to stick by his word, and thus it should only be given after due consideration. His wife and daughter will have to be consulted. 'Princess Ghamra is free to make her own choice.' So he sets out to talk to them, not aware of what has happened between Ghamra and her cousin. He is still very embarrassed about the fact that his son's female identity has now been revealed, but the idea of all those presents and the huge bride price is also very appealing. Smiling happily, he tells his wife about what has occurred. She clearly has her reservations but goes to consult her daughter. Ghamra just laughs and states in the strongest of terms that she will never be 'Āmir's wife and that he will never be her husband. If they try to force her she will kill herself in order to escape the whole affair. Her mother conveys the bad news to her husband, who summons Ghamra and mildly chides her: this is her own cousin, after all. But she is adamant, repeating that if they try to force her she will either kill herself or convert to Christianity and enrol in the Byzantine army.

It is certainly the worst threat that she can utter: becoming an apostate and being prepared to take up arms against Islam and against her own family. Nothing could make a Muslim father more miserable. The poor ʿUtārid waits another day, but then has no other option but to tell his brother and the other members of the tribe that marriage is out of the question. Ghamra will not agree to it. ʿĀmir, the prospective groom, faints upon hearing the news. Everybody pities him, and a delegation of women led by Princess Dhāt al-Himma tries to persuade Ghamra to change her mind but to no avail. She just confirms her earlier point of view.[22]

At this point in the story a messenger arrives. Enemy action has been detected and the attendance of Prince ʿAbd al-Wahhāb and Princess Dhāt al-Himma is urgently required. New adventures take place, in which, as usual, the villainous *qāḍī* ʿUqba plays his treacherous role. Ghamra takes part in battle just as she was accustomed to do when she was still thought to be Prince ʿAmr. Within her tribe, her switch to female identity makes no difference: there are a number of other prominent female warriors among the leading heroes, such as ʿAbd al-Wahhāb's wives Qannāsa, ʿUlwā and Maymūna, and also Nūra, the wife of trickster-hero al-Baṭṭāl. But now that it is known that Ghamra is a woman, she has, as we will see, become more vulnerable in confrontations with opponents. They sometimes have no qualms about showering her with verbal abuse related to her femininity.

Central in this episode stands *qāḍī* ʿUqba's capture by some of the Kilābī warriors while he is preaching in a Christian church, urging his audience to go and wage war, *jihād*, against the Muslim lands.[23] He is taken to the camp in Malatya, and the Kilābīs, led by ʿAbd al-Wahhāb, say that he must be condemned as an apostate and killed. The Banū Sulaym are deeply shocked to see their esteemed relative in chains and subject to these very serious accusations. They cannot believe what they are told: how could all this be true about ʿUqba, the leading scholar of Islam? They are further angered when the Kilābīs suggest that the best way to ascertain his identity would be to ask Ghamra to identify him as the villain who betrayed her during her earlier adventure with the Armenians, when she was still Prince ʿAmr. The Banū Sulaym refuse, asking how could they accept

> the word of a woman, a creature without intelligence and without the right to testify, and listen to what she has to say in the affair of declaring the imam of Islam an unbeliever, the man who has memorized the Book of God the Almighty as well as thirty thousand sayings of the Prophet – may God bless him and give him peace? The man with whom most of the scholars of Baghdad have studied, who can recite

the Qur'ān in all the different readings[24] and who knows all the sciences and all the languages?[25]

The Sulaymī leader, 'Amr ibn 'Ubaydallāh, writes a letter to the newly appointed caliph Mu'tasim to that effect. The caliph resents the action of 'Abd al-Wahhāb, whom he mistrusts anyway. Letters are sent by carrier pigeons to both leaders. To 'Amr ibn 'Ubaydallāh, the caliph says that he supports his views, but urges him not to oppose 'Abd al-Wahhāb to the point where it may lead to a battle between their tribes, while to 'Abd al-Wahhāb he suggests that it would be better to postpone 'Uqba's execution until they have made Constantinople the seat of the caliphate and they can crucify him there.

'Abd al-Wahhāb still insists on bringing 'Uqba to trial and on asking Ghamra to identify him. In order to test her reliability they will first show her another half-blind old man, and when she denies that this is the *qādī*, they will bring forward the real 'Uqba. 'Amr ibn 'Ubaydallāh, following the caliph's orders to go along with the plan, agrees. They all go to the field where the trial will take place, including Ash'ath and his son 'Āmir, who harbours a deep resentment against Ghamra and considers the possibility of abducting and killing her. 'Utārid arrives with Ghamra at his side. Since it became known that she is a woman, she has started to cover her face with a veil.[26] 'Uqba is brought forward on a mule, and the tension builds. Ghamra recognizes him immediately: this is the man who released the Christian prisoners during her early adventure. Objections and heated discussions follow, but Ghamra sticks by her opinion. 'Uqba mockingly says: 'What can be more stupid than listening to what someone who menstruates has to say about me, while I know very well that this all comes from my enemies?'[27]

In order to avoid further escalation of the disagreement, both parties decide to await the arrival of the caliph. When the caliph arrives, he contrives, with 'Amr ibn 'Ubaydallāh and the Banū Sulaym, to capture 'Abd al-Wahhāb and to break the power of the Kilābīs. Skirmishes between the parties ensue. Ash'ath and his son 'Āmir refuse to participate out of resentment against 'Abd al-Wahhāb, who, according to a false rumour spread by 'Uqba, has asked for Ghamra in marriage for his son. It even comes to fighting between Ash'ath and his brother 'Utārid, a fight in which Ghamra has to intervene in order to protect her father.[28] But while Ghamra may easily get the better of her uncle in combat, she is fighting a losing battle on the other front: behind her back, her uncle asks the caliph Muʿtasim to order Ghamra to marry her cousin. The caliph asks her about it, but she still flatly refuses.[29] ʿĀmir, however, manages to engage ʿUqba's support, crying to him about his misery, and the matter is soon settled: Muʿtasim, after having bestowed upon ʿAmr ibn ʿUbaydallāh the supreme command that formerly belonged to ʿAbd al-Wahhāb, suggests that it would be a good idea if he, ʿAmr, arranged the marriage between Ghamra and ʿĀmir and also gave ʿĀmir a good position within the army, should he be willing to stay on in Malatya.

Commander ʿAmr ibn ʿUbaydallāh complies and immediately gives orders for the wedding to take place. People take hold of Ghamra and she is forcibly put into bridal apparel. The marriage is concluded, and after the couple have retired to the bridal chamber, Ghamra sees her chance. She firmly ties ʿĀmir up, gets on her horse and, before anybody is aware of what is happening, she has sped off, heading for the Hijāz. They all hope that she will come back, but there is absolutely no chance of that. Princess Dhāt al-Himma especially regrets this very much, for she had become very fond of Ghamra.[30]

Keeping herself alive by hunting, Ghamra finally arrives in Yemen, her native kingdom. She, as a princess of the royal house, is received enthusiastically and soon recognized as leader. She continues in this position and does not disappear completely from view: she is the first to arrive with thirty thousand of her warriors when the tribes want to make sure that ʿAbd al-Wahhāb, who had been taken captive, has actually been released.[31] Apparently she stays around after that, for, together with her father and other champions, she also takes part in an adventure involving a Christian warrior princess, Marjāna, who later converts to Islam.[32]

The reader may be puzzled about Ghamra's marital state: was she, at this stage, a married woman? Had the marriage been consummated and, if not, what did this imply for its validity? It is important to keep in mind here the view of many jurists that it is not the actual consummation that counts, but the fact that the couple have been secluded together for a certain period of time. If this seclusion (*khalwa*) has taken place, the marriage is legally valid.[33] The fact that there is no further question in the *sīra* of love affairs involving Ghamra gives the impression that at least the narrator and audience consider her to be married.

This is the story of Ghamra so far. It illustrates how the narrators made use of familiar material, sometimes forgetting to integrate it adequately with in its new context. The reader who is not familiar with the story of Jaydā will keep wondering why Ghamra's meek and gentle father wanted to bring up his daughter as a boy. Yet her male identity, combined with her strong character, is a big support for her father in the confrontations with his unpleasant brother. When her father's brother beats him up, it is Ghamra who encourages him to leave and take the family to another country; and when, later on, her father is in danger from his brother during a combat, it is Ghamra, now recognized as female, who comes to his support. The whole story shows a curious switch of role between father and daughter, with the daughter demonstrating the pride and valour that one would expect from the father. Remarkable, too, is the role of the mother, who encourages her daughter not to assume a position of feminine weakness and helplessness, but to take her fate into her own hands.

In our view, Ghamra's behaviour also compares favourably with that of her cousin ʿĀmir, who, both physically and morally, collapses after he has fallen in love. He does, in fact, seem a fairly despicable character. Here, however, we ought to keep in mind that, according to Arab moral standards, lovesickness is one of the few more or less acceptable reasons why a man may no longer be able to stick to the rules of *muruwwa*, male virtue. *Sabr*, stoically enduring, a basic aspect of male virtue, cannot be expected of the hapless lover.

CHAPTER 6

Warrior Women in Sīrat ʿAntara *1: Ghamra the Daughter of Fāʾiz*[1]

Protagonists

- ʿAbla, daughter of Mālik, cousin and wife of ʿAntar
- ʿAntar ibn Shaddād, Arab champion, hero of the *sīra*
- Banū Khudāʿa, a tribe of Yemeni origin
- Dhū l-Khimār, see Sabīʿ Dhū l-Khimār
- Durayd, leading chief of the Arab tribes
- Fāʾiz, Arab chief, father of Ghamra
- Ghamra, daughter of Fāʾiz, Arab warrior woman, marries ʿAntar
- Ghamra, daughter of ʿUtārid, Arab warrior woman in *Dhāt al-Himma*
- Ghassūb, son of Ghamra and ʿAntar
- Hayfāʾ, sister of ʿAmr Dhū l-Kalb, marries ʿAntar
- Hind bint Qays, Arab warrior woman
- Hudhūr, Ethiopian princess, mother of Ghamra the daughter of Fāʾiz
- Ibrīza, Byzantine princess
- Jadhīma, Arab king
- Jāʾida, Arab warrior woman
- Mālik, father of ʿAbla, uncle of ʿAntar
- Maryam, Byzantine girl, supposedly killed at ʿAntar's orders
- Mubādir ibn Jabbār, Yemeni tribal leader
- Muhriya, a bride abducted and raped by ʿAntar
- Mutanaʿjiz, brother of Ghamra the daughter of Fāʾiz
- Rabāb, Arab queen
- Sabīʿ Dhū l-Khimār, Arab champion
- Shaybūb, ʿAntar's brother

- 'Umar al-Nu'mān, Arab king
- 'Unaytira, daughter of Hayfā' and 'Antar
- 'Utārid, Arab chief, father of Ghamra in *Dhāt al-Himma*
- Zarqā', Arab warrior woman, aunt of Sabī' Dhū l-Khimār

Of the Arabian epics, *The Adventures of 'Antar ibn Shaddād* is the first that became widely known in Europe, largely because it was partly translated into English in 1819–20.² In the Arab world, it was recited by professional storytellers specializing in performing this particular *sīra*. Edward William Lane, the Orientalist to whom we owe so much of our knowledge about popular storytelling, counted six professional reciters of *'Antar* in Cairo during his stay there between 1825 and 1835.³ Listening to performances of *The Adventures of 'Antar* was still a popular pastime in Cairo during the first half of the twentieth century, especially in Ramadan when storytellers recited it in coffee houses during Ramadan nights.⁴

'Antar is the archetypical Arab hero, an Arab Hercules. This is demonstrated by the fact that his name has even been used as a brand name for petrol. He is the very ideal of masculinity, a paragon of manly virtue and virility. He is a great warrior as well as a great lover. He also has some very human traits, which makes it all the easier for the (male) audience to identify with him. He rarely gives a thought to the havoc he wreaks on the lives of others by following his sexual impulses regardless of the consequences, especially the consequences for the women involved, and always tries to hide his escapades from his beloved wife. In a way, *The Adventures of 'Antar* is very much a boy's tale, boasting about 'Antar's exploits in battle, his sexual prowess and even the remarkable force with which he urinates, splitting stones in the process.

'Antar starts his life burdened by social disadvantages: he is the illegitimate black son of a tribal chief, and has to cope with disdain and unfair treatment from the other members of the tribe. That he is destined to become a very great hero is already obvious in his early youth, when he performs a number of astonishing feats.

There exist two versions of *The Adventures of 'Antar*. For our current purpose, the difference between the versions is of minor importance. Our focus in this and the next chapter will be on the role of women in *The Adventures of 'Antar*, in particular the warrior women.

The major female character in *The Adventures of 'Antar* is 'Antar's cousin 'Abla, his great love. She is the daughter of his uncle Mālik, and he falls in love with her the moment he sets eyes on her. His uncle is not at all inclined to marry his daughter to his brother's illegitimate black son, a young man whose position within the tribe is that of a slave herding cattle, in spite of his gigantic strength and martial prowess. Many adventures involving heroic deeds of 'Antar will have to occur before all the barriers have been overcome and the wedding finally takes place. By then, a third of the *sīra* is already behind us.

Relations between 'Antar and 'Abla are not always easy. In spite of his great love for her, he is frequently attracted to other women. He has many love affairs, sometimes resulting in marriage and usually also in the birth of dark-skinned sons who turn up later at unexpected moments, invariably to 'Antar's delight. This is all the more painful for 'Abla because she is childless herself.

It should be noted that there is no mention of love affairs before 'Antar's marriage to 'Abla. Such affairs would not have fitted in with the image of the faithful lover who is prepared to expose himself to all kinds of danger and discomfort for the sake of, and in order to win, his beloved. But after 'Antar's long-drawn-out trials are over and he is safely married to 'Abla, there are frequent accounts of his involvement with other women.

The way in which 'Antar behaves in his extramarital adventures is often not very delicate. He may rape a girl, excited by the discovery that his supposedly male opponent in battle is actually a woman, as happens with Ghamra; sleep with a bride whom he has abducted after a long period of forced continence, as in the case of the girl Muhrīya; or have sex in a state of intoxication with a girl offered to him, and then decide to have her murdered for fear that she may be pregnant, as with the Byzantine girl Maryam.

A continuing pattern is that he tries to hide his marriages and other affairs from 'Abla. He rarely succeeds, for, inevitably, black sons turn up at some point. His reaction to 'Abla's angry complaints is usually fairly elementary, and some might be temped to call it typically male: he just walks off, or says that she shouldn't worry, for does he not love her most of all? He argues that it is his duty to make provisions for these old paramours and their offspring, a man has to take responsibility for his lapses after all, but does 'Abla not agree that this newly discovered son is a great asset to the tribe? Then he jokes a bit, recites a poem expressing his love, sleeps with her and she is happy again.

'Abla is the leading female protagonist among the many women that figure in *The Adventures of 'Antar*. A number of these women are warrior princesses. 'Abla herself is not a warrior woman, but she is anything but a meek and subdued little lady. She is a proud, highborn Arab girl and acts the part. She strangles a woman who tries to lure her into an ambush, and, if the need arises, she is quite prepared to strike out with whatever weapon she finds at hand. Most feared, though, is her tongue. She can lash out quite fiercely, and 'Antar himself does not escape her verbal thrashings. In the end, her sharp and insulting tongue will cost her her life, when the husband she has married after 'Antar's death is no longer prepared to put up with her unkindness and her snide remarks about his sexual performance. He decides that the only way to keep his dignity is to have her killed, and, after consulting with the tribe, he has her strangled in her sleep by his slave girls.[5]

It is a strange and moving end to 'Abla's long history of love and suffering. It is told in such a way that she almost seems to seek her own destruction, and, at the same time, the narrator manages to take the audience's sympathy for her away completely.

As said above, *The Adventures of 'Antar* features a number of warrior women. The beginning of the actual epic firmly sets the tone in this respect:[6] it tells the story of Queen Rabāb, an Arab warrior queen who refused to pay tribute to the powerful king Jadhīma and was eventually killed. In the course of the narrative, several more warrior queens and princesses make their appearance: Jaydā', the Bedouin girl whose story partly follows the same pattern as that of Ghamra bint 'Utārid in the previous chapter; Hind bint Qays of the Banū Shaybān, a Bedouin girl who is not only a brave warrior, but can also read and write; and an Indian warrior queen, who (just like Princess Dhāt al-Himma in the adventure cycle of that name) is raped while she is menstruating and bears a black child as a result.

In the next two chapters, four warrior women will be treated more extensively. They are all of Bedouin stock, although one of them is, through her mother, partly of African descent, just like 'Antar himself. These women are Ghamra the daughter of Fā'iz, Hayfā' the sister of 'Amr Dhū l-Kalb, Zarqā' the aunt of Sabī' Dhū l-Khimār and finally 'Unaytira, 'Antar's daughter born posthumously. Hayfā', Zarqā' and 'Unaytira will be discussed in the next chapter.

Ghamra the daughter of Fā'iz[7]

Just like Ghamra the daughter of 'Utārid in the previously told story from *The Adventures of Princess Dhāt al-Himma*, Ghamra the daughter of Fā'iz is a proud and independent girl. In both stories the relationship between the girls and their fathers is noteworthy. In each case the girl is clearly the stronger personality, which leads to a form of role switching between father and daughter. Both fathers are keen to avoid violence, not eager to confront aggressors head on and prefer to seek a roundabout way to deal with aggressive forces. 'Utārid, father of the first Ghamra, is a noble and peace-loving man. Fā'iz, the other Ghamra's father, is a far less noble character. He is more of an opportunist, and sometimes an outright coward. And while Ghamra bint 'Utārid is often protective towards her father, Ghamra bint Fā'iz simply follows her own inclinations, not bothering about her father's views.

Antagonism between Yemeni and other Arab tribes, a prominent theme throughout the *sīra*, plays an important role in the history of Ghamra bint Fā'iz. 'Antar and Ghamra engage in combat in the course of this conflict. Ghamra is not only defeated, but also violated by 'Antar. For quite a while, the formal nature of her relationship with 'Antar will remain unclear. Is she a rape victim or a wife? The answer is both; and, as we will see, it is mainly her own perception and attitude in this respect, and, accordingly, the way she is perceived by others, that change over the course of events.

Ghamra makes her first appearance during one of the endless tribal conflicts. She belongs to the Banū Khudā'a, a tribe of Yemeni origin. Her early childhood has not been easy. Her mother Hudhūr, an Ethiopian princess, had been captured by Bedouins when she went on pilgrimage to Mecca to worship the 'gods and idols' (this is all supposed to take place in pre-Islamic times) after the death of her husband. This husband, the Negus of Ethiopia, had died before the marriage could be consummated.[8] After her capture, Hudhūr became the slave concubine of Fā'iz, chief of the Banū Khudā'a. When Hudhūr gave birth to a daughter of dark complexion, Fā'iz refused to acknowledge her as his child. Only later on, when he discovered her martial prowess, did he accept Ghamra as his daughter.

Noteworthy is the brief reference to Ghamra's unusual birth and childhood. It singles her out as a person of heroic status; the way in which she obtains a famous sword is an aspect of this.

During one of their forays, Ghamra and her brother Mutana'jiz run into a group of enemy Bedouins. One of them attempts to kill Mutana'jiz, but Ghamra and her brother manage to take them all captive. Ghamra makes quite an impression, and 'Abbās, the man who tried to kill her brother, looks at her with trepidation:

He saw that she had a dark complexion, while she was also wide of shoulders, with heavy buttocks, black eyes and long forearms, the characteristic physical appearance of someone who is black. The marks on her sides clearly indicated that she was an accomplished horsewoman and warrior, so that people were amazed about her appearance. The sight of her frightened him, and he hid between his companions in order not to be noticed.

Sabīʿ Dhū l-Khimār, a prominent warrior among the captives, remains very quiet while observing Ghamra. It is obvious that we are going to hear more about him. A messenger from the captives is sent to their tribal chief to request a ransom of three hundred camels. Meanwhile brother and sister take the captives back to their own tribe. Their father is less than enthusiastic about their action because the captives belong to a powerful conglomeration of tribes and this may lead to serious trouble.

During the night, Ghamra is woken by cries, and guards come running to her for help: Dhū l-Khimār has managed to free himself as well as his companions and they have all escaped. Ghamra summons her men and sets out in pursuit. She soon catches up with Dhū l-Khimār, and this is the start of an episode in which their mutual attraction and eagerness to demonstrate their superior martial prowess play a dominant part. The narrator cleverly uses these elements to build up tension.

Ghamra's father, worried about what might happen to his daughter, tells her to capture Dhū l-Khimār and to tie him up so that he can cut off his head. Ghamra, however, would much rather defeat him in actual combat, and so establish her reputation among the Arabs. The difference in attitude between the proud warrior daughter and the cowardly father is striking. Dhū l-Khimār, stirring up Ghamra's eagerness, remarks that he could easily defeat them if he were not so hungry and thirsty, and unarmed as well. Ghamra immediately says that he must not be killed, but fed properly and provided with arms so that she can fight him when he has recovered and thus show the tribe that she has no equal.

Meanwhile ʿAntar has heard about the affair and, together with Durayd, the leading chief of the Arab tribes, comes to rescue the captives. While Ghamra's father is away discussing the matter with the tribes, Ghamra's interest in Dhū l-Khimār grows. As her father later hears from his men, 'she went to see Dhū l-Khimār every day, visiting him, eating with him and asking him about all the brave knights and heroes that he had encountered, so that he was amazed about her and despised himself because a woman, one of the ladies, had become his opponent'.⁹ The motif of the young warrior girl fascinated by the captive hero of great renown is not unfamiliar in this kind of literature. We also encountered it, for instance, in the history of Princess Maymūna in *The Adventures of Princess Dhāt al-Himma*.¹⁰ It is clearly the prelude to a love affair, which, as we will see, does not necessarily lead to marriage.

With her father still away, Ghamra decides to free Dhū l-Khimār from his bonds and to engage in combat with him. If he wins, she will set him and his companions free; if he loses, she will cut off his forelock and let him go by himself. They battle for a whole day without conclusive result. Both secretly think that the other might be a good marriage partner. Dhū l-Khimār is slightly ashamed about the thought. They continue fighting for a second day. Meanwhile Ghamra's father has returned and approaches her, saying that this combat is a very bad idea: if she should happen to kill Dhū l-Khimār, all kinds of trouble with his tribe and with 'Antar will ensue, and, very likely, many of their tribe will be killed. The matter is further complicated by the fact that Dhū l-Khimār's people and 'Antar have captured Ghamra's brother. She would do better, he says, to put Dhū l-Khimār back into captivity straight away.

With flashing eyes Ghamra listens to her father's words, disgusted by such cowardliness. Dhū l-Khimār, standing by, comes up with a different suggestion. Why doesn't she go and fight 'Antar himself, the big champion? He is prepared to come and watch her fight, and he will do his best to get her released if she should be captured. Ghamra thinks this an excellent idea and, standing at the head of her horsemen, she recites a long poem in praise of her own courage and braveness, greatly admired by Dhū l-Khimār, who secretly hopes that he may find an opportunity to kill 'Antar himself and so enhance his reputation. Ghamra is so excited about the prospect of fighting 'Antar that she cannot stay in the tents and does not turn up to eat with her father.

Setting out, Ghamra and Dhū l-Khimār separately start to look for 'Antar. Dhū l-Khimār is attacked by someone who thinks that his opponent is Ghamra. Her reputation clearly has become widespread. Ghamra herself, however, meets 'Antar in a lonely place, recognizing him by his war cry and his black skin. 'Antar does not realize that she is a woman and they engage in combat. He is most impressed by the fight his opponent puts up. Eventually, however, their horses tire and Ghamra suffers from thirst and hunger 'because she was after all a woman'. Note how her femininity suddenly becomes an issue in the narrative: it is a prelude to events in which her gender becomes a central factor.

She proposes they interrupt the combat in order to give their horses some rest and continue fighting the next morning. 'Antar refuses, but accepts giving the horses some rest and water. He dismounts, throwing off his armour, so that they have to conduct their fight on foot with shield and spear. Ghamra also takes off some of her armour and continues to fight in a light Yemeni cloak with short sleeves, exposing the sides of her body.

The account of the woman being scantily clad and the resulting body contact clearly was an exciting element: it is a standard part of many of these stories.

'Antar suddenly realizes that she is a woman: 'You are Ghamra the daughter of Fā'iz!' She confirms this, and adds that if it had not been so hot here in the desert, she would not have revealed her identity. She has no intention of letting him get away safe and sound. Yelling loudly, she attacks, aware of the fact 'that she had confused him and that his secret thoughts and his heart were preoccupied with her'. A tremendous fight follows, and eventually Ghamra becomes exhausted. 'Antar, a man quick to follow his basic instincts, grabs her and pushes her down on her back, 'being allured by the blackness of her hair'. He straddles her, pressing her to his breast and kissing her between the eyes. His intentions are obvious, and she tries to defend herself, screaming: 'What do you want, son of a whore?' Irritated, he counters that after all she hasn't led a secluded life: having gone out on her own, leaving the area permitted to girls, this is what she may expect. He knows her sort. And while, as he says, 'Abla is, of course, his one and only love, he cannot be expected to pass up an opportunity like this.[11]

Here we have the usual rapist's defence, still all-too familiar in our own day: 'the girl really asked for it by behaving as she did'.

The narrator explains that the matter is, in fact, more complicated: it has been preordained that 'Antar would beget a male child 'in whose story there would be an admonition to those who would heed it'. In order to make this come about, the Creator contrived to make Ghamra look beautiful and attractive to 'Antar.

Realizing that she cannot escape what is about to happen, Ghamra sees only one way to avoid dishonour: she demands a dowry and the assurance that 'Antar will never make public what has happened, so that she will not lose respect. Ashamed, he swears to keep silent, and, by way of a dowry, he gives her one of his swords, named Sayf al-Riqāb, 'Sword of the Necks'. A dowry is a crucial part of the marriage contract, and so the gift of the sword gives some sort of legal foundation to his subsequent defloration of Ghamra, which is described in metaphoric terms:

> Then he set up his mangonel, and yelling 'O 'Abs! O 'Adnān!', he fixed his eye on the gate, put the stone in the swing of the mangonel, shook it, and the gate split apart. He destroyed the tower and took possession of the castle and everything that was in it. The breasts swelled with joy, and 'Antar had reached his goal. So his fire was extinguished, and 'Antar regained his composure. Then they each went their own way.

Ghamra is deeply miserable: 'Her soul was broken and she had lost the honour of virginity.' She would rather have been killed than have this happening to her 'from a black slave who originally was a shepherd'. But then the horsemen that her father had sent after her appear. They ask how she is, and she tells them that she has had a terrible fight for half the night with 'a black from the tribe of 'Abs' (a most insulting way of referring to 'Antar), and that she and her opponent had decided to pause for a while before resuming the combat. Because 'Antar is exhausted, they will easily be able to capture him, now that all these reinforcements are here. She takes a fresh horse and a lance, and they go out to look for 'Antar. They catch up with him near a pond, where he has taken off his clothes. He is captured and, at Ghamra's command, tied crosswise on his horse and taken back to the tribe.[12]

Ghamra's father is delighted, and wants to cut off 'Antar's head straight away. Ghamra points out that this is not very sensible as long as 'Antar's people hold so many of their tribe captive, including her brother. They will have to wait. First she will go out herself in order to free the captives. As we see, it is again Ghamra who plays a sensible and courageous role: her father is not only fearful and cautious but stupid as well.

Meanwhile Dhū l-Khimār, who had encouraged Ghamra to go and fight 'Antar, roams about unhappily. Feeling attracted to Ghamra (a feeling that was clearly mutual), he had hoped to impress her if she got in trouble, and maybe have the opportunity to fight 'Antar himself. Now it is Ghamra who has gained all the honour. Of course, he does not know that 'Antar has violated her. As far as he can see, his only possible course is to go to Ghamra's tribe, kill the captive 'Antar and liberate his friend 'Abbās and the other prisoners.

Ghamra goes to confront the enemy, getting involved in combat. She is very much impressed by the enemy champions. A general battle between the tribes follows, with Ghamra's father doing his usual bit of worrying instead of partaking in the action himself. He just tries to get others to go and help Ghamra: 'Whoever today brings me my daughter's opponent, to him I will marry her!'[13]

In the midst of all this, there is an unexpected turn of events: 'Antar and his brother Shaybūb rush in, yelling their war cries, and the tide quickly turns. Ghamra's people are defeated and she herself is taken captive. It soon becomes clear what has happened: Shaybūb, having seen all that had happened, had, with a ruse, helped his brother to escape. While they were sneaking away they ran into Dhū l-Khimār who, as Shaybūb knew, was on his way to kill 'Antar. They captured him and put him in chains, and, after the battle is over, he is handed over to Durayd, leader of the victorious tribes. This gives Dhū l-Khimār the opportunity to untie the captive Ghamra, and she in turn frees her father and a number of others. Then 'Antar turns up, looking for Ghamra, and she attacks him with her sword. We would have liked to hear that this was actually Sayf al-Riqāb, the very sword that he gave to her as a dowry, but no such specification is made.

Meanwhile, it becomes dark, and Dhū l-Khimār, afraid of what might happen, grabs Ghamra and flees with her, with 'Antar in pursuit. Dhū l-Khimār's fellow tribesmen are greatly puzzled by his behaviour in the whole affair, and their conclusion is that he must be in love with Ghamra and be jealous of 'Antar. With Ghamra and her father gone, they start killing the remaining captives, among them her brother.

The budding love affair between Ghamra and Dhū l-Khimār does not have a happy ending. Dhū l-Khimār returns home with Ghamra and her father, and her father promises him his daughter's hand. Then news of her brother's death arrives, and Dhū l-Khimār fears that Ghamra's excessive grief and her urge for revenge may cause her to lose interest in marriage altogether. Ghamra, however, while preparing to set out for revenge, is faced with a problem of a different nature:

> She turned out to be pregnant. Her condition changed, and she wanted to kill herself. Her belly became big and her colour paled, and she became slow and inactive. Her father frequently came to see her and kept asking her persistent questions, for he did not know about her condition. Then she told him about 'Antar, and how he had abducted her in spite of her resistance and had taken her off and steered her to

lonely valleys. She told him the story from beginning to end.

When her father heard what had happened, he absolved her from guilt and told her not to worry, saying: 'My daughter, this has happened to many an Arab girl, to very many indeed, because of the passion of men. You did this only because you were forced. Now the best you can do is to wait patiently until the baby is born and you have got rid of it. We will then slaughter it[14] under cover of the night. You will say nothing about the whole affair and resume your former position. Nobody will then know anything about this matter, and they will just say that you have been ill. In this way, you will not lose status and will not be lowered in rank.' She answered: 'If the matter is thus, then please send that man away and explain that I am no longer bothered by his despair, for never in my life will I lie with a man. I will tell nobody about my condition, so that people will not say that Ghamra has said goodbye to facing opponents in battle and has started to follow the ways of women.' Her father said: 'Dear daughter, getting rid of this man is a simple matter. I will just send him and his companions away.'[15]

So her father tells Dhū l-Khimār that he is very sorry but his daughter has gone to revenge her brother and marriage is out of the question. Dhū l-Khimār is devastated, but his companions tell him that it is time to forget about the whole affair. So the budding relationship between Ghamra and Dhū l-Khimār prematurely comes to an end.

We may wonder what sort of impression the reaction of Ghamra's father to his daughter's illegitimate pregnancy would have made on an Arab audience. We do not know whether Ghamra told him about her 'dowry', the sword, but the impression is that she simply told him that she had been raped by 'Antar. Her father's reaction, namely that this sort of thing happened to many an Arab girl, also indicates this. Arab fathers are not known for their understanding attitude and leniency towards daughters who have violated, however unwillingly, the family honour. In that context, it is remarkable that Ghamra's father does not seem to worry about the family honour, but just about his daughter's reputation and prominent position. He advises her to murder the baby in order to protect her position.

This attitude may possibly earn him some sympathy and respect with a modern audience, but it is unlikely that this would have been the reaction of a medieval Arab audience. The whole story points in a different direction. Nothing that Fā'iz, the father, does comes across as very impressive according to the Arab code of honour. Worst of all is his cowardliness, which is depicted in shrill contrast to his daughter's intrepid behaviour. In the light of this, his reaction to Ghamra's dishonour may well have earned him the contempt of the (male) audience. This is not certain, however, because a sensitivity to the feelings of women often appears unexpectedly in these popular narratives.

After this, Ghamra disappears from the scene for a long time, and her father plays no further role in the narrative. Many other adventures take place, and (this is a usual pattern) the sequel of Ghamra's story begins when, some 150 pages later, an unknown young black warrior by the name of Ghassūb appears. The narrator soon informs us that this Ghassūb is the son of ʿAntar by Ghamra, and he is referred to as such even before the formal anagnorisis has taken place.[16]

From this point on, the act that led to Ghamra's pregnancy is no longer put in a dubious light by being presented as rape, but is consistently referred to as a marriage. The narrative element of the improvised dowry, the sword, now reveals its purpose: it offers the possibility of presenting Ghassūb as the legitimate offspring of Ghamra and ʿAntar, and giving Ghamra a respectable position. If the story of her rape had been told without this clever narrative precaution, it would have been far more difficult, if not impossible, to let her play a further prominent part in the story as a respected member of the tribe.

The sad fate of Princess Ibrīza (or Abrīza) in another epic, *The Thousand and One Nights* story of King ʿUmar al-Nuʿmān and his two sons, demonstrates that narrators have trouble finding a suitable place in the story for a woman who has given birth to an illegitimate child. She is tainted, even though it may be perfectly obvious that she is the victim of circumstances beyond her control. There are no adequate models available to allow her to continue as a worthy character, and it is easier to let her come to a sad end. That is exactly what happened to Ibrīza, who had been drugged and raped by King ʿUmar, with whom she stayed as a guest invited by his son. Pregnant, she fled away from the court, assisted by a black servant. She gave birth while still on the road, and when, afterwards, she refused the sexual advances of the evil servant, he murdered her. In this way the narrative problem of what role to allot her in the sequel to the story was solved.

This makes the sequel to Ghamra's adventure with ʿAntar, and the narrator's way of dealing with her position as an unmarried mother, all the more interesting. After having introduced Ghassūb, the young black warrior, the narrator fills us in about what has happened to Ghamra and her son since Ghamra told her father about her pregnancy. We are briefly reminded of what happened between her and 'Antar: how he raped her and gave her his sword Sayf al-Riqāb as a dowry, how she found herself pregnant and how her father urged her to keep the matter secret. The story then continues:

> When the time had come for her to give birth and the labour pains that are the fate of women started, she became afraid of the neighbours and other people, and she also started to worry about the malice of enemies and jealous people. She went to a valley and gave birth to this boy in accordance with the command of the All-Knowing, the Hidden.
> When her pains abated and she saw that the baby was a boy, she began to feel tenderness for him. She wrapped him in her cloak, but not before she had seen that he was as masterful as a buffalo, had a skin blacker than ebony, a large head and senses that were quickly alerted. She saw that the corners of his eyes were red, his mouth wide, and that he cried and yelled loudly. He was, in short, the image of his father 'Antar ibn Shaddād. So Ghamra said: 'By this boy countries will be ruled, and if I stay alive till he becomes a knight, I will live all my days under the protection of his sword.'
> She stayed there until the pain of giving birth had disappeared and her strength and endurance had returned. Then she went back to the tribe with the boy on her arm. When her cousins saw her like this, they asked her what had happened. She said: 'I have been roaming far and wide, hunting and looking for prey, fully making use of every opportunity to enjoy myself. I set out for the haunts of the desert spirits [Arabic: *'afarīt*] and there I found this baby in the mouth of a lioness that was looking for its cubs. I killed the lioness and freed the baby, for I wanted to bring him up in order to gain a reward from him and to find solace for not having children.' Her people believed her, because they knew her haughtiness and her dislike of men.
> Ghamra then gave the boy to one of her women servants and ordered her to bring him up and to treat him well. She started to spend a lot of time with him and loved him just as a mother loves her child, until the years passed and he could walk. He began to hit boys stronger than himself and to make growling sounds like a knight on the battleground. His mother thought him quite marvellous and was very pleased when she saw him frown and scowl. She took him with her on her horse when she went out riding and let him watch the jousting of the Arab knights. After she had watched

the field with him, she showed him the tricks of dodging and attacking in combat.[17]

This is an extraordinary passage. Such descriptions of parental involvement in raising a small child and awakening its interests are rare in this kind of literature, indeed in pre-modern literature in general. The usual pattern in popular epic is that the story passes straight on from the mention of birth to the first exploits of the young warrior. In the case of a prominent hero or heroine, attention may be paid to unusual deeds performed in early childhood, but these rarely entail parental coaching. It is more common for a prominent hero to grow up isolated from his parents or neglected by them. In contrast, as Ghassūb grows up, Ghamra teaches him all the arts of combat in which she herself is so accomplished, until he reaches sexual maturity:

> When he was alone with Ghamra, he used to question her: 'My lady, who is my father and who is my mother?' She then answered: 'I do not know who your father and mother are. I freed you from the teeth of a lioness, felt pity on you and brought you up. You are like a son to me, and if it had not been thus I would not have taught you patience and endurance.'[18]

Then Ghamra leaves for an expedition to the land of the black people in order to rob them of their possessions and their women. Ghassūb stays at home. Ghamra has built a separate house for him, and generally bestowed all kinds of generosity on him. Ghassūb becomes a renowned hero, for whom poets compose odes and are amply rewarded. Of course, it is not long before he falls in love. When he goes to his beloved's father to propose, however, the father's answer is that he cannot give his daughter to a man of unknown parentage, and he advises Ghassūb to go to Ghamra

> 'because she is the leader [Arabic: *sayyida*] of this tribe, the one who conducts us and counsels us. Say to her that she must connect you to her parentage and make you part of her noble lineage. Let her testify that you are her son, so that I can marry my daughter to you and firmly include you in my favour.'

To the non-Muslim reader this may look like a simple suggestion that Ghassūb get himself formally adopted. But, given the ban on adoption in Islamic law, it is not very probable that the narrator would imply this, even in a supposedly pre-Islamic context. It is more likely that the narrator wants to indicate that rumours and speculations about the exact relationship between Ghamra and Ghassūb had been circulating for some time, and that the father of Ghassūb's beloved sees this as an opportunity to make Ghamra admit that Ghassūb is her son. Ghamra's reaction certainly confirms this: after Ghassūb has contrived to put her in a good mood by talking to her for a while, impressing her with his accomplished speech, he tells her about his wish to marry and about what happened when he proposed, asking her to connect him to her lineage and to testify that she is his mother. She reacts quite fiercely:

> When Ghamra heard Ghassūb's words, the light on her face turned to darkness. 'You little bastard, how dare you ask such a thing!' she said to him. 'If I had not brought you up I would take my sword to you and leave you as a bunch of decaying bones. Woe to you, child of sin! If I testified that you are my son, no Arab would consider me innocent. The least they would say is: "That woman got him by fornicating with some black slave and has kept silent about him all this time, so that she could first pretend that he was her slave and then state later that he was her son. If this were not the situation she would not have had such a close relationship with him." I know perfectly well that once they were sure about this they would no longer obey me and accept my authority. They would give the power to one of my cousins.' Shouting, she drew her sword at him. He went away and left her with tears in his eyes. She was completely broken hearted for his sake. She did not know what to do, for he was a veritable lion and his heart was stronger than a stone rock, and she could not get into a close relationship with him for fear of enemies and envious people.[19]

Ghassūb clearly has had enough. He no longer wants to stay with the tribe. He decides to leave, joined by a group of his young unmarried friends, and look for adventure on his own. Kidnapping a group of Hijāzī women is one of their first exploits. These women turn out to be accompanied by ʿAntar's brother Shaybūb, and ʿAntar's wife ʿAbla is one of them. ʿAntar, alerted by his brother Shaybūb, frees the captives and wounds the young Ghassūb, who gets away under cover of darkness. In due course, the young intruder's challenge leads to a combat between himself and ʿAntar. Before this takes place, however, ʿAntar has a strange dream: he sees himself fighting the young man, striking him thrice with his sword, but his sword turns back on him and wounds him.[20] Unsettled by the dream, he says to one of his companions that he feels that fate is looming over him.

The combat begins, and it is obvious that Ghassūb is a formidable opponent. The Yemeni people are secretly pleased, thinking that this impressive young warrior may actually be able to kill 'Antar. The fight continues until sunset, and 'Antar feels strangely emotional about his opponent. When he notices that the young man is looking pale from exhaustion, he advises him to withdraw and rest. Ghassūb's insulting retort makes 'Antar angry, but they nevertheless break off the combat in order to have some rest. They are to continue on the following day. The next morning, 'Antar enters the field practically naked, without armour, and they end up wrestling on foot. 'Antar brings the fight to an end by taking Ghassūb in a firm grasp, 'like a father embraces his son'. He carefully puts him down and lightly ties him up. Then they go back to the camp, 'Antar and his brother Shaybūb in front 'leading his son Ghassūb'.[21]

The disappointed Yemenis, who had secretly hoped that Ghassūb would be victorious, beseech 'Antar to release at least the young man, even if he wants to keep all the other prisoners. Then, however, a group of horsemen appears, with Ghamra riding in front.[22] After Ghassūb had left her she had been extremely miserable about the way she had treated him and cast him off. For 'he in any case was her son, something that fate had left her from men'. She feels sick with worry when she thinks what might happen to him. While she is in this mood, she is attacked by a huge army and driven away from her tribal land, accompanied by a thousand horsemen. They ask her where she wants to lead them, but she has no idea: she has lost all her friends and allies, and enemies are everywhere. 'And on top of everything I am not married and have not brought forth a son.'

She considers going to Mecca, to the Holy House, to spend her days there. Her men are very sorry to be parted from her and cry over her misfortune. A number of them, the wealthy, decide to go home, but those with no possessions stay and travel with her to Mecca. There they are recognized by a group of fellow Yemenis, who are delighted to see Princess Ghamra. They tell her about what has happened with 'Antar and Ghassūb. Ghamra feels as if she is in a dream, so astonishing is it all. 'If a baby would hear these things, he would become grey before he was weaned, and it would be written down with golden ink because it is so amazing.'[23]

It is indeed a miracle: after she has been violated by 'Antar and has given birth to the son whom she hoped would be her protector, but who has given her nothing but trouble, the Lord has now guided this son to his father 'Antar, and it looks as if everything is going to end well. Ghamra and her son will be able to live with 'Antar's tribe, and she will find consolation for the loss of her home and country, 'after I have made my affair public and I no longer have to worry about keeping silent'.

First, however, things have to be sorted out between 'Antar and herself, and preferably in such a way that she does not lose prestige. She considers several scenarios. First she approaches 'Antar on the battlefield where he is jousting with his friends, and asks him by messenger whether he is prepared to fight her and her men as soon as their reinforcements have arrived. She asks the messenger not to reveal her identity to 'Antar, 'so that he will not see me as someone of little importance. Better say to him: "This is one of the famous champions, a well-known knight from the land of Yemen [...], whose name is Mubādir ibn Jabbār, knight of the sea coasts."' Her request is granted: 'Antar says that tomorrow they will wipe them out and scatter them.[24]

Here Ghamra seems to lack the confidence to present herself as a female warrior. It is, of course, not without reason. For while her gender has never put her at a disadvantage in combats with other champions, her femininity, and ensuing lack of physical endurance, was stressed by the narrator during her earlier encounter with 'Antar. Moreover, 'Antar's discovery that she was a girl incited him to overwhelm her with brute force and to treat her most dishonourably. The sequel shows that on consideration, she does not even feel up to combat with him in male disguise, and she decides to avoid a martial confrontation with him altogether. She is clearly in a state of emotional turmoil concerning him.

Ghamra then has second thoughts about engaging in battle with 'Antar. She considers using the captives whom they still have as a lever to get Ghassūb released. Finally, however, she simply decides to tell her men everything, and then it is up to them whether they turn away from her or not. So she tells them that Ghassūb is actually her son and that 'Antar is his father, and how this came about, and how 'Antar 'was not allowed to come near me until he had given me Sayf al-Riqāb (Sword of the Necks) as a dowry, taking the Lord of Lords as his witness that he had married me'. She intends to tell 'Antar and Ghassūb personally about their relationship, hoping that she can then take up residence among 'Antar's tribe as a respectable woman.[25]

An interesting detail here is the new element in her account of what happened between her and 'Antar: she introduces his explicit statement that he took her as his wife, with God as witness. Clearly, the bridal gift of the sword was not a sufficient guarantee that she would be accepted as 'Antar's lawful wife.

Her companions are highly surprised and full of admiration for the way she has handled the whole affair. They decide to release the captives and send them back to 'Antar in order to tell him that Ghassūb is his son and that Ghamra is Ghassūb's mother.

'Antar is overjoyed. Then Ghamra appears with her companions. She shouts to 'Antar that he is a lucky man indeed to have this happening to him after their previous miserable meeting. 'Antar agrees. 'Then they embraced so closely and tightly that they became like indistinct shapes without souls. They wept tears of joy and happiness, and when they parted she said to him: "Unite me with my son before morning, for I have had enough of the separation and have experienced enough misery."' 'Antar's brother Shaybūb is sent to go and fetch Ghassūb. When he hears from Shaybūb who his parents are, Ghassūb is at first very angry about the way he has been treated by Ghamra and threatens to kill her. Shaybūb, clever man that he is, calms him down, explaining why Ghamra had no other choice if she did not want to run the risk of losing her authority over the tribe. Then they mount and go to Ghamra, who 'rushed towards him, pressed him to her breast and kissed him between his eyes. Then 'Antar, too, approached and pressed him to his breast, kissing his cheeks and throat and saying: "My son, this was of course the reason why I was overcome by pity for you!"'[26]

So Ghassūb is happily united with his parents, Ghamra is acknowledged as 'Antar's wife, and from now on Ghassūb and Ghamra form part of the tribe of 'Abs. This leaves just one little problem for 'Antar to solve: he has to defend his behaviour to his wife 'Abla, who is far from pleased when she hears about this newly discovered wife of his. 'Antar soothingly says that of course he has never preferred any woman over 'Abla, but, as a man of honour, he also has to do his duty by Ghamra and Ghassūb: it would be unacceptable to send them away and let them seek refuge with someone else. And just in case 'Abla is afraid that Ghamra and 'Antar will start to have an intimate relationship, there will be no question of that happening. Ghamra is much too nice a woman for that. 'Then he joked a bit with her. She began to laugh, and her heart was set at rest.'[27]

From then on, Ghassūb and Ghamra habitually take part in the expeditions and forays of the tribe. One of these adventures involves an expedition to Ethiopia, and there they discover the family of Ghamra's mother. An amulet given by Ghamra to Ghassūb, which he wears on his sword, reveals that Ghamra's mother was the sister of the Ethiopian king, who wears the twin of the amulet on his shoulder: they slot into each other 'like male and female'.[28]

On the way home from this expedition, Ghamra falls ill and dies. 'They buried her in her land. Her son Ghassūb wept over her and they kept seven days of mourning.'[29] We notice that it is Ghassūb who weeps: we hear nothing about 'Antar, although he also forms part of the company. In a way, it illustrates that Ghamra's story is basically the story of Ghamra and Ghassūb, and not that of Ghamra and 'Antar.

Then the warriors travel on, homeward bound. Just a few lines after the account of Ghamra's burial, we read about 'Antar expressing his longing for 'Abla in a song. He is much admired by his companions.

CHAPTER 7

Warrior Women in Sīrat ʿAntara 2: Hayfāʾ, Zarqāʾ and ʿUnaytira[1]

Protagonists

- Abjar, ʿAntar's horse
- ʿAbla, cousin and wife of ʿAntar
- ʿĀmir ibn Tufayl, marries ʿAbla after ʿAntar's death and kills her
- ʿAmr, brother of ʿAbla, son of Mālik
- ʿAmr, son of Umayya and Khudhrūf
- ʿAmr Dhū l-Kalb, Arab chief, brother of Hayfāʾ
- ʿAntar ibn Shaddād, Arab champion, eponymous hero of the *sīra*
- Asad al-Falā, grandson of Zarqāʾ
- Banū ʿAbs, tribe to which ʿAntar belongs
- Banū Qudāʿa, Bedouin tribe
- Battāl, Abū Muhammad al-Battāl, trickster hero in *Dhāt al-Himma*
- Dhū l-Kalb, see ʿAmr Dhū l-Kalb
- Dhū l-Khimār, see Sabīʿ Dhū l-Khimār
- Durayd, chief of the Banū Hawāzin
- Ghadanfar, son of the Roman princess Maryam and ʿAntar
- Gushasp, daughter of Rustam in the Persian *Shāhnāme*
- Hayfāʾ, sister of ʿAmr Dhū l-Kalb, marries ʿAntar
- Hubal, major deity of the pre-Islamic pagan pantheon
- Jūfrān, son of the Byzantine girl Maryam and ʿAntar
- Kabsha, sister of ʿĀmir ibn Tufayl
- Khudhrūf, cousin and husband of ʿUnaytira
- Khusrau Anūshirwān, Sassanid king

- Kūbart, Frankish king, marries the Byzantine girl Maryam, stepfather of Jūfrān
- Mālik, father of 'Abla
- Maryam, Byzantine girl, has an affair with 'Antar
- Maryam, sister of the king of Rome, marries 'Antar
- Mundhir ibn al-Nu'mān, Arab king
- Mutana'jiz, brother of Ghamra the daughter of Fā'iz
- Nuzhat al-Zamān, sister and wife of Sharkān
- Qays, Arab king
- Rabī', brother of 'Umāra, enemy of 'Antar
- Sabī' Dhū l-Khimār, Arab champion, nephew of Zarqā'
- Sharkān, son of King 'Umar [ibn] al-Nu'mān
- Shaybūb, brother of 'Antar
- 'Umāra, brother of Rabī', enemy of 'Antar
- Umayya, first wife of Khudhrūf, the husband of 'Unaytira
- 'Unaytira, daughter of Hayfā' and 'Antar
- 'Utayba, chief of the Banū Fazāra
- Wizr, enemy of 'Antar
- Zarqā', Arab warrior woman, aunt of Sabī' Dhū l-Khimār
- Zuhayr, chief of the Banū 'Abs

Three redoubtable warrior women figure in the last part of *The Adventures of 'Antar*: Hayfā', Zarqā'² and 'Unaytira, of whom 'Unaytira is by far the most important. She is 'Antar's daughter, born posthumously, and the narrative bestows full heroic status on her. The narrator provides her with all the attributes that indicate a major hero: unusual circumstances of birth; precocious physical strength; remarkable feats performed in early youth, usually involving a fight with a lion; defeating a major enemy early on; and obtaining a famous sword. She has a supportive helper of sorts in the person of her uncle Dhū l-Kalb, who, when first introduced into the narrative, reveals the sort of outrageous behaviour characteristic of the 'man of wiles', the traditional 'helper' of the hero in Arabian epic. 'Unaytira's subsequent career offers us a female version of the 'heroic cycle' as described by Peter Heath in *The Thirsty Sword*.³

Few female heroes in popular epic have been granted such a full heroic cycle. In this respect, 'Unaytira resembles Princess Dhāt al-Himma, and also because, as in the case of Dhāt al-Himma, motherhood is an essential part of 'Unaytira's career, in spite of the fact that both are reluctant to marry. Dhāt al-Himma, early in her career, is trapped into a marriage of sorts by her hated cousin and subsequently bears a son. 'Unaytira is ordered by the Prophet Muhammad to marry her cousin, with whom she is on good terms, and produces five brave warrior sons as a result.[4]

In a way, this last part is a small epic or *sīra* of its own, featuring 'Unaytira as the leading heroine. This phenomenon, a daughter following in her father's steps, is less rare than one might think. Battāl, the trickster hero in *The Adventures of Princess Dhāt al-Himma*, begets a daughter who plays a role fully worthy of her heritage in the last part of the cycle. Gushasp, the daughter of Rustam, major hero of the Persian *Shāhnāme*, has a small epic of her own. This is the *Gushaspnāme*, one of the many offshoots of the *Shāhnāme* circulating in the Persian narrative tradition.

In the case of *The Adventures of 'Antar*, a particularly significant aspect of the last volume is that the Prophet Muhammad makes an appearance in person.[5] The preceding part of the *sīra* is largely situated in a pre-Islamic background, a fact that is often emphasized by reference to un-Islamic customs such as 'Antar's frequent wine-drinking or the worship of pagan deities at the Ka'ba in Mecca. References to Islam and to the Prophet occur with increasing frequency in the later volumes, but, as a whole, the fiction of a pre-Islamic setting is maintained. In this last part, news of the emergence of a prophet with a new religious message in Mecca starts to spread widely among the tribes, and, one after another, they swear allegiance to Muhammad and convert to Islam. In the end, 'Unaytira will also become a staunch warrior in the service of Islam. Thus, in a way, she Islamizes the *sīra* as a whole, ensuring all her father's heroic deeds and adventures eventually lead to furthering the cause of Islam.

Hayfā'

'Unaytira's story starts with Hayfā', her mother. Hayfā' is the sister of 'Amr Dhū l-Kalb, leader of the Banū Qudā'a. His name, meaning 'he of the dog', refers to one of the strange ways in which he used to deal with the Arabs 'because of his tremendous pride and ignorance'. It started when his brother, a fierce hunter who had killed countless beasts of prey, usually with his bare hands and teeth, was killed by a lion. In revenge, 'Amr not only killed the lion but also vowed to slaughter a hundred more on his brother's grave. This gained him such a reputation that people started to bring their possessions to him for safekeeping. He then dressed up a hound in costly attire and gave orders for the animal to be carried around among the tribes, saying: "'This is the dog of 'Amr ibn

Jalhama of the Banū Qudā'a! He has made it the guardian of all the tribes from Syria to the Hijāz and Yemen, and also Iraq. None of you needs to fear for his possessions and children as long as the like of this dog remains your guardian.'" Everybody then hastened to come and pay him homage (whether to the dog or 'Amr himself is unclear from the Arabic text), and, in the end, the Arabs started to refer to 'Amr as Dhū l-Kalb, 'he of the dog'. It was under this somewhat embarrassing name that he became known among the tribes.[6]

This curious character had a sister by the name of Hayfā', whom he had trained in all the martial arts.[7] She grew up to be a redoubtable warrior, and did not hesitate to go out on her own to kill and plunder. She had a very handsome cousin, and, when he looked at her one day, 'she hit him with arrows from the bows of her eyebrows', as the narrator says, using a familiar poetic metaphor. Completely smitten, he recited a poem expressing his love. This made her furious: who did he think he was, treating her in such a stupid and ill-mannered fashion? Her reaction may surprise us, but in traditional Arab culture, as in many others, composing love songs for a free and respectable woman is considered unacceptable because it will give her a bad name.

The poor young man confessed his love for her, speaking of a possible union between them. Exploding with anger, she grabbed him by the neck and the feet, and beat him to death against the ground. The result is graphically described. Having completed the act, she recited a poem of her own in which she boasted that she was not a secluded woman, but a brave lioness. Thus, in this case, the young woman is especially vexed because she does not want to be treated as a conventional girl just waiting for marriage. The event gained her a fearsome reputation, and from then on she was known as Hayfā' Qannāsat al-Rijāl, Hayfā' the Huntress (or Catcher) of Men.

Following a battle between Dhū l-Kalb and a group whose leader, insulted by the offer of protection by 'the dog', has cut off the poor animal's ears, 'Antar comes across 'Amr Dhū l-Kalb. 'Amr calls 'Antar '"the killer of my cousin Mutana'jiz"', and this connects the story to that of 'Antar and Ghamra told in the previous chapter, for this Mutana'jiz was the brother of Ghamra, the daughter of Fā'iz. A combat between 'Antar and Dhū l-Kalb is inevitable, but, when it is over, friendship between their respective tribes, 'Amr's Banū Qudā'a and 'Antar's Banū 'Abs, is restored and they decide to remain allies. Eventually, 'Antar and Dhū l-Kalb will become very close friends, 'Antar finding solace in this friendship for the loss of his brother Shaybūb, whose death had occurred shortly beforehand.

In this way, Hayfā' gets to meet 'Antar's wife 'Abla and they become very close: 'They were like two souls in one body.'[8] They talk together a great deal, 'Abla telling Hayfā' about everything she has had to endure in the way of captivity and contempt, being dragged from one place to another, and all the hardship that 'Antar has had to deal with for her sake and the many brave opponents he has killed. Hayfā' is fascinated. She tries to comfort 'Abla with soothing words, 'like a mother does with her child'. 'Abla continues with further stories about the exploits of the Banū 'Abs, and about her enemy Rabī' who did such terrible things to her, intending to kill her and bury her in the sands.

In the middle of this, 'Abla's brother (also named 'Amr) comes in, weeping and deeply upset. 'Abla kisses him between the eyes and asks what can be the matter. It seems that Rabī' and his brother 'Umāra have been making mischief again, saying terrible things about 'Antar and suggesting that 'Abla will soon become a slave.[9] Were it not for fear of causing strife within the tribe, 'Amr would have killed them. 'Abla is very miserable and collapses in tears, while her brother leaves. Hayfā' is shocked, and complains to her brother Dhū l-Kalb about 'Antar's lukewarm reaction to these people's awful slander: if 'Abla had been of her kin, she would have acted as she had done with her cousin! Dhū l-Kalb tries to calm her, pointing out that they have to go along with 'Antar's judgement about what is best for the tribe.[10] Rabī' and 'Umāra continue their disgusting behaviour, while 'Antar tries to remain patient. At some point, Hayfā' offers to kill them in vengeance for what they have said about 'Abla. Of course, 'Antar cannot accept this generous offer. In the end he kills them himself, having overheard them plotting his death during a banquet given by King Qays.[11]

'Abla is in tears when she hears what has happened, afraid of what will happen to 'Antar. King Qays, dismayed, lets 'Antar know that either he or 'Antar will have to leave the tribe, and 'Antar decides to go and settle near the Euphrates. Dhū l-Kalb and Hayfā' accompany him. It is during this time that 'Antar approaches Dhū l-Kalb with the suggestion that he marry Hayfā'. Dhū l-Kalb consults his sister, who accepts the proposal with delight. The wedding soon takes place, and the celebrations continue for seven days. 'Abla is kept completely in the dark. As from his wedding night, 'Antar establishes a routine of staying with Hayfā' for most of the night and then going to 'Abla early in the morning. It works perfectly and 'Abla has no idea what is going on. The two women continue to meet as before, being 'like two souls in one body'. So much for female solidarity, at least according to the narrator's views.

Soon afterwards, Hayfā' and 'Abla have to say goodbye to 'Antar, for new adventures await him. These involve a visit to Rome, where 'Antar's assistance is required to defend the city against the Franks. He kills the Frankish king and so puts an end to the siege of Rome, which, by that time, had already lasted nine months. The ruler of Rome, a nephew of the Byzantine emperor, is so grateful that he insists on 'Antar's marrying his sister. Her name is Maryam, which is somewhat confusing, for, during an earlier visit to Constantinople, 'Antar had a relationship with a girl also called Maryam. 'Antar hesitates to accept the offer, but finally consents and stays on in Rome for a couple of months with his new wife. Then he wants to return home. Foreseeing trouble with 'Abla and Hayfā' when he brings home a new wife, he suggests leaving Maryam behind and coming to visit her every once in a while. The idea does not appeal to her so he takes her with him, making a detour to Constantinople. There he leaves Maryam with her uncle and departs, 'for he longed for 'Abla'.[12] As we will see later on, both Maryams give birth to sons of 'Antar who will make their appearance after his death.

The narrative tells us that 'Antar spent another seven years near the Euphrates after coming home from his expedition to Rome. To the reader who is not familiar with this type of literature, the chronology of these narratives is often baffling, and one certainly should not attempt to establish a chronologically plausible sequence of events on the basis of occasional specifications of time and age. The treatment of time and space in epic literature follows rules of its own. The aging of characters is rarely taken into account, and a leading hero may be just as vigorous a warrior with his married grandchildren in tow as he was in the days of his youth. Durayd, one of the leading tribal chiefs in *The Adventures of 'Antar*, is reported to be 500 years old during the events involving 'Amr Dhū l-Kalb and his sister Hayfā', but he is as active as ever and his authority remains unchallenged.

At the end of the period spent near the Euphrates, 'Antar is wounded by an arrow, shot by his blind enemy Wizr. The wound is not immediately fatal, but its effects slowly kill him over a prolonged period of time.[13] 'Abla, who realizes that he is not long for this world, is deeply upset and looks after him as well as she can. To confuse his enemies she even rides his famous horse Abjar, while he takes her *howdah*. Only when he is about to die does he manage to get up on his horse again, and long after he has passed away his enemies see him from afar, sitting on Abjar's back, blocking their path even after death.

As mentioned in the previous chapter, 'Abla married again after 'Antar's death and made the life of her new husband a misery, constantly comparing him with 'Antar and deriding him so much that finally he saw no other way to save his honour than to have her killed. As to Hayfā', before 'Antar died he gave instructions that money should be given to '"my wife Qannāsat al-Rijāl"', saying that he was sure that after his death nobody would take pity on her or help her. So he entrusted her to the care of her brother Dhū l-Kalb,[14] and, after 'Antar's death, Hayfā' and Dhū l-Kalb went away together, accompanied by the other members of the Banū Qudā'a.

'Unaytira

Sometime later, Hayfā' gives birth to a daughter 'as black as the night'.[15] She is the image of her father 'Antar. At her brother's suggestion, Hayfā' calls the child 'Unaytira, 'Little girl 'Antar'. They hope that she may grow up just as strong and brave as 'Antar, and gain a similar reputation. They bring her up with great love and care. When she is five years old she can wrestle down dogs and wolves and shoot arrows at the servants. From this age on she adopts the habit of wrapping a turban and a veil around her head when she goes out, and everybody but her close relatives thinks that she is a boy. Covering one's face, as we will see, is not an exclusively female habit: it was done by men as well.

When 'Unaytira is ten years old, her mother and her uncle take her along to the battleground and start teaching her the art of combat. She soon excels in it, and from then on she habitually rides out every morning with some of the men. She grows up thinking that Dhū l-Kalb is her father, and her mother and uncle leave everyone under that impression.

This is one of the improbable situations that regularly crop up in popular epic, together with other inconsistencies. How could the girl, once she was past early childhood, continue to think that Dhū l-Kalb was her father, while also being aware of the fact that Dhū l-Kalb and her mother Hayfā' were brother and sister? And, even more improbable, how could the other members of the tribe go along with this idea? Apparently the audience did not see a problem here, although they might have balked at the idea of an actual incestuous relationship between brother and sister. Such a case occurs in another epic, *The Story of King 'Umar al-Nu'mān and His Sons Sharkān and Dā'u l-makān*. This short epic has been included in *Thousand and One Nights*. At some point, Prince Sharkān discovers that he is married to his own sister, Nuzhat al-Zamān. They are deeply shocked, especially as she has just given birth to a daughter. He decides that the best way to cover things up is to marry her to his chamberlain.[16] Incestuous relations, mostly father–daughter relations, also occur in other popular epics, but then the context is usually Iranian and pre-Islamic, so it does not need to worry the Arab audience.[17]

It will be quite a while before 'Unaytira finds out who her real father is. By then she will already have fully established her reputation as a warrior princess.[18]

Returning to the start of her career, one day her mother and uncle, with five thousand horsemen, decide to go on an expedition to Yemen and attack the Himyarī tribe. 'Unaytira, then fifteen years old, is allowed to join them. Fifteen years old may seem very young to us, but in Arabic storytelling and poetry it signifies the acme of physical development and beauty. Comparison is often made to the moon, which reaches its fullness on the fourteenth day.

Soon after they have started out, an opportunity arises for 'Unaytira to show her valour and strength: a huge lion approaches, and while Dhū l-Kalb is still getting ready to deal with it, 'Unaytira rushes forward and attacks it. A classic lion fight scene follows,[19] in which 'Unaytira attacks the lion on foot and finally cleaves it asunder with her sword. The sword, we are told, is a very special sword: it was one of the very best, forged from lightning and presented to 'Antar by one of the kings of the Amalekites. 'Antar had given it to Dhū l-Kalb in the days of their friendship, and he in turn had given it to 'Unaytira. Her uncle is deeply impressed by what she has done, and she constantly reminds him of her father 'Antar.

So 'Unaytira has now bravely killed a fierce lion, she is equipped with an extraordinary type of sword and has demonstrated that she knows how to use it. It is clear that the narrative is launching her on a fully fledged heroic career. This is confirmed in the next part of the episode. They arrive in Yemen, in the region of San'a, and are amazed to see how fertile and prosperous the area is. It all belongs to Zarqā', the aunt of Sabī' the Himyarite. This Sabī' is better known to us as Dhū l-Khimār, the one-time suitor of Ghamra, the daughter of Fā'iz, mentioned in the previous chapter.

The Banū Qudā'a advance, 'Unaytira riding in front 'like a fierce lion', followed by her uncle and her mother Hayfā' with a crowd of others. Soon they are confronted by an impressive-looking young man whose face is covered by a veil. When he pulls it away, 'he is like the full moon, beautiful of stature and with a smile on his face'. He turns out to be Asad al-Falā, Zarqā''s grandson. He loudly challenges the advancing Banū Qudāʿa, asking them whether they have come to plunder the land of the respectable mistress of the Himyari tribe, Queen Zarqā'? 'Unaytira responds to his challenge and, as is customary in conflicts between Arab tribes, they start exchanging insults and boastful verses. A combat then follows and, when the dust clears, Asad al-Falā lies dead on the ground. One after another, 25 more champions engage in combat with 'Unaytira and she kills them all.[20]

Of course, all this cannot fail to bring out Queen Zarqāʾ, Asad al-Falā's grandmother. She is a famous warrior woman herself, 'the horse-woman of her time and the unique pearl of the age',[21] and she arrives with several thousand horsemen. When she sees how 'Unaytira and her uncle rage among the Himyarīs she cries out in anger, saying that she will show them what Queen Zarqāʾ is worth. The two armies approach. 'Unaytira, her uncle and mother close behind, is still battling in front, 'dealing with the Banū Himyar in a way that her father ʿAntar could not have achieved in his early youth'.[22]

After Zarqāʾ has been captured with fifteen hundred of her men her tribe is soon defeated and the Banū Qudāʿa are free to rob and plunder to their hearts' content. When they are done, the scattered remnants of the Himyarī tribe return to their homeland. The sight that awaits them is described in a classical Arabic literary manner: they see 'ravens croaking in their houses and wild animals grazing on their hill, sated by their masters' flesh. The whole area was a deserted wasteland, the abode of owls and ravens, not a living soul going about in it, and their dwelling places were places of ignominy.'[23]

Meanwhile, insulting words and verses are being exchanged between 'Unaytira and the captive Zarqāʾ. Among other things, 'Unaytira boasts that Zarqāʾ has been captured by 'a little young maid of the Arab warrior girls, a maid who yet is a chief of the Banū Qudāʿa by her nobility and descent. Her father subdued the chiefs of the Arabs, the Persians and the Daylamites [...]. He is ʿAmr Dhū l-Kalb, the fierce one.' Zarqāʾ, addressing 'Unaytira with appropriate courtesy, asks her to send a message to her family in order to arrange a ransom.

Meanwhile, the news of his aunt's capture and of the death of her grandson has reached Dhū l-Khimār. '"Who is the Arab king who has managed to capture my aunt?"' he asks. The answer is that she has not been taken prisoner by a man, but by 'Unaytira, the daughter of ʿAmr Dhū l-Kalb. They have heard that his aunt has been put between four ploughshares and is treated very cruelly. Of course, he immediately sets out for revenge, joined by his tribe. Travelling through areas that are familiar to him from earlier days, he is reminded of ʿAntar, and also ponders that Hubal the Most High (the major deity of the pre-Islamic pagan pantheon) may have thrown him again into the hands of a woman like this ʿUnaytira, who clearly is just such a calamity as Ghamra the daughter of Fāʾiz.[24]

They soon locate ʿUnaytira and her men. ʿUnaytira's status among her tribe has clearly risen significantly since her last exploits, and so has her reputation. Even among the Banū ʿAbs, ʿAntar's tribe, the rumour has spread that a redoubtable knight (the male form is used) by the name of ʿUnaytira has manifested himself among the Banū Qudāʿa. Why this intriguing name, 'Little ʿAntar'? They suggest that Dhū l-Kalb had given the boy this name because of his close attachment to ʿAntar.

ʿUnaytira is now sometimes addressed as *malika*, queen, and is regularly designated with the honorific Umm al-Zaʿāziʿ, Mother of Tempests.[25] She is not impressed at all by the sight of Sabīʿ Dhū l-Khimār approaching with his ten thousand horsemen: 'She bowed her head over her saddlebow and attacked, with a heart harder than stone and a soul swelling faster than the tide of the sea when it rises.'

The two parties meet and the usual torrent of insulting words and verses is launched. A brave young man of ʿUnaytira's tribe comes forward and confronts Dhū l-Khimār, asking him who he thinks he is, daring to come and fight ʿUnaytira, 'mistress of the brave, Mother of Tempests, lioness roaming the sites, about the like of whom nobody has ever heard?' He charges and attacks Dhū l-Khimār 'like a roaring lion'. He is soon defeated and taken captive. Then Dhū l-Khimār takes on ʿAmr Dhū l-Kalb himself, ʿUnaytira's presumed father. Others also engage in battle and, in the words of the narrator, to cut a long story short, the fighting just went on and on. ʿUnaytira herself is dying for an opportunity to fight Dhū l-Khimār, with whom she is much impressed. Finally she manages to engage him in combat. They fiercely attack each other but Dhū l-Khimār's horse stumbles, he falls and ʿUnaytira takes him captive. He is tied up next to his aunt Zarqāʾ.[26]

Word of all this reaches King Mundhir ibn al-Nuʿmān, head of the Arab tribes and representative of Khusrau Anūshirwān, the king of Persia. He decides to go to the Banū Qudāʿa with a large number of tribes. They set up camp in the area, and he sends a message to "ʿUnaytira the daughter of Dhū l-Kalb', telling her in no uncertain terms that she should stop acting the way she has been doing, capturing respectable heroes, otherwise they are going to devastate the lands of her tribe. She is unimpressed, and a battle ensues in which King Mundhir himself is taken captive. She addresses him in the rudest of terms: "'By the buttocks [American English might be more appropriate here: By the ass] of your mother and the mother of your father Nuʿmān, and the buttocks of Khusrau Anūshirwān and all the Arabs and kings of Khurasān, I will not stop fighting all the Arabs and all other people until I have taken possession of all the lands!'" Then ʿUnaytira sets out for home with her companions and all the captives, while the defeated parties flee the area as fast as possible.[27]

When Zuhayr, chief of the Banū ʿAbs, and ʿUtayba, chief of the Banū Fazāra, hear what has happened, they are deeply shocked. They are close associates of King Mundhir. They decide to seek ʿAmr Dhū l-Kalb, the chief of the Banū Qudāʿa, who is an old friend of theirs; their friendship dates back to the time of ʿAntar. When they arrive, the matter is soon settled. Dhū l-Kalb kisses the earth in front of Zuhayr, fondly remembering the days of ʿAntar. His tears flow freely, and his sister Hayfāʾ reacts in the same way. ʿUnaytira is speechless when she sees how her 'parents' behave to Zuhayr. Before long, Dhū l-Kalb tells her that these are the Banū ʿAbs, the family of her father ʿAntar. She is totally confused: "'Father, I see that you are denying my parentage! Are you not my father and is this not my mother?" [...] "Yes, ʿUnaytira, you are right, Hayfāʾ here is your mother, and I am your uncle. As to your father, he is ʿAntar ibn Shaddād of the excellent Banū ʿAbs, knight of the horsemen's charge and hero of the sword fight, and these are your cousins of the Banū ʿAbs, good and generous people.'"[28]

So it all ends well. Once ʿUnaytira has absorbed the astonishing news, she dismounts and greets the newcomers with the utmost courtesy. All the captives are released. Dhū l-Khimār is moved to tears when he hears that ʿUnaytira is ʿAntar's daughter, and he recounts to her all that happened between her father and himself. Finally they all ask ʿUnaytira's permission to depart, including Zarqāʾ, who does not want to be separated from her brave nephew Dhū l-Khimār. Zuhayr and his men are persuaded to stay with ʿUnaytira and her uncle, and a feast is prepared in their honour.[29] Then they hold a council and ʿUnaytira proposes to launch a campaign against the Arab tribes to punish them for all the harm they did after ʿAntar's death. They agree on this and decide to join forces. Thus begins a new series of adventures in which ʿUnaytira plays a prominent role and her mother and uncle are also in evidence.

Their first target are the Banū 'Āmir, the tribe to which 'Āmir ibn Tufayl belonged, the man who married 'Antar's widow 'Abla and who had her killed in exasperation. In due course they do indeed encounter him, accompanied by other members of his tribe, and, in a battle lasting for days, he is captured and treated harshly. Revenge also extends to his family:

> Then 'Unaytira entered the houses of 'Āmir ibn Tufayl. She and her men took all the goods that were there as spoils. She also took his mother Kabsha and his sister captive and subjected them to humiliation, thus taking revenge for her uncle Mālik, his son 'Amr and his daughter 'Abla. She also took everything that remained of 'Abla's possessions, and informed her men about this. Zuhayr ibn Qays rejoiced about what she had done. She took from him the armour that had belonged to her father 'Antar. Among it were his spiked[30] armour plate and his razor-sharp sword, al-Zāmi' ('the Thirsty'). She also took the horses that had belonged to him. Not one of them was missing except Abjar, because, as we have told, he had broken away when 'Antar fell from his back and had started to roam wild in the lonely desert. 'Abla had taken these things with her when 'Āmir married her, as 'Antar had ordered her to do.[31]

Here we see another example of the way epic literature deals with time: the passing of time hardly affects the physical condition of the creatures involved, human or otherwise. In an ordinary sequence of events, 'Antar's horses would by now have been very long in the tooth and more than likely dead. 'Unaytira, after all, had not even been born when her father died. As to 'Antar's famous sword, as we will see later, 'Unaytira will not keep this but hand it over to her half-brother. She herself had already been endowed with one of 'Antar's swords when she first established her heroic status.

When the battle is over, 'Unaytira summons all the Arabs and receives them most hospitably. It is clear that she has now fully established her authority and is accepted as her father's successor:

> The Arab chiefs talked about nothing but 'Unaytira, about the courage she had demonstrated, her strength, generosity and excellent character. "Unaytira has brought the reputation of the Banū 'Abs to life again after they had become like a thing of the past,' they said. 'Now that someone like her has appeared, their reputation is no longer dead. Did she not capture a number of knights and chiefs, such

as Dhū l-Khimār and his aunt Zarqā', and throw them down when they confronted each other in battle? She also killed Zarqā's grandson Asad al-Falā and made him vanish into nothingness.'

They kindly request her to release 'Āmir ibn Tufayl and she reacts with alacrity, bestowing upon him a robe of honour and inviting him to the gathering. He leaves soon afterwards and will come to a bad end. He starts plotting the murder of the new prophet, Muhammad, but is killed by a huge tumour in his neck that God has sent to him as a punishment.[32]

Now that 'Unaytira's relations with her father's tribe have been properly settled, we come to the last and most significant part of her story. For now that she has been acknowledged as 'Antar's heir, it falls upon her to revenge him in full. However, she will not have to do so alone. News arrives that a Byzantine leader who presents himself as Ghadanfar, the son of Queen Maryam, has made an appearance.[33] This Ghadanfar has grown up in Constantinople at the court of the emperor. His mother is Queen Maryam, the emperor's niece. Her uncle had become very fond of the strong, dark-skinned boy to whom she had given birth. This, as we know, happened after her husband 'Antar had left her at her uncle's court.[34] When the boy had grown up, his uncle put him in charge of one of the border fortresses.

During one of his forays he raids King Mundhir's delegation to Khusrau Anūshirwān, capturing the tribute that they were carrying. King Mundhir appeals to 'Unaytira for assistance. She agrees and the tribe sets out to deal with Ghadanfar. The usual battles and skirmishes ensue, and, in a final combat between Ghadanfar and herself, she 'Unaytira takes him captive, placing the strap of her sword on his neck as a sign of his utter humiliation. During the subsequent celebrations she has him brought out, looking miserable, and proposes to kill him. She draws her sword, but 'her heart refused to obey her'. She does not understand what is holding her back.[35]

To the audience, the signs are obvious: such qualms announce that a moment of anagnorisis is near. And indeed, when his mother Maryam is summoned to arrange his ransom, she is struck by the resemblance between 'Unaytira and Ghadanfar, and tells Ghadanfar that they are brother and sister, his father being 'Antar. 'Antar married Maryam when he was in Rome and left her with her uncle in Constantinople on his way back. Everybody is very much moved. Eventually, 'Unaytira will hand over 'Antar's armour and his legendary sword al-Zāmi' to Ghadanfar, who will use them in battle.[36]

Joint adventures follow. Soon there is a repeat of the previous event: a new threat announces itself in the form of a Frankish knight approaching Damascus. His name is Jūfrān. He, too, is accompanied on his campaign by his mother, who is also called Maryam. He is a very redoubtable warrior, and not only manages to capture a number of the Arab champions, but also Ghadanfar and 'Unaytira themselves. Even Duraid, the venerable chief of the Banū Hawāzin (reported to be 500 years old), is taken prisoner. Dhū l-Kalb and his sister Hayfā' battle on, Hayfā' astonishing even the bravest warriors by her courage and the feats she performs.[37]

Worried about the fate that awaits the captives, 'Unaytira's cousin Khudhrūf goes to Jūfrān's camp in disguise, hoping to free them. The plan goes wrong when Ghadanfar naively says that this is his cousin. Then Maryam, King Jūfrān's mother, appears and, upon hearing that some of them belong to the tribe of 'Abs, she becomes very interested. She starts talking to them, asking what has happened to 'Antar and to 'Abla. They tell her about the fate that has befallen them. She is excited to hear that 'Unaytira and Ghadanfar are 'Antar's children, and promises that she will see to it that they are released.[38]

That night, King Jūfrān has a dream that upsets him. Nobody is able to interpret it, which makes him very angry. At last, an old monk suggests bringing out the captives because they may be able to explain the dream. The chamberlain goes to fetch them. Meanwhile, Ghadanfar has also had a dream, which has been interpreted by old Duraid: Ghadanfar will soon meet a brother. How could that be possible? Khudhrūf, his cousin, says angrily that his mother Maryam might have married someone else and produced a son. Ghadanfar finds this remark shocking. Khudhrūf grows angrier and continues: "'Maybe this king Jūfrān is your brother! One of the women of your father 'Antar may have become pregnant by him! I should consider this possibility, for he resembles you in appearance, colour, stature and shape of body.'" Old Duraid, looking at Jūfrān, says that he is indeed the spitting image of Ghadanfar.[39]

Duraid is then asked to explain Jūfrān's dream and tells him that the dream announces that he will soon meet a brother with just such an army as his own. Jūfrān replies that this is impossible: "'Dear shaykh, my father is dead and my mother has never remarried.'" Irritated, the king is about to cut off their heads. Just in time his mother arrives, telling him to stop, for these people are his own kin. Then she explains the whole history of her brief relationship with 'Antar, her pregnancy, 'Antar's plan to kill her, his departure and her marriage to the Frankish knight Kūbart. Kūbart was unhappy when she bore a black child and proposed to kill the baby. Seeing Maryam's misery, however, he decided to let her keep it. After Kūbart died she brought up her son by herself.

Khudhrūf, 'Antar's nephew, is asked to confirm the story because he had accompanied 'Antar on his visit to Constantinople together with his father Shaybūb, 'Antar's brother. He says that it is all true, and that 'Antar had wanted to kill Maryam because he did not like the idea of a son of his growing up among the Franks. Khudhrūf is asked to pick the real Maryam from a line-up of women and says she is not among them. Then the real Maryam is brought out and recognized immediately. A poison-detecting bead once given by Maryam to 'Antar and now carried by 'Unaytira clinches the matter. It also becomes clear how Maryam survived Shaybūb's murder attempt, carried out at 'Antar's orders: Shaybūb just wounded her, and then Kūbart took her away on a ship.[40]

With all 'Antar's surviving children now reunited, they start planning an expedition of revenge.[41] Jūfrān is prepared to go to extremes: he has 'Antar's bones dug up and put on a camel so that their father can ride in front and see how his children revenge his death. 'Unaytira is somewhat taken aback: '"Brother, those old bones do not have a clue about what is going on!" "By the protection of the Arabs," he said, "if you people do not obey me, I will kill you on the spot and subsequently myself." Then they had nothing more to say.'[42]

The plan is carried out, and they deal out their revenge to all 'Antar's former enemies, asking his bones again and again whether he is satisfied. When they are done, 'Antar's remains are buried again. Then Ghadanfar and Jūfrān return to their own countries, and 'Unaytira is on her own again.

By this time, the religion of the new prophet, Muhammad, has started to spread rapidly. Tribe after tribe converts to Islam. Gradually, 'Unaytira's family members begin to convert, including her mother Hayfā', and, finally, 'Unaytira herself also accepts Islam. The Prophet Muhammad is delighted to welcome such a warrior and hopes that she will be prepared to fight for the cause of Islam. 'Unaytira's cousin Khudhrūf, meanwhile, has fallen in love with her but she refuses to consider his proposal, not because of his wife Umayya and their son, but because she prefers to stay single. Khudhrūf looks to the Prophet for help, and when he orders her to marry her cousin, 'Unaytira cannot refuse. A seven-day wedding is celebrated.[43]

What happens to poor Umayya? The narrator quickly gets rid of her. 'As to Umayya, the mother of 'Amr: after the wedding of Khudhrūf she lasted for seven days, ill with jealousy, and then passed away to the mercy of God Most High, in the religion of Islam.'[44] Her fate thus is the same as that of Prince 'Abd al-Wahhāb's first wife in *The Adventures of Princess Dhāt al-Himma*.

'Unaytira bears Khudhrūf five sons. Together with their grandmother Hayfā', they all become staunch warriors on the path of Islam. 'Unaytira dies a martyr, battling side by side with the Prophet. Muhammad mourns her, saying that God will approve of her on the Day of Judgement. Her mother Hayfā' survives her by three years.[45]

The puzzling question remains: what made the narrator decide to end the story of 'Antar, the epitome of machismo, with the history of a daughter, a female hero, even if she is a daughter as fierce and relentless as 'Unaytira? We do not know. The answer might be that in this way the audience is allowed to keep the image of their great hero 'Antar intact, unchallenged by the exploits of a new, young male hero. They do not need to divide their loyalties. A daughter does not challenge her father's image, but enhances it.

The strangest thing of all is that in the extensive article on *Sīrat 'Antara* in the venerable *Encyclopaedia of Islam*, an article that was published in the late 1950s, 'Unaytira's name is not even mentioned.[46] There, revenge is exclusively the affair of 'Antar's sons Ghadanfar and Jūfrān. In some respects, Western *sīra* scholarship reflects social attitudes just as vividly as do the popular narratives themselves.

Chapter 8

Prince Hamza al-Bahlawān: In Praise of Traditional Womanhood[1]

Protagonists

- ʿAbd al-Wahhāb, Arab champion, son of Princess Dhāt al-Himma
- Aflantūsh, enemy king
- Al-Yūnānī, see ʿUmar al-Yūnānī
- ʿAnqāʾ, daughter of the giant Tahmāz, marries Nūr al-Dahr
- Anūshirwān, see Khusrau
- Asmābarī, *jinnī* princess, marries Hamza
- Badīʿ al-Zamān, son of Hamza
- Bakhtak, vizier of Khusrau Anūshirwān
- Bālkān, son of Hassāna and Rustam
- Bihzād, king (Hamza's son Badīʿ al-Zamān)
- Buzurjmihr, vizier of Khusrau Anūshirwān
- Ghamra, daughter of Fāʾiz, Arab warrior woman in *ʿAntar*
- Ghamra, daughter of ʿUtārid, Arab warrior woman in *Dhāt al-Himma*
- Ghashshām, suitor of Qannāsa
- Hamza, son of Ibrāhīm, the governor of Mecca
- Hassāna, warrior woman
- Hindām, father of Hassāna
- Khusrau Anūshirwān, Sassanid king
- Makhlūf, highway robber
- Mihrdukār, daughter of Khusrau Anūshirwān, marries Hamza
- Nuʿmān, Arab king
- Nūr al-Dahr, son of Badīʿ al-Zamān, marries ʿAnqāʾ
- Qannāsa, warrior woman, daughter of King Nuʿmān
- Rustam, son of Hamza

- Saʿd, son of Turbān and ʿUmar al-Yūnānī
- Salwā, warrior woman, marries Hamza
- Sarkhāna, warrior princess
- Tahmāz, a giant, father of ʿAnqāʾ
- Turbān, warrior woman, daughter of Aflantūsh, marries Hamza's son al-Yūnānī
- ʿUmar, trickster helper of Hamza
- ʿUmar al-Yūnānī, son of Zahrbān and Hamza, marries Turbān
- Zahrbān, Byzantine princess, mother of al-Yūnānī
- Zūbīn, counsellor of Aflantūsh, suitor of Turbān

The story of Prince Hamza is one of the most popular heroic tales in the Muslim world. Of Persian origin, tales about Hamza's adventures spread to South Asia as well as to Turkish regions and the Arab world, and versions exist in many languages, often widely divergent in content. Some of these are marvellously illustrated, such as the famous *Hamza* manuscript that was commissioned by the Mughal ruler Akbar (d. 1605).[2]

In studies on Arabic popular epic there is often confusion about who this Hamza was. The suggestion is that the hero of the Arabic *Hamza* epic is Hamza ibn ʿAbd al-Muttalib, the uncle of the Prophet Muhammad, as in many other versions. This, however, is not the case. He is a pre-Islamic Arab prince, the son of Ibrāhīm, the governor of Mecca.[3]

Islam does not play a part in this epic or 'tale',[4] not even at the very end. There are some references to pre-Islamic monotheism, but they appear on a much smaller scale than in *Sīrat Sayf ibn Dhī Yazan*, which also features a pre-Islamic hero. A general monotheistic attitude manifests itself in expressions such as 'the one true God', but that is about all. References to pilgrimage (called *ziyāra*, indicating an occasional visit, instead of *hajj*, the yearly Muslim pilgrimage) to the holy shrine in 'Mecca the Purified' also occur, but such pilgrimages already existed in pre-Islamic times.

We do not know exactly when the Arabic *Qissat al-amīr Hamza*, 'The Tale of Prince Hamza', was composed. Most likely it goes back to Mameluke storytellers of the fourteenth to sixteenth centuries. As to language and style, the story is mostly told in straightforward, rather simple prose, occasionally interspersed with rhymed prose and also poetry. The style is much less ornate, and also much less formulaic, than in cycles such as *ʿAntar* and *Dhāt al-Himma*.

Storytellers adapted their material to the taste of each particular audience, and this is also clearly visible in the printed version of *Hamza* that I have used here. It must have been based on a fairly recent (nineteenth century?) manuscript, for at some point the narrator says that the image of a girl whom the hero saw for just one brief moment was imprinted on his mind and thought 'just as the image of someone who is photographically (*fūtūghrafī*) portrayed is imprinted in not more than a few seconds'.[5] A number of remarks made by the narrator suggest that his background was Christian, for example a quotation from Genesis 1:2; discussion of marriage in terms of 'holy matrimony'; and also a quotation from Matthew 19:6: 'they became one flesh, and what God has joined, let no man put asunder, as it is said'.[6]

The story tells us about the adventures of Hamza, a pre-Islamic Arab nobleman who leads the Arabs in their battles against a variety of enemies. The Persians, adherents of the Zoroastrian religion, play a dominant role. The Persian ruler in the story is Khusrau Anūshirwān,[7] a name which recalls the Sassanid Khusrau I, known as Anūshirwān the Just, who ruled from 531 to 579. He has two viziers, Buzurjmihr and Bakhtak, also names of historical figures. These two, rather than Khusrau himself, are fierce opponents of Hamza. Hamza falls in love with Khusrau Anūshirwān's daughter, Mihrdukār, and marries her. In the course of his adventures he visits many foreign countries, has to fight a variety of enemies and falls in love with a number of women. Like the heroes of other *sīras*, Hamza has a faithful helper, here in the shape of the *'ayyār* 'Umar, one of the most prominent trickster characters in Arabic popular epic.

Female roles

Although *The Tale of Hamza* is basically an adventure story, love plays an important part in it, as it does in many of the *sīras*. The vicissitudes of the love of Hamza and the Persian princess Mihrdukār form a leading motif. Throughout most of the story the counter-role in the love story is played by the *jinnī* princess Asmābarī. She traps Hamza, who is already married to Mihrdukār, into marriage. She is in many ways Mihrdukār's opposite: she constantly nags where the other is compliant, she schemes and contrives where the well-behaved Mihrdukār merely waits and endures. Mihrdukār ultimately gets her reward: the story ends with Hamza finally devoting himself exclusively to her.

A noteworthy aspect of *The Tale of Hamza* is that in the love episodes more than usual attention is paid to musings about unfaithfulness, jealousy, women's willingness to put up with rivals, men's susceptibility to the attractions of other women, and the allowances to be made for this weakness by their betrothed ones or wives. In line with this, heroes are sometimes described as worrying about hurting their beloveds by succumbing to the charms of other women. In short, we see in this story cycle a greater than usual preoccupation with the problems inherent to polygamous life. The happy ending of *Hamza* can be seen as a triumph of monogamy.[8] In this way *Hamza*, in its present version, illustrates that these popular story cycles, recited evening after evening in the traditional coffee houses of the Middle Eastern world, reflect the preoccupations of the audience, just like modern soap operas, and are even occasionally used as a medium for emphasizing certain norms and values.

In spite of the fact that *The Tale of Hamza* presents the conventional and polite Mihrdukār as the feminine ideal, several warrior women feature prominently in the story and not only on the enemy side. Yet the approach to this type of female character in *Hamza* is widely different from that which we saw in, for instance, the *sīras* of *'Antar* and *Dhāt al-Himma*. The difference shows itself most prominently in the attitude of the eponymous hero himself: unlike many other Arab warriors, Hamza explicitly disapproves of the activities of these enterprising females.

It is illustrative, for instance, to compare the reaction of a male protagonist in an episode from the *Sīrat Dhāt al-Himma* with that of Hamza in a similar situation: in *Dhāt al-Himma*, the hero is eager to marry Ghamra, an Arab woman who has crushingly defeated and humiliated him, because "'I want to be like 'Abd al-Wahhāb, because he has women who can defend him as well as themselves.'"[9]

Hamza's attitude in these matters is entirely different. After his daughter-in-law Turbān, seeking revenge for wrongful treatment, has fought and killed her arch-enemy, Hamza has a serious talk with her: now that she has reached her goal, she ought to give up fighting, "'for we do not want it said that we seek help from our women; nor is there any need to do so, for we are all knights and warriors and perfectly able to defend ourselves'".[10]

The *Hamza* cycle, in any case, seems to favour a more traditional role for women. The woman who is prepared to take up her traditional role and does not meddle in the affairs of men has a right to be treated with the highest respect. Here, the contrast between Hamza's behaviour towards his bossy and aggressive *jinnī* wife Asmābarī on the one hand, and his faithful and forbearing wife Mihrdukār on the other, is illustrative. He reacts to Asmābarī's attentions with rudeness, while Mihrdukār is treated with the highest respect. When, for instance, their newborn son is presented to the Arab leaders, they ask Hamza what he is going to name the boy. His answer is that the mother needs to be consulted on this matter, and he lets Mihrdukār choose a name.[11] In this respect it is also illustrative to see how the daughter of Hamza and Asmābarī tries to persuade her mother to give up her attempts to get Hamza exclusively for herself. She urges her to go and live with him like an ordinary wife, which implies, of course, the acceptance of co-wives. She sees this as the best way for her mother to earn proper respect.

Such a strong emphasis on the traditional role of women can hardly be without consequences for the treatment of the warrior woman theme. A short analysis of the episodes featuring these warrior heroines may show us what line is taken in this particular story cycle.

Warrior women in *The Tale of Hamza*

In total there are six episodes in *Qissat Hamza* in which a traditional warrior woman figures: these are, respectively, the episodes featuring the heroines Qannāsa, Salwā, Hassāna, Sarkhāna, 'Anqā' and Turbān. The episodes are quite different, but the general picture that arises clearly demonstrates the overall approach to female warriors, and to independent females in general, in this epic.

Qannāsa[12]

Early in his career Hamza meets the warrior woman Qannāsa,[13] the warrior daughter of Hamza's opponent, King Nuʿmān. She is definitely not an attractive specimen of the warrior woman genus. Hamza first hears about her when he meets a man called Makhlūf, whose tame lion he has killed. He can hardly be blamed for this, since the lion acts as Makhlūf's helpmate in highway robbery.[14] Asked to explain his amazing relationship with the lion, Makhlūf tells about his love for the warrior princess Qannāsa,[15] 'who is of exceptional beauty, and who day and night mounts her horse to go out on forays'. She had made him a promise of marriage when he bravely rescued her after she had been captured by Prince Ghashshām. The bridal contest motif, a familiar one in warrior women stories, is briefly introduced here: the combat was intended as a test for her suitor Ghashshām, because 'she only wanted to marry someone who could defeat her on the battleground'. Ghashshām, however, after defeating her treacherously, takes her away to do with her as he wants instead of honourably marrying her. He certainly would have been a good match for her, as it turns out, for she proves herself no less treacherous: in spite of her promises to her rescuer Makhlūf, she tells her father that she has freed herself, and Makhlūf's angry protests only lead to his banishment from the city. It is then that he meets the lion, which cringes, cries and wags its tail when he is about to kill it, so – recognizing a fellow victim – he dries its tears and turns it into his faithful companion.

Hamza then goes to fight Qannāsa's father, King Nuʿmān. Qannāsa advances with her army of warrior girls in order to fight the Arabs, and Hamza is outraged: how can he be expected to fight women, who have definitely not been created to that end and for whom it is a shameful thing to fight in battle? Makhlūf, who, in spite of everything, is still in love with Qannāsa, offers to take over from Hamza in duelling with Qannāsa in single combat 'in order to teach her a lesson, so that henceforth she will know her own limits and never again dare to confront brave knights'. He hopes to capture her and then force her to marry him. When he comes face to face with her, Qannāsa is furious because she had hoped to fight the famous Hamza and not her rejected lover.

She soon realizes that Makhlūf is too strong for her and decides upon a ruse: complaining about the heat she asks for a short break in order to remove some of her armour. She uncovers her face and loosens her hair, letting it fall over her shoulders. Then she opens her dress so that rivulets of sweat are seen to run between her breasts. Makhlūf, dazzled by the sight, is about to be thrown from the saddle, but Hamza sees the danger and comes to his rescue. He captures Qannāsa and forces her to marry Makhlūf, while her warriors flee back to King Nuʿmān.

Qannāsa looks for a means of escape, and when Makhlūf wants to consummate the marriage she tries to persuade him to wait until her father can give his consent and they can have a proper wedding. When this argument fails, she feigns exhaustion and falls asleep, as does Makhlūf. Then she cuts off his head and flees to her father. Hamza follows her and cuts her in two.

Compared with similar episodes in other popular epics, the role of the warrior woman here is described rather sketchily. Just a few basic elements of this type of story are included, without any of the colourful embellishments or psychological subtleties that often enrich these episodes. Of the standard elements, we find here only the suitors' contest and the unbalancing of a male opponent by an unexpected display of feminine charms. It is noteworthy that the warrior woman is met with great disapproval by Hamza, who considers her behaviour to be unworthy of a woman. As mentioned above, the attitude of male heroes in other epics, such as *Sīrat Dhāt al-Himma*, *Sīrat ʿAntar* and *Sīrat Sayf ibn Dhī Yazan*, is usually quite different. They may occasionally utter a derisory remark, but usually they treat the warrior women with great respect.

Salwā[16]

This episode is only included for formal reasons and will be discussed very briefly. It features Salwā, a valiant girl who marries Hamza and gives birth to one of his sons. Only in name, however, is she a warrior princess. She is not described in action, although she is depicted as being proud and independent.

Salwā is the beautiful sister of a horseman who has arrived to serve Hamza. She is a courageous girl and she even manages to capture Hamza's friend ʿUmar, who has sneaked into her house. When Hamza agrees to marry her, she wants to postpone the wedding until they are in Madāʾin, so she can marry Hamza at the same time as he marries his long-time beloved Mihrdukār. Until then she will just be his companion. He agrees, promising her that she can accompany him and join him in battle, for she is quite accomplished in the use of arms. In one passage, she is indeed counted among Hamza's knights.[17] Completely in line with the general trend in this epic, her role, however, is not that of a fighting companion but rather a more womanly one: she cheers Hamza up and consoles him when the need arises. Not unexpectedly, the life of a somewhat neglected second wife does not suit Salwā. She leaves Hamza, and later kills herself in order to avoid marriage to an abductor.[18] It is a sad ending for this proud and honourable girl, whose independent attitude is clearly little appreciated.

Hassāna[19]

While the general attitude in *The Tale of Hamza* is that warrior girls and women need to be put in their proper place, this does not necessarily imply that they have to end up dead. There are other ways to teach them a lesson. The episode of the princess Hassāna gives us an example. Hassāna is an endearing character, almost comical in her naive overrating of her own abilities.

Her father, Hindām, is desperate when the Arabs, led by Hamza's son Rustam, approach his country. His only hope is his daughter, a fearless young beauty who 'pretends to be a very brave warrior, a most intrepid horsewoman and wielder of the sword'. She comes to her father and tells him not to worry about '"an Arab who out of pure simple mindedness dares to fill your heart with fear"'. She promises to kill this Arab in order to set her father's mind at rest: '"I know my own worth, and I am sure that no warrior of these days can hold out against me in the field."' Her father lets her go, feebly advising her to watch her step and to send to him for help if there is any need '"so I can come to you with soldiers and heroes"'.[20] Noteworthy here is the weak role of the father, also encountered in other stories, such as that of Ghamra the daughter of 'Utārid in *Sīrat Dhāt al-Himma* and Ghamra the daughter of Fā'iz in *Sīrat 'Antar*.

Hassāna sets off with her girls, all dressed in male attire, and the Arabs do indeed take them for men. After some initial exchanges of invective, she soon comes face to face with Rustam and quickly realizes that he is too strong for her. She asks for some respite to recover and, following the same pattern as Qannāsa in the episode described above, she uncovers her hair, face and breasts. Rustam is filled with shame when he discovers that he has been fighting a woman, and she quickly takes advantage of his situation by unhorsing him and tying him up 'like a camel'. She orders her girls to defeat the remaining Arabs, which they do with alacrity. Hassāna then takes Rustam home in triumph. She is very proud of herself.

She suggests to her father that Rustam be killed at once, but the wise vizier thinks better of this and persuades her to wait, saying to Hassāna that nobody will believe that she really captured Rustam unless she can produce him alive. Her head filled with dreams of glory, she quickly agrees: '"I will not kill Rustam before the heads of the tribes, the judges and governors have come together and seen him a prisoner in my hands; then I will kill him with my own hands, and slake my father's thirst for revenge by killing him."' So Rustam is put into prison, where, in spite of the harsh treatment that he receives, he cannot get Hassāna's beauty out of his mind. If only the Arabs would come and release him, he could capture her, marry her whether she wanted to or not and keep her firmly restrained for the rest of her life.

Hamza, meanwhile, has heard what has happened. He is very distressed about the fate of his son, and so are Rustam's two wives.[21] He promises to bring their husband back, and advances on King Hindām in order to rescue his son. Hindām is deeply troubled, but Hassāna, intoxicated by her success, brags that she will have the head of Hamza at her father's feet in no time, and goes out to meet him with an army of a hundred girls, dressed as soldiers. They set up camp near the Arabs, who are greatly surprised by these proceedings and cannot help but laugh. When fighting starts, Hassāna finds herself face to face with Hamza. Of course, she is no match for him, and he is quite amazed by her lack of balance and uncoordinated movement: how in the world did this bumbling oaf of a girl manage to defeat Rustam? Hassāna then tries the same ploy that she used against Rustam. 'Her exhaustion and anxiety made her cheeks grow redder and redder.' Hamza, though by no means immune to her beauty, is no longer the hot-blooded young fellow that he once was, and has no trouble in resisting her charms. He captures her without difficulty.

Hearing that his daughter is now in the hands of the Arabs, her father hastens to avert the danger that threatens her. He offers her hand to the still imprisoned Rustam, and quickly releases him when he accepts. The fathers arrange the wedding and Hassāna is much relieved: 'She was happy about it, for the thought had never before entered her mind.' So the wedding takes place, and love soon springs up between the spouses, 'in spite of the fact that not long ago she had wanted to kill him'. So the little goose is put out of harm's way, and when, not much later, the Arabs continue their wanderings, Hassāna (who is pregnant) is left behind with her father, as is common practice in these stories, where heroes soon forget the women they married, being fully engaged in new adventures.

It will be quite a while before we meet Hassāna again in the story. She turns up, much later, in the company of her grown son, Bālkān, who has been raised in the belief that his grandfather is his father.[22] It is his grandfather, too, who has trained him in the martial arts – there is no question, apparently, of his mother taking on this task herself, as did Princess Dhāt al-Himma and Ghamra the daughter of Fā'iz. When the boy discovers that his mother worships another god than that of his fire-worshipping grandfather, he asks for explanations and thus does not only hear about the one true God, but also about his parentage. Mother and son then depart in search of Rustam. In due course they manage to locate the Arab army, and Bālkān, reunited with his father Rustam, joins the Arabs.[23]

Sarkhāna[24]

The episode concerning Princess Sarkhāna, a warrior princess who arrives with her army of women to join the Arabs, presents a warrior woman in name only. No fighting takes place, and none of the usual elements of warrior women stories are present. What remains is nothing but a romantic love story leading up to a glorious wedding. Sarkhāna is attracted by the reputation of the Arab warriors and comes to see them with her own eyes: "'I have come in the hope of seeing something[25] of the fighting of the Arabs and to see with my own eyes how brave they are.'" Neither she nor her girls, however, engage in martial activities of any kind. When she arrives near the place where the Arabs have set up their camp together with their allies, led by King Bihzād (who is, in fact, Hamza's son Badīʿ al-Zamān), the general attitude is one of amusement, fascination and protectiveness. A general ban on visiting the women's camp is pronounced by the army leaders. Bihzād himself, however, cannot resist a nightly peep, and is just in time to kill a snake about to bite the sleeping Sarkhāna. The dagger which he leaves behind finally leads to his discovery. There is an interlude similar to the scene of the fitting of the glass slipper in *Cinderella*, with a claimant turning up first whose scabbard does not fit the dagger. When it becomes clear that Bihzād wants to marry her, Sarkhāna is beside herself with joy: "'Will such a king become my husband?'"

The male warriors are encouraged to marry Sarkhāna's girls. All the girls are converted to 'the true religion' and, on the day of the wedding, 'they arrived at the camp of the girls, and saw the whole ground decked with flowers and green twigs and the pavilion of the girls decorated all over with wreaths of splendid red and dazzling white flowers. At the door stood the servant girls who had taken off their men's clothes and donned women's apparel. All the other girls had done the same.'[26]

In short, the natural order of society, briefly disrupted by the girls presenting themselves in a role reserved for men, is restored. Nothing could be further from the weddings of the warrior women in, for instance, *Sīrat Dhāt al-Himma*, which usually only come about after the considerable resistance of the girl has been overcome, often in armed combat.

'Anqā'[27]

This is a very short episode, which looks like a truncated version of an originally much longer story. The story has no relation to that which is found in a Berlin MS,[28] a fairy tale in which appear a Princess 'Anqā' as well as another 'Anqā', "Anqā' the daughter of the wind', a fairy of strange birdlike form. 'Anqā', it may be remembered, is also the name of a mythical bird, usually identified with the phoenix. Whether the 'story of al-'Anqā'' mentioned by the twelfth-century Jewish scientist Samaw'al al-Maghribī[29] is identical to the story that lies at the root of the episode in *The Tale of Hamza*, as I am inclined to believe on account of it being mentioned in connection with *'Antar, Dhāt al-Himma* and the Alexander novel, or with the 'Anqā' story from the Berlin MS mentioned above, can, as yet, only be guessed.

In this episode, another of Hamza's grandsons marries a warrior woman. This grandson is Nūr al-Dahr, the son of Badī' al-Zamān. The girl, 'Anqā', is the daughter of the giant Tahmāz, who has been killed by Nūr al-Dahr. She puts on men's clothes and sets off with a band of warrior girls to avenge her father. Hamza realizes that Tahmāz's 'son' is too strong for Nūr al-Dahr, and he takes over from his grandson in the combat with 'Anqā'. They battle for half a day before Hamza notices that his opponent shows signs of flagging. Hamza immediately takes advantage of the situation and unhorses her. She is taken captive and an attack is launched on her companions, who, however, quickly pull the veils from their faces and start shrieking for mercy: "'Do you want to fight virgin girls?'"

Hamza is quite astonished that his opponent has been a woman, and a very beautiful one at that. Too beautiful to be killed, he judges, and comes up with a particularly cruel way of teaching the enterprising girl a lesson: she can either choose death or convert to 'God, the Living, the Eternal, the All-Powerful who is present everywhere' and be married to Nūr al-Dahr, her father's killer.

'Anqā' has little choice and decides to bide her time, hoping that new opportunities for revenge will arise in the future.

The wedding takes place and the couple stay together for 15 days. Nūr al-Dahr falls truly in love with his new wife, while 'Anqā' just waits for an opportunity to kill him. No such opportunity, however, presents itself, and when her husband has to prepare for battle again and is about to leave he finds out that his wife has disappeared. Hamza is not surprised: he had worried all along about her wiliness and treacherousness, and thinks that Nūr al-Dahr is better off without her. 'Anqā' goes to Aleppo, where she stays for some time. Having killed a man, she flees to the woods, where she gives birth to Nūr al-Dahr's son. The boy will eventually become a brave hero. No more is heard about 'Anqā' and her son, although hers is clearly a story with much potential.

A noteworthy aspect in the episodes described above is that the male hero who discovers that his opponent in battle is a woman instead of a man, is invariably said to be angry or ashamed. This element is absent from similar episodes in, for instance, the *Sīra Dhāt al-Himma* or *Sayf ibn Dhī Yazan*.

It is completely in line with this that in none of these stories does the warrior woman continue to take part in fighting after her marriage. Marriage is implicitly seen as a means to put her back into the role that befits her: that of the traditional dependent female. That Hassāna does not even instruct her son in the martial arts but leaves this to her father, the old man who, in the earlier part of the story completely depended on his daughter's military prowess, nicely illustrates the epic's implicit attitude towards female roles.

Turbān[30]

The one warrior woman who does not give up without a struggle is Turbān, the girl who marries Hamza's son al-Yūnānī.[31] But, in the end, she, too, has to give in and revert to a more traditional role. The pressure to do so does not come from her husband, but from her father-in-law, Hamza. From that moment on, she has to avail herself of the usual means used by women to exert power in a male-dominated society, namely to do so through her sons.

Turbān, daughter of Hamza's enemy Aflantūsh, is first taken for a boy by the Arabs, but then Hamza is told that this is Aflantūsh's daughter, the girl called 'the Intrepid'. Hamza is quite interested to see this girl: "'Is she the one who has vowed to kill me?'"[32] Turbān at that time has not yet reached her thirteenth birthday.[33]

Turbān suffers from the attentions of her father's crony, the treacherous Zūbīn, who is madly in love with her and wants to marry her.[34] She, however, loathes him and does not bother to hide her feelings. This makes Zūbīn so angry that he decides to abduct and rape her.[35] Marriage will then be the only way out for her, and in this manner he can also take revenge for all the humiliation he has suffered from her. His servant helps him to achieve his goal by drugging all Turbān's servants with henbane and then carrying her off in a blanket. He leaves her, tied up, to go and fetch his master, but just then Hamza's son al-Yūnānī turns up and rescues her. Al-Yūnānī has just arrived in his father's camp with his mother, the Byzantine princess Zahrbān. He is about 15 years old and very handsome.[36] He and Turbān fall in love at first sight, and he persuades her to leave her people and to come back with him to the Arab camp. Hamza is very much in favour of their marriag, and asks her views on the matter.[37] Marriage to al-Yūnānī would, of course, mean conversion to the religion of the one true God, and she would have to consent to the marriage, for the religion of the Arabs demands the mutual consent of the spouses.

Turbān agrees, but worries about deserting her father. She writes him a letter to tell him what Zūbīn has done to her and how al-Yūnānī has saved her from a fate worse than death. Zūbīn, angrily called to account by the king, glibly talks himself out of this charge. Together they decide to go and get Turbān back from the Arabs.

Al-Yūnānī consoles Turbān, who is deeply upset about everything that has happened, and dries her tears.[38] They are very much in love, and, after seven days of feasting, they are married. Her father and Zūbīn soon conclude that their project is hopeless and pretend to join the Arabs. In due time Turbān gives birth to a son, Saʿd.[39]

During Hamza's absence Zūbīn attacks the Arabs and abducts Turbān and Hamza's wife Mihrdukār, as well as their sons. Plans are made to burn them as a sacrifice.[40] Luckily, ʿUmar, Hamza's trickster companion, manages to rescue them just in time.[41] It is noteworthy that nowhere during this episode does Turbān make use of her warrior skills. The heroines that appear in the *Sīrat Dhāt al-Himma*, for instance, would certainly not have acted so meekly.

Al-Yūnānī, Turbān's husband, disappears and is not heard of for several months. Turbān is very distressed and tries to find consolation in educating her son. She personally trains him in all the martial arts,[42] 'so that he looked twenty although he was not yet nine years old'.

Turbān never forgives the treacherous Zūbīn for his dishonourable behaviour, and she instils the thirst for revenge in her son from his early years. Together they join in a large-scale campaign against the Persians, who include Zūbīn and Turbān's father, Aflantūsh. Hamza is strongly opposed to this, but she says that she will obey him in anything except this: she will not return before she has taken her revenge.[43] Hamza is especially angry when he hears that she has urged her son to join her, but she retorts that 'as far as she is concerned, she would rather see him die under a cloud of swords than to see him shirk from taking his revenge, trusting others to do so'. And, disregarding Hamza's orders, they go out together at night, Turbān's ultimate wish being to find and kill Zūbīn.

In the course of their fight with the Persians she does not achieve her goal, but manages to capture her father Aflantūsh, who tries to kill her. The situation becomes so dangerous that she has to be rescued by a fellow warrior, who points out that this is just the thing that Hamza feared when he tried to dissuade them from setting out.[44] Hamza and his party finally capture Zūbīn and he is sentenced to death, although he pleads his innocence regarding the abduction of Turbān. She is allowed to carry out the sentence herself and cuts him in two, screaming for revenge.[45]

Hamza then has a serious talk with her: now that she has achieved her goal she ought to give up fighting, "'for we do not like it said that we seek help from our women; nor is there any need to do so, for we are all knights and warriors and perfectly able to defend ourselves'". Turbān promises to give in to his request, saying that until now she could not do so because the humiliation she had suffered because of Zūbīn did not allow her to set her mind at rest. This was also the reason why she raised her son in the full consciousness that his mother's honour should be revenged. Hamza addresses his son 'Umar al-Yūnānī, saying that from now on he will no longer allow him to let his wife go to war. She will have to stay in the women's quarters, just like the other women. "'I obey your command,'" says al-Yūnānī, "'but I do not want to go against her wishes by doing one of the things you ask. For she is a noble lady, prudent, well-bred, intrepid and wise; women like her do not have a master, but are their own mistress (*lā yumlaku bal yamliku*).'"

Finally Turbān's son gives his view: "'I would never in my life have let my mother set out for war if it had not been necessary.'" The matter is then decided according to Hamza's wishes and Turbān is happy about this. Now that her thirst for revenge has been slaked, she no longer feels the need to go out and fight.[46]

But although she is no longer allowed to take part in fighting herself, Turbān remains a warrior woman at heart. She maintains a lively interest in her son's affairs, urging him to go out on dangerous exploits whenever she sees fit. Hamza is quite vexed by this; upon hearing from Sa'd that his mother has incited him to go out and fight the dangerous Persian champion Hārūn, he says: "'Your mother will not stop driving you to these dangers until you fall victim to one of them and return to her in a thoroughly bad state.'" When Sa'd tells his mother about his grandfather's refusal to let him fight, she orders him to prepare for departure straight away. They will go and seek out this enemy together. Their departure is spotted and reported to Hamza, who immediately sets out on horseback. Catching up with them, he repeats his views, but Saʿd says that he is fed up with staying idle, and Turbān sticks to her familiar view: "'If my son cannot fight Hārūn, then he had better be dead. For it is better that it is said of him that he died fighting this knight than that he dies lolling on a sofa.'" Hamza argues with her at great length, but finally gives up and lets them have their way.

So they set off and Saʿd challenges Hārūn to come out and fight. They engage in combat. However, when Turbān sees that Hārūn is about to kill Saʿd she screams and throws herself between them. We then see how irrevocably she has succumbed to the pressure to adapt to a traditional female role: when Hārūn is about to turn against her she unveils, saying to him: "'Are you not ashamed to fight a woman?'" He immediately offers his apologies and allows her to take away her son. She then carries him off on horseback and manages to nurse him back to health.[47]

To us, it is a disappointing turn of events to see Turbān, formerly so proud and valiant, use the ploy of her femininity. It illustrates very well the trend that runs consistently through this whole epic: although women may feel inclined to go out on their own and act independently, it is better for society that they stay at home and leave matters of the outside world to men. If they are not inclined to do so of their own accord, as in the case of Turbān, one must try to convince them and, if necessary, force them to give up their unwomanly behaviour, which may sometimes necessitate killing them. This not only applies to women who want to take part in battle, but also to other females who do not play a passive role: Hamza, for instance, kills a female *jinnī* who has done nothing worse than pursue a man with whom she has fallen in love.[48]

Concluding remarks

As we have seen, the approach to warrior women in *The Tale of Hamza* is consistently negative. Hamza, the leading hero, repeatedly expresses his view that it is unseemly for a woman, and especially a married woman, to engage in military activities. A woman should stay at home since warfare is exclusively men's business. This point of view explicitly comes to the fore in Hamza's discussions with his daughter-in-law, Turbān, and implicitly in the way in which another warrior girl, Hassāna, is ridiculed.

In the warrior women stories that occur in *The Tale of Hamza*, the women's military prowess, elaborated upon with great relish in other *sīra*s, is played down as much as possible. The attitude taken in general is that however capable the warrior woman may be, she ought to think better of it and give up her warlike activities in favour of a more conventional female role.

Whether the Christian narrator whose influence is repeatedly visible in this Arabic version, notably in the views expressed on marriage, had anything to do with this is difficult to say. To answer this question, the Arabic *Hamza* tradition, with its different versions still only available in manuscripts, needs to be studied more thoroughly.

Chapter 9

Sīrat Baybars *1: Lionesses*[1]

Protagonists

- 'Abdallāh al-Maghāwirī, Muslim saint
- Aḥmad al-Badawī, Muslim saint
- 'Ā'isha of Bushna, female Ismaili *fedawi*, sister of Hasan
- 'Alī al-Tuwayrid, son of Sulṭāniyā and Shīha
- 'Alī Fakhr al-Dīn al-Shaftūr, Muslim champion
- Al-Ṣāliḥ Ayyūb, Ayyubid sultan, adopts Baybars and his wife
- 'Arnūs, prominent champion, son of Ma'rūf, the chief of the Ismailis
- Baybars, Mameluke sultan, eponymous hero of the *sīra*
- Fāṭima, also known as Shajarat al-Durr, wife of al-Ṣāliḥ Ayyūb, adopts Baybars
- Fāṭima al-Ḥawrāniya, sister of Ibrāhīm al-Ḥawrānī
- Fāṭima Sitt al-Shām, Damascene lady, adopts Baybars
- Ghaydā', warrior woman, mother of 'Alī Fakhr al-Dīn al-Shaftūr
- Ḥamza, eponymous hero of *Qiṣṣat Ḥamza*
- Ḥasan, Ismaili *fedawi*, brother of 'Ā'isha
- Ḥusna-with-the-tattoos, Christian girl converted to Islam
- Ibrāhīm al-Ḥawrānī, prominent Ismaili *fedawi*
- Ibrīza, daughter of the king of Bashqat, also called Qannāsa
- Jawān, a Christian often posing as a Muslim, villain of the *sīra*
- Labwa, sister of Ma'rūf, the chief of the Ismailis
- Ma'rūf, chief of the Ismailis
- Maryam al-Ḥamiqa, warrior queen, daughter of 'Arnūs
- Qannāsa, see Ibrīza
- Sa'd, cousin and inseparable companion of Ibrāhīm al-Ḥawrānī
- Saladin (Ṣalāḥ al-Dīn), Ayyubid sultan of Egypt and Syria, 1174–93
- Salbān, Christian girl, converted and named Ḥusna-with-the-tattoos

- Sayyida Nafīsa, granddaughter of the Prophet's grandson Hasan, Muslim saint
- Sayyida Zaynab, granddaughter of the Prophet, Muslim saint
- Shajarat al-Durr, see Fātima
- Shīha, trickster character, substitute Ismaili chief, helper of Baybars
- Sultāniyā, former wife of Shīha, mother of ʿAlī al-Tuwayrid
- Turbān, daughter-in-law of Hamza in *Qissat Hamza*
- ʿUqba, crypto-Christian *qāḍī* (judge), villain in *Dhāt al-Himma*
- ʿUthmān, helper of Baybars

The Mameluke sultan Baybars ruled from 1260 to 1277 over Egypt and Syria, which, in those days, included present-day Jordan, Lebanon, Israel and Palestine. His fame was such that he became the subject of many legends, culminating in the very substantial *Sīrat al-malik al-Ẓāhir Baybars*. It has rightly been said that Baybars thus had three lives: his actual life, his life as it was depicted by Arab historians of Mameluke times, and his legendary life as it appears in popular epic.[2]

In Morocco, *Sīrat al-malik al-Ẓāhir Baybars*, or *Sīrat Baybars*, 'The Adventures of Baybars', for short, is called *al-Ismāʿīlīya*. This is because intrepid warriors from the Ismaili sect, also known as the Assassins, play an important role in it. These warriors are called *fidāʾī*s, or *fedawi*s, and their first loyalty is always to the leader of their sect, who may or may not support Baybars at that particular stage of events. Female *fedawi*s, 'lionesses', also appear on the scene, as will be shown.

Sīrat Baybars is one of the later *sīra*s. The oldest known written fragment dates from the early sixteenth century, which makes it likely that the epic was originally composed in the fifteenth century and took shape in the next century. Its late origin explains the frequent use of firearms in the events. Mines explode,[3] firearms are used in battle and cannons on the ramparts are put out of action by pouring water into them.[4]

Situated largely in urban surroundings, this *sīra* is very different in character from *sīra*s such as *Dhāt al-Himma*, *ʿAntar* and *Hamza*. Chivalry of the type encountered in those epics, with knights meeting on the battleground and fighting each other in single combat, barely plays a role in *Baybars*. It is set among the popular cities like Damascus, Aleppo, Alexandria and especially Cairo. Soldiers, merchants and craftsmen feature prominently and so does the world of crime, organized or otherwise. It is full of coarse humour. Style and language are very down to earth, without complicated literary turns. There is no rhymed prose, though occasionally poems are inserted. The language is juicy and full of dialect, the particular type of dialect often depending on the background of the characters.⁵ Foreign words are freely mixed in, many of Italian and Turkish provenance.

The text is eminently suited for oral performance as it involves a lot of flamboyant acting and gesturing, and that is indeed the way it was performed in Damascus until the twentieth century. After performances had stopped there for some years, they were brought to life again in the late 1980s and still continue today.⁶

Versions

Sīrat Baybars exists in several recensions. They diverge considerably from each other, although the general storyline is the same. The three recensions that are currently most easily accessible to the wider (partly also to the non-Arabic) scholarly public, either in printed Arabic editions or in translation, clearly demonstrate the situation. One is the French translation of the 'Aleppine version' of *Sīrat Baybars* begun in 1985 by Georges Bohas and Jean-Patrick Guillaume. They used a manuscript from Aleppo, probably written in the first half of the nineteenth century.⁷ Ten volumes of the translation have appeared so far, the latest in 1998. It makes very enjoyable reading. Style and vocabulary really manage to give the reader a taste of the original.

The second is the 'Egyptian recension'. M. C. Lyons's extensive summary of the *sīra* in volumes 2 and 3 of his *The Arabian Epic* (1995) is based on a reportedly undated, five-volume Cairo edition of this recension. The edition in fact dates from 1908–9, as stated by Thomas Herzog, who also provides a summary of this Egyptian recension.⁸ The edition was reprinted in 1923–6 and again, photographically, in 1996–7, with different page numbering. This was done at the instigation of the Egyptian novelist Gamal al-Ghitani, whose affinity to *sīra* literature, especially *Baybars*, is obvious in the style, atmosphere and setting of his novel *al-Zaynī Barakāt*, set in a turbulent period of Mameluke history full of political intrigue and fear, where nothing is what it seems.

Thirdly, there is the edition of the 'Damascus recension' currently being published by L'Institut Français d'Études Arabes de Damas (IFEAD, the French Institute in Damascus). It is based on a manuscript owned by the IFEAD, written by Muhammad Adīb al-Makkāwī.⁹ The first volume was published in 2000, volume 9 in 2011 and the project continues.

These three versions of the *sīra* each represent a specific branch of the text transmission. They differ considerably, not in the general outline of the story, but in the way individual episodes are worked out. Just one example may be cited as an illustration, namely the episode in which the 'lioness' 'Ā'isha, sister of an Ismaili *fedawi*, kills a Christian tavern keeper. In the Damascene version, 'Ā'isha, disguised as a man, goes to Tripoli after a quarrel with her brother Hasan, who has decided to join the villain Jawān, Baybars's opponent. Walking around the city, she comes to a place called The Bridge. She notices a Christian sitting at the door of a tavern. Upon seeing her, he jumps up, welcoming her as the 'son' of his brother Nūr al-Masīh, and invites her in. Once inside, he confesses that he just pretended to be her uncle because of the neighbours, who otherwise might have spread slanderous rumours upon seeing him with a handsome young man. He suggests that the young man should work in the tavern by day and do a few extra chores by night, compensating him for the money that customs have relieved him of. The young 'man' agrees. When night falls, 'Ā'isha asks the tavern keeper what this little extra task might be. Sleeping together for mutual relaxation and pleasure is the answer. She goes on bantering with him for a bit, and then makes him follow her to the bedroom, where she kills him by smothering him with a cushion and squeezing his testicles 'till he broke wind and his soul flew off with the fart'.[10]

The Aleppine version, here represented by the translation of Bohas and Guillaume,[11] follows the same line but tells the episode somewhat differently: upon reaching Tripoli, disguised as a man, 'Ā'isha looks for a place to sleep. She finds a tavern. The Christian owner immediately conceives a passion for the handsome young man. He offers him a cup of wine and asks about his background. 'Ā'isha says that her name is Hibat al-Masīh, that she is from Antioch and is all alone in the world except for an uncle. He offers her his guidance and protection, suggesting that for the sake of the customers the young man should pretend to be his nephew. She agrees, is given a place to sleep and the next day she sneaks out, returning in the afternoon when the tavern is full. The owner welcomes her enthusiastically as his long-lost nephew, both of them shedding tears of joy. He gradually trains the young man in running the business, until he can control himself no longer, embraces the young man and starts playing with his belt. '"Keep your paws off me!"' says 'Ā'isha. '"Please, just this once! I'm not made of wood!"' replies the tavern owner. 'Ā'isha then has no option but to strangle him.

The Egyptian recension is quite different: arriving in Tripoli in male disguise and looking for a place to sleep, 'Ā'isha enters a tavern and sees a very beautiful girl. The narrator includes a poem to describe her beauty. The girl has a father and they run the tavern together. 'Ā'isha orders food and when it is brought she puts *banj* in it and invites them to join her, having taken an antidote herself. Once they are unconscious she kills the father. When the girl comes to, 'Ā'isha threatens her until she converts to Islam. 'Ā'isha then promises to find her a husband just as handsome as she ('Ā'isha) is herself.[12]

As we have seen, the Egyptian and the two Syrian versions are widely divergent, while the Syrian versions, although basically telling the same story, differ considerably in the way it is worked out. It all demonstrates what has been pointed out previously: in *sīra* literature, every performance and every written version has its own text, and each is just as 'authentic' as the next.[13]

Since the Damascus edition is not yet complete, I will concentrate here primarily on the Egyptian version,[14] with occasional reference to the other two recensions.

Contents

In the *sīra*, Baybars is the son of a king, who is captured and sold as a slave by scheming uncles. Baybars is 'adopted' by various subsequent masters and mistresses, among them Fāṭima Sitt al-shām, a character based on the half-sister of Sultan Saladin,[15] and finally by the Ayyubid sultan al-Ṣāliḥ Ayyūb and his wife Fāṭima,[16] known as Shajarat al-Durr.[17] Baybars soon begins to obtain the paraphernalia belonging to his heroic status: a miraculous man-slaying horse, a bow and a mace. He has a number of helpers, notably two *'ayyār* characters, 'Uthmān and Shīha, both accomplished tricksters. The leading villain is Jawān, a treacherous Christian often posing as a Muslim. He is a descendant of 'Uqba, the villain in *Sīrat Dhāt al-Himma*. It is not the only instance where we notice a connection between the epics.

The external enemies in *Sīrat Baybars* are various. Christians feature prominently in the form of Crusaders as well as kings of various Mediterranean countries. So do Mongols. Baybars's great historical feat, after all, was his decisive defeat in 1260 of the Mongols under Hulagu, Genghis Khan's grandson, in the Battle of 'Ayn Jālūt in Palestine. Then there are the Persians, who are not always clearly discerned from the Mongols.

A striking feature of the *sīra* is the overwhelming presence of the supernatural. In that respect, too, *Sīrat Baybars* is very much a product of the later medieval period. Saints, miracles and all kinds of magic and sorcery appear in the story. One can never be sure that things are what they seem.

The role of saints is especially prominent. They constantly turn up in dire situations to help and save, in actual events as well as in dreams. In those dreams, they may offer advice or even practical help, such as curing illnesses. In this respect a clear shift can be noted from an older epic such as *Dhāt al-Himma*: there the Prophet Muhammad is the one who advises or cures in dreams. He may, for instance, confirm someone's paternity, promise deliverance from a seemingly hopeless situation or restore amputated limbs. In *Baybars*, this role has been taken over completely by saints. In the *sīra*, al-Sālih himself, the Ayyubid sultan who adopts Baybars, is already revered as a saint with miraculous powers during his lifetime. He remains a powerful saint after his death and often interferes in affairs. Other Egyptian saints also appear: Ahmad al-Badawī, Sayyida Zaynab, Sayyida Nafīsa and especially 'Abdallāh al-Maghāwirī,[18] who, time and again, gets people out of difficult situations by transporting them over the sea to other countries or by offering various kinds of assistance.[19]

Just as in several other *sīra*s, an ancient book of esoteric knowledge plays an important part in *Sīrat Baybars*. This is the *Kitāb al-Yunān*, 'The Book of Yunān'. Yunān was an ancient sage who laid down his secret knowledge in a book of gold, to which his son later added silver pages with additional knowledge. The book is discovered at some point,[20] the clever Shīha learns it by heart, and henceforth it will provide crucial knowledge during future events.

To give an adequate overview of everything that happens in the *sīra* is beyond the scope of this book. For this, the reader is referred to the summaries provided by Lyons and Herzog.[21] Suffice it to say that the events and adventures are often extremely complicated, and what makes it even more confusing for the reader is the number of persons bearing identical names (a staggering number of Maryams appear on the scene) and the frantic speed with which new marriages are concluded, usually resulting in offspring unknown to the quickly departed father and likely to turn up much later under an unknown identity. While this is a common feature of most epics, heroes in *Baybars* tend to break records: 'Ārnūs, the son of Maʿrūf, the chief of the Ismailis, and a prominent hero himself, marries at least fifteen times.

Warrior women

As we have mentioned, chivalric warfare of the type encountered earlier hardly plays a role in *Baybars*. This also has its consequences for the treatment of the warrior woman theme in this *sīra*. Martial women regularly appear, but the warrior woman as we encountered her in *Dhāt al-Himma*, *ʿAntar* and *Hamza* – the woman fully trained in the art of combat, capable of meeting male knights and champions on an equal footing and duelling with them on the battleground – hardly features in *Sīrat Baybars*. The characteristic form in which the woman prepared to use violence appears in *Baybars* is that of the female *fedawi*, the *labwa* or 'lioness'.

Foreign warrior queens also appear on the scene, and sometimes they even fight the occasional duel, but there are no extensive descriptions of combat scenes elaborating on the physical qualities and martial prowess of the woman. Reference to the traditional warrior woman theme is mostly nominal, although we occasionally come across traces of the traditional motif as it appears in *Dhāt al-Himma* and *ʿAntar*.

The story of Ibrīza, daughter of the king of Bashqat, is an example. I quote from the Damascus edition.[22] Princess Ibrīza, as we are told, used to be an accomplished warrior princess, but this has not brought her much happiness.

> She used to ride horses, to go out boldly into the night, and never bothered about the number of men around her. Those whom she could not overpower by her braveness she captured by her glances, as the poet says. […] For that reason they called her Qannāsa ('Huntress' or 'Catcher'). There was not a man in that area who had not proposed to her. She said, however: 'I will only marry the man who defeats me in the turmoil of the battleground.' Nobody, however, managed to defeat her, and then the suitors started to disappear. Then she was struck by melancholia. Her father called in the doctors, but none of them knew a cure for her. They prescribed activity. So her father made for her the garden that we mentioned.[23]

Then ʿĀrnūs, the prominent Ismaili *fedawi*, passes by and discovers the garden. He falls asleep on a bench, where the princess discovers him – a familiar theme in the course of ʿĀrnūs's adventures. A love affair ending in marriage is the result. There is no question of a duel between the lovers. Ibrīza's statement that she will only marry a man who defeats her on the battleground is merely topical, and nothing in the sequel of her story suggests that she might be able to hold her own in armed combat, let alone lead an army into battle. The princess, in fact, plays a completely traditional role.

Lionesses

One of the fascinating aspects of *sīra* research is that every time one appears to have discovered a pattern or to have reached some sort of conclusion, a counter-example turns up. It is no different here. Just when we are tempted to conclude that the warrior woman theme in *Sīrat Baybars* is only a vague echo of what it was in the older *sīra*s, we hit upon a perfect gem of a warrior woman story containing all the familiar elements. Fātima al-Hawrānīya, the sister of the prominent *fedawi* Ibrāhīm al-Hawrānī, is the heroine of this episode.

Fātima's case is especially interesting because it forms a bridge between the warrior women of the earlier *sīra*s and another kind of martial woman, typical for *Sīrat Baybars*. This is not the woman trained in warfare and the chivalric arts, but the ruthless independent woman who will go her own way if she chooses and is quite prepared to use violence in order to reach her goal. She may use poison, or wield a knife, dagger or sword. Maryam al-Hamīqa, about whom we will speak later, combines the two: she starts as a foreign warrior queen, but, after this role has come to an end because she turns out to be the granddaughter of the Ismaili chief and thus belongs to the Muslims, she continues to use ruse and violence against her enemies. In this respect, she shows the characteristic mental make-up and behaviour of the fierce women of the Ismaili *fedawi*s in the *sīra*, the 'lionesses' (Arabic: *labwa*, plural *labawāt*).[24] *Labwa* is used as a personal name as well as a kind of title for these women. Fātima al-Hawrānīya is such a lioness.

Fātima al-Hawrānīya[25]

Fātima's story starts, as so often in popular epic, with the appearance of an unknown son, in this case ʿAlī al-Tuwayrid, a newly discovered son of Shīha by a long-forgotten wife. Having joined the Muslim army, ʿAlī at some point goes out hunting. Just when he is about to turn back to the castle of Hawrān, a figure emerges from the wilderness, shouting: "'Who has directed you to this place to hunt? Do you not know that this is the land of *muqaddama* [captain] Fātima al-Hawrānīya, daughter of Hasan al-Hawrānī? How dare you enter an area without permission of its owners?'" He answers that he is not a stranger, but the son of Shīha and a close friend of her brother Ibrāhīm.

> 'So you are the son of Sultānīya, and ruler of our land!' While she respectfully bowed her head, her veil slipped, showing a face as radiant in beauty as the full moon and eyes nobody could look at without feeling a burning passion. 'Oh!' said captain ʿAlī. 'God bless you, light of my eyes! Do not say Oh! If you are my beloved, then, by the Greatest Name, I am yours! Do not be afraid of me, I guarantee your safety with my life!'

They continue talking for a while, expressing their love. Then they have to part. ʿAlī immediately goes to his father Shīha, urging him to ask Ibrāhīm's consent for a marriage between ʿAlī and Ibrāhīm's sister. Shīha does so straight away. Ibrāhīm is happy with the idea, but says that there is a hitch: she must formally be defeated and taken captive.[26] Shīha thinks that this is not a major problem, given that her intentions are clear. So Ibrāhīm puts the proposal to her. She answers that she will marry ʿAlī on one condition: "'Brother, when he is suitably strong to defeat me in battle I will be his bed mate and obey his every word.'" Ibrāhīm arranges for the contest to take place formally on the battleground, the *maydān*, the following morning. Fātima does not make it too hard for ʿAlī: within an hour, he has grabbed her by the throat and forced her to dismount. "'Be my witness, sons of Ismaili!' he said. They answered: "Be worthy of it!" He said to her: "Go back to the women's quarter and do not get on horseback again."'[27]

The wedding is soon celebrated and lasts for seven days. When ʿAlī enters the bridal chamber he finds her 'a pearl not yet pierced, a steed never ridden by someone else'. One small detail remains to be solved: his mother, Sultānīya. She wants to stay with his father, Shīha. ʿAlī tells her that this is not possible. His father has found another wife, but since he, ʿAlī, cannot find another mother, she must come with him. His wife, he says, will understand that to keep his esteem she must accept this. Fātima understands that she had better agree, and says that of course she will be his mother's servant in every respect. So ends a woman's independent life. It is reminiscent of the way in which Hamza, in *Qissat Hamza*, insists that his brave daughter-in-law Turbān confines herself to the women's quarters.

ʿĀʾisha[28]

ʿĀʾisha of Bushna, part of whose history was told above to illustrate the difference between the various recensions of the *sīra*, is a typical example of a fierce and independent Ismaili woman. When her brother Hasan threatens to kill Baybars's messenger ʿUthmān, ʿĀʾisha draws her sword and rushes in, forcing him to release ʿUthmān. She then strikes him on the head with her dagger and fiercely chides him, calling him a number of offensive names. Finally she sends ʿUthmān on his way. It makes Hasan very angry: "'You shameless bitch, do you dare to laugh at men?'" He swears that he will go to Tripoli and join Jawān.[29] At that point ʿĀʾisha decides to go to Tripoli in male disguise, where, as we saw above, she kills the Christian owner of a tavern and continues running it with the dead shopkeeper's daughter, whom she has forced to accept Islam. ʿĀʾisha changes the girl's name from Salbān to Husna-with-the-tattoos. ʿĀʾisha suggests using the tavern as a trap to kill Christians. When they have killed a good number they will try to conquer the land and hand it over to the king of Islam. It seems an excellent plan, and they start luring people in by calling out: "'Free food and drink!'" Everybody hastens to the shop, but nobody comes out again: 'they would be staying there in their graves till the Day of Resurrection'.

Not only Christians come to the tavern, however. One day, the clever trickster Shīha, substitute leader of the Ismailis, arrives in the land and comes to the tavern.[30] The two girls attempt to drug him, but he sees through their plot and threatens to report them to the king. He also shocks ʿĀʾisha by addressing her by her real name. After he has revealed his identity, he joins in killing customers.

Then, at some point, two *fedawi*s, Ibrāhīm al-Hawrānī and his cousin Saʿd, appear in the tavern.[31] To get them out of the way, ʿĀʾisha makes them drunk and puts them in a dark and narrow cell. She shows an obvious predilection for Saʿd, putting heavy chains on Ibrāhīm, but tying Saʿd up with silk rope. Ibrāhīm is fed with coarse lower-class food, while a luxury meal is served to Saʿd. When, some time later, the treacherous Jawān and his sidekick Burtuqūsh also turn up and are put in the cellar with the others, Jawān quickly notices the difference in treatment and concludes that 'Ā'isha must be in love with Sa'd.

In the course of events, Ibrāhīm and Sa'd, who by this time have both fallen in love with 'Ā'isha, are freed again, and they all join Baybars. Tricking Ibrāhīm, Sa'd manages to get to Baybars first, successfully applying for 'Ā'isha's hand. A seven-day wedding is duly celebrated. She plays no further active role: shortly after, she is abducted and left in a Christian castle.

'Ā'isha is by no means the only 'lioness' to appear on the scene. Several other Ismaili *fedawi*s have formidable sisters or mothers, who, regrettably, only make a brief appearance, such as Lioness (*labwa*) Ghaydā', the mother of 'Alī Fakhr al-Dīn al-Shaftūr, a renowned champion on the battlefield. Since her husband was not around when her son was born and she did not want to be hampered on her forays by a baby, she left him to the servants during the daytime and nursed him at night.[32]

Labwa[33]

Labwa is clearly used as a title in the case of the above Lioness Ghaydā'. The sister of Ma'rūf, the chief of the Ismailis, on the other hand, is just known as Labwa: 'Lioness' is her personal name. Ibrāhīm al-Hawrānī, not exactly a weakling himself, is afraid of her and no wonder: she is a real *jabbāra*, a giantess. She rules over the castles of the Christians as well as the Muslims. She has a huge moustache, two strings of which she ties behind her head and two that she ties in the manner of tying up a camel. She eats two fully grown sheep a day, one in the morning and one in the evening.[34] No man can hold his own against her on the battleground, and when Shīha, demanding Ibrāhīm's help, plans to put his name on the castles that she rules, none of the *fedawi*s is prepared to help him. Not even Shīha's derisory remarks about Ibrāhīm's cowardliness can make them change their minds. They tell him that he will have to deal with Labwa on his own.

So this is what he sets out to do, in typical *'ayyār* manner: not by fighting her but by a wily ruse. Having drugged her maid, the one who prepares Labwa's sheep for breakfast and dinner, he puts on the woman's clothes and takes her place. This gives him the opportunity to put something in the food that makes Labwa's heart swell up and causes terrible pain. She asks her 'maid' what can be the matter, and the 'maid' answers that it must be her fear of having to fight Shīha that makes her so ill. She ought to give up the plan, for it is clearly more than her nerves can cope with: "'Drink this, it is peppermint, it will cure your heart.'" As soon as Labwa has drunk the offered concoction she feels better and shouts that tomorrow she will go out and deal with Shīha. The whole operation is then repeated several times until Labwa is no longer able to get up from the bathroom floor and does not know which way is up or down. Finally she gives up her plan and Shīha sneaks off, after having put an antidote in the drugged maid's ear to wake her up.[35] Labwa then goes to pay her respects to Ibrāhīm, who receives her with great hospitality, and Shīha's name is put on the gates of the first castle.[36]

As we have seen, the 'lionesses', however intrepid and full of zest they are, only play minor roles. Having played their part, they soon disappear into the background again. In this respect, Maryam al-Hamiqa, whom we will discuss next, is an exception. She plays the double role of a foreign warrior queen out to destroy the Muslims and that of the independent woman prepared to use all kinds of violence in order to save herself. In the latter role, she distinctly shows herself a *labwa*.

CHAPTER 10

Sīrat Baybars 2: Warrior Queens[1]

Protagonists

- 'Adhrā' al-Masīḥ, daughter of Marīn, marries 'Arnūs
- Ahmad, son of Maryam and Tuqtimur
- 'Arnūs, Muslim champion, father of Maryam, son of Ma'rūf, the chief of the Ismailis
- Bahrūna, enemy warrior queen
- Barhajān, father of Marjāna
- Baybars, Mameluke sultan, eponymous hero of the *sīra*
- Budūr, daughter of Dawāhī, marries 'Arnūs
- Buktimur, Muslim commander of the Upper Nile region
- Burtuqush, servant and helper of Jawān
- Dawāhī, enemy warrior queen, sister of Shawāhī, Sātirīn and Marīn
- Ibrāhīm al-Hawrānī, prominent Ismaili *fedawi*
- Jawān, a Christian often posing as a Muslim, villain of the *sīra*
- Marīn, enemy king, brother of Shawāhī, Dawāhī and Sātirīn, converts to Islam
- Marjāna, a *jinnī* princess
- Maryam al-Hamiqa, warrior queen, daughter of 'Arnūs
- Maymūna, daughter of Maymūna
- Maymūna, Ethiopian warrior queen, sister of Sayf al-Mulk, mother of Maymūna
- Nimr, a deserter *fedawi*
- Nūr al-Masīḥ, daughter of Shawāhī, marries 'Arnūs
- Sātirīn, enemy king, brother of Shawāhī, Dawāhī and Marīn, converts to Islam
- Sayf al-Mulk, Ethiopian king, brother of Maymūna
- Shabshīr, a *jinnī*

- Shawāhī, enemy queen (later king), sister (later brother) of Dawāhī, Sātirīn and Marīn, converts to Islam
- Tāj Nās, sorceress, wife of Shīha
- Taud, son of Tāj Nās
- Tuqtimur, brother of Baybars, marries Maryam
- Ward al-Masīh, daughter of Sātirīn, marries ʿArnūs

Maryam al-Hamiqa[2]

Maryam al-Hamiqa, Maryam the Foolish,[3] is introduced in *Sīrat Baybars* as the queen of a faraway island kingdom. She is a real warrior queen, well trained in the martial arts. Planning a campaign against the Muslims, she has ordered all the ships' captains in the area to put themselves under her command in order to sail to Muslim territory. Nothing, however, has happened for a year, and yet she does not allow the captains to leave. One of them, fed up with the year-long inactivity, has sailed away, realizing only too late that he has put himself in danger of terrible repercussions. He meets Jawān, the arch-villain, who is roaming around with his sidekick Burtuqush because he is no longer welcome anywhere. The captain explains his miserable situation and Jawān offers to plead his case with the queen. Together they go to her court, where they find her surrounded by forty kings who have all come to support her and are all eager to marry her. Jawān urges her to forgive the captain, but the queen's reaction is to draw her sword and cut the deserter in half. Jawān, however, is courteously received and quickly manages to gain her confidence, promising to arrange military assistance for her.

Abandoning her idea to attack from the sea, the queen now decides to approach over land. The captains are dismissed, and she marches off with a huge army until she comes near Muslim territory, where she sets up her camp, waiting for Jawān's promised troops. No one arrives and she realizes that he has lied to her. She decides to arrange a contest between the forty kings who accompany her in order to find out who is the strongest. She promises to marry the winner and to make him commander of the army. Meanwhile, news of her arrival has reached ʿArnūs, the prominent Muslim champion. He quickly sets off to meet her. One of his former wives will say later that it was undoubtedly the rumour of Maryam's beauty that spurred him on. He arrives just when the last two remaining kings are engaged in combat. Without hesitation he attacks, defeating them both. Queen Maryam is impressed and proposes a joint attack on the Muslims, with 'Arnūs leading half of the army against the city of Marmor (his own city, in fact) while she advances upon Aleppo with the other half. She promises to marry him when they have conquered the land. He agrees. Only then does she ask him about his background, and he tells her that he is a Christian roaming the lands to further the cause of Jesus, the Messiah.

All seems fine, but while 'Arnūs is out hunting gazelles Jawān turns up, announcing to Maryam that he has brought her a huge army. She explains that she has already found herself a formidable champion. From her description Jawān immediately recognizes 'the devil 'Arnūs'. 'Arnūs is captured and Maryam decides to entrust him, as a valuable hostage for future negotiations, to her mother. She then advances upon Aleppo. Baybars sends Ibrāhīm al-Hawrānī to her with a letter, saying:

'You, Maryam the Foolish, accursed woman, what do you think you are doing? To lead your armies against my lands, while Persians, Byzantines, Turks and Franks have been subjugated by my sword! You, a woman, made from a crooked rib and with a stammering tongue![4] If Satan has incited you to this you have called down destruction upon yourself and your army. Should you want to save yourself from going into eternity and opt for living on instead of being destroyed, I advise you to come over, bringing Jawān and Burtuqush with you. Then, if you convert to Islam, I will take care to marry you to someone of your own standing, so that henceforth you can stay home as befits a properly behaved girl. If you do not agree, the strike of the sword will be your only option. The sword is more true than books and papers covered with script. Let these words suffice you.'[5]

Ibrāhīm returns to Baybars completely overwhelmed by love for the queen. Maryam does not pay the slightest attention to Baybars's words and soon both armies are facing each other.

Single combats between champions of both parties then take place, until Maryam herself, persuaded by Jawān, comes forward in all her splendour, challenging her opponents. One champion after the other presents himself but is struck by love as soon as he sets eyes on her, saying that he has only stepped forward to offer her his services. In this way she takes twenty of them captive on the first day. After two other leading champions have suffered the same fate on the next day, Baybars tells his brother Tuqtimur to step onto the battleground, hoping that he will finally take her captive. There is no chance of this, however: 'He was unable to do that, for she started twisting her body around on her horse in a way that even a snake could not possibly have managed.' He is completely confused by this artistic display of beauty, and when she asks him whether he has learned anything to boast about when confronted with an opponent in war, his only answer is that he would like her to accept Islam, marry him and be his bedmate. She deals him a sword strike, wounding his shoulder. '"Ow!" he said. But the strike fell upon him like cool water in the mouth of a thirsty man, and he said: "Have patience! Once more, my lady! For your strike heals misery and cures illness and pain!"' This is virtually the only time that Maryam demonstrates something of her martial skills. Otherwise, her confrontation with the Muslim champions does not involve any fighting at all.

Baybars, seeing his brother's condition, is disgusted. Screaming, he attacks Maryam and takes her captive without further ado, handing her over to one of his companions. Baybars wants to have her killed, but this does not come about. Soon afterwards, 'Arnūs and his companions arrive, accompanied by Maryam's mother. It turns out that she is 'Arnūs's former wife and that Maryam is their daughter. A happy reunion takes place and they all return to Cairo. We see here again the narrative use of the many love affairs in which *sīra* heroes get involved. These affairs usually result in marriages of a brief duration, and, later on, this offers the possibility of introducing a threatening, usually Christian, enemy who then turns out to be a brave Muslim son or daughter.

Here, basically, Maryam's career as a warrior queen ends, although there are still quite a few adventures in store for her, in the course of which she will not shun the use of violence. Briefly, the sequel of her story is as follows: her father gives her in marriage to Tuqtimur, Baybars's brother, to the deep disappointment of Ibrāhīm, who has proposed to her first. Her father tries to mitigate his anger by pointing out that Ibrāhīm's huge body makes the marriage unsuitable: he would very likely crush her during the act of love. The redoubtable warrior queen, as we see, is thus reduced to a vulnerable little woman.

Then a long series of failed wedding ceremonies begins, the ceremony being interrupted again and again by the abduction of the bride. In the course of these adventures Maryam has to use all sorts of ruses and violence to save herself. At some point, after having been abducted, she roams about in a foreign country, completely on her own, until a ship arrives and the captain agrees to take her on board. It soon becomes clear to her that the captain has evil intentions towards her, and she sees no other solution than to kill him and his whole crew. She goes about it as follows. She suggests to the captain that they leave the ship for a while so that they can make love without being troubled by his crew. The captain enthusiastically agrees. Once they are alone and he is befuddled by drink, he asks her to dance for him. She agrees, but only if she is allowed to do a sword dance. She also makes him all sorts of sexual promises about making love to him Egyptian style as well as Syrian style.

> Then Queen Maryam started to dance, approached him closely and threw herself against his breast, pulling him against herself with such strength that his ribs were pressed together. As soon as she had cracked them well and truly and he was no longer able to free himself from her embrace he said: 'Please! Egyptian style!' She did not let him go till life had fled out of him. Then she put him down and sat down beside him. The first mate arrived, asking: 'How is the captain?' 'O well, he has been busy fornicating and now is fast asleep.' Of course the man was eager for a similar session. She romped about with him till she had put him down next to the captain. So she went on with one officer after another until only the common seafolk were left. She stepped on board again, sword in hand, and killed them all. Then she left the ship, without the faintest notion as to where she should go. But lo, a cloud of dust appeared in the distance ...[6]

The cloud of dust announces the arrival of a handsome young king, who takes her to his castle and introduces her to his mother. His budding feelings of love are soon smothered because his mother explains that he is Maryam's half-brother, his father being 'Arnūs.

And so on. In the course of further events, she poisons one suitor and strangles another. The situations are immensely complicated: various doubles or near-doubles play a part, three different Maryams (two of them identical in appearance) feature in the events, unknown sons and daughters, the fruit of almost-forgotten marriages (usually of 'Arnūs) turn up, among them three half-brothers of Maryam who want to marry her, not knowing that she is their sister. In the end, everything is sorted out. She returns safely and is finally married to Tuqtimur, to whom she bears three children. It is not the end of her adventures, however: her baby son Ahmad is abducted by Jawān and disappears, and, in the course of a later kidnapping, Maryam barely escapes being forcibly married to her own son, who, as it turns out, had been raised as a Christian prince.

The reader may hardly be able to make sense of it all, but clearly the audience enjoyed such complicated and improbable plot developments just as much as the modern viewer of television soap series.

Foreign warrior queens who, unlike Maryam, are not prepared to abandon their religion and accept Islam end up quite differently. They are simply killed. We will give three examples, each with its own particular slant. These are the stories of Queen Bahrūna, a naive little goose; the sisters Shawāhī and Dawāhī, two queens, both sorceresses, who in the end choose different options in religion; and two more sorceresses, Maymūna and her daughter. The latter story is noteworthy because it presents a confrontation between modern and traditional warfare.

Bahrūna[7]

The story of Bahrūna in many ways runs parallel to that of Maryam al-Hamiqa. Some episodes are even practically identical, such as the choosing of an army commander by letting all the champions duel with each other, 'Arnūs turning up, defeating the last two contestants and presenting himself as a Christian champion, and Jawān then recognizing him from the heroine's description and capturing him. The difference is that in this case the queen refuses to convert and, accordingly, is killed.

Bahrūna is a warrior queen who is planning an expedition against Muslim lands. 'She was bringing soldiers together in great numbers, since her purpose was to raid the lands of Islam, because she had much money and it was her intention to spend it all on *jihād*, obeying the Messiah.' She has raised forty elephants and intends to place iron towers on their backs upon which four cannons will be placed. Her ministers think that it would be useful to have Jawān with them, but he is usually not easy to locate. She sends people out to look for him, but after many days he has still not been found. She then decides to go ahead and choose a commander by means of the procedure described above. So 'Arnūs, under an assumed Christian name, becomes her army commander. She does everything to make his life comfortable, and all day long they play chess together. He is a very handsome man and she soon falls in love with him.[8] Then, however, Jawān turns up. Bahrūna, starry-eyed, tells him about this marvellous 'king of the whole world' who has come to help her. Jawān asks for a description and immediately says: "'That is exactly how the *diyābrū* [devil] 'Arnūs looks, the one who eats Christian girls! He is a Muslim [...] the king of the City of Marmor, the very city that you were going to attack!'" This considerably dampens her enthusiasm. Her life is in danger! She could be eaten! "'O Father, what shall we do now?'" Jawān, handing her some *banj*, the usual soporific, quickly arranges 'Arnūs's capture and takes him away to interrogate him, stating in coarse and explicit terms what he supposes 'Arnūs's sexual intentions towards Bahrūna to be.

Bahrūna may be a warrior queen but, as we see, she comes across as a little goose. She simply follows Jawān's suggestions while he makes no attempt at consulting her. He forbids her to put the iron towers upon the elephants: these are no use except on horses, he says, and the elephants will just trample the Muslims to death during the attack. She trusts his opinion and marches towards Aleppo.[9]

Jawān persuades Nimr, a *fedawi* deserter with nothing but contempt for Baybars and his lot, to act as Bahrūna's commander. He agrees, saying he will not rest before he has put Baybars and Shīha and all their followers into Bahrūna's power. Jawān is delighted and gives him a robe of honour. Bahrūna follows suit, although she has not been consulted at all about the arrangement. Captive after captive is brought in by Nimr. Bahrūna walks up to him and laughs sweetly, promising him that she will convert to Islam, marry him and then make him sultan of the castles and herself sultaness of Egypt and Syria. This drives him into a frenzy. Doubling his efforts, he captures one Muslim champion after another, including Baybars himself.[10] Of course, their captivity does not last long. Two of Bahrūna's servants discover that they are sons of Muslim champions and thus also Muslims themselves, and they free the captives. Bahrūna is captured by Shīha and asked to accept Islam. She refuses and is subsequently killed.

Shawāhī and Dawāhī: four weddings and a funeral[11]

The episode featuring the warrior queen Dawāhī is so complicated and confusing that it is hard to take it seriously. Sorceresses Shawāhī and Dawāhī,[12] two queens, each inhabiting a castle, appear together with two kings, Sātirīn and his brother Marīn, who also inhabit two castles. Later on in the episode it will become clear that they all are sisters and brothers.[13] Their castles are connected by subterranean corridors. They are all Christians. The warrior queen among them is Dawāhī. Her sister does not engage in military activities.

Each of the kings and queens has a beautiful daughter, and we see 'Arnūs in full swing: he marries all four of them. Dreams leading to conversion play a dominant role: all four girls in due course convert to Islam. In three of the cases this happens as the result of a dream in which the girl is told to go and free 'Arnūs from her father's or mother's dungeons, an action which then quickly leads to conversion and marriage. Two of the girls have fairly simple dreams, but Princess Budūr, the daughter of warrior queen Dawāhī, has a horrible nightmare: she sees her mother Dawāhī being dragged by her hair towards hellfire, wanting to take her daughter with her.

In the Cairo edition, the episode, already very complicated, is made even more confusing because, in the later part of the story, Shawāhī is consistently referred to as 'king' and 'he'. Although it is probably just a mistake, I have kept it in order to show how messy and confusing the transmission of these texts sometimes is. In the Damascus edition this part has not yet been published. We will have to see whether the episode is included there or not.

The story begins when 'Arnūs hears about the castles. He rides out to visit them. Entering a garden near one of the castles he falls asleep in a gazebo with walls of clear crystal. When he wakes up he finds himself captured and shackled. The queens had learned by geomancy that he would enter the land and bring about their destruction. He is put into a dungeon, soon to be freed by King Sātirīn's daughter, Ward al-Masīh, whom he marries straight away.

Family complications soon follow. Being already married, the princess tells her father to refuse the offer of marriage from her cousin, Marīn's son. '"You promised to marry me yourself when I would be grown up!"'[14] War between the two brother kings is the result. 'Arnūs is kidnapped. Ward al-Masīh tells her father to put on 'Arnūs's clothes and attack the enemy, shouting Islamic battle cries. Marīn is defeated, 'Arnūs returns safely, and when he hears about his daughter's marriage and conversion, Sātirīn also becomes a Muslim.

'Arnūs is soon captured again. At his wife's suggestion, he asks for the hand of her cousin 'Adhrā' al-Masīh, Marīn's daughter.[15] The girl and her father, however, pretending to accept the proposal, trick him into captivity, and King Marīn calls in the help of his sister Dawāhī to defend his land and reconquer the area lost by the conversion of his brother. Dawāhī, an intrepid army leader, is quite successful. Meanwhile, 'Arnūs is still in Marīn's dungeon. One night, to his amazement, his perfidious quasi-bride 'Adhrā' al-Masīh, Marīn's daughter, steps in. She has been converted to Islam in a dream by 'Arnūs's deceased father, who told her to go down and free his son. Together they go to see her father, who also converts along with all his officials. Upon hearing this, King Shawāhī (for Queen Shawāhī is now a king) flees.[16]

'Arnūs's new wives alert him to a third possible wife, namely their cousin Nūr al-Masīh, the beautiful daughter of Shawāhī.[17] His proposal is not accepted and 'Arnūs attacks Shawāhī's castle. Battles follow, and King Shawāhī meets up with his warrior sister Queen Dawāhī.

It is at this stage that Dawāhī's warrior nature really comes to the fore, and her contacts with the perfidious priest Jawān, who, in the meantime, has also turned up, are greatly instrumental in bringing out her fierce character. By magical means she captures 'Arnūs and her brothers Sātirīn and Marīn, now both Muslims. She wants to kill them, but they are put in prison instead. Jawān thinks it is better to kill all the Muslims together once they have captured their king, Baybars. Dawāhī is happy to follow his lead, and together they ride out to attack Marīn's castle. They find it empty, the people having fled in fear of her, meeting Baybars on the way. He talks to them reassuringly and takes them along with him. Meanwhile Dawāhī goes on to Sātirīn's castle and finds it in ruins. She gathers her advisors around her and again suggests beheading the captured Muslims. Just then gunfire is heard, announcing the arrival of Baybars.

Dawāhī returns to her own castle, Baybars following her trail. Jawān tells her to get on her horse and to ride out to the battleground, ensuring the help of the *jinn* in waging war against Baybars. She follows his advice and goes out, killing and capturing twelve emirs and five *fedawi*s in one day. Jawān urges her to behead the captives, which she does enthusiastically, throwing the bodies to the Muslims.[18] However, by this act she has gone too far. Baybars calls out, enraged, and Tāj Nās, the wife of Shīha, appears from the air. She is a powerful sorceress. She spreads a black tent over Dawāhī's people, blinding them, and her son Taud cleaves Dawāhī's head asunder with his sword.

Just before this happens, Dawāhī's daughter has the nightmare mentioned above, in which she sees her mother being dragged to hell, trying to take her daughter with her. A big grey man tells the girl that she must accept Islam if she wants to be saved. She must go down to the dungeon, free 'Arnūs and ask him to accept her conversion. This duly happens and he marries her straight away. Marriage to King Shawāhī's daughter Nūr al-Masīh soon follows, after the king has consented to follow his daughter in accepting Islam and joining the Muslims.[19]

So the outcome of the story is four weddings and a funeral, and a substantial number of new Muslims. This latter positive effect is largely due to 'Arnūs's overwhelming attraction for girls, which takes on fairly hilarious proportions in the story. One even has a fleeting suspicion that the narrator did not really bother to take his own story seriously.

Maymūna and her daughter[20]

The episode of the sorceress Maymūna and her daughter, both warrior women, also shows us a foreign warrior queen for whom conversion to Islam is out of the question, and who consequently ends up dead. The episode is especially noteworthy for the scene in which traditional brave warriors are confronted by enemy forces using firearms. On a very minor scale, it recalls the gruesome battle scene in Akira Kurosawa's epic film *Kagemusha*, where a similar confrontation takes place.

Maymūna (a common name for black women) is the sister of the Ethiopian king Sayf al-Mulk. She is a sorceress and soothsayer. So is her daughter, who can assume different shapes. King Sayf al-Mulk is in danger of being attacked by Buktimur, one of Baybars's companions, who, as the result of a complicated series of events, leads military operations in the region of the Upper Nile. Maymūna, a brave army leader, offers her brother assistance and leads her men against Buktimur's army. At first she is successful, but then Buktimur has the good fortune to meet a *jinnī* princess, Marjāna, whom he saves when she is harassed by an unwanted lover, the *jinnī* Shabshīr. It earns him not only her gratitude but also Shabshīr's magic sword, a magic eye salve from her father and a protective magic cloak from her mother. The next time that Maymūna attacks Buktimur, things do not go well for her.

> Maymūna looked at that army and knew that it was Buktimur. She ordered her armies to go out, and out they went as if they were Gog and Magog. Buktimur yelled to the regiment: 'Fetch what I asked you!' Then he went to the battlefield, the army following him like eagles. They started to attack bravely, cutting through the lines, splitting skulls and craniums, striking cutting blows and effectuating piercing thrusts. His armies were behind him like striking lions. They went on like that till the end of the day. Eventually, the drum signal to withdraw was given. The blacks went back, and the armies

of Buktimur also returned from the battleground. They slept in safety and security.

Then Maymūna said to the soldiers: 'Do you not fear shame, being the noble sons of Hām and not able to fight a weak bunch of whites?' 'Queen, it is not that we are not able to fight the whites, and it is not our intention to withdraw from fighting, but we know that this emir fights us, and during the day he fights with the whites, but when we want to fight with him at night he attacks us with something that emits fire by which the blacks are killed, something that we have never seen in our life before. We, oh sorceress of the times, cannot make a proper estimate of the whites. We are afraid of the thing that they have with them.'

She got up and went into her stargazing room, wanting to practise sorcery. They openly said to her: 'Queen, we cannot take on Buktimur the Saʻdī, for Queen Marjāna has given him the sword of the *ifrīt* Shabshīr, her father King Barhajān has smeared the salve of brightness on him so that he can see us, strike us with that sword and annihilate us. Her mother gave him that magic cloak to put on. The science of divination by arrows is no longer of any use.[21] If you kill him you will still not be successful. The only thing that you can do, oh sorceress, is to flee.'

The accursed woman became furious. She left her stargazing room, got on the back of her horse, drew her sword and shouted: 'Tribe of Hām!' Horsemen flocked to her like eagles, and they advanced upon Buktimur. Buktimur had ordered the regiment to come down and confront the enemy, and his men met the horsemen with cannons and fire. The night was dark and the cannons continued firing until many people had been destroyed. When daylight broke, everything was covered with dead bodies. All the blacks lay on the ground, having been trampled underfoot.

Marjāna was stupefied to see what cannons can do. She knew that the sorceress Maymūna had not been successful against Buktimur the Saʻdī. She left immediately and went her way. As for Maymūna, when she saw that her men had been destroyed and that the sciences of divination were of no help against her enemy, she thought it best to accept defeat, for peace of mind is better than any kind of booty.[22]

And so modernity makes its appearance in popular epic. Both Maymūna and Marjāna realize that chivalric courage and magic are no longer the means to gain victory on the battlefield. Maymūna flees. Buktimur follows her with his army and eventually comes up against her brother's forces, whom he also defeats with his cannons, chasing them off to

Khartoum. Baybars rewards him by appointing him sultan over the region of Sudan.

Yet Maymūna does not give up, and neither does her daughter, who is also called Maymūna. When Buktimur is out hunting, the younger Maymūna assumes the shape of a white gazelle and lures him away. Having lost her trail, he finally comes upon a gathering of a hundred black girls and, in their midst, an Ethiopian girl of radiant beauty. He asks her for water and she gives him some to drink. Food is also brought and a bed is spread for him. She tells him her name, Maymūna, and he asks her whether she is married. She isn't, and she tells him that he is everything that she has always wanted in a husband. The marriage is concluded and consummated, and, when he is asleep and snoring, she gets hold of his magic cloak and burns it. She also breaks the magic sword. Then she firmly ties him up. When he wakes up she tells him about the ploy, adding that a female *jinnī* had placed herself between them during their embrace, so that their marriage had not really been consummated. She puts him on a horse and takes him to her mother and uncle, whose business it is to deal with him.[23]

Of course, eventually things do not end well for the Ethiopians. Nothing more is heard about the younger Maymūna, but King Sayf al-Mulk is captured and his sister, Maymūna the elder, is killed by Shīha's son. Her head is sent to her brother: 'When he saw her head he knew that she was dead.' The sight drives him mad.[24]

These examples may serve to demonstrate how the theme of the foreign warrior queen is treated in *Baybars*. It is basically little different from what we have seen in other *sīra*s, but the theme is not worked out so extensively. This agrees with the general picture: on the whole, the standard warrior woman motifs are only fleetingly encountered in *Baybars*. The women do not enter battle in male disguise. We hear nothing about their being trained from childhood in the martial arts. They lead armies but hardly ever engage in single combat. We do not come across the extensive combat scenes presented with such relish in older *sīra*s, the scenes where a male hero battles with a foreign warrior princess who will eventually become his wife. The warrior women described in *Baybars* rarely use weapons.

In *Baybars,* the intrepid woman who does not shun the use of violence is not the chivalrous lady trained for accomplished jousting on the battlefield, but the *fedawi* woman who has no scruples at all in reaching her goal. Her appearance is usually brief, but highly memorable.

Chapter 11

King Sayf ibn Dhī Yazan, the Soft-Hearted 1: Qamarīya[1]

Protagonists

- ʿAbd al-Salām, pious shaykh
- Afrāḥ, African king, fosters the young Sayf, father of Shāma
- Akhmīm, sorcerer, father of Jīza
- ʿĀqila, sorceress, mother of Tāma
- ʿĀqisa, *jinnī* foster sister of Sayf
- ʿArnūs, Ismaili leader in *Baybars*
- ʿAyrūd, *jinnī* servant of a magical tablet
- Barnūkh, sorcerer, supports Sayf
- Būlāq, son of Takrūr and Sayf
- Damar, son of Shāma and Sayf
- Dhū Yazan, Yemeni king, father of Sayf
- Hām, son of Noah
- Ibrāhīm, Qurʾānic prophet, the biblical Abraham
- Jayyād, pious shaykh
- Jīza, daughter of Akhmīm, marries Sayf
- Maymūna, warrior woman, wife of ʿAbd al-Wahhāb in *Dhāt al-Himma*
- Miṣr, son of Munyat al-Nufūs and Sayf
- Munyat al-Nufūs, queen of the City of Maidens, marries Sayf
- Nāhid, daughter of the king of China, marries Sayf
- Noah, Qurʾānic prophet
- Qamarīya, concubine of Dhū Yazan, mother of Sayf
- Saʿdūn, enemy champion, later supporter of Sayf
- Sām, son of Noah
- Sayf ibn Dhī Yazan, Yemeni king, eponymous hero of the *sīra*
- Sayfa Arʿad, emperor of Ethiopia

- Shāma, daughter of Afrāh, marries Sayf
- Takrūr, African girl, marries Sayf
- Tāma, daughter of ʿĀqila, marries Sayf

The name of the hero of *Sīrat Sayf ibn Dhī Yazan* recalls the famous pre-Islamic Himyarite king Sayf ibn Dhī Yazan, who, with the help of the Persians, drove the Christian Ethiopians out of Yemen at the end of the sixth century. While this explains why the Ethiopians are Sayf's major enemies in the *sīra*, there is otherwise hardly any connection to the pre-Islamic historical scene. The fact that Sayf's main opponent is the Ethiopian emperor Sayfa Arʿad sufficiently illustrates this: the historical Sayfa Arʿad ruled from 1344 to 1372, a period fairly close to the *sīra*'s probable time of composition.

In the story, Sayf ibn Dhī Yazan is a pre-Islamic hero who is converted by a pious shaykh to some type of Abrahamitic monotheism, a kind of proto-Islam.[2] Pre-Islamic Yemenite history is briefly brought up at the beginning of the story, which starts with the exploits of King Dhū Yazan, Sayf's father. That, however, is about the only historical connection to Yemeni history. Unlike *sīras* such as *Dhāt al-Himma*, *ʿAntar* or *Baybars*, *Sīrat Sayf ibn Dhī Yazan* does not present an easily recognizable historical framework.[3] As one scholar aptly put it, 'the *sīra* is situated from the outset in a mythical primordial universe, where men and *jinn* associate together on familiar terms, where sorcerers, wizards and enchanters engage in dogged combat, competing for power or for the mastery of natural forces'.[4] It was for that very reason that people from the audience of Sī Mlūd, the Moroccan storyteller mentioned in Chapter 1, expressed their dislike of the *sīra*: they considered it full of sorcery and lies, and preferred historical tales such as *ʿAntar* or *Dhāt al-Himma*.[5]

An Egyptian public might have had a different outlook, for the *sīra* is closely tied with the legendary history of Egypt. Sayf himself uncovers the Citadel of Cairo, and a number of the major protagonists become the founders of Egyptian cities named after them: Sayf's wives Jīza and Takrūr (Dakrūr), his sons Misr and Būlāq, and the sorcerer Akhmīm. Sayf also unblocks the Nile, which has been diverted to Ethiopia, and he makes it run through Egypt again. Fear of tampering with the course of the Nile by the Ethiopians is deeply ingrained in the Egyptian consciousness and emerges in various legendary accounts.[6]

A full summary of the *sīra*'s contents can be found elsewhere.[7] Briefly, the outline is as follows: the Yemeni king Dhū Yazan plans to attack the Ethiopians, who worship the planet Saturn. Having marched out towards their lands, he founds a city called the Red City. He inflicts heavy taxes on trade. In order to get rid of him, the Ethiopian king Sayfa Arʿad presents him with a beautiful girl, Qamarīya, who must kill him with poison hidden in her hair. She is successful in her mission and succeeds Dhū Yazan to the throne. She is pregnant by him, and when her son is born, a beautiful boy with a mole on his cheek, a sign that he is from royal Yemeni stock, she fears that he will soon be hailed as his father's rightful successor. Since she does not want to give up the throne, she decides to get rid of him. She abandons him in the desert, dressed in silk brocade, wearing a necklace and with a bag of money beside him. He is suckled by a gazelle, and a hunter finds him and brings him to the court of a black king named Afrāh. Soon after, a daughter is born to the king who also has a mole on her cheek. Her name is Shāma.

An old prediction says that if these two marry and 'the two moles will be joined on one pillow', the curse pronounced by Noah over his black son Hām will be fulfilled and the whites, the descendants of Noah's son Sām, will forever rule over the blacks. So the Ethiopians will be subject to the Arabs. This, as has rightly been pointed out, should not be taken to imply that the *sīra* is about white supremacy. The issue at stake is the victory of Islam over paganism.[8]

At the insistence of an Ethiopian sorcerer, King Afrāh promises to keep Sayf and Shāma apart. During this period, Sayf spends three years with the family of the *jinnī* woman who, along with a gazelle, briefly nursed him when he was left in the desert as a baby. He becomes very close to his *jinnī* foster sister ʿĀqisa, who will become his great support and helper, getting him out of difficult situations again and again.

He then returns to Afrāh's court but is soon sent away again to be trained in the art of war. When his master is satisfied with his accomplishments, he sends Sayf away to embark upon his adventures. He soon meets Shāma and the two are eager to marry, but the Ethiopian sorcerer constantly tries to prevent this by sending other wedding candidates to her father or by sending Sayf on impossible quests.

In the course of these adventures, Sayf (who still does not know his name and descent) is joined by a strong helper, a warrior called Saʿdūn. He is also sent out by the sorcerer to obtain the *Book of the Nile*, which will guarantee its possessor power over the Ethiopians and the blacks. In the course of this quest he meets a venerable shaykh named Jayyād, who hails him as 'the one who will lead the Nile from the land of the Ethiopians to Egypt'. The shaykh also tells him his real name, Sayf ibn Dhī Yazan, and explains to him that the curse of Noah will be fulfilled if he marries Shāma. He also converts Sayf to pre-Muhammadan monotheism, telling him to pronounce the Abrahamitic confession of faith: "I testify that there is no God but God, that Ibrāhīm is the Friend of God and that Muhammad is the Messenger of God, the last of the prophets and their seal." Shaykh Jayyād tells Sayf that henceforth he must fight the unbelievers. If he is in dire need he must call upon God, saying "'God is the greatest! God is the greatest!'" He also explains the basic principles of Islam. These are not specified, apart from the ritual ablution (*wudū'*), which Sayf dutifully performs at the first opportunity.[9] The subjects of Islam and conversion will return frequently throughout the *sīra*, usually without explicit reference to the fact that this is a pre-Muhammadan form of Islam.

After his meeting with the shaykh, Sayf is fully equipped to set out on his heroic career. He knows his name and royal descent, has become a true believer and is fully aware of the predictions that he has to fulfil: to 'join the two moles' by marrying Shāma and to divert the course of the Nile from Ethiopia to Egypt with the help of the *Book of the Nile*.

Many fantastic adventures follow, often not directly connected to Sayf's ultimate goal. In the end, however, Sayf's mission is fulfilled. The blockade at the fifth cataract is destroyed and the Nile flows into Egypt. The Cairo citadel is uncovered and cities are built. Sayf spends his last days as a hermit in the Muqattam hills behind the Cairo citadel.[10]

As usual in this literary genre, the date of composition of the *sīra* is unknown. The historical Sayfa Ar'ad, Sayf's main opponent, reigned until 1372, and he had already become part of legendary history when the *sīra* was composed. The oldest known manuscripts date from the seventeenth century. A reasonable supposition is that it was composed in Mameluke Egypt between the fifteenth and sixteenth centuries.[11]

As to style and language, the *sīra*, as it appears in the printed versions, is an interesting mixture of formal and informal language. The narrative style is fairly simple, but rhymed prose regularly occurs, especially for emphatic utterances, and poems are included from time to time. Sometimes these are quite long; one of the odes takes up more than five pages.[12] Apart from the passages using formal style, one is often struck by the remarkably simple, modern style and manner of expression. This again reminds us of the difficulties we have with dating the text of the printed versions. They are usually based directly on a manuscript but we do not know which one. Only extensive study of the manuscripts in connection with the printed versions, such as has been done for *Sīrat Dhāt al-Himma* by Claudia Ott and by Thomas Herzog for *Baybars*,[13] can give us a clearer idea about the dating of each particular version of the text.

Women

A noteworthy aspect of *Sīrat Sayf ibn Dhī Yazan* is the remarkable number of women who play a role. Among them there are *jinn* and humans, women who act as Sayf's protectors, such as his *jinnī* foster sister 'Āqisa, as well as fierce enemies. There are sorceresses and women of monstrous appearance. Noteworthy is the fact that many of these women are very independent characters. They have a clear sense of what they want, and are prepared to act quickly and ruthlessly. Compared with them, Sayf often comes across as fairly soft-hearted and pliable, sometimes even rather naive. He frequently depends on women, in particular his foster sister, to get him out of trouble. This kind of role division between males and females is not uncommon in Arabic popular storytelling. We find it not only in the tales of *The Thousand and One Nights*, but also in the tales told in family circles up to recent times.[14]

Lena Jayyusi, in the introduction to her partial translation of *Sīrat Sayf ibn Dhī Yazan*, remarks that the treatment of women in the Sayf tale 'demonstrates that the oral narrative is a living field of negotiated identities, positions, and practices'.[15] This is exactly what transpires in Sayf's relationships with women, especially with some of his wives. Like heroes in other *sīra*s, such as 'Arnūs in *Baybars*, Sayf concludes one marriage after another. A quick survey yields some sixteen marriages, not counting the wife and family he acquires and loses during a stay in an illusory world. As to how the audience fitted this in with the Islamic rules about marriage, which only permit four simultaneous wives, one answer may be that this clearly was not a problem in the Abrahamitic form of pre-Islam to which Sayf adhered: only with the advent of Islam was polygamy restricted. Another answer, more in line with the actual reality of Islamic life, is that it was common practice for travellers in Islamic times to leave a wife behind and give her the right to divorce if her husband did not return within a certain period of time. This left the husband free to marry again and again, as can be seen in the account of the travels of the famous fourteenth-century traveller Ibn Battūta.[16]

Sayf's many love affairs are not always met with enthusiasm by his other women, and the way in which the story handles the ensuing emotions is sometimes not without psychological subtlety. Depending on her character, a wife or lover may utter death threats towards her rivals, or use the more subtle approach of deriding a co-wife's feminine attractions, such as comparing her dancing to that of a buffalo. Or, as we also saw with women in other *sīra*s, she may voice her discomfort by criticizing her husband's lack of interest in the well-being of their son, who has disappeared and not been heard of for a long time.[17] Criticism is not only uttered by wives but also by one of Sayf's sons, Damar, who bitterly reproaches his father for his never-ending interest in concluding new marriages, which has been very hurtful to his mother Shāma. At one point this even leads to an armed confrontation between them.[18]

The output from all these marriages in terms of offspring is remarkably small, certainly compared with that of 'Arnūs in *Baybars*: four sons, no daughters. Only his wives Shāma, Munyat al-Nufūs, Jīza and Takrūr bear him children.

As to warrior women, *Sayf ibn Dhī Yazan* is more a fairytale than a romance of chivalry, and this has its implications for the treatment of the warrior woman theme. Several warrior women appear on the scene, but their martial training and career are not described as extensively as in *Dhāt al-Himma* or *'Antar*. Yet there is much in the *sīra* that is of interest in this respect. Particularly noteworthy are the remnants of the classical Amazon motif in the description of a community of martial women where men are excluded. The episode in which this occurs deserves special attention.

Among the many female characters who appear in *Sayf* we will choose three who are particularly interesting, both for their own sakes and for Sayf's reaction to their behaviour: his mother Qamarīya, a thoroughly villainous character, intent on killing Sayf from the moment he is born;[19] his wife Tāma, a headstrong, single-minded girl who is a bit of an unguided missile, and actually kills one of Sayf's other wives; and his wife Munyat al-Nufūs, queen of a female community from which Sayf has to retrieve her when she has left him in anger.

Qamarīya[20]

Qamarīya, Sayf's mother, is one of the most violent and power-hungry women in *Sīrat Sayf ibn Dhī Yazan*. Motherhood is unwelcome to her, and she hates her son from the moment he is born. She consistently tries to harm him and to remove him from the scene. In this, she does not fit

Qamarîya

at all into the usual pattern of the mother figure in Arabic literature,[21] although Maymūna in *Sīrat Dhāt al-Himma* has traits in common with her. Qamarīya frequently exploits Sayf's wish to see her as a concerned and loving mother by getting him to trust her and then playing a vile trick on him. In spite of continuous warnings, he again and again gives her the benefit of the doubt, and even when his enraged foster sister finally throws Qamarīya's head into his lap he mourns the loss of his mother, although he is fully aware of her evil nature and the harm she has done to him.

Qamarīya plays a prominent part in the first quarter of the *sīra*. A full account of all the complicated adventures in which she is involved is not possible here. We will just note the main points and highlight a few episodes in which her attitude to Sayf is especially prominent.

As mentioned above, Qamarīya enters the story as part of a ploy by the Ethiopian ruler to get rid of the Yemeni king Dhū Yazan. She kills Dhū Yazan, takes his place on the throne and gives birth to a son whom she hates from the start. She realizes that, in due course, her subjects will want the boy, Sayf, to replace her on his father's throne. She fervently prays to Saturn (the Ethiopians are star worshippers) to bring about his death. She gives him hardly any milk, trying to starve him, but he just gets more and more beautiful. The nobles ask to be shown their king. She fetches the baby and throws him on the throne in their midst. She hears how they praise and welcome him, and almost explodes with anger and jealousy. She tries to cut off his head but God prevents this, paralysing her arm. Finally she abandons him in the wilds, where he is found by a hunter. He is brought up at the court of King Afrāh, whose daughter Shāma he is destined to marry.[22] King Afrāh is a vassal of the Ethiopian ruler, and so the young Sayf forms part of his entourage.

Meanwhile, Qamarīya continues to rule in her deceased husband's town, the Red City. She replaces all his chamberlains with her own men, and forms a threat to commercial traffic. Officially she is still a vassal of the Ethiopian king, but she does not properly pay her dues. Nobody knows whether her son, who by now must have reached maturity and is the real heir to the throne, is still alive. When complaints to this effect reach the Ethiopian king, he decides to send an expedition of ten thousand horsemen to bring Qamarīya into line. He appoints the young Sayf as leader of the expedition. Sayf's real identity, at that point, is not known to Qamarīya, and neither is he aware of the fact that she is his mother.

When he is close to the Red City, Sayf sends Qamarīya a message telling her about the king's displeasure and asking her to pay her dues. She, however, prefers battle, and Sayf decides that the armies will meet on the battlefield the following day. While he sits up at night praying, his servant announces that Qamarīya is at the door, wanting to speak to him. She suggests that they wrestle together in order to decide the outcome of the conflict rather than waste their soldiers' blood. Sayf thinks it a good idea, but is somewhat taken aback when she starts taking off her clothes, revealing 'a body as white as pure silver'. She only wears a very thin garment that is lifted by the lightest breeze, revealing everything that is underneath. The text describes this in minute detail.[23]

Her intention, the narrator explains, was to lead Sayf astray by suggesting illicit pleasures. She has underrated him, though: he absolutely refuses to wrestle with her while she is practically naked. She insists, saying that this is common practice in wrestling, and finally he consents to take off his clothes. By this, his necklace is revealed, which she immediately recognizes as the one she put on her baby son when she abandoned him in the wilderness.

In her foreign language she elaborately curses the fact that he is still alive in spite of her efforts. Then, effecting a quick change of role, she changes to Arabic and greets him as her long lost son, whom she had thrown out in the desert in a bout of madness. Four of his fathers' chamberlains, she says, will confirm her words, as they indeed do, recognizing the mole on his cheek.[24]

Sayf is delighted but also somewhat taken aback by the fact that she could thus abandon her own son. Qamarīya defends herself, intermittently voicing her suppressed anger in her own language, which Sayf does not understand. She apologizes for her act by referring to the madness that took hold of her, saying that she regretted it so much that she can no longer enjoy food or drink. She cries, and he feels sorry for her. He suggests that she goes back to her city to tell her soldiers that war between them is over, and then he will join her tomorrow to be presented to her people. She returns home, but first takes care to kill the four chamberlains, who are very unwelcome witnesses.[25]

Sayf wants to believe that she really is glad to have him back, but his common sense has not completely left him: he asks for his father's treasure, saying that he will not enter the city before she has given it to him. According to Qamarīya the treasure has been hidden somewhere in the wilderness, and together they depart to retrieve it. She hopes for an opportunity to kill him, but Sayf is too careful. Clearly he does not trust her yet. He also refuses to keep watch over her while she sleeps. Further and further they go, and, on the fourth day, he asks her why, for heaven's sake, she decided to hide his father's treasure so far away? She puts on a 'poor little me' act: "'If I had not done this they would have attacked me and taken it away from me. I could not have got it back, for I am a woman, a creature with a crooked rib and a stammering tongue.'"[26]

Finally, Sayf decides that he does not want to go any further, and when they come to a big tree with a spring under it he accepts her offer to watch over him while he sleeps. She puts his head in her lap to demonstrate her motherly love. Looking down at him, her anger blazes up again when she realizes that her attempt to get rid of him has all been in vain, for here he is back as a 20-year-old young man! She gets up, draws her sword and starts hacking away at him. Finally, she thinks that he is dead and, wiping her sword, she happily leaves.[27] She goes back to her city and is reconciled with the Ethiopian king, the same one who sent her on the mission to kill Dhū Yazan, Sayf's father. He agrees with the way in which she handled the affair at the time, and all is well again between them.[28]

Sayf, left for dead in the desert, wakes up in a miserable condition and prays for help. Two birds arrive and perch on a branch above his head. They utter a prayer, and then one says to the other: "'Brother, have you seen what the accursed Qamarīya has done to her son? [...] What will we do?" "Brother, do not interfere with what the All-knowing King has decided," answers the other, "Know that this Qamarīya is his mother, no doubt, and that seven times she will treat him treacherously. The first time was when as a small baby she left him in the wilderness under the burning sun [...]. This is the second time: she has attacked him with weapons and left him here out in the open country.'" Before flying away, they mention that the chewed leaves of the tree cure wounds. Sayf has heard their words and gratefully makes use of them. These two birds, as it turns out, were the spirits of Shaykh 'Abd al-Salām and Shaykh Jayyād, two pious shaykhs whom Sayf had met earlier, and whose bodies he had buried when they died.[29]

One would think that this experience would put an end to any positive expectations of Qamarīya that Sayf may have cherished. Yet his longing to have a loving mother means that he trusts her again and again, and, as the words of the bird had already predicted, there is still a lot in store for him on her account.

During his next adventure, shortly after he has been saved in this miraculous manner, he obtains a magical tablet which makes its owner the master of a *jinnī*, 'Ayrūd. When the tablet is rubbed the *jinnī* appears to do his master's bidding. Sayf's first deed is to order the *jinnī* to take him back to the Red City where he has left his army. He must also find out what is happening to his beloved Shāma. He arrives there in the nick of time. She is about to be married to someone else, and he is just in time to prevent the wedding.[30]

Their own wedding is then finally arranged. When Qamarīya's name is mentioned in his conversation with Shāma, he refers to her as 'that accursed traitress',[31] but, in spite of this, he still has not given up all hope of her. After his wedding is concluded, he meets his mother on his way to the bridal chamber. She congratulates him, wishing him well, and this makes him very happy.[32] Of course, Qamarīya has her own evil intentions: she has her eye on the magical tablet he is carrying. He enters the bridal chamber, Shāma kisses his hand and, very naively, he gives the tablet to his mother to guard while he consummates the marriage. When bride and bridegroom are asleep, Qamarīya walks off with the tablet. Having locked her door, she summons the *jinnī* and orders him to carry Sayf off to the land of the ghouls and Shāma to the Valley of the Giants. The *jinnī*, forced to do her bidding, flies off with them. Totally bewildered, Sayf asks where he is taking them and who has ordered him to do this.

> 'That tender, loving, seductive sorceress gave me the order, namely your mother, my treacherous and accursed mistress Qamarīya!' 'But 'Ayrūd, my mother repented about what she had done and had become pure of heart towards me!' 'Yes, and then you gave her authority over me and made her my mistress, although I had not complained to you or been fed up with serving you.' 'I was afraid to say that I did not want to give it to her.' 'Well, so much for her pure heartedness and repentance about her former deeds! You have acted in full knowledge of what you did and have made all your efforts go to waste. Everything that your mother said was lies and falsehood.' Sayf deeply regretted what he had done and wept about his fate. "Ayrūd, can you not take us both to the same place?' 'No, that is not possible.'

Having carried out his orders, 'Ayrūd returns to Qamarīya, who is very pleased.[33] Her third trick has been successfully accomplished and there are more to follow. Eventually Sayf and Shāma, who, in the meantime, has given birth to a son,[34] manage to get together again, but Qamarīya will not leave them in peace. She has Sayf removed again, this time to the Mountain of the Sorcerers. Here Sayf has the good luck to find that the chief sorcerer has been converted through a dream in which he met Sayf and helps him to escape.[35] Action is undertaken against Qamarīya. Barnūkh, the converted sorcerer, punishes her by means of magic, managing to make her terribly ill.[36] In spite of this she manages to summon the *jinnī* and orders him to remove Sayf again. While they are flying over the sea, a burning pain tells ʿAyrūd that she wants him to return to her immediately, and he leaves Sayf on the first island that he comes across. This is an island where the people are extremely tall and where crab shells are collected for use against blindness.[37]

Upon leaving the island, Sayf takes a crab with him, and this enables him to cure the blindness of Princess Nāhid, who then becomes his wife.[38] His peregrinations come to an end immediately after the wedding, because Barnūkh, the helpful sorcerer, manages to steal back the tablet from Qamarīya and orders the *jinnī* to take Sayf home again to the Red City, where his wife Shāma and her son also soon arrive.

Qamarīya still rules the city and is very much taken aback when she finds Sayf sitting on her throne the next morning and, moreover, discovers that the tablet has disappeared. She tries to save herself by grovelling, saying that she is such an evil person that death is the only fitting punishment for what she has done. Although his friends strongly advise him to kill her, Sayf cannot bring himself to do so, as she knows full well: "'She is my mother, and here she stands before me, humbling herself. Maybe she will repent when I have pity on her. I will never be able to kill her.'"[39]

Instead Sayf imprisons Qamarīya and she sees her chance. She pretends to be terribly ill, soiling her clothes, throwing herself on the ground and in general making such a fuss that the servant entrusted with her care is afraid that she will die and warns Sayf. His reaction is: "'The only thing that I am afraid of is that she will die while she is angry with me.'" He bursts into tears when he sees her condition and hears her confess in a very weak voice that she has done him terrible harm. He gives orders to bathe her, to dress her in the finest clothes and to put her in a comfortable place. She continues to affect utter weakness. Sayf keeps all this a secret for fear of the reaction he will get from his companions.[40]

Qamarīya manages to send a message to summon the help of two powerful sorcerers. They come to Sayf's court to ask about her condition. Sayf tells them that he has released her from prison. The news causes great consternation among his companions. Some of them want to depart as soon as possible for fear of what she might do.

What she does, in fact, is create symptoms of serious illness in herself with the help of the two sorcerers. They have two herbs, one to make her very ill and one to make the symptoms disappear on the spot. The situation looks very serious indeed and Sayf is fetched. He is very upset, afraid that his mother's death is his fault, for keeping her in prison far too long. His mother begs him to forgive her for everything she has done wrong, and he, in his turn, asks her to forgive him. They go on for a while in this vein, until Sayf is completely out of his mind, throws himself at her feet and kisses her. It was the tablet that drove them apart, he says, '"Take it if you want, and do with me as you see fit!"' She refuses, however.[41]

That night he takes the tablet, hung by a chain, from around his neck and puts it in a box, asking his wife Nāhid to lock their bedroom door. She forgets to do this and Qamarīya, miraculously recovered, steals the tablet while Sayf and Nāhid are asleep.[42] She is delighted, and she orders the *jinnī* ʿAyrūd to carry Sayf off and drop him on the points of swords and lances. ʿAyrūd cannot disobey her, but manages to put Sayf into a hollow tree trunk before dropping him so that he has a chance of survival. As it turns out, Sayf does not even reach the ground: his foster sister ʿĀqisa snatches him out of the air and flies him home. On their way back they visit an island where he meets a next wife, Munyat al-Nufūs.

Qamarīya's sixth evil trick has been accomplished successfully, but she is coming to the end of the line, although she still has the magical tablet. The sorceress ʿĀqila, about whom we will say more in the next section, gives Sayf a magic belt that makes it impossible for *jinn* to come near him.[43] Thus ʿAyrūd cannot carry out Qamarīya's orders when she wants to have Sayf removed again. Of course, Qamarīya wants to get hold of the belt at all costs, and to achieve that she needs to regain her son's confidence. She thinks up a clever ploy: to tell him that she wants to convert to Islam at the instigation of his father, who has appeared to her in a dream. As a sign of her good faith she will give him the tablet (a replica of course), saying that she no longer needs it. The plan works perfectly and Sayf is delighted, not so much about having the tablet back as about his mother's conversion.[44]

Qamarīya then approaches Sayf's wife Nāhid, realizing that the unhappy Nāhid, who feels neglected after Sayf has concluded two more marriages, is a weak spot in Sayf's defence. She persuades Sayf to spend the night with Nāhid, who is very grateful for her intervention and gladly agrees to bring the belt to Qamarīya as soon as Sayf is asleep. Qamarīya stands waiting by the bedroom door and Nāhid hastens towards her, stretching out her hand with the belt that she has taken from under her sleeping husband's head. A sword flashes and Nāhid's head rolls away, separated from her body. The sword, as it turns out, was handled by Tāma, about whom more will be said below. Qamarīya flees in panic. She orders ʿAyrūd to take her to China, to the court of Nāhid's father, where she makes her appearance in full splendour, dazzling everybody with her beauty.[45]

Qamarīya does not stay away long, though. Soon she is back to look for new opportunities but to no avail: the magical tablet is stolen back from her and she is captured by ʿĀqisa, who, after much persuasion, obtains Sayf's permission to kill her. ʿĀqisa, finally allowed to vent her rage, cuts off Qamarīya's head with the sword of Tāma, who almost manages to beat her to the task. The head lands in Sayf's lap.[46] Qamarīya is buried in Nāhid's grave, and, in spite of everything, Sayf mourns her deeply.

CHAPTER 12

King Sayf ibn Dhī Yazan 2: Tāma[1]

Protagonists

- Afrāh, African king, fosters the young Sayf, father of Shāma
- ʿĀqila, sorceress, mother of Tāma
- ʿAyn al-Hayāt, daughter of Sābik al-Thalāth, wife of Sayf
- ʿAyrūd, *jinnī* servant of a magical tablet
- Barnūkh, sorcerer, supports Sayf
- Jayyād, pious shaykh
- Munyat al-Nufūs, queen of the City of Maidens, marries Sayf
- Qamarīya, concubine of Dhū Yazan, mother of Sayf
- Qamrūn, king of the city of Qaymar
- Saqardīyūn, Ethiopian sorcerer, enemy of Sayf
- Sayf ibn Dhī Yazan, Yemeni king, eponymous hero of the *sīra*
- Tāma, daughter of ʿĀqila, marries Sayf
- Umm al-Hayāt, see ʿAyn al-Hayāt

The antics of Tāma, who will become one of Sayf's wives, make amusing but also curious reading. She is an excitable young girl who is hard to restrain once she has got something in her head, and she is inclined to act before she thinks. It is hard to believe that she is a character created in the fifteenth century: her reactions are more reminiscent of the tomboy heroines from early twentieth-century European (here I think particularly of Dutch) novels.

Tāma's wild and unrestrained behaviour curiously contrasts with Sayf's soft-heartedness, already demonstrated by his attitude to his mother Qamarīya. Sayf finds Tāma very attractive and this makes him fairly defenceless. She can do little wrong in his eyes even though one occasionally thinks that she could do with a good spanking: what to think of a man who reacts with nothing more than a little sadness and disappointment when he discovers that his intractable fiancée has killed his wife?

Is Tāma a warrior woman? She is more a travesty of a warrior girl than a real female knight. She appears in full armour, not even recognizable as a woman, but she is clueless about the rules of combat. She knows how to handle a sword, however, at least to the extent that she manages to cut off a rival's head. She is the daughter of ʿĀqila, a sorceress who decides to help Sayf and who plays an important part all through the *sīra*, meeting her death only near the very end. ʿĀqila and Tāma enter the scene when Sayf, early in his career, is engaged in his quest for the *Book of the Nile*, which is kept in the city of King Qamrūn. ʿĀqila and the sorcerers under her command help Qamrūn to guard it using all possible means.

Shaykh Jayyād, after telling Sayf his real name and mission, points the way to ʿĀqila's dwelling place and tells him that her daughter Tāma is destined to become one of his wives. ʿĀqila herself has also found out that Sayf is Tāma's predestined husband and that he will come to their city to take the *Book of the Nile*. She decides to help him.

Following the shaykh's directions, Sayf crosses the water that separates him from ʿĀqila's country on the back of a fantastic feathered beast that constantly tries to swallow the sun, following it over the water. Meanwhile, ʿĀqila and Tāma are already aware of his arrival and take action. So when Sayf sets foot on land and looks around him, he notices a cloud of dust in the distance, which comes nearer and reveals

> a knight clad from top to toe in iron, riding on a yellow golden horse with a long tail, girded with a sword as if he was the messenger of death, carrying a brown spear [...] and straight of posture. The knight wore a veil over his face and had eyes that shot arrows from the midst of passionate fury.[2] He sat on his horse full of self-conceit like a lion. When this lion was close to Sayf he shouted: 'Halt, you there! Do not move a step closer! Know that this day will be your last!' When Sayf ibn Dhī Yazan saw him, he did not give him any answer and refrained from dealing out thrusts and strikes, not paying attention to the knight's attacks and charges. Every time that the horse charged he pushed it back without lifting his sword or thrusting with his spear. This went on for a full hour. Every time that the knight struck out at Sayf ibn Dhī Yazan with his sword or thrust at him with his spear, his actions had no effect at all. Sayf parried his blows in such a way that they vanished into thin air as soon as they landed.

The knight was stupefied by the way he acted and said: 'Young man, do you not strike me like I strike you and fight me like I fight you?' Sayf answered: 'Young man, I see that you are not a warrior, that you do not know how to strike and fight and that you have not sufficient endurance to take up action against someone. In fact you are just an ignorant fool. You make a serious mistake in riding that horse while you see me walking on foot. From sheer ignorance you have said to yourself: "I am going to attack that knight and fight him!" I have nothing but contempt for you, because you are just a stupid young boy. You do not have the endurance and the stamina to fight me. If you really were a warrior who knew what is right, you would not set out to fight, order me to halt upon meeting me and attack me while you are mounted on a horse and I am walking on foot. This is not how noble knights act. If this had happened to me with a real warrior and fighter I would have thrown you headlong in the sand, flat on the ground. Just to make you understand that I really mean what I say: this is what I would have done with a champion.' He grabbed the neck of the horse with his right hand and lifted the knight with his left, saying: 'This is what men do who have experience in fighting.' Then he put him right back into the saddle.

Stupefied and completely baffled, the knight said: 'You are right, king of the kings of Yemen, lord of the fief of Sana and Aden, destroyer of those who adhere to unbelief and cause affliction, you who cleanse the earth of sorcery and discord. You are Sayf ibn Dhī Yazan.' 'Yes,' he answered, 'and you are a stupid little boy. Who is your father and what is his name among knights and champions so that you knew about me and wanted to fight with me?' He said: 'I am neither a man nor a champion, but a female, a virgin girl, one of the ladies that stay hidden behind their curtains. It was worry and compassion for you, lord of champions, that made me come to this desolate region and do this to you.

My name is Queen Tāma and my mother is a sorceress named 'Āqila the Wise. The reason why I came here is that when my mother brought me up I asked her to see whom I was going to marry. So she cast the sand figures and told me that my husband would come from the land of Yemen and that he was Sayf ibn Dhī Yazan. I asked her: "How will we be brought together, since he lives in a faraway country?" She answered: "He has asked the daughter of King Afrāh in marriage and the king has asked for the *Book of the Nile* as her dowry and wedding present. So he will come and get it from this country, and I will help him to get it. He will have to endure tremendous hardship and I will step in and save him, because I want to marry you to him."

My mother went on in this way. Every night she did her best to tell me more, until the time came that she said to me: "King Sayf has asked for marriage, but the sorcerer Saqardīyūn has opposed him. He then went to the castle of the Pleiades and his beloved has gone with him."'[3] As she told him, Tāma had then said to her mother: 'Find out who this girl is so that the sign becomes clear to us.' She answered: 'The girl is his [future] wife Shāma. Out of compassion for him and fear that he will meet his death she has gone with him to the castle of Sa'dūn and saved him from perdition after he had fallen into the traps. Subsequently they made peace with Sa'dūn.' 'Later on my mother told me: "Sayf has asked for Shāma a second time, and this time they have asked him to bring the *Book of the Nile*." Still later on my mother said to me: "Sayf is approaching this land, but he is held up in the hermit cell of shaykh Jayyād, who teaches him the confession of faith in the only God and how to say the holy name of the Lord of the pious worshippers. This evening," she said, "he will mount the *hāyisha* [a miraculous beast] that will bring him over the sea. In the morning he will come to this land, and I fear for his life when he tries to get past the defences." I asked her: "What are you afraid of, mother?"'

Her mother answers that the city of Qaymar, from which Sayf has to fetch the *Book of the Nile*, is protected with all sorts of magic devices made by ancient magicians. She describes these devices in detail. Tāma continues:

'I said to her: "What to do now, since you have promised me that you will marry me to him and will help him to get the *Book of the Nile*? Tell me what clever solutions we can think of and what actions we can undertake, so that I can go and try to do something about it. If I see that he is in trouble I will wage my life for him."

My mother said: "Get on your horse and prepare your battle gear. Go out as if setting out to hunt and go in the direction of that plain. When you see a lone man approaching, you must attack him, suggest that you will kill him and strike him with your sword. It will have no effect on him. Harass him with all your might until he plucks you from your horse with his left hand and lifts the horse with his right. Then you will know that he is the man you want. Let him know that he must be careful and that he cannot pass through the gate of the city to get below the tenth tower. I will put him onto the mangonel. Maybe God will provide a way to get us out of difficulties."

When I had heard what my mother said I saw that she was right. I got on my horse straight away and set out for the lonely desert until I saw you in the situation that she had described. Then I set out to fight and battle with you. This is what I did and things came to pass as they did. I have told you, oh King Sayf, everything that my mother has said. I have seen that what she said was right and beyond doubt or hidden meaning. So, king, what do you want to do, so that I can see how you are going to act and can observe what sort of clever plans you have thought up?'

King Sayf answered: 'To me everything that you say sounds just like a bunch of confused dreams. I thought you were just a champion knight wanting to battle with me. You started hacking away at me like a very dangerous enemy and when you saw yourself defeated and humiliated you pretended that you were a girl, one of the ladies. Then you told me a long story of which I do not understand a word – I cannot make head nor tail of it. I know nothing of the *Book of the Nile* and have not come searching for it. I am not the man you spoke about. You are wearing a veil over your face, so I really do not know what is going on.' 'You are right,' she said. 'My mother already told me that you would say this, saying "He will not believe you before you take the veil from your face." So hereby I give you the proof that I am who I said, oh imām, oh intrepid young man!'

She took off her veil, revealing a face like the full moon. It was round like a radiant disk of crystal. It had cheeks spread with roses made by the All-Forgiving King, eyes like that of the wild cow or the gazelle, glances that shot piercing arrows to hit warriors and other men, and a neck that looked as if it was moulded from precious stones put on a chest that was like a plate of marble under which a couple of breasts sprang up that would make the necks of lions bow down in reverence. When Sayf ibn Dhī Yazan looked at all that and saw the beauty and charm with which Queen Tāma had been endowed, his head reeled and he was completely perplexed. 'Hide your face, marvel of beauty and charm!' he said to her. 'The passion and unsettling emotion that you bring about make the frightening situation that I have to face even worse.' 'Never mind,' she said. 'What you see is just a gift of God to refresh your eyes. I will go back to my mother, the wise 'Āqila, and let her know that you are on your way.'[4]

She gives him instructions about going straight to the tenth tower, staying outside the city wall, and lying down in a chest that he will find waiting there, attached to a rope. He follows her instructions, is hauled over the wall and arrives in ʿĀqila's house without having been noticed by the devices guarding the city. ʿĀqila explains to him the whole situation, including her wish that he should marry her daughter. Sayf agrees to the proposal, but explains that he must first marry Shāma and to do so he needs the *Book of the Nile*. Mother and daughter immediately start devising a number of clever tricks to get him to the place where it is hidden. King Qamrūn, the ruler of the city, is not aware of the fact that ʿĀqila has switched sides and regularly consults her when strange things start to happen with the guarding devices. Her sorcerers know exactly where Sayf is, but the king does not believe them. So Sayf stays hidden in the house of ʿĀqila, and Tāma has a happy time preparing meals for him, sitting next to him and feasting her eyes on his handsome face.[5] All goes well until Sayf disregards ʿĀqila's instructions and is discovered. He is thrown into a jar-shaped dungeon, but his *jinnī* foster sister ʿĀqisa is waiting for him there and takes him away from the city.[6] Together they embark on various adventures and she takes him on a trip to see the wonders of the world. During one of their adventures he steals a cap that makes him invisible. With the help of this cap he will eventually manage to steal the *Book of the Nile*, after ʿĀqisa has brought him back to the city of Qaymar.

In Qaymar, meanwhile, ʿĀqila and Tāma wait for him. In his absence Tāma's love for him increases substantially. She can hardly bear to be separated from him. 'Mother, how could King Sayf, the man you said I was going to marry, be thrown into the jar-dungeon by King Qamrūn? How can I now be married? Go on, see what has happened to him!'[7] So ʿĀqila starts to follow Sayf's adventures by geomancy, comforting her daughter with the promise that he will be back. Finally she discovers that Sayf is on his way to their house. She tells her daughter to go and open the door:

> 'Do you really mean it? Is King Sayf coming?' Tāma ran to the door, opened it and stared at King Sayf. She went up to him and hugged him to her breast, congratulating him on his safe return and kissing him between his eyes. 'My lord,' she said, 'are we awake or is this a dream? God be praised! How did you escape from the jar-dungeon, noble lord?' King Sayf started to speak to her while, her hand in his, she went up to her mother ʿĀqila the Wise.

The next problem to be solved is how to get hold of the *Book of the Nile*. 'Āqila, accompanied by Sayf, who wears his cap of invisibility, goes to King Qamrūn, pretending that she wants to consult the book. Sayf, still invisible, follows them to the tower where it is kept and manages to steal it: the king suddenly sees it flying away and does not understand what is happening.[8]

Now that Sayf's mission is accomplished, 'Āqila wants him to marry Tāma. Sayf, however, is adamant: Tāma is a pretty darling and he certainly does not want to give her up, but first he must marry Shāma.

> 'So please mother, do not speak any longer about this and do not heap censure and blame upon me. I have let you know how it stands, and that is how it is.' 'Āqila replied, 'I will not let you marry anyone before my daughter, and you are right here with me' and Sayf answered, 'I will never do that, even if it means my death.' They continued talking for a while and then sought to rest their bodies. Sayf ibn Dhī Yazan went to bed and slept, having put the book and the cap of invisibility under his head.'

Tāma has overheard their conversation and steals the cap, refusing to give it back before Sayf has married her. 'Well, my lady, then just take it, may God bless it for you [...] I do not rely on my cap, for the one who helps me is God.' He happily disappears without the cap but with the *Book of the Nile*,[9] and it will be quite a while before they meet again. By that time, Sayf will not only have married Shāma,[10] but also two more wives, Nāhid[11] and Munyat al-Nufūs.

The next meeting of Sayf and Tāma, like their first, starts with a cloud from which a knight emerges. Sayf is in a dire situation: sorcerers have paralysed him and his companions, and they stand motionless in the palace. His wife Shāma, who has escaped their fate, is with them.

Barnūkh, a sorcerer who is on their side, is powerless himself and prays for help. A cloud of dust approaches and a knight on a black horse emerges from it, a veil over his face. In front of him flies an old woman sitting on a large brass jar. They come to the palace where Sayf and his bewitched paladins are. Shāma stands at the door, her sword in her hand. The old woman greets her politely by name and asks about Sayf, promising that all will be well. Then the unknown knight draws near and the old woman tells him that this is Shāma, Sayf's wife. The knight reacts furiously: 'Get out of the way, so that I can strike off her head!'

It is Tāma, who, as we remember, had sworn to kill every wife of Sayf that she came across. Her mother tells her to behave:

> 'This is King Sayf's wife and she is not your affair.' 'But mother, I have sworn to kill every wife of King Sayf ibn Dhī Yazan that I saw! This is the first of his wives and I absolutely must stick to my oath and kill her, so that I will not be associated with lies and void threats.' When Queen Shāma heard this she said: 'What is it that you have sworn, you shameless hussy? Am I a stray creature that you can kill at will?' She drew her sword and went up to Tāma, who did the same. 'Āqila the Wise laughed at them and ordered the servants to keep them apart.[12]

'Āqila chides her daughter, saying that they have come to help, not to cause more harm. She goes back to Shāma, very nicely and politely explaining the plan to marry her daughter to Sayf. Eventually she manages to conciliate Shāma and Tāma. With the help of a magic bowl filled with water she then undoes the spells.[13] Sayf says that now nothing stands in the way of his marrying Tāma, except the little matter of the stolen cap of invisibility. 'Āqila asks her daughter where it is, but to no avail.[14]

A stalemate results: Sayf refuses to marry Tāma before she returns the cap to him, and she refuses to hand it over before she is married. Remembering Tāma's threats to kill his wives, Sayf becomes seriously worried, especially about his beloved wife Munyat al-Nufūs, who is less protected by family connections than the others. In spite of Tāma's threats he marries yet again, this time Umm (or 'Ayn) al-Hayāt, the daughter of a newly converted former enemy. Tāma is furious, but still hangs on to the cap.[15]

There is also the matter of Jīza, another promised bride. Her father is very insistent that the marriage should not be postponed. Sayf consults his companions and 'Āqila steps in, saying that they should not worry too much about Tāma: Jīza's father is their neighbour and a friend. At her mother's insistence, Tāma promises that she will never harm Sayf's wives Shāma and Munyat al-Nufūs or the two new ones, Umm al-Hayāt and Jīza. Everybody is reassured and the wedding takes place.[16]

We notice that the name of Nāhid, the fifth wife, is not mentioned here, and she is also excluded from the arrangements for spending his nights that Sayf has made with his wives. Thus Nāhid is dissatisfied and this has dramatic consequences, as was explained above: Sayf's evil mother Qamarīya uses her to get hold of Sayf's magic belt, and this leads to Nāhid's death. When Nāhid is about to hand the belt over to

Qamarīya, all of a sudden there is the flash of a sword and Nāhid's head rolls away, separated from her body. Qamarīya flees in panic in order to escape a similar fate.

When Sayf wakes up and does not find Nāhid beside him, he gets up to investigate, only to find her dead, her body drenched in blood. He has no idea what has happened. Crying, he recites a poem of mourning. Then his thoughts turn to Tāma and her threats. She soon arrives, stands before him and greets him:

'A very pleasant evening, oh Kinglet of all times, pearl of the age, king of Yemen, exterminator of those who deal in unbelief and tribulation!' Sayf replies, 'Why do you belittle me and address me as Kinglet? This has always been a great insult among Arab kings.' Tāma answers, 'Yes, and that is because you are a lot more stupid than those kings. Neither a rich man nor a brigand would act as you do.' He became very angry and wanted to give her a good slap, but restrained himself for fear of discord. 'Tāma,' he said, 'who has killed Nāhid?' 'I have no idea, my lord,' she replies. 'By the truth of the religion of Islam, tell me the truth!' says Sayf. 'By the Creator of light and darkness, no other than myself has killed her with this sharply cutting sword,' replies Tāma. His anger rising again, he says: 'Tāma, you have killed a living being while God forbids the killing of innocent people!' She replies, 'Good God! Her crime is on your head! Do you not know that I swore dire oaths to kill everyone you married except the four? Those four that are with you are all alive, Shāma, Munyat al-Nufūs, Jīza and 'Ayn [sic] al-Hayāt. This is another woman. She was not part of the condition and she was not mentioned in the oaths.' 'But why did she deserve death without committing a crime [...]?' asks Sayf. 'Her crime was enormous! To kill her was completely justified. God, the Creator of all beings, made me afraid, because she had taken the magic belt from under your head, wanting to present it to your mother Qamarīya.'

And, she continues, when his mother had the magic belt, he would no longer be protected against the *jinnī* that his mother can order about with the help of the magic tablet. She adds that Sayf, with his good and trusting heart, may think that he himself has the tablet in his possession, but the one he has is just a copy that his mother substituted a while ago for the real one. He can hardly believe her, but when he rubs his tablet, the *jinnī* 'Ayrūd does not appear. 'O yes, the real tablet of 'Ayrūd is with your tender loving mother who has cleverly pulled the wool over your eyes, may God curse her forever.' It makes Sayf all the more sad: his wife

Nāhid is dead, killed by his fiancée Tāma, and his mother Qamarīya is at the bottom of it all, still set on doing him harm.

Nāhid is buried, and Tāma's parting shot to Sayf is that, in due course, she will fill up the grave for him with all the wives he is going to marry. He bottles up his rage but decides that he is going to get even with her, and how! He only calms down when his *jinnī* foster sister 'Āqisa insists that Tāma's act was justified.[17] Qamarīya is killed soon afterwards, as described above.

Sayf's troubles with Tāma are by no means over. Shortly afterwards, he wakes up in the middle of the night to discover Tāma at his bedside, about to kill his wife Munyat al-Nufūs.[18] He yells at her but she does not let herself be frightened, saying that this is what she swore to do: to kill this wife like she did the other. Her mother 'Āqila appears, alerted by the screams. Sayf complains, but 'Āqila defends her daughter: the poor girl is completely distracted, she cannot eat or sleep and thinks about nothing but Sayf. Love has driven her to this desperate behaviour.

In spite of this Tāma still refuses to give back the cap of invisibility, and Sayf also does not want to give in: first the cap, then the wedding. Wise counsellors have a solution: Sayf can marry Tāma but leave the marriage unconsummated as long as the cap is not handed over.[19] Thus the matter is decided. Tāma's intractable nature again shows itself when the formalities have to be arranged: no, she does not want a dowry, and what does she need a wedding feast for? She just wants Sayf and as quickly as possible. Compromises are struck: her dowry will be that Sayf will give her anything she cares to ask for, and her mother's wish for a proper wedding party for her only daughter is respected.

A big wedding is organized and Sayf's wives dance at the party, not without occasional snide remarks at each other's elegance or lack of it ('buffalo!'). Tāma is very impressed by Munyat al-Nufūs's dancing, and Munya, knowing about the wedding condition, suddenly sees a way to get back the feather bird robe that Sayf had locked away when he married her (see the next chapter), afraid that she might fly home with it. She says to Tāma that if she only had the robe, she could show her some dancing, but Sayf does not want to let her use it.[20]

It is just the kind of challenge that appeals to Tāma. She decides to make this her promised wedding wish. With careful planning, she does not bring it up during her wedding night,[21] but the following morning. Sayf is aghast and says that this is impossible. Tāma reminds him of his promise. She says that nobody would think of giving the robe to Munyat al-Nufūs, if that is what he fears, and Munya anyhow is too engrossed in her newborn son to be interested. ʿĀqila also supports her daughter, guaranteeing that the robe will be safe with her.

Sayf takes the robe out of its hiding place, entrusts it to Tāma and goes hunting. Of course, it does not take long before Munya gets hold of the robe. Putting it on to dance as promised, she quickly ties her baby to her breast in a kerchief and flies away to her own country, delighted that she still knows how to use the robe. Tāma is desperate and her mother strongly blames her for breaking her promise. Initially, Tāma tells Sayf that Munya is dead, but, seeing his desperation, her mother tells him what really happened. Remarkably, Sayf is not even very angry at Tāma. That night he sleeps with her and she, rather uncharacteristically, says that she was wrong in taking the robe. She blames it all on Munyat al-Nufūs, who tricked her into getting the robe and then used it to fly away. Sayf just laughs, saying that Munya has the right to take liberties with him. He will just have to bear it. He will try to be reunited with her even if it costs him his life. This is definitely not what Tāma wants to hear. She is secretly angry about what he has said.

The next night Sayf sleeps with Shāma, who tries to set him against Tāma. Again he says that she did it just by mistake, and that basically she is a good-hearted girl with pure intentions. He tells Shāma that she is his right eye, Tāma his left, Jīza his heart and Munyat al-Nufūs his mind.[22] The next night he says farewell to his wife Jīza and her son, and the fourth night is for his wife ʿAyn al-Hayāt. Soon afterwards, he leaves the palace to start his quest. Nobody notices him for he wears the cap of invisibility.[23]

In due course Sayf will return with Munya, and although Sayf marries many more wives in the course of his adventures, the basic set-up of his household continues to consist of Shāma, Munya, Jīza and Tāma. Remarkably, Tāma is the only one who does not have a child.[24] She remains the odd one out, even though her relations with her co-wives improve considerably over time. A brief event may illustrate this: when Tāma is visiting Shāma, the news arrives that the sons of Shāma, Munya and Jīza have disappeared from their bedrooms. Tāma immediately suggests to 'the girls', as the three wives are referred to, that she will go into enemy country and try to find them. They are impressed: does she think she can manage that? Yes, she says, for she has the cap of invisibility that King Sayf once brought her. She climbs down from the ramparts by a rope, telling the others to haul her up again when the rope is pulled three times. She returns without the boys, however, and it will be quite a while before they are found again.[25]

So much for Tāma, one of the most striking female characters of Arabic popular epic. Headstrong and sometimes violent as she may be, we cannot help liking her for the way she stands up to Sayf despite of her love for him.

CHAPTER 13

King Sayf ibn Dhī Yazan 3: Munyat al-Nufūs[1]

Protagonists

- ʿĀqila, sorceress, mother of Tāma
- ʿĀqisa, *jinnī* foster sister of Sayf
- ʿĀsim, sorcerer king, brother of Qāsim
- ʿAyrūd, *jinnī* servant of a magical tablet
- Kawkab, female prison warden
- Marjāna, viziress of Nūr al-Hudā
- Munyat al-Nufūs, queen of the City of Maidens, marries Sayf
- Nūr al-Hudā, sister of Munyat al-Nufūs, replaces her as queen
- Qāsim, sorcerer king, brother of ʿĀsim, father of Munyat al-Nufūs
- Sayf ibn Dhī Yazan, Yemeni king, eponymous hero of the *sīra*
- Shāh al-Zamān, Persian king
- Tāma, daughter of ʿĀqila, marries Sayf

As I remarked in Chapter 2, the all-female communities that we meet in Arabic popular epic contain few elements that connect them to the Amazons of classical antiquity. Occasionally, however, remnants of the classical myth turn up, and the episode of the City of Maidens in *Sīrat Sayf ibn Dhī Yazan* is such a case. The episode centres around Sayf's wife Munyat al-Nufūs. It deserves closer attention in spite of the fact that Munyat al-Nufūs is not a prominent warrior woman, although she rules an all-female kingdom. Yet the wider context of her story is interesting enough to be treated here in some detail, with occasional references to theoretical literature.[2] One reason is that the episode presents striking examples of popular epic as a 'field of negotiated identities, positions, and practices'.[3] This applies in particular to gender relations in the story. Attitudes regularly shift, making the story a maze of ambivalence towards women's freedom and independence. The ambivalence appears in the attitudes of the male as well as the female protagonists, and is found at all levels of the story.

The narrator's sympathy, and consequently his focus, constantly wavers. His inability to take a stand in the battle between the sexes is unwittingly but most pointedly expressed by his refusal to tell us unambiguously what the hero, King Sayf, does at a crucial point in the story: namely when he has the option to have sex with a tree fruit shaped like a woman in every detail. In that particular episode (discussed later) the hero, although appreciative of the independence and capability of women, finds it difficult to resist the attraction of these fruits, these completely submissive females, chattels in the most literal sense of the word. It is only his piety that urges him not to give in to seduction. Whether effectively or not, remains unclear.

King Sayf, however nicely he goes about it, does not harbour the slightest doubt that the women in the story will ultimately have to bow to his domination. They will have to accept that he, in the most literal sense, robs them of their wings. The women themselves are also ambivalent: fierce rejection of male interference alternates with a willingness to betray a fellow female at the drop of a (man's) hat, and to bend to a man's will with alacrity if there looms the slightest chance of marriage and motherhood.

Briefly, the episode in *Sayf* runs as follows: King Sayf ibn Dhī Yazan, who has been taken on a trip to see the wonders of the world by his *jinnī* foster sister 'Āqisa, comes upon a secret garden where he spies a group of women bathing. They have flown there by means of enchanted feather robes.[4] Sayf falls in love with their queen, a woman of incomparable beauty, and, at his foster sister's advice, he traps her into captivity by stealing her feather robe. Having plied her with wine and loving words, he persuades her to marry him. He then takes her to his home, where he shuts away her feather robe for fear that she may use it to escape and fly back to her country. The fear is not unfounded, for although Munyat al-Nufūs, as she is called, loves him, she never quite overcomes her resentment of him having robbed her of her freedom by trickery and not having married her in the proper manner.

Later in the story we hear more about Munyat al-Nufūs's background and the reason why she flew to this particular island. It all started when Munyat al-Nufūs refused to be married to her cousin, the son of her uncle 'Āsim, or to any other man. Her father, 'Āsim's brother, King Qāsim, did not want to go against her wishes, especially as Munyat al-Nufūs threatened to kill herself if he tried to force her. In revenge 'Āsim made his sorcerers cast spells by means of the waxen image of a girl that was placed in the middle of the city,[5] with the result that all women were lured away from his brother's city to his own. Qāsim retaliated by doing the same with 'Āsim's men.

As a consequence, there were two cities, one inhabited exclusively by men and the other by women, at least after 'Āsim passed away and Munyat al-Nufūs succeeded her uncle on the throne. Spells and complicated devices such as watchmen made of brass and armed with trumpets kept the cities inaccessible. The possible incursion of male intruders into the women's city was further obstructed by 'Āsim's decree that all the girls should learn the art of chivalrous warfare in order to be able to ward off attacks. They kept up their training after 'Āsim's death.

It is implicitly understood that, as a result of the spells cast over them, the women shunned the company of men, at least as a community, and developed a social system in which there was no place for men. The mildly lesbian scenes that are included in the story (a fairly common aspect of tales with a similar setting) preclude the question whether sexual interest had any place in this community. As to the girls' sexual interest in men, the story is ambiguous. The end of the story suggests that their sexual interest does not awaken until the spells have been undone, but the individual women who come into focus as the story develops all show an interest in relationships with men, at least in private conversation. Besides, we are also told that the sorcerers have taken care to make at least some of the girls susceptible to sexual desire for men.[6]

The men, who are all lured to the city of Qāsim, Munyat al-Nufūs's father, are stuck there without women but are not devoid of sexual interest. For that reason the sorcerers' devices include the creation of a pond between the two cities. This pond is meant to lure girls away from the other city in order to find relief by bathing, for the sorcerers make their skins itch when they start longing for men.[7] Once they are in the water they are grabbed by men laying in wait for them. They are held captive to satisfy the men's needs until a new victim turns up. King Qāsim, when proudly shown this clever arrangement, is full of praise for the ingenuity of his magicians. The fate of the poor girls subjected to communal rape for an indefinite period of time clearly does not trouble the king at all, something that curiously contrasts with his attitude towards his own daughter, whom he treats with the utmost respect, even accepting her refusal to marry.

The existence of these segregated communities does not cause the king any personal trouble, because he has found a way to continue seeing his beloved daughter: he has given her a magical feather robe, enabling her to fly so that she can come and visit him. He also makes a secret garden where she can go and bathe with her companions, also endowed with feather robes. They, at least, do not have to bathe in the pond at the risk of being sexually abused. At first Munyat al-Nufūs makes use of her privilege too freely, and her father orders her to limit her excursions to the garden to once a year. Thus, the freedom of movement that the feather robe gives her is surrounded by ambiguity. The robe has been given to her by her father, but clearly his concern is mostly that he does not want to be deprived of her company. He supports her refusal of marriage, and when her uncle's vengeful act has separated her from him he gives her the feather robe in order that she may be able to visit him, explicitly forbidding her to use it whenever she wishes.

It was during one of these visits that Sayf fell in love with her and abducted her. He shuts away Munya's feather robe when he arrives home with her, afraid that she will use it to escape. Shortly after the birth of her son, however, she manages to get it back by cleverly manipulating Sayf's new wife Tāma. She puts on the robe, flaps her wings and rises up in the air. Perching for a moment on top of the palace wall, she calls down a message for Sayf:

> 'When King Sayf ibn Dhī Yazan comes and asks for me, say to him that his wife has gone away to her own country to set her heart and mind at rest. She has taken her son with her. Say to him: It is beyond your power and that of a thousand other kings to possess Munyat al-Nufūs, the daughter of the Frowning King. One does not take the daughters of kings by stealing them, but by writing a marriage contract and establishing good relations. You have stolen me away from the girls and have caused me pain by taking other wives and leaving me alone. But what is past is past. When you really are a man of high resolve and perseverance, you can come to the Islands of Maidens, and if you long for your wife and son, you can find them on the islands of Wāq al-Wāq.'[8]

Then she ties her baby son to her breast and flies away. When Sayf returns home, his wife Tāma, who feels very guilty, first tells him that Munyat al-Nufūs has died, but, seeing his despair, Tāma's mother ʿĀqila tells him the truth. His reaction is unambiguous: he must go and retrieve his beloved wife and son from the strange and faraway world of Wāq al-Wāq, a world that cannot be reached within ordinary time limits.

His *jinnī* foster sister ʿĀqisa and ʿAyrūd, the *jinnī* servant of the magical tablet in Sayf's possession, are prepared to help him. They carry him to the outward edges of Wāq al-Wāq, an area that is inaccessible to ordinary *jinn*. Going on, he meets a saint who provides him with a number of useful objects to take along on his trip. One of them is another tablet governing a *jinnī*, this one powerful enough to take him to the Islands of Maidens. Seven islands will have to be traversed before the final goal is reached, and these are full of wonders.

Soaring through the sky, the *jinnī* tells Sayf about them. They pass an island where the trees are full of human-shaped fruit, some of which are shaped like beautiful young women. They hang from the trees by their hair, and by night these fruits raise their voices to praise the Creator. Sayf asks the *jinnī* to descend so he can see these fruits with his own eyes and hear their voices.[9]

The next day they visit an island where there are similar trees. At night they listen to the cries of the women, and when Sayf announces that he is hungry the *jinnī* says: '"My lord, can there be anything in the world that tastes better than these women?"' Sayf is shocked, but the *jinnī* picks off a woman fruit and breaks it in two. The inside is segmented like an orange and very tasty. After some persuasion, Sayf eats it and finds it delicious.[10]

Later on they come to an island where, according to the *jinnī*, the fruit is even better: the women fruits on this island are not only delicious to the taste, so that people cook and pickle them, but they are also shaped in such a way that one can have sex with them, better sex even than with ordinary women. There is no legal objection to this, he says, for their status is the same as that of slaves: they are mere chattels.

Sayf, having been away from his womenfolk for a long time, cannot suppress his curiosity and asks the *jinnī* to bring him one of these women so that he may see these astonishing creatures with his own eyes. The *jinnī* obeys and puts a woman in front of Sayf, leaving her with him. The narrator leaves us in the dark about what happens next: 'Some say that he had sex with her there, others deny this.'[11] Whatever happens, Sayf is extremely angry at his *jinnī* servant for having subjected him to this temptation and his anger continues for a long time.

The passage is most intriguing. At the upper level, it is Sayf's credibility as a devout Muslim that is at stake; but the very fact that the narrator of this particular version (for versions of these epics diverge from one storyteller to another) chose to leave the matter undecided brings it in line with the current of ambiguity that underlies the story as a whole. Sayf is here tempted to succumb to the appeal of the beautiful, totally passive and undemanding female, instead of concentrating on the quest for his beautiful but proud and independent wife and restoring their relationship.[12]

Their journey continues and finally they reach the island where the city of women is located.[13] Sayf is put down outside the city and, from then on, will have to venture forth on his own. The magical gifts obtained by Sayf prove to be highly useful, for among them are a polo mallet and ball as well as a female soldier's costume, and when the girls come out to exercise he waits until a group turns up whose costumes match his own and unobtrusively blends into the scene. This implies that he has to partake in their games and exercises. There are some initial difficulties. As is his habit, he plays to win in their ball game, constantly trying to get possession of the ball and throwing it with full strength. The girls see this as very loutish behaviour and start asking who this ill-mannered girl is.[14] His cover is almost blown, but just in time he manages to tone down his display of superior physical strength.

It is an intriguing passage. Sayf's quest here demands a complete change of attitude. If he wants to survive in this female community, he has to master his urge to compete and dominate, focusing not only on reaching his goal but also on his interaction with others. It is a tempting interpretation, but perhaps too modern. Possibly the narrator is just expressing his disdain for women's ability to play games.

Sayf's situation becomes very awkward when the women proceed to one-to-one body wrestling, and Sayf also has to take a sparring partner. It arouses his maleness to an extent where it can no longer be concealed. Luckily the woman involved is the commander of the troops, and her position allows her to accept his plea for asylum and to honour his request for help. She has no knowledge of his wife, but is prepared to help him find her and his son. She finds the matter very curious because the girls in the city are all virgins without any knowledge of men, let alone having children, and Munyat al-Nufūs could hardly have escaped notice.[15]

It soon becomes clear that, upon her return, Munyat al-Nufūs had been received less than cordially by her sister Nūr al-Hudā, who has taken her sister's place on the throne.[16] Seeing her Munyat with a small child, she remarks: "'So, you have been kicked by the stallion, and you have brought forth! This is not acceptable for virgins and maidens.'" Nūr al-Hudā asks her father Qāsim for advice. When informed by his geomancers that his vanished daughter had been abducted by a great king and had borne him a son who one day might rule over a realm even larger than his father's, he decides that if this was meant to be so, it had to be accepted. Upon hearing that Munyat al-Nufūs and her son have returned to his realm, however, we see another instance of his ambiguity: he orders Nūr al-Hudā to throw her sister into prison and to give her daily fifty lashes as punishment for bringing a possible rival male, namely her son, into the all-female world that her uncle has created and that her father allows to exist.[17]

Munyat al-Nufūs, mourning her fate, sees her plight as a punishment for leaving her husband. Some pity is shown to her by Kawkab, the female prison warden, who allows her to nurse her son.[18] Marjāna, the vizieress, secretly takes Sayf, in female disguise, to the prison so he can see his wife. Kawkab, the warden, recognizes him as a man, hears the story of his search for his beloved wife and dissuades him from seeking her out: of her former beauty nothing remains after the harsh regime she has suffered, and Sayf would do better to take her, Kawkab, as his wife instead. The narrator's view of female solidarity is obvious: it soon evaporates when there looms a chance of marriage.

Sayf rejects Kawkab's suggestion, saying that he only wants to visit his wife to chide her for her unacceptable behaviour.[19] Kawkab, reassured, guides him to Munyat al-Nufūs and an emotional reunion takes place, with Munyat al-Nufūs blaming herself for all that has befallen them. Marjāna takes them all home with her, a fact that is disclosed to Nūr al-Hudā in a dream, justly interpreted as implying that the arrival of Sayf will put an end to the existence of the segregated male and female communities.[20]

Marjāna is held to account but denies the story. Queen Nūr al-Hudā goes to her house in disguise, discovers the truth and accuses Marjāna, who pleads that she only intended to trick Sayf into captivity in order to hand him over to Nūr al-Hudā. An army of women is then sent out to capture or kill Sayf. This greatly worries Munyat al-Nufūs, but to Sayf these women are not a real threat. He attacks the female warriors with his full male force and they do not stand a chance until the queen, enraged, employs a magical device. Sayf's situation then becomes very dangerous until Munyat an-Nufūs's plea miraculously brings the Persian king Shāh al-Zamān and his warriors to rescue Sayf.

With Nūr al-Hudā's army thus defeated, Munyat al-Nufūs is reinstalled on the throne. Marjāna, the vizieress, summons all the girls to come and swear allegiance to her: "'Everyone who delays doing so will be flayed alive.'" It is not the only sign of violence in the women's dealing with the situation: Marjāna cleaves a sorceress in two with her sword,[21] and Munyat al-Nufūs plans to crucify her sister Nūr al-Hudā on the city gate, a project which Sayf wisely advises her to postpone.[22] The two sisters are eventually reconciled.[23]

Munyat al-Nufūs again thanks Sayf for his benevolence in coming to find her and not blaming her for what has happened.[24] Their relationship has obviously now been established on an orderly traditional footing. Before long Munyat will be boasting to her father and sister about her husband's impressive deeds.[25]

The problem then is how to redress the unnatural situation that exists between the two cities. This implies that the magical devices in both cities have to be deactivated. In the women's city this is quickly accomplished, and immediately 'the sadness was taken away from the eyes of all the women. They started to become aware of themselves, for a longing for sex had crept into them, and the blood stirred in their natures. The girls became aroused and started pining for the pleasures of love.'[26] After some discussion, Nūr al-Hudā flies over to the other city in order to persuade their father to deactivate the magical devices in the other city as well.

When this is done, Sayf starts marrying off the men and the women, pair for pair, just like the classical Amazons' marriages to the Scythians.[27] King Qāsim expects that his daughter Nūr al-Hudā will now also want a husband and children. This indeed turns out to be the case, but she only wants to marry a man of Sayf's choosing. Sayf suggests a marriage to the Persian king Shāh al-Zamān, who has already left, but the matter will be arranged in the near future.[28]

Order is thus restored. Female, embodying the aspects of woman that are threatening to man, has been replaced by feminine. The women will no longer act on their own for their own pleasure, but henceforth will be dutiful spouses and mothers.[29]

What, then, of the feather robes? Sayf sets out for home, heading for the place where the land of Wāq al-Wāq ends. This is the place where the *jinnī* put him down to find his way to the City of Maidens after their long flight. Home is very far away. 'When King Sayf came to that place, Munyat al-Nufūs said: "King of the Age, I can carry my son and go back to my palace in no time." "Give me that robe of yours, so that I can burn it!" answered the king. "By the religion of Islam," said Munya, "I will only put it on at your command and only visit my father and family with your permission."'

King Sayf, however, explains that it is his intention to take all the women and girls with them, so that she will never feel the urge to go back. Her father Qāsim thinks this an excellent idea. Qāsim gathers all the women together and urges his wife Marjāna to join the group. It will be nice for her to visit another country, he remarks. The powerful *jinnī*, who has been waiting for Sayf's return, constructs a sort of garden and invites them all to enter it. Hoisting the whole construction onto his back, he then flies them to the place where Sayf's foster sister is waiting for him.[30]

***

As we have seen, some basic elements of the classical Amazon myth, in its several versions, can still be found in the Arabic story. The rejection of relationships with men, particularly sexual relations, is one of them. Munyat al-Nufūs initially is adamant about not wanting to marry any man, and this leads to the separation of men and women into different cities. Nūr al-Hudā's fury against her sister is based on the fact that she has entered into a sexual relationship with a man, and this recalls the fact that, in the classical myth, loss of virginity was often seen as incompatible with being an Amazon. Combined with this there is the aversion to patriarchal marriage, a structure of male order. Aversion of male children, also an element in some Amazon stories, is here rationalized by presenting Munya's son as a possible threat to the current ruler, Queen Nūr al-Hudā.

Yet even the fiercest reaction to the returning queen's married state and motherhood does not entail the harming of her small son. It can, on the whole, be said that the position of children, and more especially sons, in the Arabic versions of Amazon stories is less problematic than it is in the classical Greek versions. Motherhood (at least in the context of marriage) and the mother–child relationship are, in the Arabic versions, stable and unchallenged phenomena.

In other respects, too, the sting has been taken out of the myth. The existence of a self-sufficient female community, the City of Maidens, is not the result of female protest against male dominance, but is the spin-off of a conflict between two men. It is entirely brought about by male power, and the same power can also undo it. It is also obvious that the whole situation is only waiting to be cleared up by a male hero who will restore the natural order disrupted by other men, a restoration which will, the assumption is, eventually lead to the women's happiness.

Patriarchal values are the be-all and end-all of everything, although the narrator occasionally pays attention to the women's angle.

Munyat al-Nufūs herself, by fleeing from her husband but challenging him to get her back, recalls the wavering attitude of the traditional Amazon towards patriarchal marriage. Munya does not, as such, object to love and marriage, but she stands on her dignity and independence. Sayf marries her as his captive and restricts her liberty of movement by taking away her feather robe. In so doing, he loses her. She manages to get it back, and only after a dangerous quest has proved him worthy of her love does she accept him again as her spouse and finally gives up her independence, in the shape of the feather robe, with only the slightest of protests.

CHAPTER 14

Final Observations

The preceding chapters present a selection of what Arabic popular epic has to offer on the subject of warrior women. Not all known epics have been included, and not all the warrior women who make their appearance in those that have, have found a place in this book.

Yet these chapters offer a fairly representative view of the literary conventions that define the genre and the various ways in which the generic motif of the martial woman has been worked out. They demonstrate how the standard elements of warrior women descriptions have been adapted to the individual cases: the early training in the art of war; the vow only to marry a man who defeats her in combat; deliberately unsettling her opponent by exposing her female charms; marriage and motherhood; and the continuing martial career after marriage.

While answers have been given to some questions, a great many more have been raised, awaiting future study. The material obviously lends itself to analysis from a variety of disciplinary angles, not only in the spheres of comparative literature, literary theory, gender studies and folklore, but also from many other perspectives, including the historical. As I said in the Preface, my aim in this book was, in the first place, to tell the stories and to emphasize how much popular epic has to offer. While occasionally bringing in the gender angle, I have tried not to let theoretical discussions dominate the discourse.

What these chapters have made clear is that although the same generic themes and motifs are used throughout the epics, the description and nature of individual warrior women differs considerably, and so does the way in which the phenomenon of the warrior woman is treated from one epic to another. There is a marked difference between the epics that have a Bedouin setting, such as *'Antar* and *Dhāt al-Himma*, and the others *sīra*s. In the 'Bedouin' epics, the existence of independently acting warrior women, foreign as well as of Arab stock, is accepted as a natural occurrence. These women have been trained in the martial arts from their youth on, and engage in combat as a matter of course. Combat and wrestling scenes involving a man and a woman are described extensively and with great relish, and the descriptions often have strong sexual overtones. Such scenes are less prominent in other epics, although they still occur, as is demonstrated by the wrestling scene between Sayf ibn Dhī Yazan and his mother Qamarīya, and also that between Sayf ibn Dhī Yazan and the female warrior in the episode of the City of Maidens.

Noteworthy in the 'Bedouin' epics is the fact that women continue to take part in forays and battles after their marriage, and that, in contrast to other epics, this never becomes an issue. The pride, self-confidence and independence with which these women conduct their martial careers and carry on discussions with their husbands are one of the most striking aspects of the warrior women stories in these epics.

In *Hamza* and *Baybars*, a change of attitude towards warrior women can be observed. In *Hamza*, traditional views of womanhood prevail, in spite of the occurrence of several brave warrior women. Prince Hamza himself is not in favour of married women taking up arms and engaging in combat. The matter is not resolved without discussion, though. Hamza's daughter-in-law Turbān, supported by her husband, does not hesitate to oppose him in this matter.

Baybars, with its distinctly urban setting, again offers us a different view: while enemy women leading armies appear quite frequently, accounts of women personally engaging in combat rarely occur, and then only in a very succinct form. Baybars himself, as his letter to an enemy warrior queen shows, is not in favour of women engaging in war: "'If you convert to Islam, I will take care to marry you to someone of your own standing so that henceforth you can stay home as befits a properly behaved girl.'" Energetic and independent women going their own way and prepared to kill if they see fit, however, occasionally play prominent roles in *Baybars*, but they are of a very different nature than the intrepid warrior girls and women, well trained in the art of formal combat, whom we encounter in *Dhāt al-Himma*, *'Antar*, and, to a lesser extent, also in *Hamza*.

Sayf ibn Dhī Yazan, dating from about the same time as *Baybars* and noteworthy for its many fantastic elements, which makes it, of all epics, closest to the tales of *The Thousand and One Nights*, again offers us a different view. A number of martial women appear in it, but the one time that a formal armed combat between a man and a woman on horseback is described, their duel turns out to be a travesty. The woman involved is almost completely clueless about the art of chivalric warfare.

A striking point in the epics, in particular the 'Bedouin' ones, is that gender roles are often reversed, or at least run counter to what the average Western reader would expect. Women defeat and humiliate men on the battlefield, causing not anger but passionate love. Daughters protect fathers or take bold initiatives where their fathers fearfully avoid confrontations and keep a low profile. Men are eager to marry strong martial women who can protect them. It would, of course, not be plausible to interpret this as a feminist development *avant la lettre*. We must assume that *sīra* literature was originally composed by men for a male audience, to be recited in the public space, a predominantly male domain. Accordingly, the martial women do not represent the female angle in a male discourse, but embody the perceptions, anxieties and desires of men.

As to what kind of anxieties and desires, we need only to look at the episode of Ghamra the daughter of 'Utārid to see a number of examples. There is the social stigma inherent in having only daughters; the reluctance to be pushed into marriage because it prevents one from engaging in manly pastimes; the utter, sexually enhanced, humiliation of the man by the woman who is his opponent; the male fascination with strong and dominant women, which, on the one hand, makes men want to defeat and sexually overpower such a woman and, on the other hand, to be protected by her; and the anxieties and risks that are connected to the wedding night, for both genders. In other episodes there is the excitement of hearing about voluptuous, almost naked women, prepared to engage in combat with men: the – not necessarily Muslim – warrior princesses of the Arabic tales often uninhibitedly display their bodies, as we saw, for instance, in the history of Karna, who, upon entering the battlefield, throws off her clothing, dazzling her male opponent by the luxurious folds of her white belly.[1] The combats between two women that we encountered in *Dhāt al-Himma*, with the powerful mother figure defeating a young and sexually threatening female opponent, are another instance.

Clearly, male audiences enjoyed hearing such stories, in spite of the fact that men were often the weaker party in them and even sometimes ridiculed. This latter aspect may seem somewhat puzzling, but what ought to be kept in mind is that audiences have no trouble identifying with a person of the opposite sex, as has been aptly explained in connection with another narrative genre involving male audiences appreciating victorious females.[2] Such cross-gender identification is sometimes made easier by the fact that the woman in question is dressed as a man, as is often the case in the Arabic stories, or otherwise has boyish aspects. The tomboy girls that we encountered in the epics, with their impulsive and rebellious behaviour, fit this pattern.

The fact that these heroic women are creatures of male fantasy, however, does not imply that the stories do not pay attention to the emotions of women. Female sensitivities are regularly brought into focus, particularly in relation to matters such as motherhood, pride and jealousy. All we can say, however, is that this tells us something about the attitudes and perceptions of the male narrators and their audience, and about the society in which they lived. The change in attitude to independently operating warrior women that we noted in the later *sīra*s offers an example. To quote Carol Glover: the girl playing a heroic role is 'female not despite the maleness of the audience, but precisely because of it. The discourse is wholly masculine, and females figure in it only insofar as they "read" some aspect of male experience. [...] She is simply an agreed-upon fiction.'[3]

We may take this as a fitting conclusion, and as a warning not to take the message conveyed by the warrior women stories too much at face value.

Notes

A Note on the Illustrations

1. The one exception is the story of King ʿUmar [ibn] al-Nuʿmān from *The Thousand and One Nights*, of which two wonderfully illustrated manuscripts exist, one in Tübingen and one in Manchester. The transmission of this particular epic tale, however, stands apart from that of the other popular epics.
2. See, for instance, the illustration to the history of Tāj al-Mulūk in Peter Heath, 'Arabische volksliteratur im Mittelalter', in Wolfhart Heinrichs (ed.), *Orientalisches Mittelalter: Neues Handbuch der Literaturwissenschaft*, vol. 5 (Wiesbaden: Aula Verlag, 1990), 430.
3. Examples in Jacqueline Sublet, *Les trois vies du Sultan Baibars* (Paris: Imprimerie Nationale, 1992), 144, 174.
4. See Basil Gray, *Persian Painting* (Geneva: Editions d'Art Albert Skira, 1995), 47.
5. Reproduced in Giovanni Canova, 'Sayf b. Dhī Yazan: history and saga', in Sabine Dorpmueller (ed.), *Fictionalizing the Past: Historical Characters in Arabic Popular Epic, Proceedings of the Workshop at the Netherlands–Flemish Institute in Cairo 28th/29th of November 2007 in Honor of Remke Kruk* (Louvain: Peeters, 2012), 107–23, 114.
6. http://majjal.wordpress.com/2012/04/14/shahrazad-and-dhat-al-himmah-epics-storytellers-and-warrior-women/ and http://wp.patheos.com.s3.amazonaws.com/blogs/mmw/files/2012/04/dhat-al-himma.jpg (both accessed 3 January 2013).

Chapter 1: Arabic Popular Epic: An Introductory Note

1. His translation appeared between 1704 and 1717.
2. Using terms devised in the West to designate genres found in classical European literature in any case is problematic, as Wen-chin Ouyang has justly remarked. She rightly points out that this, on the other hand, allows the researcher to make use of everything that Western literary theories about such genres have to offer in terms of critical perspectives, methods of analysis and technical terms. Wen-chin Ouyang, 'Romancing the Epic: "ʿUmar al-Nuʿmān as Narrative of Empowerment"', *Arabic and Middle Eastern Literatures* 3/1 (2000), 5–18, 12.

3. On various kinds of storytelling, see Robert Irwin, *The Arabian Nights: A Companion* (London: Allen Lane, The Penguin Press, 1994), ch. 4.
4. Claudia Ott, *Metamorphosen des Epos: Sīrat al-Mujāhidīn (Sīrat al-Amīra Dhāt al-Himma) zwischen Muendlichkeit und Schriftlichkeit* (Leiden: CNWS (Leiden University), 2003), 90–95. For a wider picture of reading practices in sixteenth- to eighteenth-century Cairo, see Nelly Hanna, *In Praise of Books: A Cultural History of Cairo's Middle Class, Sixteenth to the Eighteenth Century* (Syracuse, NY: Syracuse University Press, 2003), especially 96, and Boaz Shoshan, 'On Popular Literature in Medieval Cairo', *Poetics Today* 14/2 (1993), 349–365, especially the first three pages.
5. Malay and Persian versions were extensively studied by Ph. S. van Ronkel, *De Roman van Amir Hamzah* (Leiden, 1895).
6. F. C. W. Doufikar-Aerts, *Alexander Magnus Arabicus: A Survey of the Alexander Tradition through Seven Centuries from Pseudo-Callisthenes to Suī* (Leuven: Peeters, 2010).
7. See Claudia Ott, 'Finally we know ... why, how, and where Caliph al-Ḥākim disappeared! *Sīrat al-Ḥākim bi-Amrillāh* and its Berlin manuscript', in Sabine Dorpmueller (ed.), *Fictionalizing the Past: Historical Characters in Arabic Popular Epic: Proceedings of the Workshop at the Netherlands–Flemish Institute in Cairo 28th/29th of November 2007 in Honor of Remke Kruk* (Leuven: Peeters, 2012), 63–72.
8. Peter Heath, 'Arabische Volksliteratur im Mittelalter', in Wolfhart Heinrichs (ed.), *Orientalisches Mittelalter: Neues Handbuch der Literaturwissenschaft*, vol. 5 (Wiesbaden: Aula-Verlag, 1990), 423–439, and also Wilhelm Ahlwardt, *Verzeichniss der arabischen Handschriften der königlichen Bibliothek zu Berlin*, 10 vols (Berlin: Schade, 1887–99); vol. 8: *Die grossen Romane* (1896). Some unedited epics mentioned include: 99–101: *Al-Arqat*; 102: *Al-Badr Nār*; and 144–146: *Muhammad al-Kurdī*.
9. Al-Wāqidī, *Futūh Ifrīqīya*, 2 vols (Tunis: Maktabat al-Manāra, 1966). The author is not actually the historian al-Wāqidī, and therefore is generally referred to as pseudo-al-Wāqidī. See also René Basset, 'Le livre des conquètes de l'Afrique et du Maghreb', in Charles de Harlez, *Mélanges Charles de Harlez* (Leiden, 1896), 26–34.
10. Martin Schreiner, 'Samau'al b. Jahjā al-Magribī und seine Schrift "Ifḥām al-Jahūd"', *Monatszeitschrift für die Geschichte und Wissenschaft des Judentums* 3 (1898), 123–133, 127. Text: Samaw'al ibn Yahyā al-Maghribī, *Badhl al-majhūd fī ifḥām al-yahūd*, ed. Muh. al-Fiqqī (Cairo, 1358/1939), 16 – Dalhama is an older form of the name Dhū l-Himma or Dhāt al-Himma.
11. His name was Abū l-Mu'ayyad ibn al-Sā'igh. Ibn abī 'Usaybi'a, *'Uyūn al-anbā' fī tabaqāt al-atibbā'*, ed. A. Müller, 2 vols ([Cairo] Konigsberg? 1884), 1: 290–297.
12. The oldest MS of *Sīrat 'Antar* dates from 1466 (Peter Heath, *The Thirsty Sword: Sīrat 'Antar and the Arabic Popular Epic* (Salt Lake City: University

of Utah Press, 1996), 28); the oldest MS of *Sīrat Dhāt al-Himma Sīrat al-Mujāhidīn* from 1430 (Ott, *Metamorphosen*, 237).

13. On this figure, see the extensive study by Malcolm Lyons, *The Man of Wiles in Popular Arabic Literature: A Study of a Medieval Arab Hero* (Edinburgh: Edinburgh University Press, 2012).

14. Giovanni Canova, 'Twenty years of studies on Arabic epics', in Giovanni Canova (ed.), *Studies on Arabic Epics, Oriente Moderno* 22/83, n.s., 2 (2003), v–xxii.

15. Peter Heath's analysis of the episode in which 'Antar hangs his *Muʿallaqa* demonstrates how close this connection sometimes is ("Antar hangs his *Muʿallaqa*: history, fiction, and textual conservatism in *Sīrat ʿAntar ibn Shaddād*', in Dorpmueller (ed.), *Fictionalizing the Past*, 9–24, especially 17–18).

16. An exception is an otherwise unknown printed epic that I recently discovered in the New York Public Library, *Sīrat al-Iskandar Dhī l-Qarnayn* or *Sīrat al-amīr ʿArūs*. In this *sīra*, the story of a certain Prince ʿArūs is connected to that of al-Iskandar (about the *Sīrat al-Iskandar*, see Doufikar-Aerts, *Alexander Magnus Arabicus*, 2010). From Book 5 on, the story is identical to part of the *Sīrat al-Iskandar*. The copy does not contain the complete story. I am currently preparing an article on the text.

17. C. Brockelmann, *Geschichte der arabischen Litteratur*, Suppl. 2 (Leiden: Brill, 1936–42), 64 n.1, in this context mentions the polemics between the Egyptian poet Muh. Hāfiz Ibrāhīm (d. 1932) and the Englishman Wilfrid S. Blunt, who had dared to characterize the *Sīra Hilālīya* as an Arabic *Iliad*. Brockelmann refers to *Dhikrā al-Shāʿirayn* (Damascus, 1356), 139.

18. Dwight F. Reynolds, *Heroic Poetry, Poetic Heroes: The Ethnography of Performance in an Arabic Oral Epic Tradition* (Ithaca: Cornell University Press, 1995), 7. His source: Taqī al-Din Subkī, *Muʿīd al-niʿam* (1908), 186, as cited in Muhammad Zaghlūl Salām, *Al-Adab fī l-ʿasr al-mamlūkī* (1971), 121.

19. Ibn Taymīya, *Minhāj al-Sunna*, 4 parts, 2 vols (Būlāq, 1322/1904), 4: 12.

20. Ibn al-Kathīr, *Al-Bidāya wa-l-nihāya* (Beirut, 1989), 9: 347. Quoted after Dwight Reynolds, 'Popular prose in the post-classical period', in Roger Allen and D. S. Richards, Cambridge History of Arabic Literature, vol. 5: *Arabic Literature in the Post-Classical Period* (Cambridge: Cambridge University Press, 2006), 245–269, 260.

21. The *fatwā* was from Ibn al-Qaddāh. For reference, see M. Canard, *EI2*, 2: 238.

22. Exceptions occurred in the Arab world, as is demonstrated by the case of Ahmad al-Rabbāt al-Halabī and his collection of popular literature, which is currently being studied by Ibrahim Akel (Institut national des langues et civilisations orientales, Paris).

23. First published in 1836. An expanded version appeared in 1860.

24. Alexander Russell, *The Natural History of Aleppo* (London, 1794), 148–149: description of a storyteller disappearing at a cliff-hanging point in the story, leaving the audience in a state of suspense.
25. Remke Kruk and Claudia Ott, '"In the Popular Manner": *Sīra*-Recitation in Marrakesh Anno 1997', *Edebiyat* 10 (1999), 183–198.
26. Roger LeTourneau, *Fès avant le protectorat: Étude économique et sociale d' une ville de l'occident musulman* (Casablanca: Société marocaine de librairie et d'édition, 1949), 555–556.
27. Khaled Abouel-lail, 'The *Sīrat Banī Hiāll:* new remarks on its performance in Upper and Lower Egypt', in Dorpmueller (ed.), *Fictionalizing the Past*, 73–93.
28. Thomas Herzog, 'Présentation de deux séances de hakawātī et de deux manuscrits de la Sīrat Baybars recueillis en Syrie en 1994', MA thesis, University of Aix-en-Provence, 1994.
29. For a more extensive report on these sessions, see Kruk and Ott, '"In the Popular Manner"', and Ott, *Metamorphosen,* ch. 5.
30. Ahmad Sefrioui, *La boîte à merveilles* (Paris: Le Seuil, 1954).
31. Emile Habibi, *Luka' ibn Luka': Thalāth jalasat amāma sundūq al-'ajab: hikāya masrahīyah* (Beirut: Dār al-Fārābī, 1980).
32. For a demonstration of the process: http://awaheed.wordpress.com/2010/05/14/abu-el-ajab-preserving-the-land-of-storytellers/ (accessed 26 January 2012).

Chapter 2: Warrior Women in the Arabic Tradition

1. See http://www.the99.org/ (accessed 24 September 2012). My thanks to Wim Raven for drawing my attention to these comics.
2. AK Comics, founded by the Egyptian Dr Ayman Kandeel, see http://www.racialicious.com/2008/08/26/female-muslim-and-mutant-a-critique-of-muslim-women-in-comic-books-part-2-of-2/ (accessed 4 August 2013).
3. In this respect, the fact that none of the heroines discussed in this book are included in Jessica A. Salmonson's *The Encyclopedia of Amazons* (New York: Paragon House, 1991), is significant.
4. Torquato Tasso, *La Gerusalemme liberata*, ed. Giorgio Cerboni Baiardi (Modena: Franco Cosimo Panini, 1991), Canto 12. The episode formed the basis for Monteverdi's operatic scena *Il Combattimenti di Tancredi e Clorinda*, composed in 1624.
5. The Persian literary tradition has been well covered by John R. Perry, 'Blackmailing Amazons and Dutch Pigs: A Consideration of Epic and Folktale Motifs in Persian Historiography', *Iranian Studies* 19/2 (1986), 155–165, which deals not only with literary but with historical material, and, more recently, Marina Gaillard, 'Héroïnes d'exception: Les femmes *'Ayyār* dans la prose romanesque de l'Iran médiéval', *Studia Iranica* 34/2 (2005), 163–198.

6. Jeannine Davis-Kimball with Mona Behan, *Warrior Women: An Archaeologist's Search for History's Hidden Heroines* (New York: Warner Books, 2002), 55–66.
7. Hippocrates, *On Airs, Waters and Places*. In the Arabic tradition, it circulated as part of Galen's commentary on the text. This commentary has been lost in Greek. The reference to the Amazons does not occur in all the Arabic manuscripts, and is not found in the edition of J. N. Mattock and M. C. Lyons, *Kitāb Buqrāt fī-l-amrād al-bilādiyya. Hippocrates: On Endemic Diseases (Airs, Waters and Places)*, ed. and trans. with notes, intro. and glossary (Cambridge: Cambridge Middle East Centre, 1969).
8. V. Minorsky, *Sharaf al-Zamān Tāhir Marvazī on China, the Turks and India. Arabic text (circa AD 1120) with an English translation and commentary* (London: The Royal Asiatic Society, 1942), 38.
9. Sharaf al-Zamān Tāhir Marwazī, *Kitāb Tabā'iʿ al-hayawān*, MS UCLA Ar. 52, ff. 58a–60a. This chapter is not included in Minorsky's partial edition and translation mentioned in the previous note.
10. The Battle of the Camel, which took place in 656, owes its name to the fact that 'A'isha, widow of the Prophet, participated in it, seated on a camel.
11. F. C. W. Doufikar-Aerts, *Alexander Magnus Arabicus: A Survey of the Alexander Tradition through Seven Centuries from Pseudo-Callisthenes to Surī* (Leuven: Peeters, 2010), 85.
12. Doufikar-Aerts, *Alexander Magnus Arabicus*, 314–19.
13. Antonia Fraser, *The Warrior Queens: The Legends and the Lives of the Women Who Have Led their Nations in War* (London: Mandarin Books, 1989), 116. Fraser bases her account on the fourth-century author Trebellius Pollio.
14. See, for instance, al-Tabarī, *The History of al-Tabarī (Ta'rīkh al-rusul wa-l-mulūk)*, vol. 4: *The Ancient Kingdoms*, trans. and annot. Moshe Perlmann (New York: SUNY Press, 1987), 138–150.
15. M. Canard, 'Les reines de Géorgie dans l'histoire et la légende musulmanes', *Revue des études islamiques* 1 (1969), 3–20.
16. J. Déjeux, 'La Kahina: de l'histoire à la fiction littéraire: Mythe et épopée', *Studi Maghrebini* 15 (1983), 1–42.
17. They have been the subject of a popular book by Fatima Mernissi, *The Forgotten Queens of Islam* (Minneapolis: University of Minneapolis Press, 1993).
18. She lived from 1048 (less probably, 1052) until 1138 CE. See Farhad Daftary, 'Sayyida Hurra: The Ismaʿīlī Sulayhid queen of Yemen', in Gavin R. Hambly (ed.), *Women in the Medieval Islamic World* (New York: St Martin's Press, 1998), 117–130.
19. See Taef Kamal el-Azhari, 'Dayfa Khātūn, Ayyubid queen of Aleppo 634–640 A.H./1236–1242 A.D.', *Annals of Japan Association for Middle East Studies (JAMES)* 15 (2000), 27–55.
20. V. Vacca, 'Sadjāh', in *EI2*, 8: 738–739.

21. al-Ṭabarī, Ta'rīkh al-rusul wa-l-mulūk, 15 vols (Leiden: Brill, 1879–1901), 1: 2100–2101.
22. Ilse Lichtenstädter, Women in the Aiyām al-'Arab: A Study of Female Life during Warfare in Preislamic Arabia (London: The Royal Asiatic Society, 1935), and literature given there.
23. Ibn al-Athīr, al-Kāmil fī al-ta'rīkh, 14 vols (Leiden: Brill, 1867–1876), 5: 372.
24. Abū l-Faraj 'Alī al-Husayn al-Isbahānī, Kitāb al-Aghānī, 24 vols (Cairo: Dār al-Kutub al-Misrīya, 1345–94/1927–74), 12: 96. The passage is mentioned, without source reference, by Fuad Matthew Caswell, The Slave Girls of Baghdad: The Qiyān in the Early Abbasid Era (London and New York: I.B.Tauris, 2011), 191, who lets Yazīd strike with his sword instead of his spear.
25. Niall Christie, 'Noble Betrayers of their Faith, Families and Folk: Some Non-Muslim Women in Mediaeval Arabic Popular Literature', Folklore 123/1 (2012), 84–98, 91, referring to the Memoirs of Usāma ibn Munqidh, trans. Paul M. Cobb (2008), 137.
26. K. Ciggaar, 'La dame combattante: thème épique et thème courtois au temps des croisades', in Hans van Dijk and Willem Noomen (eds), Aspects de l'épopée romane: Mentalités, idéologies, intertextualités (Groningen: Forster, 1995), 121–130.
27. Abū Shāma, Kitāb al-Rawdatayn, Recueil des Historiens des Croisades: Historiens Orientaux, 5 vols (Paris, 1872–1906), 4: 434, as quoted by Carole Hillenbrand, The Crusades: Islamic Perspectives (Edinburgh: Edinburgh University Press, 1999), 348–349.
28. For these, see Elena Lourie, 'Black Women Warriors in the Muslim Army Besieging Valencia and the Cid's Victory: A Question of Interpretation', Traditio 55 (2000), 181–209.
29. The so-called maghāzī and futūh literature, such as Futūh al-Shām and Futūh Ifrīqiyya of pseudo-al-Wāqidī, the anonymous Futūh al-Yaman and related stories.
30. Franz Rosenthal, 'Fiction and reality: sources for the role of sex in medieval Muslim society', in Afaf Lutfi Sayyid-Marsot (ed.), Society and the Sexes in Medieval Islam (Sixth Giorgio Levi della Vida Biennial Conference, May 13–15, 1977) (Malibu, CA: Undena Publications, 1979), 3–22, 13–14; his reference about the Battle of the Yarmūk is to Futūh al-Shām, 2 vols (Cairo 1354/1935), 1: 133.
31. Qissat futūh al-Yaman al-kubrā al-shahīr bi-Ra's al-Ghūl (Cairo: Maktabat al-jumhūrīya al-'arabīya, n.d.), 132–150.
32. See John Renard, Islam and the Heroic Image: Themes in Literature and the Visual Arts (Columbia, SC: University of South Carolina Press, 1993), who (p. 56) refers to pp. 129–177 of William Hanaway's unpublished dissertation, 'Persian Popular Romances before the Safavid Period', Ph.D. dissertation, Columbia University, 1970.

33. William Blake Tyrrell, *Amazons: A Study in Athenian Mythmaking* (Baltimore and London, 1989), especially ch. 3.
34. Dwight F. Reynolds, *Heroic Poetry, Poetic Heroes: The Ethnography of Performance* (Ithaca: Cornell University Press, 1995), 17.
35. Reynolds, *Heroic Poetry*, 76.
36. Dwight Reynolds, 'Sīrat Banī Hilāl', in R. Allen and D. S. Richards (eds), *Cambridge History of Arabic Literature*, vol. 6: *Arabic Literature in the Post-Classical Period* (Cambridge: Cambridge University Press, 2006), 313.
37. So far, little research has been done on this epic and its relation to the Persian, and possibly also the Turkish, tradition, apart from a short article: Kenneth Grant, '*Sīrat Fīrūzshāh* and the Middle Eastern epic tradition', in Giovanni Canova, *Studies on Arabic Epics, Oriente Moderno* 22/83, n.s., 2 (2003), 521–528.
38. Anonymous, *Qissat Fīrūzshāh ibn al-Malik Dārāb*, 4 vols (Beirut: Maktabat al-tarbīya, 1984/1404) 3: 289.
39. *Fīrūzshāh*, 1: 77, 83.
40. Jan de Vries, *Heroic Song and Heroic Legend*, trans. B. J. Timmer (London: Oxford University Press, 1963), 211ff.
41. Peter Heath, *The Thirsty Sword: Sīrat ʿAntar and the Arabic Popular Epic* (Salt Lake City: University of Utah Press, 1996), 67–100.
42. This is not the same sword as ʿAntar's famous al-Zāmi', 'The Thirsty'.
43. An example among many is *Sīrat Baybars*, reprint Cairo 1996–97, 2: 1106–1107, where a girl has been converted in a dream, falls in love with the Muslim who has just killed her father and, at his request, kills her mother to prove the sincerity of her conversion.
44. For instance, *Dhāt al-Himma* 43: 12.
45. *Dhāt al-Himma* 33: 24.
46. *Dhāt al-Himma* 6: 60–74.
47. A typical characteristic of the *ʿayyār*, the trickster character, is that he can appear out of the blue when his name is called.
48. *Dhat al-Himma* 13: 44–45.
49. *Dhāt al-Himma* 61: 25ff.
50. *Dhāt al-Himma* 3: 73ff. Their marriage takes place in *Dhāt al-Himma* 4: 35. Alūf is one of the most engaging female characters of the *sīra*. Her history has been studied by Claudia Ott in 'Der falsche Asket: Ursprung und Entwicklung einer Romanfigur aus der sīrat al-amīra *Dhāt al-Himma*', MA thesis, University of Tübingen, 1992.
51. 'yamīlu qalbī ilā rabbāt al-hijāl', *Dhāt al-Himma* 4: 6.
52. *Dhāt al-Himma* 1: 13–17.
53. *Alf Layla wa-Layla* [A Thousand and One Nights], 2 vols (Baghdad: Maktabat al-Muthannā, n.d.; photographic reprint of the edition Būlāq: Matbaʿat Būlāq, 1252 AH).

54. There is even a veiled reference to her pubic hair, which must have been particularly shocking to the audience.
55. *Alf Layla wa-Layla*, Nights 44–106.
56. *Dhāt al-Himma* 5: 8–16.
57. *'Antar* 8: 336–358.
58. *Dhāt al-Himma* 48: 50–58.

Chapter 3: *Sīrat Dhāt al-Himma* 1: Princess Dhāt al-Himma and Her Many Battles

1. The edition I used (referred to as *Dhāt al-Himma*) is *Sīrat al-amīra Dhāt al-Himma wa-waladihā 'Abd al-Wahhāb wa-l-amīr Abū Muhammad al-Battāl (etc.)*, 7 vols, 70 parts (Cairo: Maktabat 'Abd al-Hamīd Ahmad al-Hanafī, n.d.). References are to parts (*ajzā'*).
2. See Chapter 1, 11.
3. That people, especially illiterate people, actually perceived *sīra* literature to be an account of their historical past was observed by Susan Slyomovics, *The Merchant of Art: An Egyptian Hilali Oral Epic Poet in Performance* (Berkeley and Los Angeles: University of California Press, 1987), ch. 3, and Remke Kruk and Claudia Ott, '"In the Popular Manner": *Sīra*-Recitation in Marrakesh Anno 1997', *Edebiyat* 10 (1999), 183–198.
4. For an extensive study of the manuscripts and printed versions, see Claudia Ott, *Metamorphosen des Epos: Sīrat al-Mujāhidīn (Sīrat al-Amīra Dhāt al-Himma) zwischen Muendlichkeit und Schriftlichkeit* (Leiden: CNWS, 2003).
5. Shawqi Abd Al-Hakim, *Princess Dhat Al Himma: The Princess of High Resolve*, trans. and intro. Omaima Abou Bakr (Cairo: Ministry of Culture, 1995).
6. The narrator sometimes refers to the work as *Sīrat al-Mujāhidīn* in the printed text that has been used here, the Cairo edition of 1327/1909, reprinted in the 1960s, although the edition itself does not have this title. About the title, see Ott, *Metamorphosen*.
7. In the Cairo edition of Maktabat al-Hanafī, the name sometimes alternates with the older form Dhū l-Himma and the still older Dalhama or Dhalhama. Regarding the question of these names, see Marius Canard, 'Dhū l-Himma', in *EI*2, 2: 233–239.
8. See, for instance, Jan de Vries, *Heroic Song and Heroic Legend*, trans. B. J. Timmer (London: Oxford University Press, 1963), 211ff., and for Arabic popular epic, using the life of 'Antar as an example, Peter Heath, *The Thirsty Sword: Sīrat 'Antar and the Arabic Popular Epic* (Salt Lake City: University of Utah Press, 1996), 68–69.
9. See Chapter 1, 6.
10. *Dhāt al-Himma* 45: 23.

11. *Dhāt al-Himma* 61: 23–24.
12. *Dhāt al-Himma* 69: 90.
13. *Dhāt al-Himma* 6: 14.
14. *Dhāt al-Himma* 6: 14.
15. *Dhāt al-Himma* 6: 15–16.
16. Arabic text: *shaddād*, probably a misprint for *samawāt*.
17. Antonia Fraser, *The Warrior Queens: The Legends and the Lives of the Women Who Have Led their Nations in War* (London: Mandarin Books, 1989), 116.
18. *Dhāt al-Himma* 6: 17–19.
19. Curiously, the chief of the tribe is regularly referred to as king, which does not fit Bedouin custom at all.
20. *Dhāt al-Himma* 6: 18.
21. On the matter of the names, see also Wen-chin Ouyang, 'Princess of resolution', in Lena B. Ross (ed.), *To Speak or Be Silent: The Paradox of Disobedience in the Lives of Women* (Wilmette, IL: Chiron Publications, 1993), 197–209, especially 205.
22. *Dhāt al-Himma* 6: 19.
23. *Dhāt al-Himma* 6: 24.
24. *Dhāt al-Himma* 6: 25.
25. *Dhāt al-Himma* 6: 27.
26. *Dhāt al-Himma* 6: 30.
27. Arabic: *hurma*.
28. *Dhāt al-Himma* 6: 33.
29. *Dhāt al-Himma* 6: 35–36.
30. *Dhāt al-Himma* 6: 36.
31. *Dhāt al-Himma* 6: 53.
32. Arabic: *ʿālamīn*.
33. *Dhāt al-Himma* 6: 59.
34. *Dhāt al-Himma* 6: 60.
35. *Dhāt al-Himma* 7: 9–10.
36. *Dhāt al-Himma* 7: 11.
37. *Dhāt al-Himma* 7: 12–13.
38. *Dhāt al-Himma* 7: 13.
39. *Dhāt al-Himma* 7: 14.
40. *Dhāt al-Himma* 7: 20.
41. *Dhāt al-Himma* 7: 34.
42. Apart from being a renowned scholar, Jaʿfar al-Sādiq is also famous in the popular tradition for his supernatural powers and wisdom.
43. *Dhāt al-Himma* 7: 39–43.
44. *Dhāt al-Himma* 7: 64–65.
45. On this stock character of Arabic popular epic, see Chapter 1.
46. *Dhāt al-Himma* 26: 8.
47. *Dhāt al-Himma* 24: 47.

48. *Dhāt al-Himma* 51: 54–55.
49. *Dhāt al-Himma* 32: 7–8.
50. Arabic text: *khilāl*, skewer; probably a misprint for *khayāl*, ghost, cf. *Dhāt al-Himma* 45: 22, paen.
51. *Dhāt al-Himma* 32: 12–13.
52. *Dhāt al-Himma* 36: 5–6.
53. *Dhāt al-Himma* 39: 27.
54. *Dhāt al-Himma* 40: 37.
55. *Dhāt al-Himma* 69: 106–108.
56. Also written as Ghaydūrus.
57. *Dhāt al-Himma* 45: 21.
58. *Dhāt al-Himma* 45: 22.
59. The text is very specific, and this is functional in the story: Dhāt al-Himma is reciting Sura 33, *al-Ahzāb*, and has just reached verse 44: 'O Prophet, We have sent thee as a witness, and good tidings to bear and warning.'
60. *Dhāt al-Himma* 45: 33.
61. See also Remke Kruk, 'The bold and the beautiful: women and *fitna* in the *Sīrat Dhāt al-Himma*: the story of Nūrā', in Gavin R. Hambly (ed.), *Women in the Medieval Islamic World: Power, Patronage and Piety* (New York: St Martin's Press, 1998), 99–116.
62. *Dhāt al-Himma* 13: 58–60.
63. *Dhāt al-Himma* 19: 34–35.
64. Cf. the forced defloration of the drugged Dhāt al-Himma herself and the princess who is drugged by Battāl in order to enable Zālim, Dhāt al-Himma's grandson, to deflower her. *Dhāt al-Himma* 70: 141–142.
65. *Dhāt al-Himma* 37: 34–40.
66. *Dhāt al-Himma* 20: 19.
67. *Dhāt al-Himma* 70: 146.
68. *Dhāt al-Himma* 70: 145.
69. The order of events is somewhat unclear. According to the final page (*Dhāt al-Himma* 70: 147) it is still 'Abd al-Wahhāb who informs al-Wāthiq's successor, Mutawakkil, of the Byzantine recapture of Malatya.
70. *Dhāt al-Himma* 70: 146.

Chapter 4: *Sīrat Dhāt al-Himma* 2: Prince 'Abd al-Wahhāb and His Warrior Wives

1. For the Arabic text that was used, see Chapter 3, n.1.
2. *Dhat al-Himma* 6: 64–65.
3. *Dhāt al-Himma* 7: 62.
4. *Dhāt al-Himma* 12: 22–24.
5. *Dhāt al-Himma* 13: 5.

Notes to pages 66–83

6. *Dhāt al-Himma* 13: 6–7.
7. *Dhāt al-Himma* 7: 71.
8. *Dhāt al-Himma* 8: 15.
9. *Dhāt al-Himma* 8: 15.
10. *Dhāt al-Himma* 11: 34.
11. *Dhāt al-Himma* 11: 71.
12. Also spelled as Ashmītīs or Ashmītāsh. *Dhāt al-Himma* 12: 22–24.
13. *Dhāt al-Himma* 12: 54–13: 8.
14. *Dhāt al-Himma* 14: 8.
15. *Dhāt al-Himma* 14: 8.
16. *Dhāt al-Himma* 14: 35–36.
17. *Dhāt al-Himma* 15: 2–3.
18. *Dhāt al-Himma* 41: 21.
19. *Dhāt al-Himma* 42: 46.
20. *Dhāt al-Himma* 70: 31.
21. *Dhāt al-Himma* 31: 21–25.
22. *Dhāt al-Himma* 23: 30.
23. *Dhāt al-Himma* 31: 27.
24. *Dhāt al-Himma* 17: 54–56.
25. *Dhāt al-Himma* 8: 77–9: 14.
26. *Dhāt al-Himma* 8: 78–9: 3.
27. *Dhāt al-Himma* 9: 6.
28. *Dhāt al-Himma* 9: 5.
29. *Dhāt al-Himma* 9: 7.
30. *Dhāt al-Himma* 9: 5–8.
31. Also called Sayf al-Hanafīya.
32. This section is partly based on my 'Warrior Women in Arabic Popular Romance: Qannāsa bint Muzāhim and other Valiant Ladies', Part 1, *Journal of Arabic Literature* 24/3 (1993), 213–230; Part 2, ibid. 15/1 (1994), 16–33. Part 2 gives a full translation of the expedition against Qannāsa led by 'Abd al-Wahhāb and Dhāt al-Himma, *Dhāt al-Himma* 11: 11–26.
33. *Dhāt al-Himma* 11: 11.
34. *Dhāt al-Himma* 11: 26.
35. *Dhāt al-Himma* 20: 59.
36. *Dhāt al-Himma* 20: 72.
37. *Dhāt al-Himma* 21: 9.
38. *Dhāt al-Himma* 21: 26–27.
39. *Dhāt al-Himma* 21: 30–31.
40. *Dhāt al-Himma* 36: 32–34.
41. *Dhāt al-Himma* 22: 40.
42. *Dhāt al-Himma* 22: 58–59.
43. *Dhāt al-Himma* 68: 28.

44. This section is partly based on my 'The Princess Maymūnah: maiden, mother, monster', in Giovanni Canova (ed.), *Studies on Arabic Epics, Oriente Moderno* 22/83, n.s. 2 (2003), 425–442.
45. *Dhāt al-Himma* 44: 14.
46. Cf. for instance the cases of Alūf (Kruk, 'Warrior Women' (1993), 222) and Zanānīr (ibid., 224).
47. *Dhāt al-Himma* 37: 46.
48. *Dhāt al-Himma* 36: 44.
49. *Dhāt al-Himma* 37: 9–11.
50. *Dhāt al-Himma* 37: 34–36.
51. *Dhāt al-Himma* 40: 3.
52. *Dhāt al-Himma* 43: 36.
53. *Dhāt al-Himma* 43: 46–47.
54. *Dhāt al-Himma* 43: 48.
55. *Dhāt al-Himma* 43: 50, 54.
56. *Dhāt al-Himma* 44: 4–5.
57. *Dhāt al-Himma* 44: 5–6.
58. *Dhāt al-Himma* 44: 6–13.
59. *Dhāt al-Himma* 44: 14–15.
60. *Dhāt al-Himma* 44: 15.
61. *Dhāt al-Himma* 44: 23.
62. *Dhāt al-Himma* 53: 41. His name is mentioned later on.
63. *Dhāt al-Himma* 46: 47.
64. *Dhāt al-Himma* 50: 2–9.
65. *Dhāt al-Himma* 53: 56.
66. *Dhāt al-Himma* 54: 8.
67. *Dhāt al-Himma* 55: 13.
68. *Dhāt al-Himma* 55: 17.
69. *Dhāt al-Himma* 55: 30.
70. *Dhāt al-Himma* 55: 31–33.
71. *Dhāt al-Himma* 55: 33.
72. In some respects Maymūna reminds us of 'Arūs al-'Arā'is' the thoroughly depraved heroine of a story in the *Kitāb al-hikāyāt al-'ajība*, translated by Hans Wehr in his *Wunderbare Erlebnisse – Seltsame Begebnisse: arabische Erzählungen*. (Hattingen, Ruhr: Hundt, 1959). See also Ulrich Marzolph, 'As Woman as Can Be: The Gendered Subversiveness of an Arabic Folktale Heroine', *Edebiyat* 10 (1999), 199–218, and Malcolm C. Lyons, 'Qissat 'Arūs al-'Arā'is', in Canova (ed.), *Studies on Arabic Epics*, 559–573. Yet Maymūna is surpassed in depravity by Qamarīya, the mother of Sayf ibn Dhī Yazan (see Chapter 11).
73. Peter Eversteyn, director of the popular Dutch soap series *Goede tijden, Slechte tijden*, in *VPRO Gids* 15 (14–20 April 2001), 6. The English translation of the quotation is mine.

Chapter 5: *Sīrat Dhāt al-Himma* 3: The History of Ghamra the Daughter of ʿUṭārid

1. For the Arabic text that was used, see Chapter 3, n. 1.
2. Marius Canard has pointed out that ʿAmr ibn ʿUbaydallāh takes the name of ʿUmar al-Nuʿmān in the related Turkish *Battālnāme*, and also in the story of King ʿUmar al-Nuʿmān and his two sons that has been incorporated in *The Thousand and One Nights*. See Marius Canard, 'Dhū l-Himma', *EI*2, 2: 233–239, and, more recently, Yorgos Dedes, 'Battālnāme', Ph.D. dissertation, Harvard University, 1996.
3. The story of Jaydāʾ and Khālid is not found in all the versions of *Sīrat ʿAntar ibn Shaddād*. It is included in the partial translation of *Sīrat ʿAntar* made by Terrick Hamilton, *ʿAntar, a Bedoueen Romance*, 4 parts, 2 vols (London: John Murray, 1819–20), Part 1, 2: 133–155.
4. *Dhāt al-Himma* 40: 43.
5. For example, in the story of Hind and Rabīʿa in *Sīrat ʿAntar ibn Shaddād* (Cairo: Maktaba wa-matbaʿa Mustafā al-Bābī al-Halabī, 1961–2), 8: 336ff.
6. *Dhāt al-Himma* 40: 45.
7. A strong soporific made from black henbane, *Hyoscyamus niger*. It is traditionally used by trickster characters in the Arabic popular epics.
8. Arabic: *māhā*, wild cow.
9. *Dhāt al-Himma* 40: 48.
10. *Dhāt al-Himma* 40: 51.
11. *Dhāt al-Himma* 40: 51.
12. *Dhāt al-Himma* 40: 52.
13. *Dhāt al-Himma* 40: 53.
14. *Dhāt al-Himma* 40: 54.
15. Hans Hinrich Biesterfeld and Dimitri Gutas, 'The Malady of Love', *Journal of the American Oriental Society* 104/1 (1984), 21–55; for the impact of this idea, through Arabic sources, on medieval Europe, see Mary Frances Wack, *Lovesickness in the Middle Ages: The Viaticum and its Commentaries* (Philadelphia: University of Pennsylvania Press, 1990).
16. Arabic: *aʿlam*.
17. *Dhāt al-Himma* 50: 55.
18. *Dhāt al-Himma* 40: 56.
19. *Dhāt al-Himma* 40: 57.
20. *Dhāt al-Himma* 41: 3.
21. *The Book of Dede Korkut: A Turkish Epic*, trans. and ed. Faruk Sümer, Ahmet E. Uysal and Warren S. Walker (Austin: University of Texas Press, 1972), 99.
22. *Dhāt al-Himma* 41: 4.
23. *Dhāt al-Himma* 41: 5.
24. Arabic: *riwāyāt*, the various canonical ways of reciting the Qurʾān.
25. *Dhāt al-Himma* 41: 12.
26. *Dhāt al-Himma* 41: 15.

27. Dhat al-Himma 41: 15–16.
28. Dhāt al-Himma 41: 23.
29. Dhāt al-Himma 41: 28.
30. Dhāt al-Himma 41: 31–32.
31. Dhāt al-Himma 42: 26.
32. Dhāt al-Himma 43: 10, 13.
33. See, for instance, Susan A. Spectorsky, *Chapters on Marriage and Divorce: Responses of Ibn Hanbal and Ibn Rahwayh* (Austin: University of Texas Press, 1993), 21.

Chapter 6: Warrior Women in *Sīrat ʿAntar* 1: Ghamra the Daughter of Fāʾiz

1. The edition of *Sīrat ʿAntar* used here (referred to as *ʿAntar*) is *Sīrat ʿAntar ibn Shaddād al-ʿAbsī. Riwāyat abī Saʿīd ʿAbd al-Malik ibn Qarīb al-Asmāʿī* (Cairo: Maktaba wa-matbaʿa Mustafā al-Bābī al-Halabī, 1381/1961–2). The text is divided into 12 vols, 58 parts (*ajzāʾ*). References are to volumes, not parts. Consulting is somewhat complicated by the fact that the 12 vols of the text are bound in various ways, the binding not necessarily coinciding with the volumes into which the text itself is divided. For wider information and analysis of *Sīrat ʿAntar*, the reader is referred to Peter Heath, *The Thirsty Sword: Sīrat ʿAntar and the Arabic Popular Epic* (Salt Lake City: University of Utah Press, 1996), which also contains an extensive summary.
2. Terrick Hamilton, *ʿAntar, a Bedoueen Romance*, 4 parts, 2 vols (London: John Murray, 1819–20).
3. Edward William Lane, *An Account of the Manners and Customs of the Modern Egyptians. The Definitive 1860 Edition. Introduced by Jason Thompson* (Cairo and New York: American University in Cairo Press, 2003), ch. 22 (reprinted from the London 1860 edition. First, less complete, edition of the work: London, 1836).
4. Armand Abel, 'Formation et constitution du Roman d' Antar', in Albert Bates et al. (eds), *Atti del Convegno internazionale sul tema: La Poesia Epica e la sua Formazione* (Rome: Accademia Nazionale dei Lincei, 1970), 717–730. Followed by comments by R. Paret, 731.
5. *ʿAntar* 12: 36–38.
6. As noted earlier, in one of the versions the actual epic is preceded by an introduction connecting ʿAntar's tribal history to pre-Islamic prophets.
7. The history of Ghamra starts in *ʿAntar* 6: 126, continuing until 6: 216; it is then taken up again in 7: 383 until 7: 412. From there on, Ghamra simply forms part of the cast, participating in battles, until the episode of the expedition to Ethiopia, which leads to the disclosure of her family background (8: 267). She dies of an illness on the way back from this expedition (8: 302).

8. These details are only revealed much later in the story: ʿAntar 8: 267-268.
9. ʿAntar 6: 142.
10. See my 'The Princess Maymūnah: maiden, mother, monster', in Giovanni Canova (ed.), *Studies on Arabic Epics*, Oriente Moderno 22/83, n.s., 2 (2003), 425-442.
11. ʿAntar 6: 149-150.
12. ʿAntar 6: 150.
13. ʿAntar 6: 156.
14. The Arabic word *nadhbahuhu* does indeed have this crude meaning.
15. ʿAntar 6: 215.
16. ʿAntar 7: 383-384, 387, 394ff.
17. ʿAntar 7: 387ff.
18. ʿAntar 7: 389.
19. ʿAntar 7: 390.
20. ʿAntar 7: 394.
21. ʿAntar 7: 400.
22. ʿAntar 7: 403.
23. ʿAntar 7: 403-405.
24. ʿAntar 7: 406.
25. ʿAntar 7: 408.
26. ʿAntar 7: 412.
27. ʿAntar 7: 444.
28. ʿAntar 8: 267ff.
29. ʿAntar 8: 302.

Chapter 7: Warrior Women in *Sīrat ʿAntar* 2: Hayfāʾ, Zarqāʾ and ʿUnaytira

1. For the Arabic text that was used, see Chapter 6, n.1.
2. The spelling of her name in the text alternates between Zarqā and Zarqāʾ. I have opted for the latter form.
3. See Chapter 2.
4. Vol. 12, the last four sections, *ajzāʾ*, 56-59, of the Cairo 1962 edition used here.
5. ʿAntar 12, final part.
6. ʿAntar 11: 405-406.
7. ʿAntar 11: 407.
8. ʿAntar 11: 433.
9. ʿAntar 12: 434.
10. ʿAntar 12: 437.
11. ʿAntar 12: 445-448.
12. ʿAntar 12: 10-11.
13. ʿAntar 12: 17-32.
14. ʿAntar 12: 23.

15. *'Antar* 12: 53ff.
16. 68th–69th Night in the Calcutta edition of 1839. 68th–69th Night in the Būlāq edition of 1252 AH, or: *Alf Layla wa-Layla* (Būlāq, 1252) 68th–69th Night.
17. See Geert Jan van Gelder, *Close Relationships: Incest and Inbreeding in Classical Arabic Literature* (London and New York: I.B.Tauris, 2005), especially 36–38.
18. *'Antar* 12: 101.
19. Killing a lion is a familiar way for the hero in popular epic to demonstrate his (or her) prowess. On the lion fights in *'Antar*, cf. Peter Heath, *The Thirsty Sword: Sīrat 'Antar and the Arabic Popular Epic* (Salt Lake City: University of Utah Press, 1996), 249–253.
20. *'Antar* 12: 56.
21. *'Antar* 12: 61.
22. *'Antar* 12: 62.
23. *'Antar* 12: 66.
24. *'Antar* 12: 65.
25. *'Antar* 12: 80.
26. *'Antar* 12: 84–90.
27. *'Antar* 12: 95.
28. *'Antar* 12: 101.
29. *'Antar* 12: 104.
30. Arabic: *ahyajī*. I am not quite sure about the meaning of this word.
31. *'Antar* 12: 124–125.
32. *'Antar* 12: 121–128.
33. *'Antar* 12: 124.
34. *'Antar* 12: 136.
35. *'Antar* 12: 150.
36. *'Antar* 12: 195.
37. *'Antar* 12: 204.
38. *'Antar* 12: 212.
39. *'Antar* 12: 215.
40. *'Antar* 12: 221–227.
41. *'Antar* 12: 235.
42. *'Antar* 12: 249.
43. *'Antar* 12: 319ff.
44. *'Antar* 12: 321.
45. *'Antar* 12: 322.
46. B. Heller, 'Sīrat 'Antar', in *EI2*, 1: 518–521.

Chapter 8: Prince Hamza al-Bahlawān: In Praise of Traditional Womanhood

1. This chapter is a reworking of part of my earlier article 'Back to the boudoir: versions of the *Sīrat Hamza*, women warriors, and literary unity', in

Notes to pages 147–156   243

Ludo Jongen and Sjaak Onderdelinden (eds), 'Der muoz mir süezer worte jehen': Liber amicorum für Norbert Voorwinden (Amsterdam and Atlanta, GA, 1997), Amsterdamer Beiträge zur älteren Germanistik, 48: 129–148. The Arabic version that I used (referred to as Hamza) is Qissat al-amīr Hamza al-Bahlawān al-maʻrūf bi-Hamzat al-ʻArab, 4 vols (Cairo: Maktaba wa-Matbaʻat al-mashhad al-Husaynī, n.d.), which presents a text that is basically the same as the edition used by Malcolm Lyons in The Arabian Epic: Heroic and Oral Storytelling, 3 vols (Cambridge: Cambridge University Press, 1995).

2. John Seyller, The Adventures of Hamza: Painting and Storytelling in Mughal India (Washington, DC: Smithsonian Institution, 2002).
3. The matter is further complicated by the fact that there exist two Arabic versions, which differ considerably but have the same eponymous hero. For the many versions of the Hamza tradition and relevant literature, see Ph. S. van Ronkel, De Roman van Amir Hamzah (Leiden, 1895); U. Marzolph, 'Hamza-Name', in Enzyklopädie des Märchens 6, 2/3 (1990), 430–436; and Kruk, 'Back to the boudoir'.
4. This epic is not called a sīra but a qissa, or tale.
5. Hamza 1: 180.
6. Hamza 3: 229.
7. Khusrau is also spelt as Chosroe or Chosroes.
8. See also my 'Click of needles: polygamy as an issue in Arabic popular epic', in Manuela Marin and Randi Deguilhem (eds), Writing the Feminine: Women in Arab Sources (London and New York: I.B.Tauris, 2002), 3–23.
9. Dhāt al-Himma 41: 3.
10. Hamza 3: 258.
11. Hamza 2: 139.
12. Hamza 1: 21–26, 34–39.
13. This is a familiar name for warrior women. Cf. Qannāsa in Sīrat Dhāt al-Himma and 'Antar's wife Hayfā', nicknamed Qannāsat al-Rijāl, 'Huntress (or Catcher) of Men'.
14. Hamza 1: 26.
15. Hamza 1: 21.
16. Hamza 1: 2–50; 2: 89, 95; 3: 144.
17. Hamza 1: 250.
18. Hamza 3: 144.
19. Hamza 3: 21–28, 208–12.
20. Hamza 3: 21.
21. Hamza 3: 25.
22. This may seem strange to us, because clearly his mother is not married to his grandfather, but the same situation occurs repeatedly in popular epic. It is obviously an accepted narrative device.
23. Hamza 3: 208–212.

24. *Hamza* 4: 72–86.
25. Arabic: *atafarraju*, a colloquial word meaning 'to look at something for one's own amusement'.
26. *Hamza* 4: 84–85.
27. *Hamza* 4: 176–177.
28. W. Ahlwardt, *Verzeichnis der arabischen Handschriften der königlichen Bibliothek zu Berlin* (Berlin, 1896), 8: 104–107, n.9.
29. See Chapter 1, page 11.
30. *Hamza* 2: 95–258; 3: 51–54.
31. He is called al-Yūnīnī in the edition used by Lyons, *The Arabian Epic*.
32. *Hamza* 2: 95.
33. *Hamza* 2: 105.
34. *Hamza* 2: 97.
35. *Hamza* 2: 107.
36. *Hamza* 2: 119–122.
37. *Hamza* 2: 129.
38. *Hamza* 2: 132.
39. *Hamza* 2: 141.
40. *Hamza* 2: 151–153.
41. *Hamza* 2: 191.
42. *Hamza* 2: 194–197.
43. *Hamza* 2: 248.
44. *Hamza* 2: 251.
45. *Hamza* 2: 256.
46. *Hamza* 2: 259.
47. *Hamza* 3: 51–53.
48. *Hamza* 2: 157.

Chapter 9: *Sīrat Baybars* 1: Lionesses

1. The edition that I used (referred to as *Baybars*, Cairo 1996–7) is *Sīrat al-Zāhir Baybars*, intro. Gamāl al-Ghitānī, 5 vols (Cairo: al-Hay'a al-misrīya al-'āmma li-l-kitāb, 1996–7). This edition is a reprint, with added introduction and different paging from the 2nd edition (Cairo, 1923–6).
2. Jacqueline Sublet, *Les trois vies du Sultan Baibars* (Paris: Imprimerie Nationale, 1992).
3. Malcolm C. Lyons, *The Arabian Epic: Heroic and Oral Storytelling* (Cambridge: Cambridge University Press, 1995), vols 2 and 3: *Baybars* episode 63.
4. *Baybars*, Cairo 1996–7, 2: 1145. For further discussion of methods to date *Sīrat Baybars* and other *sīra*s I refer to Jean-Claude Garcin's article 'Siras et histoire/Siras and History', ed. Katia Zakharia, Part 1, *Arabica* 51/1–2 (2004),

55–76; *Sīrat al-malik al-Zāhir Baybars/s*: de l'oral à l'écrit/From Performance to Script', Part 2, *Arabica* 51/3 (2004), 223–257.
5. Heidi Toelle and Katia Zakharia, *À la découverte de la littérature arabe du VIe siècle à nos jours* (Paris: Flammarion, 2003), 167.
6. T. Herzog, 'Présentation de deux séances de hakawātī et de deux manuscrits de la Sīrat Baybars recueillis en Syrie en 1994, MA thesis, University of Aix-en-Provence, 1994.
7. Georges Bohas and Jean-Patrick Guillaume, *Roman de Baïbars. Traduit de l'arabe et annoté par Georges Bohas et Jean-Patrick Guillaume*, vol. 1: *Les enfances de Baïbars* (2nd edn, Paris: Éditions Sindbad, 1985), 1: 35.
8. Thomas Herzog, *Geschichte und Imaginaire: Entstehung, Überlieferung und Bedeutung der Sīrat Baibars in ihrem sozio-politischen Kontext* (Wiesbaden: Harrassowitz, 2006), 861–905.
9. *Sīrat al-malik al-Zāhir Baybars hasaba al-riwāya al-shāmīya. Haqqaqahu wa-ʿallaqa ʿalayhi George Bohas wa-Katya Zakharīya* (Damascus: IFEAD, 2000), 9.
10. *Baybars*, Damascus 2000–11, 4: 247–248.
11. Georges Bohas and Jean-Patrick Guillaume, *Roman de Baïbars. Traduit de l'arabe et annoté par Georges Bohas et Jean-Patrick Guillaume*, vol. 9: *Échec au roi de Rome* (2nd edn, Paris: Sindbad/Actes Sud, 1997), 110–113.
12. *Baybars*, Cairo 1996–7, 2: 1237–1238.
13. For a wider view of the MSS of *Sīrat Baybars* and their variation, see the extensive concordances in Herzog, *Geschichte und Imaginaire*.
14. I used the reprint of 1996–7, which contains many printing errors (or scribal errors, as one might call them).
15. Toelle and Zakharia, *À la découverte*, 173.
16. The historical al-Sālih Ayyūb was the last effective Ayyubid ruler of Egypt. He reigned briefly in 1240 and again from 1245 to 1249.
17. This is not a real adoption as we know it, for adoption of this kind is not allowed in Islam. The 'adoption' referred to in the *sīra* was a practice among the Mamelukes to incorporate specially selected slaves into noble families.
18. According to Herzog, *Geschichte und Imaginaire*, 182–184, the Maghribi saint al-Maghāwirī of the *sīra* was a corruption of a twelfth-century Alexandrian saint called al-Mughāwir and al-Maghāwarī, the legendary founder of the Bekhtashi order in Egypt in the fourteenth century, who is buried in the *takīya* near the caves (*maghāwir*) in the Muqattam hills. See also Frederick De Jong, 'The takiya of ʿAbdallah al-Maghāwiri in Cairo', in his *Sufi Orders in Ottoman and Post-Ottoman Egypt and the Middle East* (Istanbul: Isis Press, 2000), 40–54, 40.
19. See also Denis Gril, 'Du sultanat au califat universel: le rôle des saints dans le *Roman de Baybars*', in Jean-Claude Garcin (ed.), *Lectures du roman de Baybars* (Marseille: Éditions parenthèses, 2003), 173–197.
20. *Baybars*, Cairo 1996–7, 1: 947.

21. Lyons, *The Arabian Epic*, 2: 45–119 and 3: 77–236; Herzog, *Geschichte und Imaginaire*, 861–905.
22. The parallel episode in the Cairo version runs quite differently. The princess involved there, ʿAyn al-Masīḥ, has no warrior past, unlike Ibrīza (*Baybars*, Cairo 1996–7, 3: 1970–1971).
23. *Baybars*, Damascus 2000–11, 9: 21–22.
24. Cf. Toelle and Zakharia, *À la découverte*, 173.
25. The episode is found in *Baybars*, Cairo 1996–7, 4: 2531–2534.
26. This suggests that among these Ismailis there was a tradition of bride kidnapping.
27. The fact that the defeated girl is being forced to walk recalls the episode of Hind and Rabīʿa in *Sīrat ʿAntar* (see Chapter 2).
28. *Baybars*, Cairo 1996–7, 2: 1237–1249.
29. *Baybars*, Cairo 1996–7, 4: 1235–1236.
30. *Baybars*, Cairo 1996–7, 4: 1242.
31. *Baybars*, Cairo 1996–7, 2: 1240–1241.
32. *Baybars*, Cairo 1996–7, 4: 2600–2061. Her name also occurs as al-Jaydāʾ, cf. Herzog, *Geschichte und Imaginaire*, 897.
33. *Baybars*, Cairo 1996–7, 2: 1147–1157.
34. *Baybars*, Cairo 1996–7, 2: 1151.
35. *Baybars*, Cairo 1996–7, 2: 1151–1153.
36. *Baybars*, Cairo 1996–7, 2: 1156.

Chapter 10: *Sīrat Baybars* 2: Warrior Queens

1. For the Arabic text that was used, see Chapter 9, n.1.
2. *Baybars*, Cairo 1996–7, 4: 2475–2487, when she is recognized as ʿArnūs's daughter; 2475–2522 for the first attempted wedding of Maryam and Tuqtimur to the birth of their children.
3. It is not clear to me why she bears this nickname. She is the granddaughter of Maryam al-Zunnārīya, Maryam the Girdlemaker, the mother of ʿArnūs; cf. *Baybars*, Cairo 1996–7, 4: 2338 and 4: 2439, which connects her to Maryam the Girdlemaker in the story of Nūr al-Dīn and Maryam in *The Thousand and One Nights*.
4. This is a common way in popular epic to refer to the inadequacy of women.
5. *Baybars*, Cairo 1996–7, 4: 2480–2481.
6. *Baybars*, Cairo 1996–7, 4: 2498.
7. *Baybars*, Cairo 1996–7, 4: 2435–2445.
8. *Baybars*, Cairo 1996–7, 4: 2439.
9. *Baybars*, Cairo 1996–7, 4: 2440.
10. *Baybars*, Cairo 1996–7, 4: 2444–2445.
11. *Baybars*, Cairo 1996–7, 4: 2217–2243.

Notes to pages 181–188   247

12. The names recall Shawāhī Dhāt al-Dawāhī, the fearsome grandmother of Princess Ibrīza in the story of King 'Umar al-Nu'mān and his sons in *The Thousand and One Nights*; see Chapter 2. For 'sorceress', the Arabic here uses the terms *kāhina* (soothsayeress), *sahira* (sorceress) and *hakīma* (wise woman).
13. *Baybars*, Cairo 1996–7, 4: 2242.
14. *Baybars*, Cairo 1996–7, 4: 2218–2219.
15. *Baybars*, Cairo 1996–7, 4: 2224.
16. *Baybars*, Cairo 1996–7, 4: 2238.
17. As from 4: 2225 she is *al-babb Shawāhī*, the *hakīm*.
18. *Baybars*, Cairo 1996–7, 4: 2240.
19. *Baybars*, Cairo 1996–7, 4: 2242.
20. *Baybars*, Cairo 1996–7, 4: 2404.
21. *Baybars*, Cairo 1996–7, 4: 2411.
22. *Baybars*, Cairo 1996–7, 4: 2410–2411. On the use of firearms by the Mamelukes and their attitude to them, see David Ayalon, *Gunpowder and Firearms in the Mamluk Kingdom* (London: Valentine, Mitchell, 1956).
23. *Baybars*, Cairo 1996–7, 4: 2414.
24. *Baybars*, Cairo 1996–7, 4: 2418.

Chapter 11: King Sayf ibn Dhī Yazan, the Soft-Hearted 1: Qamarīya

1. The edition used here (referred to as *Sayf*) is *Sīrat fāris al-Yaman al-malik Sayf ibn Dhī Yazan al-batal al-karrār wa-l-fāris al-mighwār sāhib al-batsh wa-l-iqtidār al-ma'rūf bi-l-ghazawāt al-mashhūra*, 4 vols (Cairo: Maktaba wa-matba'at al-mashhad al-Husaynī, 1391/1971).
2. Arabic: *millat al-khalīl*, 'the community of the Friend', i.e. Abraham. *Sayf* 1: 138. According to Islam, Abraham was the founder of Islam, but his religion was later corrupted by Jews and Christians until the Prophet Muhammad restored the true religion.
3. Yet the connection of the *sīra* to the historical background is highly interesting, as has been demonstrated by Aboubakr Chraïbi in his analysis of the structure of the *sīra* in connection to geographical location ('Le Roman de Sayf ibn dhī Yazan: Sources, Structure and Argumentation', *Studia Islamica* 84 (1996), 113–134), and recently by Giovanni Canova's analysis of Arabic historical sources relevant to the historical Sayf ibn Dhī Yazan ('Sayf b. Dhī Yazan: history and saga', in Sabine Dorpmueller (ed.), *Fictionalizing the Past: Historical Characters in Arabic Popular Epic. Proceedings of the Workshop at the Netherlands–Flemish Institute in Cairo 28th/29th of November 2007 in Honor of Remke Kruk* (Leuven: Peeters, 2012), 107–123).
4. J.-P. Guillaume, 'Sayf ibn Dhī Yazan', in *EI2*, 9: 101.
5. Remke Kruk and Claudia Ott, '"In the Popular Manner": *Sīra*-Recitation in Marrakesh Anno 1997', *Edebiyat* 10 (1999), 189.

6. See Emery van Donzel, 'The legend of the Blue Nile in Europe', in Haggai Erlich and Israel Gershoni (eds), *Histories, Cultures, Myths* (London and Boulder, CO: Lynne Rienner Publishers, 2000), 121–130.
7. R. Paret, *Sīrat Saif ibn Dhī Jazan. Ein arabischer Volksroman* (Hanover, 1924; augmented English translation: Gisela Seidensticker-Brikay, 2006); Malcolm Lyons, *The Arabian Epic: Heroic and Oral Storytelling*, 3 vols (Cambridge: Cambridge University Press, 1995), 2: 239–265; 3: 586–641.
8. Lena Jayyusi (tr.), *The Adventures of Sayf Ben Dhi Yazan: An Arab Folk Epic*, intro. Harry Norris (Bloomington and Indianapolis: Indiana University Press, 1996), xxiii–iv.
9. *Sayf* 1: 69–72.
10. Just like the caliph al-Hākim bi-Amr Allāh in the *sīra* of that name, see Claudia Ott, 'Finally we know ... why, how, and where Caliph al-Hākim disappeared! *Sīrat al-Hākim bi-Amrillāh* and its Berlin manuscript', in Dorpmueller (ed.), *Fictionalizing the Past*, 63–64.
11. J.-P. Guillaume, 'Sayf ibn Dhī Yazan', *EI2*, 9: 101–102.
12. *Sayf* 1: 145–150.
13. Claudia Ott, *Metamorphosen des Epos: Sīrat al-Mujāhidīn (Sīrat al-Amīra Dhāt al-Himma) zwischen Muendlichkeit und Schriftlichkeit* (Leiden: CNWS, 2003); T. Herzog, *Geschichte und Imaginaire: Entstehung, Überlieferung und Bedeutung der Sīrat Baibars in ihrem sozio-politischen Kontext* (Wiesbaden: Harrassowitz, 2006).
14. See my introduction in Jamal Sleem Nuweihed, *Abu Jmeel's Daughter and Other Stories: Arab Folk Tales from Palestine and Lebanon*, preface by Salma Khadra Jayyusi, trans. by members of her family with Christopher Tingley (New York and Northampton: Interlink Books, 2002), xii–xix.
15. Jayyusi, *Sayf Ben Dhi Yazan*, xxiii.
16. See Remke Kruk, 'Ibn Battūta: Travel, Family Life and Chronology. How Seriously do We Take a Father?' *Al-Qantara* 16/2 (1995), 369–385.
17. For instance *Sayf* 3: 119–120: Jīza cries about her missing son Nasr, her only child, and complains that Sayf has not asked about him.
18. *Sayf* 4: 200–201.
19. In character she resembles Maymūna in *Dhāt al-Himma* during the later part of her career (see Chapter 3).
20. It is often difficult to decide on the most plausible vocalization for personal names in the epics. In this case, Qumrīya, referring to the dove to which women are often compared, is a possibility. Qamarīya, connecting her to the Mountains of the Moon near her country of origin, is another. This is the vocalization chosen by most scholars and I follow it here.
21. Cf. Jayyusi, *Sayf Ben Dhi Yazan*, xxiii.
22. *Sayf* 1: 26–30.
23. *Sayf* 1: 137–138.
24. *Sayf* 1: 138–140.

25. *Sayf* 1: 144.
26. The more usual expression is: 'made from a crooked rib'. This is a common way in popular epic to refer to the inadequacy of women.
27. *Sayf* 1: 152–154.
28. *Sayf* 1: 181.
29. *Sayf* 1: 154–156.
30. *Sayf* 1: 178.
31. *Sayf* 1: 180.
32. *Sayf* 1: 199.
33. *Sayf* 1: 202.
34. *Sayf* 1: 212.
35. *Sayf* 1: 240.
36. *Sayf* 1: 253. The practice described involves drawing an image of a female on a brass plate with a stylus of steel, writing the name Qamarīya on it, putting the plate in a leaden tube and burying it at the city gate.
37. *Sayf* 1: 256. Pounded crab shells were actually used in medicines against eye disease in medieval Arabic pharmacopoeia.
38. *Sayf* 1: 362–363.
39. *Sayf* 1: 264–265.
40. *Sayf* 1: 268.
41. *Sayf* 1: 270–274.
42. *Sayf* 1: 275–279.
43. A belt of gazelle hide (*mantiqa wa-hiya min jild al-ghazāl* (*Sayf* 1: 350); later on in the text it is referred to as *thawb min riqq al-ghazāl*, on which names and spells (*talāsim*) were written in Greek script.
44. *Sayf* 1: 354–355.
45. *Sayf* 1: 363–366.
46. *Sayf* 1: 368.

Chapter 12: King Sayf ibn Dhī Yazan 2: Tāma

1. For the Arabic text that was used, see Chapter 11, n.1.
2. Arabic: *min wast al-junūn*. I am not sure whether the text is correct.
3. The castle of the champion Saʿdūn, whose head Sayf was supposed to get as a dowry for Shāma, see *Sayf* 1: 53.
4. *Sayf* 1: 72–74.
5. *Sayf* 1: 84.
6. *Sayf* 1: 75–93.
7. *Sayf* 1: 112.
8. *Sayf* 1: 113.
9. *Sayf* 1: 114.
10. *Sayf* 1: 199.
11. *Sayf* 1: 263.

12. *Sayf* 1: 347.
13. *Tāsa*: a remarkable reference, for although magic bowls were frequently used in daily life (and sometimes still are), references to them in written sources, even magical handbooks, are rare.
14. *Sayf* 1: 348–349.
15. *Sayf* 1: 356–357.
16. *Sayf* 1: 359–360.
17. *Sayf* 1: 361–365.
18. *Sayf* 1: 369.
19. *Sayf* 1: 371.
20. *Sayf* 1: 372–373.
21. Nothing more is said about the cap of invisibility, but clearly Tāma has handed it over, for not much later Sayf puts it on.
22. Arabic: '*aql*.
23. *Sayf* 1: 375–381.
24. Sayf has another son by one of his later wives, Takrūr.
25. *Sayf* 2: 382–383.

Chapter 13: King Sayf ibn Dhī Yazan 3: Munyat al-Nufūs

1. For the Arabic text that was used, see Chapter 11, n. 1. This chapter contains reworked parts of my earlier article 'Clipped Wings: Medieval Arabic Adaptations of the Amazon Myth', *Harvard Middle Eastern and Islamic Review* 1/2 (1994), 132–154.
2. For my analysis of this episode I have made use of William Blake Tyrrell's *Amazons: A Study in Athenian Mythmaking* (Baltimore and London: Johns Hopkins University Press, 1989). I find his views quite workable, in spite of the criticism raised by gender specialists such as Batya Weinbaum, *Islands of Women and Amazons: Representations and Realities* (Austin: University of Texas Press, 1999), 66ff. Of the other studies dealing with the episode that I have consulted I specifically mention here Jamel Eddine Bencheikh, Claude Bremond and André Miquel, *Mille et un contes de la nuit* (Paris: Gallimard, 1991), 143–258, and Richard van Leeuwen's discussion of a parallel version, the story of Hasan of Basra in *The Thousand and One Nights*, in his *The Thousand and One Nights: Space, Travel and Transformation* (London and New York: Routledge, 2007), 105–118.
3. Lena Jayyusi (tr.), *The Adventures of Sayf ben Dhi Yazan: An Arab Folk Epic*, intro. Harry Norris (Bloomington and Indianapolis: Indiana University Press, 1996), xxiii.
4. *Sayf* 1: 287. The feather robe is a widespread motif in folklore all over the world, for example the swan woman (Aarne–Thompson motif classification no. 402).
5. *Sayf* 1: 384.

Notes to pages 215–225   251

6. *Sayf* 2: 4.
7. *Sayf* 2: 4.
8. *Sayf* 1: 378.
9. *Sayf* 1: 11. Of the vast literature on the Wāqwāq (or Wāq al-Wāq) women, I will just mention here Fedwa Malti-Douglas, 'Sexual geography, asexual philosophy', in Fedwa Malti-Douglas, *Woman's Body, Woman's Word: Gender and Discourse in Arabo-Islamic Writing* (Princeton: Princeton University Press, 1991/American University in Cairo Press, 1992), 85–111, and Jean-Louis Bacqué-Grammont et al. (eds), *L'arbre anthropogène du Waqwaq, les femmes fruits et les îles des femmes* (Naples: Università degli studi di Napoli 'l'Orientale' and Institut français d'études anatoliennes, 2007).
10. *Sayf* 2: 12.
11. *Sayf* 2: 20.
12. Cf. Ulfa al-Idlibī (Adlabi), *Nazar fī adabinā al-shaʿbī: Alf layla wa-layla wa-sīrat al-malik Sayf ibn Dhī Yazan* (Damascus: Manshūrāt ittihād al-kuttāb al-ʿarab, 1974), 130–132, who briefly comments upon this episode.
13. *Sayf* 2: 23.
14. *Sayf* 2: 26.
15. *Sayf* 2: 28.
16. *Sayf* 2: 37.
17. *Sayf* 2: 37.
18. *Sayf* 2: 37–38.
19. *Sayf* 2: 35.
20. *Sayf* 2: 41.
21. *Sayf* 2: 45.
22. *Sayf* 2: 46.
23. *Sayf* 2: 49.
24. *Sayf* 2: 45.
25. *Sayf* 2: 50.
26. *Sayf* 2: 47.
27. Cf. Tyrrell, *Amazons*, 41–42.
28. *Sayf* 2: 48–49.
29. Cf. Tyrrell, *Amazons*, xvi.
30. *Sayf* 2: 49–51.

Chapter 14: Final Observations

1. *Dhāt al-Himma* 33: 34.
2. Carol J. Glover, *Men, Women and Chainsaws: Gender in the Modern Horror Film* (Princeton: Princeton University Press, 1992). Glover analyses the relationship between the male audience of the horror movie, in particular the slasher movie, and the female victim who eventually plays a heroic role,

defeating her attackers. My attention was drawn to this book during a seminar meeting at Yale in 2008 by a participant whose name unfortunately is not known to me. I want to thank him anonymously.

3. Glover, *Chainsaws*, 53.

Bibliography

Sīra and qissa texts

'Antara ibn Shaddād:
: Sīrat abī l-fawāris fāris fursān al-jazīra 'Antara ibn Shaddād battāl al-jazīra al-'arabīya wa-fāris fursānihā al-mushtamil 'alā a'jab al-akhbār wa-l-hawādith, 8 vols (Beirut: Al-maktaba al-sha'bīya, n.d.).

: Sīrat 'Antar ibn Shaddād al-'Absī. Riwāyat abī Sa'īd 'Abd al-Malik ibn Qarīb al-Asmā'ī, text divided into 12 vols, 58 parts (ajzā'), bound in 6 (sometimes 8) bindings (Cairo: Maktaba wa-matba'a Mustafā al-Bābī al-Halabī, 1381/1961–2).

: Sīrat 'Antar ibn Shaddād ibn Mu'āwīya ibn Qarrād al-'Absī, man sārat bi-hadīthihi al-rukbān wa-tamayyaza bi-dhikrihi al-zamān [...] wa-fāris al-hayjā'. Bi-qalam al-mu'ammar fī al-jāhilīya wa-l-islām al-Alma'ī 'Abd al-Malik ibn Qarīb al-shahīr bi-l-Asmā'ī, 8 vols (Cairo: Maktaba wa-matba'at al-mashhad al-Husaynī, 1971).

: Sīrat fāris fursān al-hijāz abī l-fawāris 'Antara ibn Shaddād wa-hiya al-sīra al-fā'iqa al-hijāzīya al-mushtarika 'alā l-akhbār al-'ajība wa-l-anbiyā' al-jalīya, 8 vols (Beirut: Al-maktaba al-'ilmīya al-hadītha, n.d.).

Banī Hilāl:
: Taghribat Banī Hilāl al-Kubrā al-shāmīya al-aslīya (Cairo: Maktaba wa-matba'at al-mashhad al-husaynī, n.d.).

Baybars:
: Sīrat al-Malik al-Zāhir Baybars (Beirut: Dār al-kutub al-sha'bīya, n.d.).

: Sīrat al-Zāhir Baybars, intro. Gamāl al-Ghitānī, 5 vols (Cairo: al-Hay'a al-misrīya al-'āmma li-l-kitāb, 1996–7). Reprint, with added introduction and different paging, of the 2nd edition Cairo, 1923–6.

: Sirat al-Malik al-Zahir Baybars, Texte arabe de la recension damascène, ed. Georges Bohas and Katia Zakharia (vols 1–7) and Georges Bohas and Salam Diab (vol. 8) (Damascus: L'Institut Français d'études arabes de Damas (IFEAD), 2000-11). Arabic title: *Sīrat al-malik al-zāhir Baybars hasaba al-riwāya al-shāmīya*. Haqqaqahu wa-'allaqa 'alayhi George Bohas wa-Katia Zakharīya (vols 1-7), George Bohas wa-Salam Diab (vols 8-9) (Damascus: IFEAD, 2000-11).

Dhāt al-Himma:

Sīrat al-amīra Dhāt al-Himma wa-waladihā 'Abd al-Wahhāb wa-l-amīr Abū Muhammad al-Battāl wa-'Uqba shaykh al-dallāl wa-Shūmdaris al-muhtāl, 7 vols, 70 parts (Cairo: Maktaba 'Abd al-Hamīd Ahmad al-Hanafī, 1327/1909).

Sīrat al-amīra Dhāt al-Himma wa-waladihā 'Abd al-Wahhāb wa-l-amīr Abū Muhammad al-Battāl wa-'Uqba shaykh al-dallāl wa-Shūmdaris al-muhtāl. Akbar ta'rīkh li-l-'arab wa-khulafa' banī Umayya wa-l-khulafa' al-'abbāsīya. Jama'at hādhihi al-sīra akhbār al-'arab wa-hurūbihim wa-akhbār mulk masr wa-l-shām wa-Baghdād wa-ghayrihā min bilād al-islām wa-bilād al-ifranj wa-fīhā min al-futūhāt ma yabharu al-'uqūl, 7 vols, 70 parts (Cairo: Maktaba 'Abd al-Hamīd Ahmad al-Hanafī, n.d.). Reprint of 1909 edn, with slight differences in paging.

Sīrat al-amīra Dhāt al-Himma wa-waladihā 'Abd al-Wahhāb wa-l-amīr Abū Muhammad al-Battāl wa-'Uqba shaykh al-dallāl wa-Shūmdaris al-muhtāl. Akbar ta'rīkh li-l-'arab wa-khulafa' banī Umayya wa-l-khulafa' al-'abbāsīya. Jama'at hādhihi al-sīra akhbār al-'arab wa-hurūbihim wa-akhbār mulk masr wa-l-shām wa-baghdād wa-ghayrihā min bilād al-islām wa-bilād al-ifranj wa-fīhā min al-futūhāt ma yabharu al-'uqūl. Ta'līf: 'Alī ibn Mūsā al-Muqānibī wa-bn Bakr al-Māzinī wa-Sālihal-Ja'farīwa-Yazīdibn'Ammāral-Muznīwa-'AbdallāhibnWahb al-Yamānī wa-'Awf ibn Fahd al-Fazārī wa-Sa'd ibn Mālik al-tamīmī wa-Ahmad al-shamshātī wa-Sābir al-Mur'ishī wa-Najd ibn Hishām al-'Amirī, 7 vols (Beirut: Al-Maktaba al-thaqāfīya, 1400/1980).

Fīrūzshāh:

Qissat Fīrūzshāh ibn al-malik Dārāb, 4 vols (Beirut: Maktabat al-tarbīya, 1404/1984).

Futūh al-Yaman:

Qissat Futūh al-Yaman al-kubrā al-shahīr bi-ras al-ghūl wa-mā jarā li-l-imām 'Alī al-fāris al-karrār [...] (Cairo: Maktabat al-jumhūrīya al-'arabīya, n.d.).

Hamza al-Bahlawān:

Qissat al-amīr Hamza al-Bahlawān al-ma'rūf bi-Hamzat al-'Arab, 4 vols (Cairo: Maktaba wa-matba'a al-mashhad al-Husaynī, n.d.).

Qissat Hamza al-Bahlawān fāris barrīyat al-Hijāz wa-sultān al-ʿarab (Damascus: Dār al-karam, n.d.).

Sayf ibn Dhī Yazan:
Sīrat fāris al-Yaman al-malik Sayf ibn Dhī Yazan al-batal al-karrār wa-l-fāris al-mighwār sāhib al-batsh wa-l-iqtidār al-maʿrūf bi-l-ghazawāt al-mashhūra (this is the title as given in vol. 1; vols 2–4 give the following title: *Sīrat fāris al-Yaman al-malik Sayf ibn Dhī Yazan ibn Tubbaʿ ibn Asad al-Baidāʾ ibn Fāris al-natīja ibn Wahsh al-Barr al-fāris al-karrār wa-l-batal al-mighwār sāhib al-batsh wa-l-iqtidār wa-huwa min salālat l-tubbaʿ Hassān wa-fātih kunūz sayyidinā Sulaymān al-maʿrūf bi-l-ghazawāt al-mashhūra wa-l-hurūb al-hāʾ ila al-madhkūra man tāra sītuhu fī l-bilād wa-kharrat li-haybatihi al-abtāl al-shidād fī maʿāmiʿ al-hurūb wa-l-tirād fa-hiya qissa tawīla ʿajība wa-umūr jarat fīhā gharība* (number of volume). *Rūjiʿat ʿalā l-nuskha l-amīrīya wa-qad hallaynāhā bi-l-suwar wa-l-rusūm* (apart from the addition of *wa-l-rusūm*, this latter title is identical to that of the Cairo edition of 1930), 4 vols (Cairo: Maktaba wa-matbaʿat al-mashhad al-Husaynī, 1391/1971).

Sīrat Fāris al-Yaman al-malik Sayf ibn Dhī Yazan (Beirut: Dār al-kutub al-shaʿbīya, n.d.).

Sīrat al-malik Sayf ibn Dhī Yazan Fāris al-Yaman, 4 vols (Beirut: Maktabat al-tarbīya, 1404/1984).

Other literature

Abbott, Nabia, 'Pre-Islamic Arab Queens', *American Journal of Semitic Languages and Literature* 58 (1941), 1–22.
Abd Al-Hakim, Shawqi, *Princess Dhat Al Himma: The Princess of High Resolve*, trans. and intro. Omaima Abou Bakr (Cairo: Ministry of Culture, 1995).
Abel, Armand, 'Formation et constitution du Roman d'Antar, in *La Poesia Epica e la sua Formazione* (Rome: Accademia Nazionale dei Lincei, 1970), 717–730 and 731 (comment R. Paret).
Abou Bakr, Omaima, *see* Abd Al-Hakim, Shawqi.
Abouel-lail, Khaled, 'The Sīrat Banī Hilāl: new remarks on its performance in Upper and Lower Egypt', in Sabine Dorpmueller (ed.), *Fictionalizing the Past: Historical Characters in Arabic Popular Epic. Proceedings of the Workshop at the Netherlands–Flemish Institute in Cairo 28th/29th of November 2007 in Honor of Remke Kruk* (Leuven: Peeters, 2012), 73–93.
Ahlwardt, W., *Verzeichnis der arabischen Handschriften der königlichen Bibliothek zu Berlin*, vol. 8 (Berlin: Schade, 1896).

Allen, R. and Richards, D. S., *Cambridge History of Arabic Literature*, vol. 6: *Arabic Literature in the Post-Classical Period* (Cambridge: Cambridge University Press, 2006).

Ayalon, David, *Gunpowder and Firearms in the Mamluk Kingdom* (London: Valentine Mitchell, 1956).

Ayoub, Abderrahman and Galley, Micheline, *Images de Djāzya. À propos d'une peinture sous verre de Tunisie* (Paris: Éditions du CNRS, 1977).

el-Azhari, Taef Kamal, 'Dayfa Khātūn, Ayyubid Queen of Aleppo 634–640 A.H./1236–1242 A.D.', *Annals of Japan Association for Middle East Studies (JAMES)* 15 (2000), 27–55.

Bacqué-Grammont, Jean-Louis et al. (eds), *L'arbre anthropogène du Waqwaq, les femmes fruits et les îles des femmes* (Naples: Università degli studi di Napoli 'l'Orientale' and Institut français d'études anatoliennes, 2007).

Bencheikh, Jamel Eddine, Bremond, Claude and Miquel, André, *Mille et un contes de la nuit* (Paris: Gallimard, 1991).

Biesterfeld, Hans Hinrich and Gutas, Dimitri, 'The Malady of Love', *Journal of the American Oriental Society* 104/1 (1984), 21–55.

Bohas, G. and Guillaume, J.-P, *Le Roman de Baibars. Traduit de l'arabe et annoté par Georges Bohas et Jean-Patrick Guillaume*, vol. 1: *Les enfances de Baibars* (1985), vol. 2: *Fleur des Truands* (1986), vol. 3: *Les bas-fonds du Caire* (1986), vol. 4: *La chevauchée des fils d' Ismaïl* (1987), vol. 5: *La trahison des émirs* (1989), vol. 6: *Meurtre au Hammam* (1990), vol. 7: *Rempart des Pucelles* (1992), vol. 8: *La revanche du Maître des Ruses* (1996), vol. 9: *Échec à l'empereur* (1997), vol. 10: *Le procès du moine maudit* (1998) (2nd edn, Paris: Sindbad/Actes Sud).

Brockelmann, Carl, *Geschichte der arabischen Litteratur*, vols 1–2 and supplements 1–3 (Leiden: Brill, 1936–42).

Canard, Marius, 'Dhū l-Himma', *EI2*, 2: 233–239.

——, 'Les reines de Géorgie dans l'histoire et la légende musulmanes', *Revue des études islamiques* 1 (1969), 3–20.

Canova, Giovanni, 'Twenty years of studies on Arabic Epics', in Giovanni Canova (ed.), *Studies on Arabic Epics, Oriente Moderno* 22/83, n.s., 2 (2003), v–xxii.

——, 'Sayf b. Dhī Yazan: history and saga', in Sabine Dorpmueller (ed.), *Fictionalizing the Past: Historical Characters in Arabic Popular Epic. Proceedings of the Workshop at the Netherlands–Flemish Institute in Cairo 28th/29th of November 2007 in Honor of Remke Kruk* (Leuven: Peeters, 2012), 107–123.

—— (ed.), *Studies on Arabic Epics, Oriente Moderno* 22/83, n.s., 2 (2003).

Caswell, Fuad Matthew, *The Slave Girls of Baghdad: The Qiyān in The Early Abbasid Era* (London and New York: I.B.Tauris, 2011).

Chauvin, Victor, *Bibliographie des ouvrages arabes ou relatifs aux Arabes, publiés dans l'Europe chrétienne de 1810 à 1885*, 12 vols (Liège: Vaillant-Carmanne, 1892–1922).

Chraïbi, Aboubakr, 'Le Roman de Sayf ibn dhī Yazan: Sources, Structure and Argumentation', *Studia Islamica* 84 (1996), 113–134.

Christie, Niall, 'Just a bunch of dirty stories? Women in the "Memoirs" of Usamah ibn Munqidh', in Rosamund Allen (ed.), *Eastward Bound: Travel and Travellers, 1050–1550* (Manchester: Manchester University Press, 2004), 71–87.

——, 'Noble Betrayers of their Faith, Families and Folk: Some Non-Muslim Women in Mediaeval Arabic Popular Literature', *Folklore* 123/1 (2012), 84–98. Available at: http://dx.doi.org/10.1080/0015587X.2012.642988 (accessed 1 June 2013).

Ciggaar, K., 'La dame combattante: thème épique et thème courtois au temps des croisades', in: Hans van Dijk and Willem Noomen (eds), *Aspects de l'épopée romane. Mentalités, idéologies, intertextualités* (Groningen: Forster, 1995), 121–130.

Daftary, Farhad, 'Sayyida Hurra: the Ismaʿīlī Sulayhid queen of Yemen', in Gavin R. G. Hambly (ed.), *Women in the Medieval Islamic World* (New York: St Martin's Press, 1998), 117–130.

Davis-Kimball, Jeannine and Behan, Mona, *Warrior Women: An Archaeologist's Search for History's Hidden Heroines* (New York: Warner Books, 2002).

Dede Korkut, Sümer, *The Book of Dede Korkut: A Turkish Epic*, ed. and trans. Uysal Faruk, E. Ahmet and Warren S. Walker (Austin: University of Texas Press, 1972).

Déjeux, J., 'La Kahina: de l'histoire à la fiction littéraire. Mythe et épopée', *Studi Maghrebini* 15 (1983), 1–42.

De Jong, Frederick, 'The Takiya of ʿAbdallah al-Maghāwiri in Cairo', in *Sufi Orders in Ottoman and Post-Ottoman Egypt and the Middle East* (Istanbul: Isis Press, 2000), 39–54.

Donzel, Emery van, 'The legend of the Blue Nile in Europe', in Haggai Erlich and Israel Gershoni (eds), *Histories, Cultures, Myths* (London and Boulder, CO: Lynne Rienner Publishers, 2000), 121–130.

Dorpmueller, Sabine (ed.), *Fictionalizing the Past: Historical Characters in Arabic Popular Epic. Proceedings of the Workshop at the Netherlands–Flemish Institute in Cairo 28th/29th of November 2007 in Honor of Remke Kruk* (Leuven: Peeters, 2012).

Doufikar-Aerts, F. C. W., *Alexander Magnus Arabicus: A Survey of the Alexander Tradition through Seven Centuries from Pseudo-Callisthenes to Surī* (Leuven: Peeters, 2010).

Encyclopedia of Islam, new edition (*EI2*). 12 vols and index vol. (Leiden: Brill, 1960–2009).

Enzyklopädie des Märchens: Handwörterbuch zur historischen und vergleichenden Erzählforschung, ed. Kurt Ranke, Hermann Bausinger et al. (Berlin [etc.]: De Gruyter, 1975–).

Fraser, Antonia, *The Warrior Queens: The Legends and the Lives of the Women Who Have Led their Nations in War* (London: Mandarin Books, 1989).

Gaillard, Marina, 'Héroïnes d'exception: Les femmes 'Ayyār dans la prose romanesque de l'Iran médiéval', *Studia iranica* 34/2 (2005), 163–198.

Galley, Micheline and Ayoub, Abderrahman, *Histoire des Beni Hilal et de ce qui leur advint dans leur marche vers l'ouest. Versions tunisiennes de la geste hilalienne* (Paris: Armand Colin, 1983).

Garcin, Jean-Claude, 'Siras et histoire/Siras and History', ed. Katia Zakharia, Part 1, *Arabica* 51/1–2 (2004), 55–76; '*Sīrat al-malik al-Ẓāhir Baybars*/ṣ: de l'oral à l'écrit/From Performance to Script', Part 2, *Arabica* 51/3 (2004), 223–257.

—— (ed.), *Lectures du roman de Baybars* (Marseille: Éditions parenthèses, 2003).

Gelder, Geert Jan van, *Close Relationships: Incest and Inbreeding in Classical Arabic Literature* (London and New York: I.B.Tauris, 2005).

Glover, Carol J., *Men, Women and Chainsaws: Gender in the Modern Horror Film* (Princeton: Princeton University Press, 1992).

Grant, Kenneth, '*Sīrat Fīrūzshāh* and the Middle Eastern epic tradition', in Giovanni Canova, *Studies on Arabic Epics, Oriente Moderno* 22/83, n.s., 2 (2003), 1–8.

Gray, Basil, *Persian Painting* (Geneva: Editions d'Art Albert Skira, 1995).

Gril, Denis, 'Du sultanat au califat universel: le rôle des saints dans le *Roman de Baybars*', in Jean-Claude Garcin (ed.), *Lectures du roman de Baybars* (Marseille: Éditions parenthèses, 2003), 173–197.

Guillaume, J.-P., 'Sayf ibn Dhī Yazan', *EI2*, 9: 101–102.

Habibi, Emile, *Luka' ibn Luka': Thalāth jalasat amāma sundūq al-'ajab: hikāya masrahīyah* (Beirut: Dār al-Fārābī, 1980).

Hambly, Gavin R. (ed.), *Women in the Medieval Islamic World* (New York: St Martin's Press, 1998).

Hamilton, Terrick, *'Antar, a Bedoueen Romance*, 4 parts, 2 vols (London, 1819–20).

Hanna, Nelly, *In Praise of Books: A Cultural History of Cairo's Middle Class, Sixteenth to the Eighteenth Century* (Syracuse, NY: Syracuse University Press, 2003).

Harlez, Charles de, 'Le livre des conquêtes de l'Afrique et du Maghreb', in Charles de Harlez *Mélanges Charles de Harlez* (Leiden, 1896), 26–34.

Heath, Peter, 'Arabische volksliteratur im Mittelalter', in Wolfhart Heinrichs (ed.), *Orientalisches Mittelalter: Neues Handbuch der Literaturwissenschaft* (Wiesbaden: Aula Verlag, 1990), 5: 423–439.

——, *The Thirsty Sword: Sīrat 'Antar and the Arabic Popular Epic* (Salt Lake City: University of Utah Press, 1996).

——, "Ayyār: The companion, spy, scoundrel in premodern Arabic popular narrative', in Beatrice Gruendler (ed.), *Classical Humanities in their*

Own Terms: Festschrift für Wolfhart Heinrichs on his 65th Birthday Presented by his Students and Colleagues (Leiden and Boston: Brill, 2008), 20–39.

———, "Antar hangs his *Muʿallaqa*: history, fiction, and textual conservatism in *Sīrat ʿAntar ibn Shaddād*', in Sabine Dorpmueller (ed.), *Fictionalizing the Past: Historical Characters in Arabic Popular Epic. Proceedings of the Workshop at the Netherlands–Flemish Institute in Cairo 28th/29th of November 2007 in Honor of Remke Kruk* (Leuven: Peeters, 2012), 9–24.

Heller, B., 'Sīrat ʿAntar', *EI2*, 1: 510–521.

Herzog, Thomas, 'Présentation de deux séances de hakawātī et de deux manuscrits de la Sīrat Baybars recueillis en Syrie en 1994', MA thesis, University of Aix-en-Provence, 1994.

———, *Geschichte und Imaginaire: Entstehung, Überlieferung und Bedeutung der Sīrat Baibars in ihrem sozio-politischen Kontext* (Wiesbaden: Harrassowitz, 2006).

Hillenbrand, Carole, *The Crusades: Islamic Perspectives* (Edinburgh: Edinburgh University Press, 1999).

Ibn abī Usaybiʿa, *ʿUyūn al-anbāʾ fī tabaqāt al-atibbāʾ*, ed. A. Müller, 2 vols ([Cairo] Königsberg, 1884).

Ibn al-Athīr, *al-Kāmil fī al-taʾrīkh*, 14 vols (Leiden: Brill, 1867–76).

Ibn Taymīya, *Minhāj al-sunna*, 2 vols, 4 parts (Būlāq, 1322/1904).

Ibrāhīm, Nabīla, *Sīrat al-amīra Dhāt al-Himma: Dirāsa muqārina* (Cairo: Dār al-Kātib al-ʿArabī li-l-Ṭibāʿa wa-l-Nashr, 1968).

al-Idlibī, Ulfa, *Nazara fī adabinā al-shaʿbī; Alf layla wa- layla wa-sīrat al-malik Sayf ibn Dhī Yazan* (Damascus: Manshūrāt ittihād al-kuttāb al-ʿarab, 1974).

Irwin, Robert, *The Arabian Nights: A Companion* (London: Allen Lane, The Penguin Press, 1994).

al-Isbahānī, Abū l-Faraj ʿAlī al-Husayn, *Kitāb al-aghānī*, 24 vols (Cairo: Dār al-Kutub al-misrīya, 1927–74).

Jayyusi, Lena (tr.), *The Adventures of Sayf Ben Dhi Yazan: An Arab Folk Epic*, intro. Harry Norris (Bloomington and Indianapolis: Indiana University Press, 1996).

Jong, Frederick de, *see* De Jong, Frederick.

Kosegarten, J. G. L., *Chrestomathia Arabica* (Leipzig, 1825).

Kruk, Remke, 'Warrior Women in Arabic Popular Romance: Qannāsa bint Muzāhim and Other Valiant Ladies', Part 1, *Journal of Arabic Literature* 24/3 (1993), 213–230; Part 2: ibid. 25/1 (1994), 16–33.

———, 'Clipped Wings: Medieval Arabic Adaptations of the Amazon Myth', *Harvard Middle Eastern and Islamic Review* 1/2 (1994), 132–154.

———, 'Ibn Battūta: Travel, Family Life and Chronology. How Seriously do we Take a Father?', *Al-Qantara* 16/2 (1995), 369–385.

———, 'Back to the boudoir: versions of the *Sīrat Hamza*, women warriors, and literary unity', in Ludo Jongen and Sjaak Onderdelinden (eds), *ʿDer muoz mir süezer worte jehen*': *Liber amicorum für Norbert Voorwinden*, Amsterdamer Beiträge zur älteren Germanistik, vol. 48 (Amsterdam and Atlanta, GA: Rodopi, 1997), 129–148.

—— , 'The bold and the beautiful: women and *fitna* in the *Sīrat Dhāt al-Himma*: the story of Nūrā', in Gavin R. Hambly (ed.), *Women in the Medieval Islamic World: Power, Patronage and Piety* (New York: St Martin's Press, 1998), 99–116.

—— , 'Click of needles: polygamy as an issue in Arabic popular epic', in Manuela Marin and Randi Deguilhem (eds), *Writing the Feminine: Women in Arab Sources* (London and New York: I.B.Tauris, 2002), 3–23.

—— , 'The Princess Maymūnah: maiden, mother, monster', in Giovanni Canova (ed.), *Studies on Arabic Epics, Oriente Moderno* 22/83, n.s., 2 (2003), 425–442.

—— and Ott, Claudia, "In the Popular Manner": *Sīra*-Recitation in Marrakesh Anno 1997', *Edebiyat* 10 (1999), 183–198.

Lane, Edward William, *An Account of the Manners and the Customs of the Modern Egyptians. The Definitive 1860 Edition*, intro. Jason Thompson ([London 1836, 1860] Cairo and New York: American University in Cairo Press, 2003).

Leder, Stefan, 'Religion, Gesellschaft, Identität – Ideologie und Subversion in der Mythenbildung des arabischen "Volksepos"', in Christine Schmitz and Anja Bettenworth (eds), *Mensch – Heros – Gott: Weltentwürfe und Lebensmodelle im Mythos der Vormoderne* (Stuttgart: Franz Steiner Verlag, 2009), 147–180.

Leeuwen, Richard van, *see* Van Leeuwen.

Le Tourneau, Roger, *Fès avant le protectorat: Etude économique et sociale d'une ville de l'occident musulman* (Casablanca: Société marocaine de librairie et d'édition, 1949).

Lichtenstädter, I., *Women in the Aiyām al-ʿArab: A Study of Female Life during Warfare in Preislamic Arabia* (London: The Royal Asiatic Society, 1935).

Long, John E., 'Futūh Ifrīqīya: Analysis, Arabic Text and Translation', Ph.D. dissertation, Brandeis University, Waltham, MA, 1978.

Lourie, Elena, 'Black Women Warriors in the Muslim Army Besieging Valencia and the Cid's Victory: A Question of Interpretation', *Traditio* 55 (2000), 181–209.

Lyons, Malcolm C., *The Arabian Epic: Heroic and Oral Storytelling*, 3 vols (Cambridge: Cambridge University Press, 1995).

—— , 'The crusading stratum in the Arabic heroic cycles', in Maya Shatzmiller (ed.), *Crusaders and Muslims in Twelfth-Century Syria* (Leiden: Brill, 1993), 148–161.

—— , 'Qissat ʿArūs al-ʿArāʾis', in Giovanni Canova (ed.), *Studies on Arabic Epics, Oriente Moderno* 22/83, n.s., 2 (2003), 559–573.

—— , *The Man of Wiles in Popular Arabic Literature: A Study of a Medieval Arab Hero* (Edinburgh: Edinburgh University Press, 2012).

Marin, Manuela and Deguilhem, Randi (eds), *Writing the Feminine: Women in Arab Sources* (London and New York: I.B.Tauris, 2002).

Marwazī, Sharaf al-Zamān Ṭāhir, *Kitāb tabā'iʿ al-hayawān*, MS UCLA Ar. 52.

Marzolph, U., 'Hamza-Name', in *Enzyklopädie des Märchens* 6, 2/3, (1989), 430–436.

——, 'As Woman As Can Be: The Gendered Subversiveness of an Arabic Folktale Heroine', *Edebiyat* 10 (1999), 199–218.

Malti-Douglas, Fedwa, 'Sexual geography, asexual philosophy', in Fedwa Malti-Douglas, *Woman's Body, Woman's Word: Gender and Discourse in Arabo-Islamic Writing* (Princeton: Princeton University Press, 1991; Cairo: American University in Cairo Press, 1992).

Masmoudi, M., *La peinture sous verre en Tunisie* (Tunis: Cérès, 1972).

Mattock, J. N. and Lyons, M. C. (eds. and tr.), *Kitāb Buqrāṭ fī-l-amrāḍ al-bilādiyya. Hippocrates: On Endemic Diseases (Airs, Waters and Places)* (Cambridge: Cambridge Middle East Center, 1969).

Mernissi, Fatima, *Sultanes oubliées: Femmes chefs d'état en Islam* (Paris: Albin Michel, 1990). English trans. Mary Jo Lakeland: *The Forgotten Queens of Islam* (Minneapolis: University of Minneapolis Press, 1993).

Minorsky, V., *Sharaf al-Zamān Ṭāhir Marvazī on China, the Turks and India. Arabic text (circa A.D. 1120) with an English translation and commentary* (London: The Royal Asiatic Society, 1942).

Nuweihed, Jamal Sleem, *Abu Jmeel's Daughter and Other Stories: Arab Folk Tales from Palestine and Lebanon*, preface Salma Khadra Jayyusi, trans. members of her family with Christopher Tingley (New York and Northampton: Interlink Books, 2002).

Ott, Claudia, 'Der falsche Asket: Ursprung und Entwicklung einer Romanfigur aus der *sīrat al-amīra Dhāt al-Himma*', MA dissertation, University of Tübingen, 1992.

——, *Metamorphosen des Epos: Sīrat al-Mujāhidīn (Sīrat al-Amīra Dhāt al-Himma) zwischen Muendlichkeit und Schriftlichkeit* (Leiden: CNWS, 2003).

——, 'Finally we know ... why, how, and where Caliph al-Ḥākim disappeared! *Sīrat al-Ḥākim bi-Amrillāh* and its Berlin manuscript', in Sabine Dorpmueller (ed.), *Fictionalizing the Past: Historical Characters in Arabic Popular Epic. Proceedings of the Workshop at the Netherlands–Flemish Institute in Cairo 28th/29th of November 2007 in Honor of Remke Kruk* (Leuven: Peeters, 2012), 63–72.

Ouyang, Wen-chin, 'Princess of resolution', in Lena B. Ross (ed.), *To Speak or Be Silent: The Paradox of Disobedience in the Lives of Women* (Wilmette: Chiron Publications, 1993), 197–209.

——, 'Romancing the Epic: "Umar al-Nuʿmān as Narrative of Empowerment"', *Arabic and Middle Eastern Literatures* 3/1 (2000), 5–18.

Paret, R., *Sīrat Saif ibn Dhī Jazan: Ein arabischer Volksroman* (Hanover, 1924).

—— , *Der Ritter-Roman von 'Umar an-Nu'mān und seine Stellung zur Sammlung von tausendundeine Nacht. Ein Beitrag zur arabischen Literaturgeschichte* (Tübingen, 1927).

—— , *Die Geschichte des Islams in der arabischen Volksliteratur* (Tübingen, 1927).

—— , *Die legendäre Maghāzī-literatur* (Tübingen, 1930).

—— , 'Die legendäre Futūh-Literatur, ein arabisches Volksepos?' *Atti del convegno internationale sul tema La poesia epica e la sua formazione (Roma, 28 marzo–3 april 1969)*, ed. Albert Bates et al. (Rome, 1970), 735–747.

Perron, A., *Glaive des Couronnes (Sef el-Tīdjān), roman traduit de l'arabe* (Paris, 1862).

Perry, John R., 'Blackmailing Amazons and Dutch Pigs: A Consideration of Epic and Folktale Motifs in Persian Historiography', *Iranian Studies* 19/2 (1986), 155–165.

Qissa: for various *qissa* works, see section 'Sīra and *qissa* texts' above.

Renard, John, *Islam and the Heroic Image: Themes in Literature and the Visual Arts* (Columbia, SC: University of South Carolina Press, 1993).

Reynolds, Dwight F., *Heroic Poetry, Poetic Heroes: The Ethnography of Performance* (Ithaca: Cornell University Press, 1995).

—— , 'Popular prose in the post-classical period', in Roger Allen and D. S. Richards (eds), *Cambridge History of Arabic Literature*, vol. 6: *Arabic Literature in the Post-Classical Period* (Cambridge: Cambridge University Press, 2006), 245–269.

—— , 'Sīrat Banī Hilāl', in Roger Allen and D. S. Richards (eds), *Cambridge History of Arabic Literature*, vol. 6: *Arabic Literature in the Post-Classical Period* (Cambridge: Cambridge University Press, 2006), 307–318.

Ronkel, Ph. S. van, *De Roman van Amir Hamzah* (Leiden, 1895).

Rosenthal, Franz, 'Fiction and reality: sources for the role of sex in medieval Muslim society', in Afaf Lutfi Sayyid-Marsot (ed.), *Society and the Sexes in Medieval Islam (Sixth Giorgio Levi della Vida Biennial Conference, May 13–15, 1977)* (Malibu, CA, 1979), 3–22.

Ross, Lena B. (ed.), *To Speak or Be Silent: The Paradox of Disobedience in the Lives of Women* (Wilmette, IL: Chiron Publications, 1993).

Russell, Alexander, *The Natural History of Aleppo* (London, 1794).

Salmonson, Jessica A., *The Encyclopedia of Amazons* (New York: Robinson, 1991).

Samaw'al al-Maghribī, *Badhl al-majhūd fī ifhām al-yahūd*, ed. Muh. Hāmid al-Fiqqī (Cairo 1358/1939).

Schreiner, Martin, 'Samau'al b. Jahjā al-Magribī und seine Schrift "Ifhām al-Jahūd"', *Monatszeitschrift für die Geschichte und Wissenschaft des Judentums* 3 (1898), 123–133.

Sefrioui, Ahmad, *La boîte à merveilles* (Paris: Le Seuil, 1954).

Seidensticker-Brikay, Gisela (tr., comment and annotation), *Siirat* [sic] *Sayf ibn Dhi Yazan: An Arabic Folk Epic by Rudi Paret* (Maiduguri: University of Maiduguri, 2006).

Seyller, John, *The Adventures of Hamza: Painting and Storytelling in Mughal India* (Washington, DC: Smithsonian Institution, 2002).
Shoshan, Boaz, 'On Popular Literature in Medieval Cairo', *Poetics Today* 14/2 (1993), 349–365.
Sīra: for various *sīra* works, *see* section '*Sīra* and *qissa* texts' above.
Slyomovics, Susan, *The Merchant of Art: An Egyptian Hilali Oral Epic Poet in Performance* (Berkeley and Los Angeles: University of California Press, 1987).
Steinbach, Udo, *Dhāt al-Himma. Kulturgeschichtliche Untersuchungen zu einem arabischen Volksroman* (Wiesbaden: Harrassowitz, 1972).
Sublet, Jacqueline, *Les trois vies du Sultan Baibars* (Paris: Imprimerie Nationale, 1992).
al-Tabarī, Muhammad ibn Jarīr, *Ta'rīkh al-rusul wa-l-mulūk*, 15 vols (Leiden: Brill, 1879–1901).
——, *The History of al-Tabarī (Ta'rīkh al-rusul wa-l-mulūk)*, vol. 4: *The Ancient Kingdoms*, trans. and annot. Moshe Perlmann (New York: SUNY Press, 1987).
Tasso, Torquato, *La Gerusalemme liberata*, ed. Giorgio Cerboni Baiardi (Modena: Franco Cosimo Panini, 1991).
Toelle, Heidi and Zakharia, Katia, *À la découverte de la littérature arabe du VIe siècle à nos jours* (Paris: Flammarion, 2003).
Tyrrell, William Blake, *Amazons: A Study in Athenian Mythmaking* (Baltimore and London, 1989).
Vacca, V., 'Sajāh', *EI2*, 8: 738–739.
Van Leeuwen, Richard, *The Thousand and One Nights: Space, Travel and Transformation* (London and New York: Routledge, 2007).
Vermeulen, U., "Unaytara [sic], la fille d''Antar', in Adriana Fodor (ed.), *Proceedings of the 14th Congress of the Union Européenne des Arabisants et Islamisants, Budapest, 29th August–3rd September 1988*, 2 vols (Budapest: Eötvös Loránd University Chair for Arabic Studies, 1995), 1: 305–312.
Vries, Jan de, *Heroic Song and Heroic Legend*, trans. B. J. Timmer (London: Oxford University Press, 1963).
Wack, Mary Frances, *Lovesickness in the Middle Ages: The* Viaticum *and its Commentaries* (Philadelphia: University of Pennsylvania Press, 1990).
al-Wāqidī, pseudo-, *Futūh Ifrīqīya*, 2 vols (Tunis: Maktabat al-Manāra, 1966).
Wehr, Hans, (trans. and afterword), *Wunderbare Erlebnisse – Seltsame Begebnisse: arabische Erzählungen* (Hattingen, Ruhr: Hundt, 1959).
Weinbaum, Batya, *Islands of Women and Amazons: Representations and Realities* (Austin: University of Texas Press, 1999).
Zakharia, Katia (ed.), '*Sîrat al-malik al-Zâhir Baybars/s*: de l'oral à l'écrit/ From Performance to Script', *Arabica* 51/1–2 (2004).
Zeggaf, Abdelmajid, 'Le Conte Oral Marocain: Thèmes et Structures (l'exemple de Marrakech)', unpublished Ph.D. thesis, University of Toulouse-Le-Mirail, 1978.

Internet sources

http://awaheed.wordpress.com/2010/05/14/abu-el-ajab-preserving-the-land-of-storytellers/ (accessed 26 January 2012).

http://www.the99.org/ (accessed 23 September 2012).

http://majjal.wordpress.com/2012/04/14/shahrazad-and-dhat-al-himmah-epics-storytellers-and-warrior-women/ (accessed 3 January 2013).

http://wp.patheos.com.s3.amazonaws.com/blogs/mmw/files/2012/04/dhat-al-himma.jpg (accessed 3 January 2013).

http://www.racialicious.com/2008/08/26/female-muslim-and-mutant-a-critique-of-muslim-women-in-comic-books-part-2-of-2/ (accessed 4 August 2013).

Index

'Abbās 119
'Abd al-Ḥakīm, Shawqī xx, xxi, 40, 234 n.5
'Abd al-Salām 187, 195
'Abd al-Wahhāb vii, 3, 25, 26, 28, 33, 37, 38, 40, 42, 52–91, 93, 94, 96–8, 104–8, 146, 147, 150, 187, 234 n.1, 236 n.69, 237 n.32
'Abdallāh al-Maghāwirī 163, 168, 245 n.18
'Abdallāh ibn Ja'far xviii, xxi, 3,
Abjar 131, 136, 142
'Abla xvii, xviii, xix, xx, xxi, xxii, 12, 111–14, 118, 125, 128, 129, 131, 132, 135–7, 142, 144
Abrīza, *see* Ibrīza
'Abs 119, 128, 144
Abū al-'Ajab 12
Abū Muḥammad al-Baṭṭāl 3, 6, 28, 33, 34, 37–40, 42, 52–65, 68–75, 77, 78, 82–4, 93, 106, 131, 133, 236 n.64,
Abū Sufyān 18
Abū Zayd al-Hilālī xxi, 6, 22
Aden 203
'Adhrā' al-Masīḥ 175, 182
'Adnān 119
Aflanṭūsh 147, 148, 158, 160
Afrāḥ 187–9, 193, 201, 203
Aḥmad al-Badawī 163, 168
Aḥmad, son of Tuqtimur 175, 179
'Ā'isha of Bushna 163, 167, 172, 173.
    See also Hibat al-Masīḥ

'Ā'isha the daughter of Abū Bakr 16, 231 n.10
Akbar xviii, 148
Akhmīm, father of Jīza 187, 188
Aleppo 18, 158, 164, 165, 177, 188
Alexander the Great 2, 17, 23, 157
Alexandria 164
'Alī al-Ṭuwayrid 163, 164, 170
Ali Bey xix
'Alī Fakhr al-Dīn al-Shafṭūr 163, 173
'Alī ibn abī Ṭālib 110
'Alī Zaybaq 3
Almoravids 19
Alūf 28, 63, 83, 233 n.50, 238 n.46
Amāzūnas 16
'Āmir ibn al-Ash'ath 93, 97–100, 102–9
'Āmir ibn Ṭufayl 131, 142, 143
'Amr Dhū l-Kalb 111, 114, 131–41, 144
'Amr ibn Mālik 131, 135, 142
'Amr ibn 'Ubaydallāh 63, 74, 75, 93, 94, 96, 105, 107, 108, 239 n.2
'Amr, son of Umayya and Khudhrūf 131, 145
'Amr, the 'son' of 'Uṭārid 94–9, 101–4, 106. *See also Ghamra the daughter of Uṭārid*
Ankūrīya (Ankara) 61
'anqā', mythical bird 157
'Anqā' the daughter of Ṭahmāz 147, 148, 151, 157, 158
'Anqā' the daughter of the wind 157
al-'Anqā, 'The Phoenix' 3

265

Anqūsh 63, 83
'Antar (or 'Antara) ibn Shaddād al-
    'Absī xvii, xviii, xxi, xxii, 2, 3,
    4, 8, 12, 24, 25, 37, 38, 41, 94,
    111–46, 229 n.15, 233 n.42, 234
    n.8, 240 n.6
al-'Antarī 3
Anūshirwān, see Khusrau
'Āqila 187, 198, 201–11, 213, 216
'Āqiṣa xix, xxiii, 12, 187, 189, 191, 198,
    199, 206, 210, 213, 214, 217
al-'Aqṣarā'ī, Muḥammad ibn 'Īsā xvii
Armānūs 63, 87–90
'Arnūṣ 7, 163, 168, 169, 170, 175–84, 187,
    191, 192, 246 n.2, 246 n.3
Arwā 17
Asad al-Falā 131, 139, 143
'Ash'ath ibn 'Awf 93, 96–8, 102, 104,
    107
Ashmīṭūs 63, 68, 69
'Āṣim 213–15
Asmābarī 147, 149–51
Aybak 18
'Ayn al-Ḥayāt 23, 201, 208, 211
'Ayn Jālūt 167
'Ayrūḍ 187, 196–9, 201, 209, 213, 217
ayyām al-'arab 18
'ayyār 3, 6, 21, 30, 42, 52, 53, 149, 167,
    173, 233 n.47

Ba Dris 10
Badī' al-Zamān 147, 156, 157
Bāgha, daughter of Lāwūn 27
Baghdad 40, 49, 54, 69, 70, 106
Baḥrūn 37, 56, 63, 84–9
Baḥrūna 175, 180, 181
Bakhtak 147, 149
Bakhṭūsh 29
Bālkān 147, 155, 156
banj (Hyoscamus niger) 97, 167, 181
Banū 'Abs 119, 128, 131, 132, 134, 135,
    140–2, 144
Banū 'Āmir 37, 46, 142

Banū Fazāra 132, 141
Banū Hawāzin 131, 144
Banū Hilāl (or: Hilālī tribe) xxi, 1,
    2, 8, 22
Banū Khudā'a 111, 115
Banū Kilāb 37–107 *passim*
Banū Quḍā'a 131, 133, 134, 137–41
Banū Shaybān 114
Banū Sulaym 37–9, 50, 54, 63, 64,
    93–7, 101, 104–7
Banū Ṭayy 37, 38, 44, 46, 47
Barhajān 175, 185
Barmacids 39
Barnūkh 187, 197, 201, 207
Baryānūs 17
al-Baṭṭāl, see Abū Muḥammad al-
    Baṭṭāl
Baybars xxii, 2, 163–8, 172, 173, 175–8,
    181, 183, 184, 186
Bihzād 147, 156
Bilqīs 96, 101
Bohas, Georges 165, 166
Book of Dede Korkut 105
Book of the Nile 189, 190, 202–7
Book of the Orphans 22
Book on the Natures of Living Beings 16
Budūr 175, 182
Būhinmā (Bohemond) 63, 88, 89
Buktimur 175, 184–6
Būlāq, son of Sayf ibn Dhī Yazan
    187, 188
Burtuqush 172, 175–7
Buzurjmihr 147, 149

Cairo xxv, 9, 10, 112, 164, 178, 188, 190
Canard, Marius 40, 239 n.2
Canova, Giovanni 7
Castle of the Pleiades 204
Catwoman 15
Citadel of Cairo 188, 190
Clorinda 15
Constantinople 45, 60, 75, 86, 107,
    136, 143, 145

Dāhiyat banī Ṭayy 37, 46. *See also*
    Fāṭima Dhāt al-Himma
Dā'u l-Makān 39
Dakrūr, *see* Takrūr
Dalhama 3, 37, 41, 54, 228 n.10. *See
    also* Fāṭima Dhāt al-Himma
Damar 187, 192
Damascus xxi, 10, 144, 164, 165
Damdamān 63, 83
Dante 8, 9
Dār al-Barūd 11
Dawāhī 175, 176, 180–3
Day of the Camel 16
Ḍayfa Khātūn 18
Daygham 63, 67, 71, 72
De Vries, Jan 24
Dhalhama 37, 41, 48, 234 n.7. *See also*
    Fāṭima Dhāt al-Himma
Dhāt al-Dawāhī, *see* Shawāhī Dhāt
    al-Dawāhī
Dhāt al-Himma, *see* Fāṭima Dhāt
    al-Himma
Dhū l-Himma, *see* Fāṭima Dhāt al-
    Himma
Dhū l-Kalb, *see* 'Amr Dhū l-Kalb
Dhū l-Khimār, *see* Sabī' Dhū
    l-Khimār
Dhū Yazan 187, 188, 189, 193, 195, 201
Digenes Akritas 40
Divina Commedia 8
dīwān 54
Dīwān al-Aytām 22
Durayd 111, 116, 120, 131, 136, 144

El Cid Campeador 19
Eleanor of Aquitaine 19
Eski Malatya 50

Fā'iz 41, 111, 114, 115, 118, 121, 132, 134,
    138, 140, 147, 154, 155
Fāṭima Dhāt al-Himma xx, 2, 3, 4,
    6, 17, 24–95 *passim*, 104, 106,
    108, 114, 132, 147, 155. *See also*

Dāhiyat banī Ṭayy, Dalhama,
    Dhalhama, Sharīḥa
Fāṭima al-Ḥawrānīya 163, 170, 171
Fāṭima Shajarat al-Durr 163, 164, 167
Fāṭima Sitt al-Shām 163, 167
Fīrūzshāh 2, 23
Fraser, Anthonia 45
futūḥ 3, 18, 232 n.29
Futūḥ Ifrīqīya 232 n.29
Futūḥ al-Shām 11, 232 n.29
Futūḥ al-Yaman 232 n.29
futuwwa 21

Galland, Antoine 1
George, St xviii
Gerusalemme liberata 15
Ghaḍanfar 131, 143–6
Ghamra the daughter of Fā'iz 29, 41,
    111–29, 132, 134, 138, 140, 147,
    154, 155. *See also* Mubādir ibn
    Jabbār
Ghamra the daughter of 'Uṭārid 31,
    37, 60, 63, 64, 69, 78, 93–115,
    150, 154, 225. *See also* 'Amr,
    the 'son' of 'Uṭārid
Ghashshām 147, 151, 152
Ghaṣṣūb 111, 122, 124–9
Ghaydā', mother of 'Alī Fakhr al-Dīn
    al-Shaftūr 163, 173
Ghaydā', wife of Hayyāj al-Kurdī 26
Ghaydurūs 37, 38, 56, 57, 236 n.56
al-Ghitani, Gamal 165
Grizzle, the 29
Guillaume, Jean-Pierre 165, 166
Gushasp, daughter of Rustam 131, 133
Gushaspnāme 133

Habibi, Emile 12
Hadlāmūs 37, 55
Hām, son of Noah 187, 189
Ḥamza al-Bahlawān, son of Ibrāhīm
    2, 23, 147–64, 172, 224
Ḥamza ibn 'Abd al-Muṭṭalib 148

Hanaway, William 21
Hardūb 30
al-Ḥarīrī, al-Qāsim ibn ʿAlī xvii
Ḥārith, cousin and husband of Dhāt al-Himma 38, 48–52, 63, 65
Ḥārith of the Banū Ṭayy 38, 45–7
Hārūn, Persian champion 160, 161
Hārūn al-Rashīd, caliph 18, 38, 40, 58, 63, 71, 75, 79
Ḥasan al-Ḥawranī 171
Ḥasan, brother of ʿĀʾisha of Bushna 163, 166, 172
Ḥasan, brother of al-Jāzīya 22
Ḥasan, grandson of the Prophet 164
Ḥassāna 147, 151–5, 158, 161
Hayfāʾ (Qannāṣat al-Rijāl) 111–14, 131–8, 141, 144–6
hāyisha 204
Hayyāj al-Kurdī 26, 64, 81
Heath, Peter 24, 132
Herzog, Thomas 165, 168, 191
Hibat al-Masīh 166. *See also* ʿĀʾisha of Bushna
Hind 31–4, 111, 114, 239 n.5, 246 n.27
Hindām 147, 154, 155
Hippocrates 16
Hubal 131, 140
Ḥudhūr 111, 115
Humāy xviii
Humāyūn xviii
Ḥusna-with-the-tattoos, *see* Salbān

Ibn al-Athīr, ʿAlī ʿIzz al-Dīn 18
Ibn Khaldūn 8
Ibn Taymīya 8
Ibrāhīm (Abraham) 178, 190
Ibrāhīm al-Ḥawranī 163, 170–8
Ibrāhīm, governor of Mecca 147, 148
Ibrāhīm, son of ʿAbd al-Wahhāb 64, 67–71, 82
Ibrīza (Qannāṣa), daughter of the king of Bashqat 163, 169, 170

Ibrīza, daughter of Hardūb 27–30, 111, 122
Iftūnā 38, 56, 57, 64, 87, 88
Islands of Maidens 216, 217
al-ʿIsmāʿīlīya 164. *See also Sīrat al-malik al-Ẓāhir Baybars*

Jadhīma 111, 114
Jaʿfar al-Ṣādiq 38, 52, 64, 65, 235 n.42
Jalila 15
Jawān 163, 166, 167, 172–81, 183
Jawdar 93, 95. *See also* Jaydāʾ
Jaydāʾ (Ghaydāʾ) xxi, 31, 93–5, 99, 108, 109, 111, 114, 239 n.3, 246 n.32. *See also* Jawdar
Jayyād 187, 189, 190, 195, 201, 202, 204
Jayyusi, Salma 12
Jāziya (Zāziya) xxi, 22, 23
Jerusalem 15
Jesus 177
jihād 26, 106, 180
Jīza, daughter of Akhmīm 187, 188, 192, 208, 209, 211, 248 n.17
Jūfrān 131, 132, 144–6
Junduba 29
Juwayrīya 18

Kabsha 131, 142
Kagemusha 184
al-Kāhina 17
Karfanās 64, 87, 89, 90
Karna 27, 225
Kawkab, a female prison warden 213, 219
Kawkab, a fortress 64, 72
Khālid 93–5
Khartoum 186
Khudhrūf 131, 132, 144–6
Khusrau Anūshirwān 131, 140–3, 147, 149
Kilābī, *see* Banū Kilāb
Kitāb al-Yunān 168
Kūbart 132, 144, 145

Kurosawa, Akira 184
Kurpershoek, Marcel 13
Kūshanūsh 38, 54

Labwa 163, 170, 173, 174
labwa, plural *labawāt* 169, 170, 173
La boîte à merveilles 12
Lane, Edward William 9, 112
La peinture sous-verre en Tunisie xvii
Lawless, Lucy xx
Lāwūn (Leo) 27
Laylā, daughter of Ṭarīf 18
Le Tourneau, Roger 10
Leo, *see* Lāwūn
Louis VII 19
Lubāba 18
Lyons, Malcolm C. x, 4, 7, 40, 42, 165, 168

Madā'in 153
Madhbaḥūn 34, 35, 84
maghāzī 3, 18
Makhlūf 147, 151, 152
al-Makkāwī, Muḥammad Adīb 165
Malaṭya, city 27, 39
Malaṭya, daughter of Lāwūn 27, 50, 61, 67, 71, 74, 94, 96, 98, 103–6, 108
malhama 1
Mālik, father of 'Abla 111, 112, 131, 132, 142
malika x, 27, 140
Ma'mūn, caliph 38, 40, 55, 64, 93, 81, 94
Manṣūr, caliph 38, 40, 49
Marīn 175, 176, 181–3
Marjāna 1, Christian princess 93, 108
Marjāna 2, Christian princess 64, 85, 86
Marjāna, *jinnī* princess 175, 184, 185
Marjāna, vizieress of Nūr al-Hudā 213, 219–21
Marrakesh 11, 38, 40, 64

Ma'rūf 163, 169, 173, 175
Marwazī, Sharaf al-Zaman 16
Maryam al-Ḥamiqa 163, 170, 174–80, 246 n.3
Maryam, daughter of Qayṣar 147
Maryam the Girdlemaker 246 n.3
Maryam, Byzantine concubine of 'Antar 111, 113, 131, 132, 136, 144, 145
Maryam, sister of the king of Rome 131, 132, 136, 143
Marzūq 38, 42, 43, 44, 50, 51
Maslama 28
Masmoudi, Mohamed xvii
Maymūna, daughter of Damdamān 37, 38, 55, 59, 60, 63, 64, 69, 72, 83–93, 106, 117, 187, 193, 238 n.72, 248 n.19
Maymūna, daughter of queen Maymūna 175, 180, 184, 186
Maymūna, queen, sister of Sayf al-Mulk 175, 180, 184, 185, 186
Mayrūna 64, 72, 74, 75
Maẓlūm 38, 43, 46, 47, 48, 63, 64, 74
Mecca xviii, 52, 61, 65, 76, 79, 115, 126, 133, 147, 148
Medina 18
Melitene 50, 94
Midlāj 31
Mihrdukār 147, 149, 150, 151, 153, 159
Mihrdukht xxii
Miṣr, son of Sayf ibn Dhī Yazan 187, 188
Miskawayh, Aḥmad ibn Muḥammad 3
Mu'taṣim, caliph 38, 40, 42, 61, 64, 70, 85, 93, 94, 107, 108
Mubādir ibn Jabbār 111, 127. *See also* Ghamra the daughter of Fā'iz
Muḥammad, the Prophet 18, 26, 44, 52, 65, 73, 74, 87, 106, 110, 133, 143, 145–8, 164, 168, 190, 231 n.10, 247 n.2

Muhrīya 111, 113
Mundhir ibn al-Nuʿmān 132, 140, 141, 143
Munyat al-Nufūs vii, 187, 192, 198, 201, 207–22
muqaddama (captain) 171
Musaylima 18
Mutanaʿjiz 111, 115, 132, 134
Mutawakkil, caliph 38, 39, 61, 236 n.69

Nāfiʿ 64, 72
Nāhid xix, xxiii, 187, 197, 198, 199, 207–10
Naʾif al-Mutawa 15
Negus of Ethiopia 115
Nile 29, 175, 184, 188–90. *See also* Book of the Nile
Nimr 175, 181
Noah 187, 189
Nuʿmān 147, 151, 152
Nūr al-Dahr 147, 157, 158
Nūr al-Hudā 213, 218–21
Nūr al-Masīḥ, brother of tavern keeper 166
Nūr al-Masīḥ, daughter of Shawāhī 175, 183
Nūr al-Nār 28, 64, 88
Nūra 28, 38, 58–60, 64, 69, 71, 72, 81, 83, 84, 93, 106
Nuzhat al-Zamān 132, 138

Palmyra 17, 45
Paret, Rudi 7
Prophet, the, *see* Muḥammad
Protector of The City of All Faiths 15

Qamarīya 187, 189, 192–210, 224, 248 n.20
Qamrūn 201, 202, 206, 207
Qannāṣa 163, 169. *See also* Ibrīza
Qannāṣa, daughter of Muzāḥim 38, 59, 60, 64, 69, 70, 72, 76–83, 86, 91, 94, 106

Qannāṣa, daughter of Nuʿmān 147, 151–4
Qannāṣat al-Rijāl 134, 137. *See also* Hayfāʾ
Qarāqūnā 64, 84
Qashʿam 33, 34, 64, 67, 71
Qāsim 213–15, 218, 220, 221
Qaymar 201, 204, 206
Qays, Arab king 132, 135
Qays ibn Masʿūd 31, 32, 33, 111, 114
Qiṣṣat al-amīr Ḥamza al-Bahlawān 2, 148,
Qiṣṣat al-Zīr Sālim 13
Qiṣṣat Fīrūzshāh ibn al-malik Dārāb 31
Qurʾān 22, 51, 56, 88, 96, 104, 107

Rabāb 111, 114
Rabīʿ 132, 135
Rabīʿa ibn Zayd 31–3
Rāḍīya 17
Raʾs al-Ghūl xvii, 20
Rāshid ibn Damra 64, 67
Red City, the 189, 193, 196, 197
Rosenthal, Franz 19
Rustam, Persian hero 131, 133
Rustam, son of Ḥamza 147, 154, 155, 156

Sabīʿ Dhū l-Khimār 111, 112, 114, 116, 117, 120, 121, 131, 132, 138–41
Sābik al-Thalāth 148
Saʿd, cousin of Ibrāhīm al-Ḥawrānī 163, 172, 173
Saʿd, son of ʿUmar al-Yunānī 148, 159–61
Saʿdūn 187, 189, 204
Sajāḥ 18
Saladin (Ṣalāḥ al-Dīn) 163, 167
Ṣalbān (Ḥusna-with-the-tattoos) 163, 172
al-Ṣāliḥ Ayyūb 163, 167, 245 n.16
Ṣāliḥ ibn ʿAlī 18
Salwā 148, 151, 153

Sām, son of Noah 187, 189
Samaw'al al-Maghribī 3, 39, 54, 157
Sana 203
Saqardīyūn 201, 204
Sarkhāna 148, 151, 156
Sāṭirīn 175, 176, 181–3
Sayf al-Ḥanīfīya (also: Sayf al-Ḥanafīya) 64, 75, 82, 89. See also Sayf al-Nasrānīya
Sayf al-Mulk 175, 184, 186
Sayf al-Nasrānīya 64, 75. See also Sayf al-Ḥanīfīya
Sayf al-Riqāb 118, 120, 123, 127
Sayfa Arʿad 188, 189
Sayf ibn Dhī Yazan xix, xxii, xxiii, 2, 12, 29, 187–224
Sayyida Ḥurra, see Arwā
Sayyida Nafīsa 164, 168
Sayyida Zaynab 164, 168
Sefrioui, Aḥmad 12
Shabshīr 175, 184, 185
Shāh al-Zamān 213, 219, 220
Shajarat al-Durr, see Fāṭima Shajarat al-Durr
Shāma xix, 187–90, 192, 193, 196, 197, 201, 204, 206–9, 211
Shamṭāʾ, see Grizzle, the
Sharīḥa 38, 44, 45. See also Fāṭima Dhāt al-Himma
Sharkān 39: 132, 137
Shawāhī Dhāt al-Dawāhī, mother of Hardūb 29, 30
Shawāhī, queen (later king), sister (later brother) of Dawāhī, Sāṭirīn and Marīn 175, 176, 180–3, 247 n.12
Shaybūb 111, 120, 125, 126, 128, 132, 134, 145
Shaytaban 54
Sheba 96, 101
Shīḥa 163, 164, 167, 168, 171–4, 176, 181, 183, 186
Shūma 38, 40, 60

Shūmdaris 38, 40, 55, 60
Sī Mlūd 10, 11, 38, 40, 188
Sīra Hilālīya 1, 2, 4, 6, 9, 10, 11, 13, 22, 229 n.17
sīra shaʿbīya 1, 3
Sīrat al-amīra Dhāt al-Himma xx, xxi, 2, 6, 8, 9, 11, 17, 22, 25, 27–31, 33, 38–109, 114, 117, 131, 133, 146–59 passim, 164, 167–9, 187, 188, 192, 193, 223–5
Sīrat al-Ḥākim bi-'amr Allāh 2, 248 n.10
Sīrat al-Iskandar 2, 23, 229 n.16
Sīrat al-malik Sayf ibn Dhī Yazan xix, xxiii, 2, 7, 21–9, 39, 148, 153, 158, 188, 191, 192, 213, 214, 224
Sīrat al-malik al-Ẓāhir Baybars 2, 7, 9–11, 18, 22, 23, 164–70, 176, 186–8, 191, 192, 224
Sīrat al-mujāhidīn 9. See also Sīrat al-amīra Dhāt al-Himma
Sīrat ʿAntar, see Sīrat ʿAntara ibn Shaddād
Sīrat ʿAntara ibn Shaddād xvii, xviii, xix, xx, 4, 9, 10, 11, 13, 22, 24, 29, 31, 33, 37, 38, 94, 112–48, 150, 153, 155, 157, 164, 169, 188, 192, 223, 224
Sīrat Banī Hilāl, see Sīra Hilālīya
Sīrat Baybars, see Sīrat al-malik al-Ẓāhir Baybars
Sīrat Dalhama, 9. See also Sīrat al-amīra Dhāt al-Himma
Sīrat Dhāt al-Himma, see Sīrat al-amīra Dhāt al-Himma
Sīrat Sayf ibn Dhī Yazan, see Sīrat al-malik Sayf ibn Dhī Yazan
Sīrat Sayf al-Tījān 29
Suʿdā 38, 43, 44, 47, 57
Sulaymī, see Banū Sulaym
Sulṭānīya 163, 164, 171
sundūq al-ʿajab 12
sunduq al-furja 12

al-Ṭabarī, Muḥammad ibn Jarīr
    3, 18
Ṭaha (the Prophet Muḥammad)
Ṭahmāz 147, 148, 157
Tāj Nās 176, 183
Takrūr, wife of Sayf ibn Dhī Yazan
    187, 188, 192, 250 n.24
*Tale of Prince Ḥamza, see Qiṣṣat al-
    amīr Ḥamza al-Bahlawān*
Ṭama vii, xix, xxiii, 187, 188, 192, 199,
    201–13, 216
Tancredi 15
Ṭaud 176, 183
The 99 15
*The Adventures of the Holy Warriors,
    see Sīrat al-mujāhidīn*
Thousand and One Nights, The ix,
    xvii, 1, 10, 23, 27, 29, 39, 122,
    137, 191, 224, 227 n.1
Torquato Tasso 15
Trebellius Pollo 45
Trickster, *see ʿayyār*
Tuqṭimur 175–9
Ṭurbān 148, 150, 151, 158–61, 164, 172, 224
Tyrrell, William Blake 250 n.2

ʿUdhayba 6
ʿUlwā 38, 57, 64, 67–72, 80, 82, 83, 86,
    91, 94, 106
ʿUmar [ibn] al-Nuʿmān 23, 27, 39,
    112, 122, 239 n.2, 247 n.12,
ʿUmar, trickster helper of Ḥamza
    148, 149, 153, 159
ʿUmar al-Yūnānī, son of Ḥamza 147,
    148, 158–60
ʿUmāra 132, 135
Umayya 131, 145
Umm al-Ḥayāt, *see ʿAyn al-Ḥayāt*
Umm ʿĪsā the daughter of ʿAlī 18
ʿUnaytira 24, 25, 38, 41, 112, 114, 131–3,
    137–46
ʿUqba 38–97 *passim*, 106–8, 164, 167
Usāma ibn Munqidh 19

ʿUṭārid ibn ʿAwf 31, 37, 60, 63, 64, 69,
    78, 93–101, 104–7, 111–15, 147,
    154, 225
ʿUtayba 132, 141
ʿUthmān, trickster helper of Baybars
    164, 167, 172

Valencia 19

al-Wahhābīya 11, 40, 64
Walīd ibn Ṭarīf 18
al-Wansharīsī, Aḥmad ibn Yaḥyā 8
Wāq al-Wāq 216, 217, 220, 251 n.9
Ward al-Masīḥ, daughter of Sāṭirīn
    176, 182,
Wāthiq, caliph 38–40, 56, 61, 236 n.67
Wizr 132, 136
Wonder Woman 15

Xena xx

Yāmina xviii, xxi
Yarmūk 18, 19
Yūnān 168
al-Yūnānī (al-Yūnīnī), *see ʿUmar
    al-Yūnānī*

Zahra 31, 33, 34
Zahrbān 148, 159
Zalfā, daughter of Raʾs al-Ghūl 20
Ẓālim, father-in-law of Dhāt al-
    Himma 38, 43, 48, 49
Ẓālim, son of ʿAbd al-Wahhāb 60,
    64, 69, 79, 80, 82–4, 86, 94, 96
al-Ẓāmiʾ 142, 143
Zanānīr 64, 81, 83
Zarqāʾ 112, 114, 131–41, 143
al-Zaynī Barakāt 165
Zāziya, *see Jāziya*
Zenobia 17, 45
Zubayda 40
Zūbīn 148, 158–60
Zuhayr ibn Qays 142

Plate 1. ʿAbdallāh ibn Jaʿfar, the hero of pseudo-al-Wāqidī's *Futūḥ Ifrīqīya,* fleeing with his beloved al-Yāmina. Reverse glass painting.

Plate 2. Combat scene. Cover of a Cairo edition of the *Taghribat Banī Hilāl*.

Plate 3. Abū Zayd al-Hilālī killing al-Harrās, al-Nāʿisa looking on. Reverse glass painting.

Plate 4. Alexander fighting the Amazons. Painting from a manuscript of Qazwīnī's *'Ajā'ib al-makhlūqāt*.

Plate 5. Jāziya (or Zāziya), leading female protagonist of the *Sīra Hilālīya*. Reverse glass painting.

Plate 6. Cover of the 1980 Beirut edition of *Sīrat al-amīra Dhāt al-Himma*. Note the emphasis on her femininity instead of her martial prowess.

Plate 7. Cover of an Egyptian book on Princess Dhāt al-Himma. The image recalls Xena, the warrior princess from the American television series popular in the Middle East in the 1990s.

Plate 8. 'Antar and 'Abla. Reverse glass painting.

Plate 9. A Bedouin tribe travelling through pre-Islamic Arabia. This illustration from a Beirut edition of *Sīrat 'Antara* makes use of the images used in Egyptian murals celebrating the pilgrimage to Mecca. In these murals, elements such as trains, ships, planes, armed soldiers and dangerous animals are symbolic of travel to and in Arabia.

Plate 10. 'Antar killing an enemy with 'Abla looking on. Poster print. The same image is used to depict Abū Zayd al-Hilālī (see Plate 3).

Plate 11. Princess Jaydā' captured by 'Antar. Illustration from a Beirut edition of *Sīrat 'Antara*.

Plate 12. ʿAntar killing a dragon. Reverse glass painting. The picture shows a close resemblance to images of Saint George, a saint who is popular in the Christian Middle East, Egypt and Ethiopia. It demonstrates that well-known images were regularly adapted to illustrate popular epics. The episode is, in fact, of very minor importance in the epic, and would otherwise hardly merit a prominent illustration. Cf. *Sīrat ʿAntara* (Cairo: Maktaba wa-matbaʿa Mustafā al-Bābī al-Halabī), 9: 348–349.

Plate 13. ʿAbla kills the Persian ruler Ardashîr with a knife. Illustration from a 1971 edition of *Sīrat ʿAntara*.

Plate 14. Cover of a modern Beirut edition of *Sīrat ʿAntara*, showing a woman awkwardly brandishing a sword with her left hand.

Plate 15. Two girls wrestling on a roof. Painting from a Mughal manuscript of the Persian version of *The Adventures of Hamza*.

Plate 16. Princess Mihrdukht shoots her bow. Painting from a Mughal manuscript of the Persian version of *The Adventures of Hamza*.

Plate 17. The woman Khos-Kiram beheads a spy. Painting from a Mughal manuscript of the Persian version of *The Adventures of Hamza*.

Plate 18. Baybars and his four companions Saʿd ibn Dabl, Ibrāhīm al-Hawrān, ʿImād al-Dīn ʿAlqam and Sulaymān al-Jāmūs. Print on thin cardboard.

Plate 19. Cover of an abbreviated modern version of *Sīrat Baybars* featuring a seductive type of dancing girl.

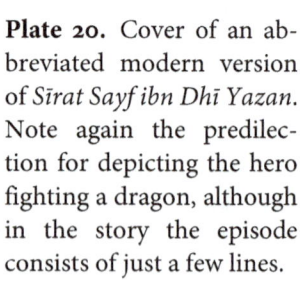

Plate 20. Cover of an abbreviated modern version of *Sīrat Sayf ibn Dhī Yazan*. Note again the predilection for depicting the hero fighting a dragon, although in the story the episode consists of just a few lines.

طامة تفاجيء ناهد بضربها بالسيف وفي يدها حزام سيف المسحور قبل اعطائه الى قمرية

Plate 21. Tāma threatening Nāhid. Illustration from an abbreviated modern version of *Sīrat Sayf ibn Dhī Yazan*.

عاقصة تتلقى قمرية بالسيف

Plate 22. ʿĀqisa attacking Qamarīya. Illustration from an abbreviated modern version of *Sīrat Sayf ibn Dhī Yazan*.

Plate 23. Cover of a 1984 edition of *Sīrat Sayf ibn Dhī Yazan*. Note the choice of a picture of a stereotypically seductive female.

www.ingramcontent.com/pod-product-compliance
Lightning Source LLC
Chambersburg PA
CBHW071232230426
43668CB00011B/1405